Andy McNab joined the infantry as a boy soldier. In 1984 he was 'badged' as a member of 22 SAS Regiment and was involved in both covert and overt special operations worldwide.

During the Gulf War he commanded Bravo Two Zero, a patrol that, in the words of his commanding officer, 'will remain in regimental history for ever'. Awarded both the Distinguished Conduct Medal (DCM) and Military Medal (MM) during his military career, McNab was the British Army's most highly decorated serving soldier when he finally left the SAS in February 1993. He wrote about his experiences in two phenomenal bestsellers, *Bravo Two Zero*, which was filmed starring Sean Bean, and *Immediate Action*.

He is also the author of the bestselling novels *Remote Control*, *Crisis Four*, *Firewall*, *Last Light*, *Liberation Day*, *Dark Winter* and *Deep Black*. His new novel, *Aggressor*, is now available from Bantam Press. Be........... lectures to security and intellig........... USA and the UK.

Praise for *Immediate Action*:

'This book paints a richly detailed picture of life in the SAS'
Sunday Telegraph

'Andy McNab's new memoir is the real thing ... The strength of *Immediate Action* lies in its detail ... much more than a jingoistic adventure story'
The Times

'A joy ... it gives an absorbing insight into the controlled thuggery and intimate comradeship that are the hallmarks of the SAS'
Daily Telegraph

www.**booksattransworld**.co.uk/andymcnab

Also by Andy McNab

IMMEDIATE ACTION

Andy McNab
DCM MM

CORGI BOOKS

For Nick, Al, Andy, Joe and Paul
Lest We Forget

1

The windows and doors of the building were boarded up and bristled with barbed wire but that wasn't going to keep us out.

An old sheet of corrugated iron nailed over the frame of a small door on the side was loose. Jamming a length of wood into the gap, I heaved with all my weight. The nails gave. Several pairs of hands gripped the corner of the sheet and pulled. The metal folded on itself sufficiently to create a hole that we could crawl through.

Murky light spilled down from a run of six or seven sky-lights in the flat roof 30 feet above our heads. In the gloom I could see lumps of metal here and there on the bare concrete floor, but apart from that the place seemed empty. There was a dank smell of mould and rotten wood and plaster. It was totally, eerily silent; had we made the slightest noise it would have echoed around the vast space. Probably nobody on the outside would hear it and raise the alarm, but I didn't want to take the chance. I looked at the others and nodded in the direction of the stairwell at the far end. As I took a pace forward my foot connected with a tin can. It went skidding across the floor and clattered into a lump of metal. From over my shoulder came a whispered curse.

I could see that the stairwell would take us up to the offices on the half-floor, then up again to a hatch that was open to the sky. Once we were on the roof, that was when the fun and games would start.

It felt colder 30 feet up than it had at ground level. I exhaled hard and watched my breath form into a cloud. I started to shiver. I walked to the edge of the flat roof and looked down at the tops of the lampposts and their pools of light. The street was deserted. There was no-one around to see us.

Or to hear the crash of breaking glass.

I span round and looked at the three figures standing near one of the skylights. There should have been four.

A split second later, there was a muffled thud from deep inside the building.

'John!' somebody called in a loud, anxious whisper. 'John!'

I knew even before I looked through the jagged hole that he would be dead. We all did. We exchanged glances, then ran back towards the roof hatch.

John was lying very still; no sound came from his body. He was face down on the concrete, a dark pool oozing from the area of his mouth. It looked shiny in the twilight.

'Let's get out of here,' somebody said, and as one we scarpered for the door. I just wanted to get home and get my head under the covers, thinking that then nobody would ever find out – as you do, when you're just eight years old.

The next afternoon there were police swarming all around the flats. We got in league to make sure we had the same story because, basically, we thought we were murderers.

I'd never felt so scared. It was the first time I'd ever seen anybody dead, but it wasn't the sight of the body that disturbed me; I was far more concerned about what would happen if I got nicked. I'd seen Z Cars; I had visions of spending the rest of my life in prison. I thought I'd rather die than have that happen to me.

I'd had a very ordinary childhood up until then. I wasn't abused, I wasn't beaten, I wasn't mistreated. It was just a normal, run-of-the-mill childhood. I had an older brother, who was adopted, but he'd left home and was in the army. My parents, like everybody else on our estate in Bermondsey, spent lots of time unemployed and were always skint.

My mum's latest job was in a chocolate factory during the week, and then at the weekend she'd be in the launderette doing the service washes. The old man did mini-cabbing at night, and anything he could get hold of during the day. He would help mend other people's cars, and always had a fifteen-year-old Ford Prefect or Hillman Imp out the front that he'd be doing things to.

We moved house a lot, always chasing work. I'd lived at a total of nine different addresses and gone to seven schools.

My mum and dad moved down to Herne Bay when I was little. It didn't work out, and then they had to try and get back on the council. My mother got pregnant and had a baby boy, and I had to live with my Aunty Nell for a year. This was no hardship at all. Aunty Nell's was great. She lived in Catford, and the school was just around the corner. Best of all, she used to give me a hot milk drink at night – and, an unheard-of luxury, biscuits.

From there we went on the council and lived quite a few years on the housing estates in Bermondsey. Aunty Nell's husband, George, died and left my mum a little bit of money, and she decided to buy a corner café. We moved to Peckham, but the business fell through. My mum and dad were not business people, and everything went wrong – even the accountant ripped them off.

We went on to private housing, renting half a house. My Uncle Bert lived upstairs. Mum and Dad were paying the rent collector, but it wasn't going to the landlord, so eventually we got evicted and landed up going into emergency council housing.

Money was always tight. We lived on what my mum called 'teddy bear's porridge' – milk, bread and sugar, heated up. The gas was cut off once and the only heat source in the flat was a three-bar electric fire. Mum laid it on its back in the front room and told us we were camping. Then she balanced a saucepan on top and cooked that night's supper: teddy bear's porridge. I thought it was great.

I joined my first gang. The leader looked like the lead singer of the Rubettes. Another boy's dad had a used-car lot in Balham; we thought they were filthy rich because they went to Spain on a holiday once. The third character had got his eyes damaged in an accident and had to wear glasses all the time, so he was good for taking the piss out of. Such were my role models, the three main players on the estate. I wanted to be part of them, wanted to be one of the lads.

We played on what we called 'bomb sites', which was where the old buildings had been knocked down to make way for new housing estates. Sometimes we mucked around in derelict buildings – the one on Long Lane was called Maxwell's Laundry. We used to sing the Beatles song 'Bang, Bang, Maxwell's Silver Hammer' and muck about inside it, throwing stones and smashing the glass. There were all the signs up: NO ENTRY, and all the corrugated iron, boards and barbed wire, but that just made it more important that we got inside. We'd get up on the roof and use the skylights as stepping stones in games of dare. It was fun until the kid fell and died.

I changed gangs. For the initiation ceremony I had to have a match put to my arm until the skin smoked and there was a burn mark. I was dead chuffed with myself, but my mum came home from her shift at the launderette, saw the state of my arm and went apeshit. I couldn't understand it.

She dragged me off to the house of the gang leader to moan at his old girl. The two mums had a big shouting thing on the landing, while we just stood there giggling. As far as I was concerned I was in the gang – let them argue as much as they like.

10

As I mixed more with the other kids I started to notice that I didn't have as much stuff as they did. The skinhead era started and everybody had to have Docker Green trousers and Cherry Red boots. I said I didn't want any.

We'd go to the swimming-pool once a week and the routine afterwards was to go and buy a Love Heart ice cream or Arrowroot biscuits out of a jar. I never had the money for either, and had to try and ponce half a biscuit off somebody. I never tasted a Love Heart, but one day I scrounged enough money from somewhere and made a special trip to buy one – only to find that they had been discontinued. I bought an Aztec bar instead, and felt very grown up. Unfortunately, there was nobody to show it off to because I was on my own.

I tried the Cubs once but never got as far as having a uniform. We had to pay subs each week, but I managed to lie my way out of paying the first few times. Then, on Tuesday nights, we had to have plimsolls to play five-a-side. I didn't have any so I nicked somebody else's. I got caught and had the big lecture: 'Thieving's bad.' That was the end of Cubs.

I knew that older boys got money by earning it, so I got chatting to the milkman and persuaded him to let me help with his Sunday round on the estate. He'd give me half a crown, which I used to buy a copy of *Whizzer & Chips*, a bottle of Coke and a Mars bar. That left me with just sixpence, but it was worth it. It was all very important to me, buying the Coke and the Mars bar, because it was grown up stuff, even if it was only one day a week.

One of the gang wore 'wet look' leather shoes, which were all the rage. His hair, too, was always shiny, like he'd just stepped out of a bath. At our house, we only had a bath on Sundays. He had one every night, which I thought was very sophisticated. We used to go into his bedroom messing around; one day, I noticed that he had a ten shilling note in his moneybox. As far as I was concerned he was loaded, and wouldn't miss it. I nicked it, and nothing was ever said.

11

I started nicking more and more. My mum used to have a load of stuff on the slate in the Co-op. When she sent me for milk and other bits and pieces, I'd take some extras and put them on tick; I knew she wouldn't check the bill, she'd just pay it when she had money.

I'd never lived with my older brother. All I could remember was him coming home from the army with presents. I didn't really know him and he didn't really know me. One time when he was home on leave, though, he noticed that my reading was crap and he started teaching me. I must have been about eight or nine and I still didn't know my alphabet. He sat me down and made me go through it. It made me feel special that he was spending time with me. However, the short lesson wasn't enough to change me. When I got to secondary school, I had a reading age of seven.

I came into school late one day and was walking down the corridor. The house master collared me and said, 'Where are you going?'

'To my classroom.'

'Where are your shoes?'

I looked down at my plimsolls. I didn't understand what he meant. Then it dawned on me.

'I haven't had any shoes this year.'

I had to go and get a form for my parents to sign for grants. I was on a free bus pass, free school dinners. I even had to stand in a special 'free dinners' queue in the school canteen. It wasn't just me: the main catchment areas were Brixton and Peckham, so a lot of kids were in the same boat. But all the same, it was one particular gang I wanted out of.

The thieving got stupid. We started by nicking pens from Woolworth's for our own use, and soon we were stealing stuff for selling. We walked past a secondhand furniture shop with a few new bits and pieces amongst the display on the pavement. A small, round wine table caught my eye; we ran past and picked it up, then went down to another secondhand place and sold it for ten bob. We spent it

12

straightaway in Ross's café on cheese rolls and frothy coffees.

I stole money one day off my Aunty Nell's neighbour. I took the pound note to the sweet shop, and my Aunty Nell was behind me without me knowing. She didn't say anything at the time, but phoned up the school.

The headmistress summoned me to her office and said, 'What were you doing with all that money?'

'I found this old mirror,' I said. 'I got some varnish, done it up, sold it and got two quid for it.'

I got away with it. I thought I was so clever; everybody else was a mug for letting me steal from them.

Because my mum and dad were working hard, I had a lot of freedom. I repaid them by being a complete shit. My mum had broken her leg and was sitting in the front room one night watching *Peyton Place*. She said, 'Don't eat the last orange, Andy, I'm going to have it for my dinner later on.'

I knew she couldn't get up and hit me, so I picked it up and started peeling it, throwing the peel out of the window. My mum went apeshit but I ate the orange in front of her, then ran out of the house when my father appeared. I slipped on the orange peel and broke my wrist.

After school, and sometimes instead of school, we used to go thieving in places like Dulwich Village and Penge, areas that we reckoned deserved to be robbed.

We'd saunter past people sitting on park benches, grab their handbags and do a runner. Or they'd be leaving their cars unattended for a minute or two while they bought their children an ice cream; we'd lean through the window and help ourselves to their belongings. If a car was hired or had a foreign plate, we'd always know there was stuff in the boot. And as we learned, they were easy enough to break into.

In school lunchbreaks we often used to take our school blazers off and hide them in holdalls so no-one could identify us when we stole. We thought we were dead

clever. The fact ours was the only comprehensive school in the whole area didn't really occur to us. Then we'd go around looking for things to steal. We got into a car one day, took a load of letters, and discovered that they contained cheques. We were convinced that we'd cracked it. None of us had the intelligence to realize that we couldn't do anything with them.

We broke into a camping shop one night in Forest Hill. There were three of us, and we got in through the flat roof. Again, we didn't really know what we wanted. It was one of the places where you could go and buy swimming ribbons to put on your trunks. So the priority was to get a few of those and all become gold medal swimmers. After that we didn't know what to do, so one of us took a shit in the frying pan in the little camping mock-up that they had as a window display.

At the age of fourteen I was starting to get all hormonal and trying to impress the girls that I was clean and hygienic. You could buy five pairs of socks for a quid in Peckham market, but they were all outrageous colours like yellow and mauve. I made sure that everybody saw I was wearing a different colour every day. I also started to have a shower every night down at Goose Green swimming baths. It cost 5p for the shower and a towel, 2p for soap and 2p for a little sachet of shampoo.

I wore clean socks, I was kissably clean, but I was over-weight. The girls didn't seem to go a bundle on fat gits in orange socks. Then the Bruce Lee craze swept the country. People would roll out of the pubs and into the late night movie, then come out thinking they were the Karate Kid. Outside the picture houses, curry houses and Chinese take-aways of Peckham of a Friday night, there was nothing but characters head-butting lampposts and each other to Bruce Lee sound effects.

I took up karate in a big way and got into training three times a week. It was great. I was mixing with adults as well

as people of my own age, and I started to lose weight. I was also doing a bit of running.

The schooling and all things academic were still bad. I got in with a fellow called Peter, who wore his cuffs and big, round butterfly collars outside his blazer, just like Jason King. I thought he was smooth as fuck in his big baggy trousers. He asked if I wanted to do a couple of weeks' work for his dad, and I jumped at the offer.

His old man owned a haulage firm. Peter and I loaded electrical goods into wagons, then helped deliver them. We made a fortune, mainly because we nicked radios, speakers and anything else we could get our hands on when the driver wasn't looking.

I earned more than my old man that month. Even in adult life people would have perceived that as a good job. My attitude was, 'Get out of school because it's shit, get a job, earn some money,' and that was it. I didn't realize how much I was limiting my horizons, but there was no guidance from the teachers. They were having to spend too much time just trying to control the kids, let alone educate us. They had no opportunity to show us that there was anything beyond the little world we lived in. I didn't realize there was a choice, and I didn't bother to look.

In the sort of place that we lived, a really good job would be getting on the print or the docks. Next level down would be an underground driver on London Transport, or a panel beater. Other than that, you went self-employed.

I landed up working more or less full time for the haulage contractor, delivering Britvic mixers and lemonade during the summer. I managed to get extra pallets of drinks put on the wagons, sold them to the pubs, and pocketed the proceeds.

In the winter time, I delivered coal. I thought I was jack the lad because I could lift the coal into the chutes. I couldn't move for old ladies wanting to make me cups of tea. I thought I knew everything I needed to know. I pitied the poor dickheads at school, working for nothing. I was

making big dough; I had all the kit that I'd wanted two years ago.

I lost my virginity on a Sunday afternoon when I was fifteen. My mate's sister was about seventeen. She was also willing and available, but very fat. I didn't know who was doing whom a favour. It was all very fumbly, all very quick, and then she made me promise that I wasn't going to tell anybody. I said that I wouldn't, but as soon as I could, like the shit that I was, I did.

The contract work finished and I started working at McDonald's in Catford, which had just opened. Life there was very fast and furious. I was sweeping and mopping the floors every fifteen minutes. I could have a coffee break, but I had to buy all my own food. There was no way I could fiddle anything because it was all too well organized. I hated it. The money was crap, too, but marginally better than the dole – and besides, the McDonald's was nearer to home than the dole office.

I started to get into disappearing for a while. A bloke and I did his aunty's gas meter and travelled to France on day passes, telling the ferries our parents were at the other end to collect us. On the way back we even stole a life-jacket and tried to sell it to a shop in Dover.

I had no consideration whatsoever for my parents. Sometimes I'd come back at four in the morning and my mum would be flapping. Sometimes we'd have the police coming around, but there was nothing they could do apart from give me a big fearsome bollocking. I thought I was the bee's knees because there was a police car outside the house.

I started going off the rails good style, sinking as low as tipping over Portaloos so I could snatch the occupants' handbags. One day, three of us were coming out of a basement flat we'd just burgled in Dulwich when we were challenged by the police. We got cornered near the railway station by a handler and his dog.

As soon as the police gripped me I was scared. I bluffed

in the van, because the other two weren't showing any fear. But as soon as we got separated at the station I wanted to show the police that I was flapping. I wanted them to take pity on me, I wanted them to see that I wasn't that bad, just easily led.

The station was a turn-of-the-century place with high ceilings, thickly painted walls and polished floors. As I sat waiting in the interview room I could hear the squeak of boots in the corridor outside.

I wanted so badly for somebody to come in; I wanted them to know that I wasn't bad; I'd fucked up, but it was the other two's fault.

My heart was pumping. I wanted my mum. It was the same horrible feeling in the pit of my stomach that I'd had running home from Maxwell's Laundry.

I had visions of ending up in Borstal or prison, or being the new young meat in an overcrowded remand wing. I'd always looked up to the local characters who'd been in prison, and I thought they were really hard. Now I knew that they must have hated it too. All their stuff about 'being inside' must have been hollow bravado; it wasn't glamorous and it wasn't exciting. It was horrible.

When my parents came up to the police station and I saw the shame and disappointment in my mum's eyes, I thought: is this it? Is this what I'm going to be doing for the rest of my life? Having a cell door slammed behind me was bad enough; it was claustrophobic and lonely in there, and I was very scared. But I'd never seen Mum like that before and I felt terrible.

I decided I was going to change. Alone in the interview room, I said to myself: 'Right, what am I going to do? I'm going to start getting myself sorted out.'

There had been one brief spell at school when I'd really got into English. I did a project on Captain Scott and got an A. I thought it was really great, but then I just dropped it. I got into history for a short while and enjoyed making a model of an Anglo-Saxon village. Maybe I could make a go

of it. I didn't want to land up as just another local nutter who thought he was dead cool because he had a Mark III Cortina and a gold chain around his neck.

So what was I going to do? There was no way I could get a decent job in south London. Academically I wasn't qualified, and certainly didn't have the aptitude to work in a factory.

In the back of my mind there had always been ideas about the army. When my Uncle Bert had lived upstairs, I'd heard him talking to my mum once about the army. He'd joined just before the Second World War because they were going to feed him three meals a day. And I knew they educated you because my mum had said so about my brother. Aunties and uncles would say, 'John's away now. ' My parents would reply, 'Oh yes, make a man of him.'

I'd seen all the adverts for the army – blokes on wind-surfers who always seemed to have loads of money, going places and doing stuff. And at least it would educate me. Why not do three years, I thought, and see what it's like? My brother had enjoyed it, so why not me? If nothing else, it would get me out of London.

As soon as the interview started I said, 'Please, I don't want to be in the shit, because I want to join the army. It wasn't my idea going in the flat. I was just dragging along. They told me to keep dog. Then they came running out and I ran with them.'

And I kept on bubbling.

I got put into a remand hostel for three days while I waited to go in front of the magistrates. I hated every minute of being locked up and I swore to myself that if I got away with it I'd never let it happen again. I knew deep down that I really would have to do something pretty decisive or I'd end up spending my entire life in Peckham, fucking about and getting fucked up.

On judgement day, the other two got probation, I got let

off with a caution. I was free to carry on where I'd left off, or I could show everybody, including myself, that this time I meant business.

I jumped on a bus that would take me past the army recruiting office.

'I want to fly helicopters,' I said to the recruiting sergeant. 'I want to go in the Army Air Corps.'

I took a simple test in English and Maths, which I failed.

'Come and try again in a month's time,' the sergeant said. 'The test will be exactly the same.'

I went down to the public library and studied a book on basic arithmetic. If I could master multiplication, I told myself, I'd never again have to hear the sound of a cell door slamming.

Four weeks later I went back in, sat the same test, and passed – by two points. The sergeant gave me a pile of forms to take home.

'What are you going in?' my dad said.

'Army Air Corps.'

'That's all right then. We don't want any of that infantry shit. You don't learn anything in that.'

I was given a travel warrant and went off to Sutton Coldfield for the three-day selection process. We were given medicals and simple tests of the 'If this cog turns this way, which way does that cog turn?' variety, and did a bit of sport. We watched films and were given talks about teeth arms and support arms, and where the army was in the world. I was loving it. The Army Air Corps seemed to operate everywhere; Cyprus and Hong Kong looked good for starters.

As I was going through the tests, though, the terrible

truth dawned on me that there was no way I was going to become a pilot. A lot of the other candidates were in the brain surgeon bracket, loaded down with O levels and going for junior apprenticeships to become artificers and surveyors. You'd have to be in the same league as them to go for pilot training, and I didn't have a qualification to my name. All the time I had wasted humping coal and lemonade flashed in front of me as if I was a drowning man. For the first time since I'd been old enough to do something about it, I was surrounded by blokes who had something that I wanted – but this time it was something that couldn't be nicked.

At the final interview, an officer said to me, 'You can go into the Army Air Corps, and train as a refueller. However, I don't think you would be best suited to that. You're an active sort of bloke, aren't you, McNab?'

'I suppose so.'

'Probably fancy a bit of travelling, seeing a bit of the world?'

'That's me.'

'Well then, have you considered a career in the infantry? There's a lot more potential – the battalions move every two or three years, so you're going to different places. It's a more exciting life for a young man. We have vacancies in the Royal Green Jackets.'

'Right, I'll have some of that.'

I was quite proud of myself. I thought I'd cracked it, I was a man, I was in the army now. I couldn't wait to get home and tell my parents the news.

'What did you land up in then?' the old man asked, looking up from his paper.

'The Royal Green Jackets.'

'What's that?'

'Part of the Light Division,' I beamed. 'You know – light infantry.'

'You wanker!' he exploded, hurling his newspaper to the

floor. 'You're not going to learn anything. All you're going to do is run around humping a big pack on your back.'

But I was not going to be deterred. A couple of days later, when it was clear that my mind was made up, my mum handed me an envelope and said, 'I think you need to know all about this.'

I opened the envelope and pulled out my adoption certificate. It wasn't a shock. I knew my brother was adopted, and I'd always just taken it for granted that I was, too. I wasn't really fussed about it.

'I met your natural mother when you were about a year old,' my mum said. 'She told me that she worked for a Greek immigrant who'd come over to England in the Fifties and was running a nightclub in the West End. She sold the cigarettes in the club, and was seventeen when she fell pregnant by him. She told me neither of them wanted a baby so she left you on the hospital steps in a carrier bag.'

My mum and dad had fostered me more or less straight-away, and eventually adopted me.

'She wasn't really concerned about you, Andy,' my mum said. 'She said to me, "I can always have other kids." '

In September 1976 I had what I thought was the world's most fearsome haircut and boarded the train to Folkestone West. Double-decker buses were waiting to take everybody to the Junior Leaders' Battalion camp at Shorncliffe. As soon as we got there all 1,100 of us were given another hair-cut. A really outrageous, bone haircut – all off, with just a little mound on the top like a circle of turf. I knew straight-away I was going to hate this place.

The first few days were a blur of bullshit, kit issue, and more bullshit. We couldn't wear jeans, they were un-gentlemanly. We had to stand to attention if even a private came into the room.

I thought I was hard but there were people here who made me look like the Milky Bar Kid. They had home-made tattoos up their arms and smoked roll-ups. If they

couldn't find somebody to pick a fight with they'd just scrap amongst themselves. Shit, I thought, what's it going to be like when I get to the battalion? I wanted out.

It was a very physical existence. If we weren't marching, we'd be doubling. We were in the gym every day, running and jumping. I actually got to like it. I found out I was quite good at running and started to get more and more into sport.

As a young soldier, milling was part of any selection or basic training at the time. They'd put four benches together to make a square and say, 'Right, you and you, in you go,' and in we'd go and try to punch hell out of each other. Most blokes just got in there and swung their arms like idiots. The hardnuts from Glasgow and Sheffield were a bit more polished, but I was amazed to find that one of the best punchers of all came from Peckham. Before I knew it, I was in the company boxing team.

One good thing about getting into any sports team in the army is that you're excused all the other training. Another is that you get to walk around in a maroon tracksuit all day, looking and feeling a bit special.

I won my two bouts at welterweight and my company won the battalion championships. We got to the army finals and I won the welterweight title. As far as I was concerned, my future was sealed: I'd go to 1RGJ, the boxing battalion, be a boxer for three years, then get out. What was even better, 1RGJ were off to Hong Kong.

A lot of the other blokes resented us sports people. Maybe it was the colour of the tracksuit – or maybe it was because we were allowed straight to the front of the dinner queue as a privilege.

The boxing team swaggered in one lunchtime, went to the head of the queue, and started slagging off the other blokes.

'You think you're fucking it, don't you?' said one of the Glasgow boys.

I answered with a smirk and walked on to the front and waited for the doors to be opened.

A Glaswegian mouth came very close to my ear and said, 'What's the difference between your leg and maroon track-suits?'

I shrugged.

'None,' he said, 'they're both full of pricks,' and with a massive grunt he rammed his fork straight into my thigh.

I staggered back a pace and looked down. The fork was embedded in my leg right up to the ends of the prongs. I grabbed hold of it and pulled gently but my leg muscle had gone into rigid spasm and I couldn't get the thing out. I wrenched as hard as I could and pulled it free. The prongs were red with blood as I did an about-turn and marched from the canteen. There was no way I was going to say anything. It wasn't until I got around the corner that I covered my mouth with my hand and screamed.

Boxing finished. I went back to the platoon, still with at least six months to do with the same intake. I was way behind. I'd done the weapon training, but I hadn't had time to consolidate it. I was really brought down to earth; they knew a lot more than me. But I worked hard at it, and even got a promotion. For the last three months we were given ranks, from junior lance corporal to junior RSM (*regimental sergeant major*). It meant jack shit really.

On Friday mornings we had the colonel's cross-country over a 6-mile course in and around the camp. The whole battalion had to race. If you came behind the colonel, you had to do it again on Sunday, whether you were staff or a junior soldier.

After that, we'd go to a training area to practise being wet, cold and hungry. I enjoyed it; at least we were away from the camp. I got better and better at it, and it made me feel good.

There was a ritual. The provo sergeant would come out of the guardroom and greet everyone back. It was the first time we had been given any respect. We would be staggering back as a platoon, with our silly tin hats on, kit

hanging off us, stinking, our faces covered in cam cream, and he would come out and give praise.

'Well done! Keep it going!' he'd boom.

It gave me a sense of pride that I'd never felt before, especially as he spent the rest of his time bollocking us.

Then came the weapon cleaning, which took until the end of Saturday or Sunday morning. Then – the weekend! We couldn't go home, and we were allowed out only until ten o'clock – and only to the local town. To the lads in Folkestone we were a nuisance, because we had money. You could show a girl a really good time on three quid a week. I met a girl called Christine at the Folkestone Rotunda and we started to see each other as often as we could.

I really started to enjoy it all. I'd finally got to grips with the system of 'bullshit baffles brains' – just do what they say, even if you know it's a bag of shit, and it keeps everybody happy. And the more I enjoyed it, the more I didn't mind working at it, and the better I got.

The exercises started to get more and more intense. We'd be out one or two nights a week, culminating in a two-week battle camp where all the different phases of war were practised, with live firing attacks. Now, at last, I started to understand what I was doing. Before, I had just dug a hole and sat in it. Now I knew why I was sitting in it.

Every eight weeks we had leave. I met up with my old mates in Peckham when I went back one time, but there was a distinct change. We'd drifted apart. Even after such a short length of time our world views had changed. All they were interested in was what I had been interested in when I left: mincing around. I didn't feel superior – the other way round, if anything. I thought I was missing out. They were talking about getting down to Margate, but on Sunday I'd have my best dress uniform on, marching down to the garrison church. Nonetheless, I couldn't wait to get to my battalion.

I got chosen to take one of the passing-out guards and

received a letter saying, 'Congratulations on being presented with the Light Division sword. Well done, and I really hope your career goes well.'

I didn't have a clue what the Light Division sword was. I discovered that each regiment had this award, presented to the most promising young soldier. I also discovered that it meant a day's rehearsal where I had to practise going up, shaking the hand, saluting, taking the sword, turning around, and marching back off. At last the whole battalion had to get into the gym for presentations by the colonel to all the different companies.

I thought the sword was marvellous, and looked forward to seeing it mounted on my bedroom wall. But as I left the podium a sergeant took it off me and gave me a pewter mug in exchange. The sword went back to the regimental museum.

The passing-out parade was quite a big affair. My parents came down, and my older brother and his family. It was quite strange, because they'd never been really that into it – Mum and Dad never even used to go to parents' evenings at my school. In fact, it was the first time any of my family had ever turned up to anything.

It really was the day I thought I'd become a soldier. We wore IJLB (*Infantry Junior Leaders Battalion*) cap badge and belt, and as soon as we came off the passing-out parade we could put on our own regimental kit – the Green Jacket beret.

There was another little matter to be attended to. Our beautifully bulled hobnail boots had to be returned to the stores, apart from those of the Guardsmen who were going to take them to their battalion for ceremonial duties. So we all lined up and bashed them on the pavement until the bull cracked like crazy paving. No other fucker was going to get their hands on them and have it easier than we did.

3

I went on leave for a couple of weeks, then reported to the Rifle Depot at Winchester. I felt a mixture of excitement and worry as the eleven of us joined a platoon of adult recruits on their last six weeks of training.

Compared to IJLB the discipline was jack shit. Once we'd finished our work for the day, we could get changed and walk out of the guardroom and down town.

At the end of the six weeks we got our postings. If you had brothers in particular battalions they could claim you; otherwise, you just stated a preference and kept your fingers crossed. 3rd battalion were known as 'the Cowboys' and the 1st were the 'Fighting Farmers'. 2RGJ were in Gibraltar, but due to come back to the UK quite soon for a Northern Ireland tour.

I asked to go to 1RGJ because of the boxing, and because they were due to go to Hong Kong. So of course, I was sent to 2RGJ. I wasn't best pleased – especially when I found out that they were called 'the Handbags'.

'Where do you come from?' the colour sergeant asked me on the barrack square, as I stood blinking in the brilliant Mediterranean sunshine.

'London.'

'I can hear that, you dickhead. Whereabouts in London?'

'Peckham.'

'Right, go to B Company.'

My rifle platoon consisted of sixteen blokes. We'd been told that when we got to the battalion they would get hold of us for 'continuation training' – indoctrination into their special way of doing things. But 2RGJ was snowed under with commitments; they were all over the Rock, on ceremonial and border duties. Everybody was too busy to give the five of us any attention and our first couple of weeks were spent just bumming around.

I went into the main street the morning after I arrived. As far as the eye could see there was nothing but shops full of cheap watches and carpets from Morocco, most of them run by Asian or Arab traders. I bought my mum a peacock carpet for a fiver, with a pair of flip-flops bunged in. I thought, this is wonderful; I've only been here a couple of days and already I'm cutting major league deals down the kasbah.

Full of enthusiasm after my year of training, I was raring to go. I thought the posting was brilliant – we were in the Mediterranean, there were beaches, there was sun. It was the first time I'd ever been abroad, apart from my day trips to France, and I was getting paid for it. So the attitude of some of the other blokes came as a bit of a surprise. Some of the old hands seemed so negative: everything was, 'Shit', and 'For fuck's sake'. Or, very mysteriously, it would be, 'I'm just going to do some business,' and off they'd go. It took me a while to find out what they were doing.

The majority of teenagers who joined the army had been exposed to some illegal substances. It was part of the culture, and they took that culture in with them when they joined. I had never been interested in drugs myself, mainly because I hated smoking and had never been exposed to them. I'd heard all the terms, but didn't exactly know what was what. And now when I did get exposed to the drug business, it scared me; it was something totally alien.

Drugs, I was told, had always been a bit of a problem. Once, when the battalion came back from an overseas exercise, a fleet of coaches had turned up at two-thirty in

the morning. It was the local police, come to raid the battalion as a matter of course. They didn't find any illegal substances on this occasion, but they did find an officer who was engaged in an activity that was even more naughty in the eyes of military law. He was in bed with a corporal from the mortar platoon.

We seemed to have the culture of the Seventies but the army of the Fifties. It felt as if I was living in one of the black-and-white movies I sometimes used to watch on a Saturday afternoon. Each morning we had to drink a mugful of 'screech', the old army word for powdered lime juice. The colonel must have been reading a book about Captain Cook and thought it would stop us getting scurvy. I heard about an officer who joined the Irish Guards. The adjutant pulled him to one side and said, 'As a young subaltern, these are the rules. One, never wear a brown suit. Two, always call the underground the underground and not the tube. Three, never travel on a red bus. Four, always wear a hat and have an umbrella, and five, never carry a brown paper parcel.' Nothing about how to approach the soldiers he was going to have under his command.

Gibraltar in the summertime was packed with tourists, and because we were doing all the ceremonial stuff we were God's gift to a pretty girl who liked a uniform. That was my theory anyway, and I set off one afternoon for the main street, wearing civvies and in my own mind very much our man in Gibraltar. I found a place called the Capri bar, with plastic palm trees inside and semicircular booths with tables. All very dark and sophisticated, I thought. To be as suave as the surroundings demanded, I ordered a Southern Comfort and lemonade, a very international drink at the time.

As I sat there listening to songs by the Stylistics and the Chi-lites, I could see now and again blokes that I recognized from the battalion walking past, looking at me through the window.

The fellow who owned the bar was a Brit. He came over to join me for a chat. He had perfect, greying hair that had been sprayed, and looked to be in his forties, but probably still thought he was seventeen. He was wearing a blue jumper with a big red star.

'Hello,' he said sliding into the booth next to me. 'What, are you in the Navy?'

'No, I'm with the battalion up the road.'

'Just got here?'

'Yeah.'

It was all rather nice. We chatted away, and then this Chinese woman came in. She was absolutely stunning. Flared trousers, high heels, and my boy was off in raptures. She sat and joined us.

'You in the Navy?'

'No, I'm with the battalion.'

After a drink or two she moved over a place and I thought – I've cracked it, it must be the sight of my drink, a woman like this was bound to feel comfortable in the company of an international jet-setter. More people were coming in, and the bar started filling up. The jukebox started playing slow Donny Osmond numbers.

I was slowly getting pissed, and I didn't really pay that much attention when my new friend said, 'Call me Pierre.'

To me, Pierre was a French bloke's name, I hadn't realized it was also a Chinese woman's. Then, very very slowly, I started to get the picture. I looked around and realized that everybody in the bar was a bloke. I looked again at Pierre – and the awful truth sank in.

'Just going to the toilet,' I said, disentangling her hand from my thigh.

I did a runner, haunted by the faces of all the blokes I'd seen looking at me through the windows. I was going around for days afterwards laughing manically and saying, 'They do the best Spanish omelette in Gibraltar down the Capri. It's full of dodgy characters, of course, but it's worth it for the food.'

The battalion were coming back to England in November and heading more or less straightaway for South Armagh. I would be too young to go with them immediately: you had to be eighteen, because years before there had been too many seventeen-year-olds getting shot. It was bad PR, so they'd upped the age limit. I'd have to wait until after my birthday.

We went to Lydd and Hythe for infantry build-up training. We spent a lot of time on the MUF (*marksmanship under fire*) range and were trained in all the different scenarios we were likely to meet.

'We are going to be based in South Armagh – bandit country,' said our company commander, 'and B Company are going to Crossmaglen – a town that makes the rest of bandit country look like Camberwick Green.'

We were issued with street maps and told to 'learn' South Armagh. There was a shooting during the build-up training and for the first time I started to read more of the newspaper than the TV page.

Towards the end of the training we were issued with an optic sight for our weapons. I'd never seen this bit of kit before, but I knew that it existed. That was it, I thought I was the international sniper.

In the infantry at that time all the clothing was incredibly basic. We had a uniform, but no effective waterproofs or warm clothing. If you wanted stuff like that you had to buy your own. The most exotic item we were given to help us through the rigours ahead was a pair of thick Arctic socks.

I was eighteen years old. I'd already been in the army for coming up to two years but this was my first operational tour. Everything was great. The way I looked at it was I was having a good experience, I was with the battalion, I thought I was hard as fuck, and I'd have enough money to buy a car and show Christine a good time when I got back.

Crossmaglen, a cattle market town known to us as XMG,

was right on the border. This meant the players could prepare in Dundalk on the other side, then pop over and shoot
at us. There was a big square in the centre, with a number
of small buildings with metal railings in front to hold the
livestock. It was overlooked by Baruki sangar, which was
less than 100 metres away from the security forces base that
we lived in. Named after a paratrooper called Baruki who
got blown up, the sangar was a big corrugated iron and
steel structure. Inside were three GPMGs (*general purpose
machine-gun*), an M79 grenade launcher, smoke dischargers,
radios and, more importantly, flasks of tea and sandwiches,
because we were up there for ever. There was one electric
heater. Stag duty in the sangar was incredibly cold and
very, very boring. It had to be manned by two of us all the
time. To get to it there used to be this mad dash – the two
men on duty in the sangar would man the guns, we'd go
out and run down the road, the two we were replacing
would get out and run back.

I was in Baruki sangar one day with a lance corporal
called Bob, short for 'Billy One Bollock' – I never knew
where the nickname came from, because he looked as if he
was complete. A foot patrol came out of the base, and after
the usual pound of running feet, all I could hear was 'click,
click, click'. What the hell is that? I wondered, and looked
out of the side hole. Standing nearby was the smartest man
alive, posing in front of a camera for the battalion
magazine.

'That's Johnny Two-Combs,' Bob said. 'Comes from the
Midlands, loves football. Plays for the battalion. Looks
good, doesn't he?'

Indeed he did. No-one wore rank in XMG, and normally
looked a bag of shit, wet, cold and covered in mud. But this
guy was wearing corporal's stripes, and his uniform was
immaculate. He was about 5'10", with blue eyes and perfect
teeth, and not a single blond hair out of place.

'He was playing in an army cup match and the battalion
started throwing combs onto the pitch,' Bob went on. 'He

picked one up and used it, asked if he was looking good, then carried on. I think he scored the winning goal.'

I watched as Johnny carried on posing, winning the war on his own for the camera. 'The thing is,' Bob said, 'he is really switched on – you're looking at a future RSM there.'

The rifle company lived in 'submarines' in the security forces base, long corridors three beds high but without lockers. Where you were, that was your space. You put your kit on your bed or under the bottom bed. I shared an area with Reggie, a corporal and my patrol commander, and Gaz, a newly married rifleman who kept his photo album under his pillow.

Reggie was twenty-five and ran the company seven-a-side rugby team. He was tall and well-built; his legs were so large he walked like a body builder. He had black curly hair and the world's biggest arse, and bad breath that he was forever making excuses about.

Gaz was aged about twenty. If he hadn't been in the army he would have been a male model. He was very fit, and had a perfect body. His ambition was to become a PTI (*physical training instructor*); every morning he would jump out of his bunk and shout, 'Twice round my beautiful body – go!'

The security forces base was laid out in a spider configuration, with submarines coming off a central area. All the support troops, plus any of the rifle company who couldn't fit in the submarines, lived in garden sheds in the compound, linked by duckboards over the mud that was ankle deep. The whole compound looked like a building site, which it was, covered by anti-mortar mesh.

The atmosphere inside the main base was very smoky, and at any time of night or day I could smell the odour of egg banjos (*fried egg sandwiches*) and chips coming from the cookhouse. There was a permanent smell, too, of damp clothing and wet floors. The heating didn't work very well, so it was either very hot or very cold. There were no windows.

In the late Seventies it was very much a foot-soldiering

conflict in South Arrnagh. If we weren't in the town patrolling we'd be in the cuds (*countryside*) patrolling, just us and the mud and the rain, our rifles and our bergens (*back packs*), out for however many days the task took. Being the nig (*new boy*), I had to carry the GPMG.

For the first month or so I was quite switched on by it all. Then it started to get very boring. I didn't feel I was achieving anything, because nothing ever happened. I'd just done all this training where every time you take a footstep something happens and you've got to react to it, but now that we were here nothing seemed to be happening. We patrolled, watched, stopped cars, put protection out at VCPs (*vehicle checkpoint*), and carried out house searches, and that was it.

We used to go out on patrol in the cuds with welly boots on because of the mud. There was a four-day routine – picked up by helicopter and taken out for four days, living in the field. Then we'd have four days on town patrol, wearing boots rather than wellies. This was a twenty-four-hour presence; there were always three patrols in the town. Then we'd do four days in sangars, doing cookhouse fatigues, cleaning the bogs out, and doing the area cleaning – a military term meaning work for work's sake. On one memorable occasion the sergeant major ordered me: 'McNab, you are to go out and sweep up all unwanted puddles.'

Everything we needed had to come in by helicopter – food, ammunition, letters, people. The helipad was a structure of wooden slats outside the camp; when a helicopter was due sangars had to stand to, and the aircraft would swoop in quickly. There was a housing estate next door and the boys used to take pops at anything that moved. The Navy crews were the best, in their Wessexes; they were more daring, and always on time – which was important after a long patrol, when you were waiting to be extracted.

I was the doorman in the sangar one day, which meant that as people jumped from the helicopter and ran towards

the door I'd open it just wide enough for them to run inside. I didn't have a clue who the character was that was running towards me. All I could see was a figure bent double, with a pile of paperwork in a wicker shopping bag with a handle like the ones grannies do their shopping with.

'Who are you?' he said.

'McNab, sir.'

'I'm Corden-Lloyd,' he beamed as he shook my hand. Then, in a brilliant piss-take of the sort of bone questions senior officers seem to need to ask squaddies when they visit, he said, 'Enjoying yourself? Mail getting through? Food all right? Any problems?'

This was great, a colonel shaking my hand, taking the piss out of himself, asking me how I was, what platoon I was in.

There were no military vehicles in the cuds to back up patrols because too many had been taken out by culvert bombs. However, there were two Saracen armoured vehicles that stayed in the town. They had anti-armour metal mesh over them to stop RPGs (*rocket-propelled grenade*) penetrating; the mesh would initiate the rocket before it penetrated the armour. They were called 'cans' and they never went outside of the town. We could move from position to position around the town in them, which was great, especially when it was pissing down. The can crews themselves had a pretty shitty job. They just sat, and the gunners just stood. The cans were essentially firm fire-bases for when we had big contacts, with a turret-mounted machine-gun. Their most useful feature, however, was secured to the rear. It was a thing called a Norwegian container, which held about two gallons of tea, with a plastic mug hanging off. The can drivers used to fill them up before a patrol, so we could go around the back for a brew. After about two hours it was lukewarm, stewy stuff, but in the early hours of the morning it was nectar.

I was on foot patrol in Crossmaglen in the early spring of 1978, at a time when the policy was to pull down any republican tricolours we saw. It wasn't a question of just going up and lifting it. It had to be done carefully, because there was always a possibility that it might be a come-on, or it could be a booby trap.

One had been put up on the Newry road leading out of Crossmaglen by the church, right on the edge of town, at the start of the cuds. It was a typical rural scene of undulating fields and hedgerows. The road was lined by telephone poles, from one of which hung a tricolour.

There were four patrols out from my platoon. On the net, the commander said, 'When we get the changeover, one patrol will take down the tricolour and we'll carry on patrolling.'

My patrol was getting ready to go out. The weather was cold and damp. All the concrete was wet and there were unwanted puddles everywhere. We were wearing nylon flak jackets on which each bloke had written his blood group. I had a civilian duvet jacket underneath my combat jacket.

There was a quick five-minute briefing in one of the garden sheds by the multiple commander.

'You take the centre of the town, you take the left, you take the right. The other patrol will stay out and take down the tricolour. Once that's done, they'll come back in and we'll carry on our patrol.'

It was no big deal; it was just another tricolour to be taken down. We got by the main gate, and four at a time the patrols would come forward into the loading bay and load their weapons. The guard commander would then get on the radio to Baruki and tell them that the patrols were ready. Their job was to cover us as we were coming out. Patrol by patrol we bomb-burst out. It would be just another routine patrol, three hours in the town, back for four, then go out again for another three hours.

We were going to be the centre patrol, around the town

square, the nearest patrol to the one that was going to take down the tricolour.

Nicky Smith, being search-trained, was told that he was going to go and take it down. The plan was that once we had come out on the ground, we would provide an outer cordon for his patrol, just be milling around the area.

They called for one of the cans that were on the opposite side of town. The plan was for Nicky to climb up on the mesh, have a quick look at the flag, and if it was all right, bring it down. It was no problem. He'd done it scores of times before, and it was in broad daylight.

The traffic was stopped either side in VCPs; we were manning the VCP that was stopping people coming out of the town along the Newry road. We checked driving licences and number plates, and asked them where they were going and where they had just been. I was stuck in a doorway, covering the two blokes who were running the VCP. I was 'ballooning' – bunching down, then standing up, making sure I didn't present a static target. After a minute or two, I would walk into another doorway, or get between two cars. It was important to keep moving.

I wasn't paying much attention to Nicky Smith and the search team. All I was concerned about was that the sooner it was finished, the sooner the can would be free, and then maybe we could get a quick cup of tea out of the Norwegian.

The can drove up to the base of the telephone pole. The gunner was manning the Browning to give cover, because the location was exposed, right at the edge of town – it could be a come-on. The driver had the armour plate that protected his face down so that he could see what was going on.

Nicky climbed on top, had a good look, and gave a tug. There was a fearsome explosion.

As an eighteen-year-old squaddy, I'd never heard the quick, sharp, piercing bang of high explosives. There was a moment of disbelief. I thought, nah, can't be. I didn't know

what to do, and was looking around for some direction. Reggie had been checking a car; he had the boot open and was taking some stuff out. He stopped, looked up, and looked around. The civilians caught in the VCP knew what was going on. They had more experience than I did of explosions going off.

Reggie slammed the boot down and the car shot off. He called us to him and we went running down the road. As we arrived at the Saracen we saw the body being pulled down by the platoon sergeant. There was screaming coming from inside the can. The back doors were open and people were trying to sort out the crew.

What remained of Nicky's body was now lying by the rear wheel of the Saracen. His head was cut off diagonally at the neck, and his feet were missing. All the bit in the middle was intact – badly messed up, but intact. The mesh was clogged with bits of his flesh and shreds of his flak jacket. Bits and pieces were hanging off every edge. The whole can seemed to be covered in blood.

'Get a poncho!' the platoon sergeant shouted.

Up on the hill on the opposite side, there were people visiting the graveyard. They stood still; cars were doing U-turns; nobody wanted to be involved. They'd seen all this before; they knew that if the rounds started flying they might become casualties themselves.

Was it a simple booby trap? Or was it command detonated by somebody in the vicinity?

All I saw was people getting on radios; all I heard were lots of orders being shouted. I didn't know what to do. I was scared. I felt really happy that there were loads of other people around me who had the appearance of knowing what they were doing.

There was a fellow in the brick (*patrol*) at the time who was a right pain in the arse; he would be AWOL on a Monday morning, come back Tuesday night, go on a charge. He never wanted to do anything. But he was really switched on this day. When we got there, the sergeant in

charge of the brick was sorting everything out and this fellow just ran up and started stitching all along the hedgerows with an LMG (*light machine-gun*). If it had been detonated by a control wire, maybe the bomber was still in range. This bloke was a renegade, always in trouble, but when he had to do this stuff, he knew what he was doing.

The QRF (*quick reaction force*) had run out of the base and were going to put roadblocks all around the town at pre-set points to stop anybody coming in or going out.

The bomb had taken Nicky out severely, spreading him out over fifty to sixty metres. All we wanted to do was to get the main bits of what was left of him onto a poncho and get him back to the base.

I was picking up the remains of the person I'd been eating breakfast with, who used to sit next to me honking about the state of the food. I was extremely angry, extremely scared, and real life hit me in a big way.

The locals were coming out of the pubs and their houses, clapping and cheering. They were chuffed; there was a Brit squaddy dead. I was flapping like fuck. I started to get angry at these people.

Four of us carried the poncho, one at each corner. The others gave protection as we went through. The poncho was soaking wet with blood. He was literally a dead weight. I was soaked up to my elbows in blood.

We got him back, but then we had to return and clear the area. Helicopters were arriving from Bessbrook to pick up the other casualties. We were sweating and panting, drenched with red. We had to use big, hard yardbrooms to get all the bits and pieces off the wagon and throw them into a bag. We burned the brooms afterwards. Then came the indignity of having to go out and look for one of his feet, because it wasn't accounted for. It was found half a street away.

The welts of our boots had his dried blood in them. Our hands had ingrained blood around the nails. All our

39

equipment was full of his blood. Even the map in my pocket was red with blood.

Nicky Smith was twenty years old. He was a nice bloke, with a mother and a girlfriend. I'd seen him write in a letter just the week before: 'Only forty-two more days and I'll be home.'

My vision of the army at the beginning was getting money, travelling, and all the other things I'd seen in the adverts – you're all on a beach, windsurfing and having fun. Maybe they were Nicky's visions as well. Even going to Northern Ireland was exciting because it was another experience. Maybe, I now thought, they needed a few posters in the recruiting office of dead boys in ponchos.

All too often, British soldiers who died on active service in Northern Ireland would get a brief mention on the news – 'Last night a British soldier . . .' – and then go unremembered. But I resolved to myself that I would never forget Nicky Smith. I would always keep the newspaper cuttings. I would always have his blood stains on my map.

I was haunted by images of disembodied feet and the Saracen spattered with blood like a child's painting. It made me fucking angry, and I personally wanted to put the world to rights. I wanted to get the people responsible. I suddenly felt that I had a cause, that I was doing something, not just for political shit or because I was saving money to buy a car; I was there because I wanted to do something for my own little gang.

4

A Saracen armoured car had got bogged down in the cuds near Crossmaglen and me and another rifleman, Gil, were put on stag to guard it.

Council estates in rural parts of Northern Ireland consisted of nice bungalows, paid for by subsidies from the EEC. A new one was under construction; the Saracen had gone into the site to turn around, and had got bogged down in the mud. Another Saracen was trying to drag it out. The company were called out and were in all-round defence with an inner and an outer cordon, but split up into groups of two and three. All our arcs overlapped each other, giving us 360 degrees cover around the vehicles.

As we took over, the other fellows told us where our arcs were, what they'd seen, what they hadn't seen, where we were in relation to other people on stag.

We lay in the hedgerow looking out; it was cold, and the grass was soaking. My trousers were wet through. My feet started to go numb, my hands were already frozen, and I couldn't cover my head up because my ears had to be exposed so I could listen. I was bored, I was pissed off, and I spent two solid hours slagging down can drivers for burying their vehicles in the mud.

The SLR (*self-loading rifle*) at the time had a bipod attached to the barrel that was like a pair of chopsticks with a spring at one end. It was a necessary bit of equipment because the rifle was too heavy to hold properly with its

cumbersome nightsight on. Every now and then I'd have a look through to see what was going on.

In the early hours of the morning, as I scanned the countryside yet again, I saw some movement. I refocused the nightsight and blinked hard. I recognized what I was seeing but I didn't believe it.

I quietly said to Gil, 'We've got two blokes coming down the hedgerow here.'

Gil said, 'Yeah, OK, fuck off, big nose.'

'I'm telling you – we've got two blokes coming down. Have a look.'

They were skulking down in front of us, maybe just over 100 metres away – not that far away at all.

'Fucking hell, you're right!'

As they got closer and came into direct line of sight, I could clearly see that one of them was carrying a long (*rifle*).

'What the fuck do we do?' Gil said.

I didn't know. Did we issue a challenge? After all, they might be two of our blokes. But what if they weren't and they went to ground? There was no way of contacting an officer or NCO. We were riflemen, so we couldn't be trusted with a radio. Shouting at the inner cordon would just create confusion; we might as well just do it, do what we'd been taught – issue a challenge, and then, if necessary, fire.

Easier said than done. We weren't allowed to have a round cocked in our weapon; we would have to issue a challenge, cock our weapons at the same time, and then get back into the aim.

I pulled the bolt back and shouted, 'Halt! Stand still! This is the army!'

The characters turned.

We fired.

The inner cordon saw the tracer and thought we were being fired at. They opened up on us because that was where the fire was coming from. It was the first time I'd

ever fired at people, and the first time I had been fired back at – and it didn't help that it was our own boys.

We had been taught a thing called 'crack and thump': when somebody's firing at you, what you're supposed to do is listen for the crack, and then the thump as the round hits the ground. From that you can work out distances – an interval of one second, for example, would mean that the weapon was about 100 metres away. However, the theory wasn't working out. I didn't hear any cracks; all I could hear was the thumps. Gil and I got our heads down in a ditch and yelled at the inner cordon to stop.

The firing increased. Reggie had gone up into one of the half-finished buildings to get a better perspective. He followed the line of the inner cordon's tracer and opened up with an LMG, giving it the good news down on us.

After what seemed like hours, there was a deafening silence. Moments after that, there was shit on. The world and his wife were trying to get in on the contact. People in the security base had been listening on the radio and legged it down towards the border, hoping to cut them off.

Pockets of little contacts were starting all over the place. Patrols were opening up on cows, trees and each other. It was chaos. I could see tracer flying. If it hit something solid it would ricochet and then *whizz!* – straight up into the air.

Soon the follow-up was in full swing. Dogs were helicoptered in to try and pick up the scent, and off we went: me and Gil, the company commander, the company commander's escort and the dog handler, traipsing through the fields, rivers and swamps of South Armagh.

The dogs picked up blood but the players were good at their trade.

'The way to evade dogs is to get on flat, open ground,' the handler said. 'If you start running along river beds, it just keeps the scent in those areas.'

'Running over a stream is jack shit use, too,' he panted as we jogged along behind the dogs. 'All the dog does is a thing called casting on the other side, and he'll pick up the

scent again. If you get into a wide open field, the scent is dispersed. You want to do a lot of zig-zagging, which slows the dog down, makes it harder for him to pick up your scent.'

Sometimes the dogs lost the scent and sniffed around aimlessly. The handler sent them forward to cast for it. They'd pick it up again and off we'd go. It was exciting stuff, like hare and hounds. It brought out a really basic human instinct.

It was exciting to be part of something so much bigger than my own little rifle company. There were two helicopters going around on Night Sun, a fearsome big floodlight, with people on the ground directing them by radio. The effort put in to get these two people was massive, and I was a part of that: I was one of the two who instigated it, and it felt really good.

We were out all night and came back well into first light, empty-handed. Our trousers had been shredded by barbed wire fences. I was soaking wet, cold and hungry, and totally knackered. We still had to carry on work the next day; there were still stags to do, patrols to go out. But it didn't worry me at all because I felt so excited; at last, I had done what I was there to do.

Two days later, a character turned up at a hospital in the south with a 7.62 wound in his leg. We were sparked up. Gil and I were the local heroes for the next day or two. In a rifle company we were just two dickheads, but now we had our fifteen minutes of fame because we were the latest ones to have had a contact.

Then all the banter started about who claimed the hit. Both of us were crap shots; it was a surprise that anybody had been hit at all.

The rest of our time in Ireland was just as busy. We had a bomb put outside Baruki sangar one night. It was an old trick, and it always worked: two slappers came by, hollering and shouting at the boys inside, flashing their arses and

working parts. While the lads were checking out the special of the day, a player walked behind the sangar and placed a bomb. When the stag changed, as they opened the door, the bomb should have gone off. The two blokes inside didn't have a clue what was going on. Luckily the bomb was discovered just in time and there was a controlled explosion.

Our colonel, Corden-Lloyd, was very keen on individualism. As far as he was concerned, we all had to wear the same outer clothing, purely so that we'd be recognized in the field. But what we wore underneath was down to us.

In theory, we should have worn army-issue shirts, thick woolly things that were a pain in the arse. The UN shirt was a much more comfortable alternative, but it was expensive. Corden-Lloyd worked out a deal with the manufacturers and took a vote – 'If everybody buys two UN shirts, we'll wear UN shirts when we get back to Tidworth,' he said. They would work out at £16 for two – quite a lot, but money well spent.

Very sadly, the purchase could not be completed. Colonel Corden-Lloyd was aboard a Gazelle helicopter that came down – PIRA say that they shot it down, MoD said it was mechanical failure. Whichever, the best officer I'd ever met was dead.

When I joined the battalion in Gibraltar there were one or two blokes that were getting ready to go on Selection, running around the Rock on a route called the Med Steps, but, being the nig, I'd no idea what it was all about. Then I heard they were going for the SAS, pronounced 'Sass'. It was only much later that I found out that to people in it, or who work with it, it's not the 'Sass' or even the SAS. It's just called the Regiment.

A fellow called Rob lived in a little room in the base at XMG that was no bigger than a cupboard. Sometimes I'd go past and I'd hear the *hish* of radios and catch a glimpse of piles of maps of South Armagh all over the place. The room

was like a rubbish tip – there were bergens, beltkit and bits and pieces everywhere. Then Rob would go missing and nobody saw him for weeks and weeks.

He turned up in the washrooms one day, so I was scrutinizing, seeing what he looked like. He wasn't 6'6" tall and 4' wide, as I'd expected. He was about 5'6" and quite normal looking. He was wearing a pair of skiddies, a T-shirt and flip-flops. His washing and shaving kit consisted of a bit of soap in a plastic teacup from a vending machine, a toothbrush, and that was it. He had his wash and left, and that was my introduction to the Regiment.

There was a warning one day that a chopper was due in ten minutes. All the spare hands that were on cookhouse fatigues had to come running out to pick up the load, so the helicopter would have the minimum amount of time on the ground. It could be delivering anything from equipment to food. Sometimes it would have a patrol on board.

As the nig I was simply told, 'There's a helicopter due in in ten minutes and there's some plastic bags. I want you to pick up the plastic bags and bring them into the camp.'

The chopper came in, the corrugated iron gates were flung open and everybody ran like idiots to pick up whatever was going to get dropped and then run back into the camp. I picked up two black plastic bags. Both contained what felt like Armalites. Then four or five blokes jumped from the helicopter. They had long curly hair and sideburns that came down and nearly met at the chin like the lead singer of Slade, and they were wearing duvet jackets, jeans and dessies (*desert boots*).

Basically the donkeys, which was us, picked the kit up and legged it in with them. We were told not to speak to these people, just to let them get on with what they were doing. Not that any of us wanted to speak to them anyway – we didn't know how they'd react. All we knew was that they were the Special Air Service – big hard bastards and they were going to fill us in. Me, the eighteen-year-old, I wasn't going to say jack shit.

46

There was only one TV in the whole camp, and that was in a room full of lockers and bits and pieces of shit all over the place. So everybody used to get in really early and book a place, sitting on top of lockers and hanging off chairs, getting on wall units and all this, to watch. Even if blokes were asleep, you'd wake them up for *Top of the Pops*.

The cookhouse was no bigger than a room in an ordinary house, and that included the cooking facilities. We'd get a tray, go in and get four slices of bread, make big sandwiches and a mug of tea, and go and claim our places for the show. Blokes would be there straight from the shower, squashed up next to blokes in shit state straight from the field. Everybody would be getting stuck into a fistful of egg banjo. The room stank of cigarettes, sweat, mud, cowshit and talcum powder.

At the time, just after Christmas 1978, Debbie Harry and Kate Bush were on the same *TOTP*. Debbie Harry was singing 'Denis', and Kate Bush was doing 'Wuthering Heights'. When Kate Bush came on the whole rifle company used to shout, 'Burn the witch!'

Then these blokes turned up as well, and I thought, they're only human after all because they've come in to watch Debbie Harry and Kate Bush. They didn't push in, they didn't get the prime spot, they just slotted in where they could, then they pushed off again. Their behaviour amazed me: they came in with respect.

I envied them their apparent freedom to come and go as they pleased. I thought, it must be an amazing life, just flying in, doing the job, then going back to wherever they live. But there again, I thought, there was no chance whatsoever of a lowly rifleman like me making the grade, and that was that.

5

There were eight infantry battalions at Tidworth, our new base in Wiltshire. The entertainment facilities in the town consisted of three pubs (one of which was out of bounds), two chip shops, a launderette, and a bank.

The army spent all day teaching us to be aggressive, and then we'd go down to the town, get bored and drunk, and use our aggression against each other. We'd then get prosecuted severely as if we'd done something wrong.

We did all the garrison sort of stuff like field firing exercises, then we started training again for Northern Ireland. The battalions would rotate, on average, one tour a year. I saw it as a great opportunity to save money. As a rifleman I could save a grand a tour because there was even less to do over the water than in Tidworth. There were three other bonuses. One, we got 50p extra pay per day, and two, we got soft toilet paper instead of the hard stuff in UK garrisons. It was actually dangled as a carrot during training: 'Remember, it's soft toilet rolls over the water.' And three, it was a pleasure to get away from Tidworth again. For the next three years the routine was going on exercises, getting drunk in Tidworth and Andover, and going over the water.

People were coming back with their grand and getting ripped off buying cars that promptly fell apart. One bloke bought a hand-painted cream and chocolate brown Ford Capri for £900, and within two days things were falling off

it. I looked at buying a Capri myself, but the insurance was more than the car was worth.

I was still going out with Christine. She was living in Ashford, so I got down there weekends and whenever else I could. There was certainly no way she wanted to come and live in Tidworth. She had a job and still lived at home. We were in love – 'we think' – and everything was coming up roses.

There began to be talk of the battalion going to Germany for five years and I knew this would present a problem for our relationship. If you were 'wife of', accommodation was provided; if you were just 'girlfriend of', then it was up to you to go and rent a place downtown. We'd never be able to afford the German rents, so I thought, what the hell, let's do it, and that was us married. It was a white wedding; the plan was that she would stay in Ashford, and after the next Northern Ireland tour we could get a quarter in Tidworth.

I got made up to lance corporal in time for the next tour. Still based in South Armagh, I was now a 'brick' commander, in charge of a four-man patrol. As such, I had to write a short patrol report after each patrol – what we had seen, what we had done, what we would like to have done. While I was on my way to the operations room one night, three or four blokes turned up in a car with all their equipment. I saw on the map that certain areas had been put out of bounds; I knew these boys were going to go and do some stuff. It made me think that as the infantry battalion we were working our arses off here, but these guys were working to a very different agenda. We used to come back from a patrol and think, we've done this and we've done that, it's really good stuff, but at the end of the day we were just walking Figure 11s (*standard target, depicting a charging enemy soldier*). We were so isolated in our own little world. Seeing these guys suddenly made me think: hey, what else is going on that we'll never get to hear about? I felt what was almost a pang of jealousy.

I went into the briefing room to pick up a patrol report.

There was masses of kit strewn everywhere on the floor. The thing that really struck me was an Armalite that was painted weird and wonderful camouflage colours, dappled with bits of black and green. In the infantry there was no way we could tamper with our weapons like that. Weapons were sacred; we could clean them, but that was about it. There was a torch mounted under the Armalite, held on with bits of masking tape on the furniture (*stock*). I thought, that's quite Gucci, I wouldn't mind one of those.

As I turned, I found myself face to face with one of the Regiment blokes. Or rather, face to arse. He had no kit on, and all I could see was the crack of his bum as he was bending over to put his trousers on. I could see he had a fearsome suntan, and had obviously been away somewhere nice before he'd come on this job.

He turned around and said, 'All right, mate?'

I went, 'Hello.'

He said, 'You can go now if you like.'

I said, 'OK, I think it's time for me to go now.'

That was the last time I saw any of these particular SAS men. Again, I was surprised at how they looked. One of them was positively skeletal – he was the only man I'd ever seen with the veins on the outside of his body.

We were patrolling one Saturday evening as a multiple, two four-man patrols. The multiple commander was Dave, a corporal, and I was the 2 i/c (*second-in-command*), in command of the other brick.

I had first met Dave in XMG but didn't have too much to do with him as he was in another platoon. On promotion I was sent to 6 platoon and became his 2 i/c. Dave was known as a maverick and was always on the edge of being demoted or fined. He came from the East End of London and kept very close contact with his family and friends. He was in his mid-twenties and his arms were covered in tattoos. He had a girlfriend back in London but the more I got to know him, the more I saw him as single for the rest

of his life, wrecking any car that he had after two months and having dealings with dodgy people from the Mile End Road. We got on very well and he became a close friend.

We were going out at six o'clock in the evening and assembled for a quick five-minute brief. Dave told us the direction we were going to go out, whether we were going to use the front gate or the back gate, information on any activity in the town, anything that we needed to know from the patrol that had just come in.

'There seem to be a lot more people running around the community centre than usual,' he said. 'And perhaps some activity in the derelict house on the corner of Liam Gardens. We'll check it out as we pass.'

Derelicts were usually to be avoided, since they were natural draw points for booby traps. Something had looked different in that house to the last patrol; it could be just an old mether in there, or it could be something put in as a come-on.

We loaded our weapons in the loading bay and stood behind the main gate, waiting for the order to go. It was a lazy, hot summer evening, not much traffic and the birds were singing. We listened on the net to the other patrol who were in the town, speaking in code words and numbers because our comms were not secure and the players had scanners.

You don't saunter out of a security forces station, you bomb-burst out – which means that you run like a fucking idiot for about twenty-five metres to get out of the immediate vicinity, before regrouping. If they were going to put a shoot in on it, or had a bomb rigged up, the one place they definitely knew soldiers were going to be was near the gates as they started a patrol.

We all bomb-burst out. Rather than going directly into the town, the route we'd decided to take was around the edge of it, in wasteground. We wanted to use the ground as much as possible to keep us away from the eyes of 'dickers' (*IRA observers*) in case they had something for us.

We didn't go through obvious features like holes in hedgelines or natural crossing points, which could be targeted and used to place bombs. We'd never touch anything military-looking either, like a shiny bit of kit which was out on the ground. Soldiers had been blown up picking up water bottles, thinking that another patrol had lost them and they'd do them a favour by retrieving them.

We came to a small river that we had to cross. No problems, we patrolled through that. Then we started to come up onto the wasteground just short of a housing estate. This was literally right on the edge of town, and from there it was cuds all the way down to a place called Castle Blaney on the other side of the border.

At that time of a Saturday night the streets were full of coaches that had come up to the estate to pick up the locals and take them down to Castle Blaney for 'the crack'. They'd go for a night out, then come rolling back at two o'clock in the morning. And quite rightly so; if I was stuck in Keady on a Saturday night I'd want to put the kit on and go over there on the piss.

We were patrolling along in dead ground. They couldn't see us, and we couldn't see them, but I was expecting that once we got nearer the housing estate I'd see a few people. We'd leave them alone. It was pointless going through crowds, because it just incited them. Our intention was to go round them, have a quick mooch around the housing estate and see what was going on.

More information was picked up when a patrol was stood still than when it was on the move. It was called 'lurking': we'd get to a position and just stop. It might be in somebody's back yard on a housing estate; we'd stop, get in the shadows and wait and listen, and see what was going on. It used to be great entertainment for the squaddies; we'd watch everything from domestic rows in kitchens to young couples groping in the mother's front room.

Dave's patrol was to the right of me, about 150 metres

away, and he was in dead ground to us. There was no need to talk on the radio. We'd been out there quite a few months already now, and we were working really well together, supporting each other.

Once we came near the estate we were hidden from view by a row of three or four shops – houses, basically, but with shop fronts. We turned right and went along the back of the buildings until we came to the fenceline and the gate. By now, the wasteground was more like disused farmland; there were old wrecked cars on it, tin cans, bags of garbage. There were goats and horses running around all over the place, so the ground was gungy and churned-up. It was summer but we still had rain at least once a week and the ground was wet. There were large puddles everywhere.

We got to the fenceline and I got lazy. If I crossed the fence, there would be all this car wreckage and rubbish in the way, and I didn't want to negotiate that. So I took the easy route.

As I started to come through the gate I came into view of the people in the street. I heard hollering and shouting and screaming all over the place, which was unusual. Normally there would just have been talking and lots of laughing, from groups of people smelling of Brut and hairspray, the girls in sharply ironed blouses.

As I looked up at the crowd I realized that everybody was shouting, grabbing hold of kids, pulling them out of the way. Something was up, but I didn't know what. I started to pan around to have a look. Still there was chaos; there must have been maybe 120 people there waiting for the coaches, and they were all reacting to my presence. I looked directly over the road, and as I then started to pan left towards the shops, crossing the road, again there was just the normal group of vehicles – three or four saloon cars and a cattle truck, which was not unusual in the area.

But then, just as I passed that, I saw a group of characters with masks on and weapons. The one that I really latched on to was a boy with his fist in the air, doing a Che Guevara

53

with his Armalite, chanting away. I couldn't have been more than 20 metres away from him. I saw his eyes open wide with alarm inside his mask.

He started to shout and fumbled with his weapon. I also shouted, fumbled for mine and cocked it. His weapon was already cocked, so he just started blatting like an idiot. I blatted back, getting the rounds down at him and the other masked people. Another fellow came up from behind the wagon and started to fire down in my general direction. They were flapping as much as I was, in a frenzy to get into the cattle truck and get away.

One of the boys got into the back of the wagon and started firing and the others clambered in. I got rounds into one of them. He was screaming like a pig as he went over the other side. Then there was lots of screaming coming from inside the vehicle, where other people were also taking rounds.

By this time, Scouse, another fellow from the patrol, had come up from the dead ground but couldn't get over the fence because of the firing. So he was firing from that side of the fence. The other two were down in the dead ground, totally confused about what was going on. It had all happened so quickly.

Lots of firing was going down. Everybody was screaming and shouting; I was kneeling and firing away. In my twenty-round magazines I always made sure that the top two were tracer. I worked on the theory that when we were in the cuds I could use my tracer to identify targets for other people. I had another tracer halfway down the magazine, so when that went off I'd know I'd fired ten rounds. The last two of the magazine were tracer again; when the fourth tracer fired off, I'd know I'd fired my second to last round and the working parts had come back and picked up the last round. I'd take the magazine off, put on another one, and that would be my reloading drill done. Time and time again I'd practised all this, until I could almost do it blindfolded. Come the day, it all went to ratshit. For one

thing, I was far too close for the tracer to ignite. And I certainly wasn't counting the rounds, I was just firing like a man possessed.

Then: *bang, bang, bang, click*. The dead man's click.

The working parts still worked, but there wasn't a round in the chamber to fire. I was flapping like fuck. I got on the floor, screaming my head off: 'Stoppage! Stoppage!' to let everyone else know I wasn't hit, but unable to fire. I could hear the different noises of the weapons: the SLR made a loud, bass sound as it fired; the Armalite was not as loud, and they were firing burst.

I tried to get hold of another magazine out of my pouches, and everything seemed sort of slow and deliberate; it wasn't, it was all really fast, but it was as if I was outside of myself, watching myself going through the drills.

I knew what to do, but the faster I was trying to do it, the faster I was fucking up. I had that feeling I'd had when the kid fell through the roof: I wanted to pull the covers over my head and wait for it all to go away. I concentrated on my mags; I didn't want to look up and see what was going on. If I didn't look, maybe I'd be all right.

What I should have been doing was getting into a position where I could look at the enemy; I was supposed to be so good at changing mags that there was no need to look at what I was doing. But I wasn't. I couldn't get the pouch opened up, I was fumbling inside getting my magazine out. It was the wrong way round. I had to turn it round, put it in, cock my weapon. It was all done in a matter of seconds, but it felt like for ever. I could hear some firing, I heard shouting; but loudest of all was the sound of me hollering and shouting inside my head: 'I don't like this! I know I've got to do it!'

I knew if I just lay there, 20 metres from him, the chances were that I'd be killed; as long as I was firing, things would be OK. My chest was heaving up and down. I knew I had to do it, I knew I couldn't just lie there.

I rolled over and started firing again. The stoppage had taken me out of action for no more than three to five seconds.

Twenty rounds later, bang, bang, bang, click.

The vehicle was moving, and by this time Scouse was firing into the cab area of the wagon, hoping to drop the driver. But these cattle trucks were armoured. They were sandbagged up with steel plates welded in to give them some form of protection.

I was still the only one that side of the fence. As the vehicle started to move off, I got up and ran forward, past the shop.

I didn't know if there was anybody left outside the wagon who'd done a runner. Had they run into the housing estate? Had they run into the shops? Had they run down to the junction which was only about ten metres away, and turned left? Or turned right, up an old disused railway line? Who knew? I had no idea what was going on.

In my peripheral vision I saw a group of people on the floor of the shop, cowering. A man stood up quickly. As far as I was concerned he could have a gun. I turned around and gave it a couple high through the window so he got the message. The glass caved in and the bloke threw himself to the floor.

'And stay down!' I shouted. I didn't know who was more scared, the people in the shop or me. It was a stupid, bone reaction of mine to shoot through the glass but I didn't know what else to do; I was so hyped up that anything that moved was a threat.

I ran up to a left-hand junction about ten metres away from the point of the contact. Time and time again during the build-up training we'd practised two ways of looking around corners. You can get very low and look round, close up to it, or, better still, you can move away from the corner and then gradually bring yourself round so you present less of a target. It was all very well in training, because I knew there was nobody round the other side with an

56

Armalite aimed at me. But here, there could be. I took a deep breath, got down on my belly with the weapon ready to swing round, and had a quick squint. There was nobody there. I brought myself round and followed on down the road a bit, just to check that there weren't any runners that way. Then I returned to the scene.

One poor fellow who had been part of the crowd was now halfway up the street. He had been in a wheelchair; the chair was lying on its side and he was crawling towards the housing estate, cursing and shouting. People were running from their houses to help him.

I could hear mothers shouting at their children, doors slamming, the sound of people running. A woman in the shop was screaming, 'There's nobody in here, there's nobody in here!' They knew that we were wound up, and they didn't want to be killed by faulty judgement.

By this time Scouse was with me and the other two blokes who had come over the fenceline. I went up to the bloke who was carrying the LMG and started kicking him.

'Where were you?' I shouted.

I had been all hyper; I'd wanted someone else there, and they weren't. But it wasn't their fault; they couldn't get there.

We started to go forward, looking for runners, at the same time getting on the radio and talking to the SF base to tell them there had been a contact. No need, they'd heard it anyway. All they wanted to know was, 'Any casualties? Any casualties?' At this stage I didn't know if any of us had been hit or not. The patrol that was to the north were running like loonies to get down to us. People were pouring out of the SF base; Land Rovers were turning up with people in tracksuits and flak jackets.

There was a massive follow-up. The dog handlers arrived within minutes, roadblocks were thrown up. The police had to be informed what they were looking for. I got on the net and was trying to describe the vehicle. All I knew

was that it was a dirty, old, yellow cattle truck, and because I had been on the floor looking up at it, I had seen that it had a fibreglass top to let the natural light in.

All the cars parked in the area were riddled with rounds – 5.56 from the players, 7.62 from us. There were empty cases all over the road.

One of the blokes from the sangars at the SF base reported that he had seen somebody running up the disused railway. We couldn't see jack shit.

A dog did his casting around and picked up the scent. The handler said, 'OK, let's go!'

There was myself, the platoon commander who'd come out of the SF base, the dog handler and his mutt, and two other blokes, and off we went. It was a very tense time. It was our job to protect the dog handler, and at the same time, we didn't know what the hell was up there. Was somebody behind cover, waiting to fire?

We ran across fields. There was an old pig hut at the top of a hill and the dog got agitated. The dog handler said, 'We've got something here.'

'He's got to be inside,' said the platoon commander.

The dog handler stayed where he was and the other fellows stayed to protect him as the rupert (*officer*) and I started to move up towards the shack.

The officer shouted, 'Any fucker in there, get out now! Otherwise we are coming in for you!'

Nothing happened.

He turned to me and said, 'Right, when you're ready, get in there.'

I thought, oh, good one – delegation of tasks.

We'd done plenty of FIBUA (*fighting in built-up areas*) in training, but this was for real. I put my weapon in the shoulder, flicked off the safety catch, took a deep breath, kicked the door open, and went for it. The shack was empty.

We cast around with the dog, but it was getting nothing. By the time we got back down into the town, the incident

had been contained. The area had been cordoned off and all the forensic people had arrived and were doing their stuff. There was activity everywhere, sirens blaring, helicopter rattling overhead.

As the colonel arrived with his team we heard on the radio that a body and two wounded had been dropped off at Monaghan Hospital in the south. The boy had taken rounds. Two others had gunshot wounds. Everybody around the area who had radios was going, 'Yes! Well done! Good shit!'

A few days later, we learned what had happened. The cattle truck and a Ford Granada had driven into that side of Keady. The people in the Ford Granada got out, and were going to get into this cattle truck and then drive past the other patrol to the north and drop as many as they could, then carry on driving over the border.

When the contact was initiated it must have been very confusing for them. The player who was firing at me was also trying to give information to his team. As they got into the cattle truck, they were firing from a step which gave them higher elevation, and what they would have seen was Dave's patrol about 200 metres away, moving through the river. Dave's patrol started to get incoming but he couldn't fire back because he knew we were in the middle. The people in the truck didn't know that we were there; if they had, they would have been able to put some heavy fire down onto us.

They got outside of Keady and went to a house that was run by an ex-prison officer. They tried to hijack his car but he came out with a shotgun and gave them the good news, so they then moved off again in the cattle truck, and got to Monaghan to drop off the boys who were dead and injured.

It was the first time I'd ever killed somebody. I was 19 years old and I couldn't have cared less. They were firing at me, and I was doing my job by firing back. I did what I was taught. No matter what a person does in the infantry – he can be a signaller, driver, whatever – what he's basically

doing is getting himself or someone else into a position where he can put the butt of a weapon into the shoulder, aim, and kill somebody.

I'd spent months and months training for this sort of situation. I'd learned the drills, I was proficient. But when the shit hit the fan, all I could think about was that the other character was trying to kill me. I just knew there were a lot of people firing, and I knew I had to get fire back, and that was about it. I considered myself very fortunate to have survived. It wasn't skill that had got me through, it was loads of rounds down the range, and loads of luck.

6

We came back to the UK and I went away on a course called an NCO's Cadre. I got an 'A' and was promoted the same day, making me the youngest corporal in the infantry at that time.

Next came 'Junior Brecon', an eight-week section commander's course at Sennybridge training area. There was no bullshit about it, just tactics and training, training and more training. It was a really intense two months, lots of physical stuff, running around with a helmet and bayonet on all the time, giving orders. I found it really hard, but I got a distinction.

By now I was totally army barmy, and was letting my married life come a very poor second. I was immature, and I was a dickhead. I came back from the course on a Saturday morning, said hello, and went out for a run. Then I got up early on Sunday morning and went for another run, trying to keep fit for whatever course I was going to go on next – and I was putting my name down for every course that would have me.

For young wives in a garrison town like Tidworth, life could be very boring. It was difficult to get decent work because employers knew they were not there for long, and that made it almost impossible for married women to have a career. The battalions liked to promote a family atmosphere, but for the wives it didn't really work out like that. There was a hierarchy, and there were more wives who

wore their rank than blokes: 'I'm Georgina Smith, wife of *Sergeant* Smith.'

The marriage started going to ratshit in about 1980. Christine was in Tidworth, in quarters, ready to go to Germany, sitting there and thinking: sod this. The ultimatum was delivered one morning during the corn-flakes: 'Are you going to come back with me or are you going to stay here in Tidworth in the army?'

No contest.

'I'm staying here,' I said. 'Away you go.'

That was it. Over and done with, sorted out over bits of paper, and I didn't give a damn. I threw myself into all the bone bravado; I was out with my mates now, I was going to stay in the army for ever, I didn't need a wife. There were many like me; I was not the only one.

There was a NAAFI disco every Tuesday night at RAF Wroughton near Swindon. It was a great event, but then, so was anything that took place outside of Tidworth. Six or seven of us in freshly pressed kit would pile into the chocolate and cream Capri, everybody stinking of a different aftershave.

One Tuesday night I met a telephonist called Debbie and forgot all my resolutions about not needing women any more.

A posting came up as a training corporal at Winchester and I grabbed it. Germany could wait. Career-wise the job was known as an E posting – a good one to get. By the time I came back I'd be a sergeant.

My platoon commander was a lieutenant; under him he had the platoon sergeant and three training corporals. Each of us full screws (*corporals*) was responsible for between twelve and fifteen recruits.

One or two of the lads were fairly switched on with life and really wanted to join the infantry for what it offered. Most of them, however, were there because they wanted to be in the army but lacked the

intelligence to be anything but riflemen – a bit like me, really.

A lot of them hadn't got a clue what they were doing when they turned up. They'd been looking at the adverts of squaddies skiing and lying on the beach surrounded by a crowd of admiring women. They had the impression that they were in for three years lolling around on a windsurfer, then they'd come out and employers would be gagging to get their hands on them.

We had to show them how to wash and shave, and use a toothbrush. I'd get into the shower and say, 'Right, I'm having a shower now,' taking with me the socks that I'd been wearing that day. I'd put them on my hands and use them like flannels – so I was washing my socks at the same time as my body. Then I had to show them how to shower, making sure they pulled their foreskin back and cleaned it, and shampoo'ed their hair.

Every one of them had to do it exactly the same way, cleaning their ears, cleaning their teeth in the shower at the same time, cleaning the shower out afterwards. I'd then show them how to cut their toenails correctly. A lot of them didn't cut them at all, and they were minging – or they just got the edge and then pulled it away so they were destroying the cuticle. In the infantry, if your feet are fucked, then the rest of you is fucked.

A lot of them had never done their own washing. We even had to show them how to use an iron. But soon, everybody was all squared away and they knew what they were doing and, more importantly, why.

The idea of the training was to keep them under pressure, but make it enjoyable. The training corporals had to do everything that they did, leading by example. And all the time we were also aiming to create competition, a sense of achievement for their group, building up team work.

The results of the section reflected directly on us, so we had that extra incentive to do the job as best we could. But

it came to the stage where I was so involved in it that incentives weren't necessary.

I didn't believe in giving a boy who was slow a hard time, because it wouldn't help him at all. All it would do would make him feel worse; if he needed extra training, we had to give it to him. I would encourage other people in that section to make sure they gave him extra training as well. I would tell them, 'He's a part of your section – he's as much a responsibility to you as he is to me.'

When a recruit got to the battalion, the first thing anybody would ask was, 'Who was your training screw?' If we were sending tossers to the battalion, we'd be in for a hard time.

The bullying that was supposed to be going on in these infantry battalions and training establishments could only have been very isolated incidents. I certainly never saw any of it. If you're doing your job right you don't need to bully, you don't need to push and shove, punch and kick. What you've got to do is lead by example, show them the skills that they need to know, make it enjoyable, give them incentives – and they'll do it. By the same token, the culture within the army is quite aggressive and close to the bone. There is a need for hard, physical work, and a hard, physical existence. But that's not bullying. If people can't actually survive that or adapt to it, or simply don't have the aptitude, that's when they should go. As the saying goes, train hard, fight easy; train easy, fight hard – and die.

Within the battalion, if people weren't performing they'd get decked. I had been filled in a few times, and after a while I always understood the reasons why. As for these daily scenes of regimental baths and scouring with Vim, I never saw it. I never went through any sort of initiation, and was never present at one. People had better things to do with their time than run around playing stupid games. They wanted to finish work, go down town and get legless.

* * *

64

I still enjoyed the army but it was all the niggly bits that pissed me off. I went shopping in the town one dinner time with another of the training corporals, a bloke in his early thirties – married, three kids, responsible. He wanted to buy a three-piece suite. He chose the suite and sat down with the manager to do the paperwork. The manager took a cheque for the deposit but then said, 'I'm sorry, but you can't have credit without your commanding officer's permission.'

'I beg your pardon?'

'You have to get this form signed by your commanding officer.'

'You're joking?'

'No, I'm afraid if you're military, that's it.'

So here was a boy with responsibilities, a house, family, all the normal things. Yet he couldn't get credit to buy a three-piece suite until somebody who was probably up to his eyeballs in debt had had a chat with him and said, 'Well, do you think you can afford this three-piece suite – do you think you're responsible enough to buy it?'

If there was any problem with the credit, they wouldn't go to the bloke who was getting the credit, they'd go straight to the commanding officer and say, 'This man isn't paying.' He'd then go on OC's orders and it would get taken out of his pay.

I had been overdrawn once in my life, for £2.50 when I was nineteen. The letter from the bank wasn't sent to me, it was sent to the battalion. I had to go on OC's orders and explain why I was £2.50 overdrawn to somebody who probably owed the bank half his annual salary.

I asked Debbie to move to Winchester and rent a flat with me, but I had to get permission from the OC for that as well.

I pondered a bit more about Selection and the life of a Special Forces soldier. From the limited amount I had seen, these people in Hereford seemed to have a much freer existence; I doubted very much that in the Special Air

Service a platoon commander aged about twenty-one or twenty-two had to say whether a thirty-year-old sergeant should be allowed to take a credit application form to his commanding officer.

I started to do a bit of bergen work just to see, and found I could move over the ground pretty fast.

Debbie and I lived together for about six or seven months. I had a great relationship with her and her family. Then came crunch time, my posting back to the battalion. She now had a problem: was she going to stay in the UK, or come over to Germany for three years? Exactly the same as last time, I thought: what the heck, we'll get married – and we did, in August 1982. This time, being a corporal, I got a quarter straightaway.

7

As soon as I got to Germany I started to dream about a return ticket.

2RGJ were now a mechanized battalion, which didn't grip my shit at all. I was supposed to be a section commander but I didn't even know how to get into an APC (*armoured personnel carrier*), let alone command one. I had about a week to sort myself out, and then the battalion was off to Canada for two months of Battle Group training. All the tanks and infantry came together to form the battle group, screaming over the vast Canadian prairies in live-firing attacks. It was probably good training but I hated bumming around in these turn-of-the-century machines. They were falling apart; most of the time was spent drinking tea while half the REME (*Royal Electrical & Mechanical Engineers*) were underneath them with spanners. Out of four vehicles in my platoon it was a safe bet that at least one of them would not even make it to the start line. The crew would spend days on the roadside waiting for recovery.

After three or four weeks back in Germany the quarter was ready and Debbie flew out. Almost immediately we started having to do two- or three-week exercises. We'd drive to a location, dig in, stay there for a couple of days, jump in our APC again, go somewhere else, and dig in again. It was incredibly boring and as far as I was concerned we weren't really achieving that much. Certainly none of us at the coal-face was ever told what the big plan was.

As in Canada, most of these exercises were spent at the roadside – either broken down, or grounded for two days because the Germans wouldn't allow armoured vehicles to move at weekends. A fair one if you were the indigenous population, I supposed, but if you were the squaddy parked up just 10 kilometres from the comforts of home it was a downright drag.

The general level of bullshit was outrageous, and it started to wear me down. Any time we weren't trundling around in geriatric APCs we were doing battalion duties. At least five times a month I'd be on guard. Then we'd have all the other regimental duties, which were twenty-four-hour duties. Then we had brigade duties.

Because it was the British Army on the Rhine, we had to look good at all times. Princess Anne was going to visit the camp one day and there were yellow marks where some boxes and bits of wood had been resting on the grass. The management ordered it to be painted green. I realized then that all the royal family must think the world smells of shoe polish, floor wax and fresh paint.

We were practising for the sake of practising and the soldiers were getting pissed off. When we'd got the promise of a posting to Germany it sounded very attractive – local overseas allowance, tax-free car, petrol concessions, all this sort of thing. But at the end of the day, the quality of life for a single soldier was not that good. We hadn't really got the time to go out and explore the place. It wasn't as if we could just jump in a car and travel down to the south of Germany to go skiing for a weekend; chances were we'd be on some weird and wonderful duty, such as being the barrier technician on the gate.

Life in Germany was unpleasant in other ways. There were a few rows with the other battalions, and plenty of rows with the Turks, who ran all the sex operations, bars and discos. Then there were all the inter-battalion horizontal manoeuvres. As soon as a battalion was away over the water, all the singlies were straight over to check

out the wives. Boxes of OMO appeared in the windows to advertise Old Man Out. I didn't find it funny. None of the married blokes did.

The army seemed to promote smoking and drinking, because the only recreational facilities available were cheap fags and drink at the NAAFI and the company clubs. If weight training facilities had been available, the lads would have used them – not because they thought that upper body strength would make them better soldiers, but because of a reason far more fundamental to an eighteen-year-old: if you look fit, you'll pull more.

I felt my morale being slowly eroded. I sat down one day and asked myself: what am I going to do – am I going stay here or fuck off? I was doing pretty well, I was coming up towards platoon sergeant, but I felt compelled to make that decision. It was a right pain in the arse sweeping up unwanted puddles, painting grass that had been discoloured by boxes, and maintaining vehicles that were falling apart.

By this time Debbie had got a job at the local military hospital. She enjoyed it very much, but we really didn't get much time together. If I had free time, I'd be training for Selection, coming home late at night. It just wasn't really happening between us. The social life was fine, and we had become good friends with Kev and his wife. He was in B Company and now a corporal. His wife worked in the same hospital as Debbie.

By now Dave was back in battalion after a posting and we'd all go out together. Kev's idea of a good Saturday would be football and a few pints. He was a fair player himself, and represented the battalion in the same team as Johnny Two-Combs. He'd joined the army when he was in his mid-twenties, and had a flat, a car and a good job. We thought he must have joined for a bet.

I became obsessed with getting into the Regiment. In the long term it would be better for our relationship, because the Regiment was permanently based in Hereford. We'd be

able to buy a house and settle down. There would be continuity in Debbie's life, and she could get a decent job. That was how I rationalized it to her, anyway. In reality, I wanted it for me.

I filled in an application form and started really working on my fitness, but at first didn't tell anyone but Kev what I was up to.

'I was thinking about doing it myself,' he said. 'I'll join you.'

Then I talked to Dave, who said, 'Yeah, fuck it, let's all do it.'

We got our bergens on, did some running and circuit training. Then Dave introduced us to a captain, a Canadian called Max, who wanted to throw in his lot with us as well. He'd been away to Oman for two years on secondment to the Sultan's forces; he'd met some of the Regiment and had got a taste for it. His family owned farmland near Winnipeg and he spoke with a distinctive twang. He planned to do the tour with the Regiment, go to Staff College, and carry on his career. The ultimate aim was to go back to the farm. He was married and very down to earth, not at all the officer type. The great thing from our point of view was that he'd have the authority to get us places.

We spoke to everybody we could think of who knew somebody who'd danced with somebody who'd done Selection. 'What's the best stuff for hardening the feet?' we'd ask when we tracked them down. 'Any hints on special food or drink?'

'I know somebody in Third Battalion who passed Selection and he swore by Neat's Foot oil,' was the furthest we got.

We tried it for two weeks, then switched back to meths.

Once the buzz started going around the battalion that there were people going for Selection, a fellow called Bob came forward. A bricklayer from London, he had joined the army late in life. He was 5'7" and strongly built; fitness seemed to come very naturally to him. Nothing fazed Bob, he laughed everything off.

'If I don't pass I'll get out anyway,' he said. 'I've had enough; I'll go back on the sites.'

Bob had a diary written by a fellow called Jeff, who had just passed Selection and at twenty-one was one of the youngest people ever to get into the Regiment. It contained details of routes used in the Brecon Beacons, and became our bible.

The captain, having more money than us, decided to buy a VW camper van so we could get over to the UK for training; we chipped in for petrol. We were helped enormously in our training programme by Alex, the anti-tank platoon commander, who had been in the Regiment himself and was now back with the battalion. He organized a three-week exercise in Wales for us as an excuse for us to get up on the hills. We drove through the night, caught the early-morning ferry, and reached one of the military transit camps near Brecon by breakfast the next day.

We met up with Johnny Two-Combs. He'd already done Selection at the same time as Jeff, and had failed. He'd made the commitment to go straight back and do the next Selection, and was doing his own training. It was great; he had more information.

'Try witch hazel on the feet,' he said. 'And if you get blisters, sort them out with iodine.'

It was all desperation stuff, trying to find some magic formula that would save our feet. Name the old wives' tale, we'd be trying it. Some people, we heard, wrapped orthopaedic tape round their heels and toes. Anything was worth a try, because if we started getting injuries, there wouldn't be time for them to heal. We'd just have to carry on day after day.

As we learned the hard way, bugger-all worked. All it took was two pairs of socks and a decent pair of boots. The inner sock was thin and the outer was a thick woollen one, and that stopped the friction rub.

Every day we were trying something different to make the bergen comfortable.

Johnny said, 'Half a roll-bed put down the back of the bergen works wonders.'

I tried it and it was just uncomfortable for me. I still got bergen sores, and they were really painful. They wore me down more and more each day. We tried other precautions, including bandages strapped around the chest to protect our backs. I had tried padding out the actual straps on the bergen but that was no good, it just wore away and rode up the masking tape. I experimented with cutting up a bit of foam roll-bed but that just used to slip along the back of it. What I found was best was simply to leave the thing alone. At the end of the day what you've got is your world stuck on your back, two straps over your shoulders, and the thing digging in. You've just got to put up with it and crack on.

Then it came to drinking water. How were we going to get water down our necks? Did we want to have to stop every five minutes and take the bergen off? There were weird and wonderful devices coming out of people's bergens. Max was the Mister Gadget Man. He had everything dangling off him. He'd worked out that water stops robbed us of a lot of time, and turned up one day with a large water bottle of the kind that cyclists use, with a long tube coming out. He'd sellotaped the tube onto the straps of his bergen so all he had to do was put the tube in his mouth and suck it. I had tried all that and it was all a bag of shit – it would go wrong, the piping would break or pull out of the bottle. What it boiled down to was that you had water on your belt and some more in your bergen. You drank from your beltkit water bottle, stopped to fill it up from the kit in your bergen, and off you went. None of the Heath Robinson kit worked – unfortunately.

Then there was the question: how are we going to carry our map? Max had a plastic orienteering map-case that hung around his neck. I tried that, and found that I spent most of my time with it blowing in my face or wrapped around my neck because it was so windy up there. What

was best was to put the map in a clear plastic bag and carry that in the map pocket on your leg.

We tried all the energy drinks, electrolytes and such that were starting to come in. People were buying Lucozade and natural body composite drinks as if they were going out of fashion, but at the end of the day, I reckoned it didn't matter what you had, as long as you had fluids down you. I still drank gallons of Lucozade, however; I loved the taste.

The only thing everyone agreed on was painkillers, and plenty of Brufen to stop the swelling. I planned to throw them down my neck like a man possessed if I had to: get rid of the pain, get rid of the swelling, and carry on.

The weather was a mixture of rain, low cloud and mist, and always overcast. If the sun was out, it was cold; if it wasn't, it was raining. We were tabbing hard anyway, so we didn't need much clothing on. We were getting really fit and confident. I felt I had stamina now with the bergen, and I knew the ground. When I looked at the map, I had every feature imprinted in my mind – where all the little pathways were, what I could see from the high ground. I felt I wouldn't have to worry about the map reading, I could just concentrate on making the distance in the time allowed.

Time spent on reconnaissance is seldom wasted. We were sure that getting up on the Beacons had been a must. It gave us the time to tune in and know the ground, to feel more confident if the weather started to clag in. Before I went to Wales I had looked on the map at Pen-y-Fan and Fan-Fawr, the major features over the Beacons, and thought: hmm, that's pretty steep. But until I got there and saw it for myself, I wouldn't have believed how vertical a hill could be. Being there for three weeks got us over that initial shock, and we soon built up confidence. And despite the weather, we had a really good laugh. I knew the pubs in Brecon anyway from the course that I'd done down there. We met people that were on the Junior and Senior Brecon courses and it was wonderful to be out of the battalion. I loved it.

Back in Germany, we spent every spare minute training. Passing Selection had become my complete and utter focus. I'd go to sleep at night thinking about Pen-y-Fan and all the other places that we'd gone to. When I woke up, my first thought was, what am I going to do if I fail? The more I thought about my life in the battalion, the more desperate I was to escape.

There was a massive ridge that ran all the way from Minden to Osnabruck. It was a really steep feature, and we used to get our arses up there nearly every day. As well as that, if another company were doing a BFT (*basic fitness test*), we'd turn up and do it with them. Then we'd go circuit training. Fitness was all; we knew that the first month of Selection was the killer, with 80 per cent of candidates gone by the end of it.

I knew I was kidding myself when I told Debbie that it would be better for us in the long term if I could get into the Regiment. She was enjoying the existence in Germany. She had a good job, friends, and she was establishing herself. If I passed Selection, I would be away from her for at least seven months of the year.

And so it was that on a hot sunny day in July 1983, the four of us boarded the old camper van for what we hoped was the last time, and set off for Hereford.

8

They didn't give us directions to Stirling Lines, for obvious reasons. If you can't even find your way to the camp, it's going to be a waste of time trying to join Special Forces. We had made sure we knew where we were going, which was just as well. One or two blokes were late, having got off the train at Hereford station and asked the locals for directions. Nobody told them. Apparently the town was very security conscious, and the police were always alerted if anyone was seen as suspicious.

We chugged up to the main gate on a Sunday. Apart from the high wire fence surrounding it and the military policemen at the gates, the camp looked like a deserted college campus. I'd expected to find a hive of activity, but instead saw only one or two characters mooching around in track-suit bottoms and T-shirts. They took no interest in us whatsoever.

We signed in and did a pile of documentation, all the usual stuff – name, date of birth, qualifications, rank. We were then directed down to the stores to draw a bergen, sleeping bag, water bottles, twenty-four-hour rations, cookers, and a survival kit.

'When you're up in the hills,' the quartermaster told us, 'all the weight that's in your bergen must be weight that's usable – food, water, bivvi bag, spare clothes. The days of carrying bricks for the sake of it are well gone.

'You are only allowed to wear an army-issue boot. The

argument is, you can wear a pair of Gucci walking boots now, but what happens if you've been in the jungle for three months and your boots start to rot and fall off? When you get a resupply parachuted into the jungle they're sure as hell not going to be size eight and a half in your favourite Go-faster Guccis.'

Our names were on a board in alphabetical order and we were allocated to eight-man rooms. The Green Jackets were split up, and we wandered off with a casual, 'See you later.'

Another couple of guys had already arrived in my room; we nodded a greeting to each other but not much more. As I unpacked the kit I'd brought with me, I cast a quick eye over what gear of theirs I could see. I wasn't the only one with boxes of electrolyte drinks, bottles of Neat's Foot oil just in case, strapping for my legs, and a party-pack of Brufen.

I wandered off to find the others. Everybody was doing their own thing, sorting themselves out, then perhaps, like me, going to see a mate who was in another room. There were one or two radios on.

It seemed everybody was amongst strangers, from different units. People were saying hello, but not really chatting to each other. There wasn't that friendly room thing that there usually was when soldiers got together on a course. There were little mumblings going on of, 'All right, mate, how you going?' but the atmosphere felt rather tense. Naturally it would take a while to know each other, as in any group, but I sensed there was more to it than that. The slightly furtive unpacking and guarded responses reminded me of boxers in a shared changing room before a bout. Polite, but wary. I thought it was rather odd. As far as I was concerned, the only person I was competing against was myself.

First thing Monday morning, all 180 of us assembled in the gym. Before the course even started we had to do the army's BFT, a 3-mile run in boots and clothing.

'You've got fifteen minutes to do the first mile and a half,' the DS (*directing staff*) said. 'The rest is up to you. Don't be last man home.'

We set off at a fastish pace. However, without kit, it was a piece of cake. A reasonable jogger wouldn't have broken out in a sweat. I couldn't believe it when I saw people falling by the wayside, holding their sides and fighting for breath. I'd seen old ladies who were fitter. Yet the basic fitness test was a basic requirement throughout the army; in theory, even the plumpest pastry cook should have passed. As the cripples limped in, the DS took their names and told them to go and get changed. They had been binned on the spot, even before the start of Selection proper. They'd obviously been reading too many James Bond books; by the looks on their faces the three miles had come as quite a shock to them.

For the next couple of days we did basic map-reading revision.

'If you can't read a map and you're stuck on top of the hill, the weather comes down and it's freezing, you're going to die,' the DS said. 'We don't want you dying: number one because of the expense of putting people on Selection, and number two, we don't want the inconvenience of having to ask the standby squadron to get their arses up trying to look for bodies – and three, it isn't good for you as you'll have failed Selection.'

Unbelievably, some people had turned up just about knowing the difference between north and south. Part of this map-reading refresher was orienteering with the bergens on, which was prepping us for the time in the mountains. I was amazed at how many people were starting to get fed up with it already. Whatever their idea of what Selection was, it wasn't this.

I didn't see much of Kev and the others, except in passing. The occasional quick chat at meal times, however, revealed that everybody was doing fine.

We did quite a lot of running, 5-milers mostly, in groups

77

of twenty to thirty. We'd do a map-reading class, then be sent off for a run; the people that had just come in off a run, leaking (*sweating*) and panting, would then do map reading. There were still people binning it and getting binned after these runs.

They got progressively more arduous: 5 or 7 miles in boots, followed by sit-ups and press-ups, then 100-metre piggyback races and fireman's carries up hills. More people jacked. I reckoned the DS were weeding out the people who wouldn't be capable of doing the first real test at the end of the week, the Fan Dance.

Another of the regular runs was an 8-miler in boots in hilly country, to be done in under an hour. I reasoned that as long as I stayed tucked in behind the DS I'd be fine, but for reasons best known to themselves everybody else seemed to want to be up the front. I couldn't see that it mattered.

We did more orienteering, this time carrying bergens. I got to one checkpoint and sat by the wagons, having a brew. One of the DS was sitting nearby, watching the rest of the gang stagger in. One of them, a tall, smart-looking bloke that I knew to be a cavalry officer, was wearing sweatbands on his wrists, a bandana around his head and, to top it all, a cravat. He looked as if he was going off for a game of squash. The DS got up and went and talked to other members of the training wing. They were all having a look at this boy and obviously discussing him. The thought struck me then that this was about being a grey man; getting noticed, I guessed, was probably only a few steps away from getting binned.

The Fan Dance is a 24-kilometre run with bergens, done with DS in groups of about thirty, with no map-reading requirement. It starts at the bottom of Pen-y-Fan, goes up onto the hill, and right to the top, which is the highest point in that part of the country. Then it's back down, around another mountain called the Crib, and along the Roman road, a rubbly old track, then down to a checkpoint at a

place called Torpanto. Then it's the whole lot again, in reverse.

One group started at Torpanto, mine at the Storey Arms mountain rescue centre at the base of the Fan, and in theory we crossed over at the top.

The bergen weighed 35lbs. We didn't know the cut-off time, but the DS did. The only advice we were given was, 'If you keep with us, you're all right. If you don't, you're fucking late.'

The DS went, he really motored. Within five minutes the tightly packed group was strung out along the track. I noticed several very fit-looking faces that I hadn't seen before, and which were overtaking me. It was the first time I'd seen people from the squadrons; apparently there was an open invite for anybody who happened to be in camp to go and do the Fan Dance. All these characters turned up in Range Rovers, with flasks of tea. They got the bergens on and off they went. I was feeling really fit and confident, but these blokes were just steaming past, especially on the uphill sections. It really pissed me off; they'd jog up alongside the DS, have a bit of a chat, then accelerate over the horizon.

My chest heaved up and down until I got my second wind, and then I started to sweat. It started to get in my eyes and sting the sores on my back. Within twenty minutes I was soaking wet but my breathing was regulated and I was feeling good. I knew where I was going, and though it was wet underfoot the weather was fine.

I arrived at Torpanto in good shape, huffing and puffing, but confident. It wasn't too hot a day, and I wasn't having to stop too often for a drink. I gave my name to the DS, turned around, then did the whole route in reverse. I sang the same song to myself in my head, over and over. It was a rap song; the music was just coming to the UK and I hated it. I still sang it, though.

It was a matter of running downhill and on flat ground, and tabbing as hard as we could uphill. That was all there

was to it, arms swinging, legs pumping. I passed Max on the way. He was going well, with the water-pipe flailing behind him in his slipstream.

Out of the 180 who had started the week, 100 of us had got as far as the Fan Dance. By the end of the day, another 30 had been binned. The Fan, we were told, was a bench mark. If we couldn't do the Fan, there was no way we had the stamina or physical aptitude to carry on.

That night Peter, the chief instructor, walked around the room. He was about 5'5" tall and looked like everybody's favourite uncle. He inspected all the weird and wonderful drinks that were lying on the lockers, and said, in a very slow Birmingham accent that never got above 2,000 revs: 'All this shit, you can take it if you like – it's up to you. But the best thing is, two pints of Guinness and a bag of chips at the end of each day.'

Dutifully, we went down to the town and sank two pints of Guinness and bought a bag of chips each at the chippie.

Everybody was sorting out their feet with whatever magic potion and strapping their toes up. I put orthopaedic felt on my heels and sorted out my blisters. The army was full of recipes for how to get rid of the things, but I had always found that the best thing was to pierce them at the edge with a needle sterilized in a flame, squeeze all the muck out, and just throw a plaster over. There wasn't a lot more that could be done.

The second week started. I reached the wagon after a particularly gruelling run and took stock. My feet and legs ached, my thigh muscles were killing me. My shoulders were badly sore and felt almost dislocated, as if they had dropped. I had a pain in the small of my back; as I carried the bergen uphill, I leaned forwards to push against the weight. When I finished and dropped my bergen, it felt as if I was floating on air. I pulled my tracksuit on and got all nice and warm drinking my flask of tea as we were driving back.

As we relaxed on the wagons, our muscles seized up.

Getting off again we looked like a load of geriatrics as we stumbled off the tailgate and hobbled back to our rooms, dragging our sleeping bags along the ground. I looked in the mirror. I looked just how I felt. My hair was sticking up where I had been sweating, and it was covered in mud and twigs.

We kept our bergens by our beds. There was a drying room for all the wet clothing but it was pointless washing it – it was only going to get soaking wet and filthy again, so we put it in the drying room for a while, then rested it on our bergens for the next day.

After a while we did start talking to each other, but the only topic was Selection. Every time I came back off a day's tabbing I wanted to find out how many people had been binned. The more people the better. I was chuffed that thirty people failed the Fan Dance. Great, I thought, it made me feel as if I was doing well.

The daily tabs now ranged from 15 to 64 kilometres, and night marches were introduced. Day after day, it was the same routine. We'd get the timings to go on the wagons in the morning, go to where the tab was going to start, do it, and get back at night. Then the Darby and Joan Club would go shuffling back to the rooms, dump their kit, put their stuff in the drying room, have a bath or a shower, have something to eat, and get their heads down. The days of Guinness and chips were over.

Nobody told us the timings for the day, so we didn't know how far we were going, where we were going, what route we were taking, or how long we had; we had no option but to go as fast as we could, and that was where the map-reading skills came in. If I came to a re-entrant (*valley*), I didn't go down and then up, I'd see if it might be worth contouring around the longer distance.

Discipline was uncalled for. All they'd say was, 'Be in the quadrangle for six o'clock.' We'd turn up, they'd call out our names and tell us what trucks to get on. The majority of people were getting in their sleeping bags or putting their

bobble hats on, resting and drinking flasks of tea. Then, all too soon, we'd get to the checkpoint, clamber out, and they'd call us forward one by one and send us on our way.

The training team told us nothing. We were the ones that wanted to be there, they weren't soliciting for our custom. Their attitude seemed to be: the course is here if you want to do it.

'Red fifteen?'

I went over to the DS.

'Name?'

'McNab.'

'Where are you?'

I had to show him on the map where I was. If you put your finger on a map you're covering an area of 500 or 600 metres – unless you've got big stubby fingers, in which case it might be a kilometre. You've got to point exactly where you are with a blade of grass or a twig.

'You are going to Grid 441353. Show me where that is.'

I showed him.

'Show me what direction you are going in.'

I took my bearing, and showed him.

He said, 'Well you'd better get started, because the clock's running.'

There was one bloke in my group, Trev, who was so hyper and revved up that he ended up doing everything the wrong way round. Instead of going north he would go south. He got off the wagon one day and got called over by the DS.

They said, 'Where are you?'

He showed them on the map.

'Which way are you going?'

He pointed the way he was going, which was correct, then went off in totally the wrong direction.

The DS turned around to us and said, 'Where the hell's he going?'

They let him go for about a hundred metres, then shouted:

'Oi, dickhead, come back here! For fuck's sake, where are you going? Show us your bearing.'

Trev showed him and the DS said, 'Then fucking go in that direction. You've already wasted three minutes.'

A lot of the time, if I was going for a high point, I could see it and it never got any closer. My mind would start wandering off onto different things. Sometimes I'd start singing stupid songs to myself in my mind; or little advertising jingles that I'd always hated anyway.

I'd get to the checkpoint and lean forward, my hands on my knees to rest the shoulders.

They'd say, 'Show me where you are.' Then, 'You are going to Grid 345678. Show me what direction that is.'

Off I'd go.

Sometimes I'd get to a checkpoint where they'd have a set of scales. For that day's marches, perhaps the bergen had to weigh 40lbs. They'd check the weight, and if a bloke was under, they'd put a big rock in his pack, sign it with a lumicolour and radio on to the next couple of checkpoints that Blue 27 had a rock in his bergen because he was a snidey bastard. It meant that instead of carrying 40lbs he would now be humping around with 55lbs for the rest of the day. When measured in sweat and blisters 15lbs is a lot of difference.

The big mistake was to take 40lbs as the all-in start weight of the bergen, including the water. As soon as you'd drunk one pint you'd be underweight. When they said 40lbs they meant 40lbs at the end of the day, not the beginning.

When we came in off the hills, we'd be sorting ourselves out. The training team would come around, calling out names. These, we soon learned, were the people who were getting binned.

If we'd had a bad day, we'd get a 'gypsy's warning'. The sergeant major would say, 'The following people, come and see me.' Those people would gather round him. He'd say, 'You didn't do very well yesterday. This is a gypsy's; you'd

better sort your shit out, because next time you'll be gone.'

If anybody had already had a gypsy's and their name was called, they could assume the worst.

I'd be feeling fairly confident if I was in the first wagon on the way back. Second wagon, I was unsure but not too worried. Third wagon, I would have been shitting myself. It only happened to me once. Most days, however, I was looking at other people, chuffed that these 6'4" blond-haired, good-looking thoroughbreds were getting the shove.

I'd say, 'That's a shame,' but inside I'd be thinking, good shit! Everybody was for themselves, everybody wanted to pass.

'The point is,' the DS said, 'if you've got to be in a position to give covering fire with your GPMG in six hours and forty-five minutes' time, it's no good being there in six hours, forty-five and a half minutes, because you're late. You might as well be ten hours late. If you're given a timing, you must be there. The attack group might have to go in without fire cover because their attack might be time co-ordinated with another attack that's going in three or four kilometres away. You must keep your timings, lives might depend on it one day.'

The training team did the course every day as well, and they would vary the time limit according to the conditions. If there was a 40-mile-an-hour wind, they took it into consideration. It was then up to us to be as good as them.

The big thing was Platform 4. At Hereford railway station, Platform 4 went to London. 'It's Platform Four for you' was the Regiment's way of saying, 'Thank you and goodnight.'

Of course, by the time people got back to their units, the reason they left Selection was because of a 'back or leg injury' – but they shouldn't have been embarrassed: they had more guts turning up for Selection in the first place than the people they were giving excuses to.

The Royal Signals people definitely had the edge on

tuning in and being happy with the environment. At that time, if a bloke wanted to go for the Regiment from the Signals he first had to be in 264, the Signals squadron in Hereford. So these guys were in the environment to begin with, and they had the Black Mountains forty-five minutes up the road to train on. A lot of them were going home of an evening. In the beginning, I felt they had an unfair advantage. Then I came to see that when it came down to it, they didn't – they still had to get the boots on and go up the hill with everyone else.

I was looking at the blokes who'd done Selection once already – maybe they had got up to the jungle phase of Continuation training and then failed. I was hoping that they were going to pass this first stage again. If I got to the jungle as well – and hopefully with them – they would know what was going on.

Some people had turned up looking fearsomely fit. I judged myself all the time against them. A fellow called Andy Baxter was one of the training team. We went out for a run with him one day, stopping to do press-ups and sit-ups. Andy took his shirt off and revealed that besides film-star good looks he had a superb physique. He should have been on the cover of *Playgirl*. I'd always been really fit in the battalion, but I thought, there's no way I'm going to pass this – I don't stand a chance here, how the hell am I going to be like him? Nothing fazed him at all. We'd come back off the runs gasping for breath, and he'd saunter back in, laughing and joking, and have a cup of tea. It annoyed me that compared to some of these blokes I was a bag of shit, sweating and knackered. I had to keep reminding myself that it wasn't Baxter I was competing against, it was McNab.

If passing Selection had been an obsession before I arrived at Stirling Lines, it was now a pathological fixation. The longer I was there, the more I wanted to stay. The atmosphere was so different from an infantry battalion, so laid back, so reliant on self-discipline. Everybody was on

first name terms. No-one hassled us; all they would say was, 'Parade is twelve o'clock,' and just expect us to be there. If we weren't, it must mean we didn't want to be there, so we could go. Each night I said to myself: I really want to be here, this is the place I want to be.

If I didn't pass Selection, I'd get out of the army. There was no way I could see myself fitting back in the battalion. I'd seen how the other half lived, and I wanted my share. All the facilities were there, everything from a library to a swimming pool. The medical centre was open for us every night when we got back. I went there to get some bandages for my feet. It wasn't like going into a medical centre in the battalion, where I'd have been hanging around so long my feet would have healed of their own accord. They treated me as a person rather than a soldier; as I limped back to my room, I said to myself again: I want to stay here!

All of us Green Jackets got up to the third week, then Bob got binned. His timings weren't good enough. He didn't seem too worried about it as he packed his gear to leave.

Next day, we had finished one march and were moving to a forestry block to spend the next few hours sorting ourselves out and having something to eat before a night tab. Dave was not feeling too good about it, and he had already had a gypsy's. As we sat around a hexy burner and sorted our feet out, waiting for dark, he said, 'What pisses me off is that they don't tell us if we've failed straightaway. I might be doing this sodding night march for nothing.'

He was. The next day, almost the end of the third week, he was also sent to Platform 4; timings not good enough. And Max, who was starting to look the worse for wear, got a gypsy's.

'It was because I kept falling over,' Dave said to me. 'And the reason I keep falling over is that my feet aren't big enough to support me. I've only got size sevens.'

I shook his hand and watched him go. I'd miss the silly bastard.

A couple of days after that, in the final week, I was

coming off Fan-Fawr and saw Max still on his way up, water tube waving in the wind, wearing a T-shirt with a motif on it, something to do with oranges. His big bushy moustache was full of snot and he was in shit state.

He said, 'I'm having a bad time here, Andy. My timings are bad.'

He was well and truly out of it – as if he was drunk, but without the happiness.

I nodded and said, 'Sorry,' but obviously I still had to crack on myself.

That night he went. Out of the original six Green Jackets three were left for the last three days of Test Week.

Kev went the next day. As usual, he wasn't that fussed.

'I tried and failed,' he grinned. 'At least I don't have to think of it again. Back to football and a few good nights out at Longbridge, that's me.'

I was sad to see them all go. I would miss their friendship and banter.

Johnny Two-Combs was still there and no way was he not going to pass. I didn't see that much of him as he was in a different block and by now, if I wasn't tabbing, I was sleeping.

'Just got to carry on the way I'm going,' I kept saying to myself. 'Just don't get an injury.'

I got a gypsy's the next day.

We were on a 35-kilometre tab in the Elan valley and I'd had a really bad day. I had no injuries but I just found it hard going. It was as if my legs didn't want to play; my body was going at 100 mph but my legs were moving at 50. I used to have a dream as a child that I was running away from something and though my whole mental state was in a frenzy, my body would be in slow motion. Now it was happening in real life. I was on the second group of wagons, which was dodgy ground.

The following morning we were waiting to be called on the vehicles. The chief instructor started to call out the names of people he wanted to see. I was one of them.

'Your timings were not good enough yesterday,' he said. 'You will have to pull your finger out for the last two days or it's Platform Four.'

It pissed me off, but there were only the Sketch Map and Endurance marches left.

'Sketch Map' involved using a hand-drawn map rather than a proper one. We had to cover 35 kilometres over different checkpoints. No problem, I was cruising. I thought I'd cracked it. I knew the ground because I'd done all the recces, I'd been up there, I knew where I was going.

I was coming up towards the Fan and came to a forestry block about a kilometre square that I would have to go around: it wasn't a fluffy little wood; this was a major Forestry Commission fir plantation. Looking down on it from the high ground, I could see that a firebreak went right through the middle. I started to push through, and made good progress for about the first 200 metres. Then I got disoriented. I had to stop for several minutes and take a bearing. I was severely pissed off with myself. I had to get on my hands and knees and start pushing myself through because the trees were planted so closely together. I was shouting and hollering to myself. I'd gone too far in to come back out and go round; it was just a matter of cracking on. Deep down, I knew I was going to be late. I knew I had fucked up.

By the time I came out I had cuts on my face and hands, and I was covered in blood. But I still went on. There might be a chance.

Making my way up to the next checkpoint, which was on the top of Pen-y-Fan, my legs were aching something fierce. I was badly out of breath and drenched with sweat, blood and mud. But the worst injury was to my pride. I knew I'd fucked up good style by being too cocky.

The sun was out and it was quite hot. Half of Wales seemed to be walking on the Fan with their families – small kids with two-litre bottles of lemonade in their hands and mothers and fathers strolling along in shorts and sandals,

enjoying the view. I screamed through them, pissed off and muttering to myself, trying to make up as much time as possible.

The DS looked at my cut face and torn trousers and said, 'You all right?'

I said, 'Yeah, I've had a bad last leg.'

'Never mind, just get down to the vehicle, that's your next checkpoint.'

I had been the last man to the top of Pen-y-Fan. Now I had to go back down to the last checkpoint. I ran. I ran faster than I'd ever imagined I could, but when I arrived there was only room on the third wagon.

That night, my name was called. It was the day before Endurance, the last big test, and I was binned. It was my fault; being cocky, thinking I'd cracked it, rather than just going around the forestry block and being sure of where I was.

Before you leave for Platform 4, you hand all your kit back to the stores. Then there is an interview with the training major. You can only try twice for Selection, unless you break a leg on your second attempt, in which case they might be lenient.

As I waited to go into the office, I wasn't alone. Eight of us were sitting on a long wooden bench. I felt very much as I had done as a kid, waiting to see the headmistress, or to go into a police station interviewing room. It was a hive of activity, people walking purposefully past, doing their own stuff. Nobody was taking any notice of us.

I felt dejected. Everything was happening around me but I wasn't a part of it any more.

The major looked up from his desk and said, 'So what was the problem? Why were you so late on the last leg?'

'Too cocky. I went through the forestry block and that slowed me down severely.'

'Ah well,' he smiled. 'If you come back again you'll make sure you go round that one, won't you?'

'Yeah.'

'Fine, maybe we'll see you again.'

'I hope so.'

An hour later, I was standing on Platform 4.

We boarded the train to Paddington. When we got to London I would go to Brize Norton, and from there I'd get an RAF flight back to Minden.

As I lifted my holdall into the luggage rack and sat down, I found myself looking straight at the word 'Hereford' on the station sign. It hit me that I hadn't felt so devastated – and so determined – for a long, long time.

9

Failing Selection was a bit like falling off a horse, only it hurt a hell of a lot more. I somehow knew that if I didn't get straight back on I'd never try again, because I was so pissed off.

Debbie was less than thrilled when I applied again, but the battalion were really good about it. They didn't give me any time off for training this time, however, because there were too many commitments – i.e. more bone exercises.

I made up my mind that if I failed Selection a second time, I'd get out of the army. I was writing away, in my naivety, to companies that had a lot of Middle East contracts: 'Dear Sirs, I can work a mortar.' As an infantryman, I thought I was God's gift to industry because I could fire a mortar, and couldn't understand it when the polite letters came back: 'Dear Sir, Fuck off!'

Alex, the captain who'd done so much to help us get some training, took me aside one day and said, 'Every morning when I was shaving, I got the soap and wrote on the mirror – Battalion No, Regiment Yes.'

It had obviously worked for him. I was encouraged.

I did all the training I could in the free time I had. It was much the same as before – lots of bergen work, circuit training and running – building up the endurance of my heart, lungs, legs and mind.

The only free time I had to get some more work in over the Beacons was during the Christmas leave period, which

obviously pissed Debbie off severely. We started to have rows about it. Our marriage was in name only. She came home one evening and we had a massive set-to.

'We're hardly ever together,' she said. 'And when we are, all you're interested in is Selection.'

'I'm pissed off with myself for failing,' I said.

'Then that makes two of us.'

I started to say that she had no idea about what was happening to me, that my whole world had fallen in, and if I didn't get in next time our future was uncertain, because I would leave the army and have to look for work.

It was a big all-nighter, with enough shouting and slamming of doors to wake up half the block. I was just feeling sorry for myself and couldn't handle being rejected by the Regiment. My only vent was Debbie, and she, I thought, didn't understand. The Regiment was what I wanted, and if she wasn't with me, then as far as I was concerned she was against me. I told her she was overreacting, that if I got in everything would be all right again and we would get back to where we were before. But Debbie was a bright girl and she must have seen the writing on the wall.

What had started as an obsession and become a fixation, was now a passion. I was no longer concerned about anything that happened within the battalion, unless it was physical. Then I'd throw myself into it, purely because it was more training.

My mind was focused completely on the first month of Selection. I wasn't worried about the continuation training at all; once I'd got over that first month, everything else was the unknown, so I couldn't prepare myself for it. But I could prepare myself for the first month. I knew I could pass it. I *knew*.

During Christmas leave Debbie stayed with her family and I went to Crickhowell, the training depot for the Prince of Wales Division. Early each morning I put the bergen in the back of the motor and screamed up to the Black Mountains.

I had a rusty old black Renault 5. One of the wings was falling off and had to be kept on with a rubber bungee. Some mornings it lacked the power even to get up the hill to my start point. When the roads were icy, I ended up more than once in a hedge.

I'd train hard all day up on the hills, then drive back down to Crickhowell, have my two pints of Guinness and a bag of chips, drink huge amounts of electrolytes and strap myself up for the next day.

On Christmas Day I treated myself to a few hours off, staying where I was and watching all the old Number Ones on *Top of the Pops*. I had Christmas dinner at one of the pubs and gave Debbie a call. There was no reply.

Next day, I did the Fan Dance. As I tabbed hard up Pen-y-Fan with this big house on my back, sweating away, four or five blokes come sprinting past with tracksuits and day sacks on. As they went piling past the bag of shit – me – they said, 'Trying for January, are you? Good luck.'

I was expecting the winter Selection to be more severe than the summer one. Cold can be so debilitating; it would be tougher to wade through snow than move over the ground, and poor visibility would make the navigation a lot harder. People died on winter Selection. Even senior officers in the Regiment had perished on the hills. I'd heard that a major set off once with a bergen full of bricks rather than warm clothing. The weather came down and he failed to return. The standby squadron got up onto the hill and found the body, but they couldn't get down themselves because the weather was so bad. They had to get the bivvi bags out, and they used the frozen rupert as a windbreak. When the weather cleared they laid him on his back, piled their bergens on top, and sledged him down the hill.

I arrived back at Stirling Lines in mid-January. I sensed that people were more apprehensive than the summer intake had been. I knew I was.

As it turned out, the weather was a great leveller. In thick mist or driving snow, everybody had to rely on their

navigation. The elements slowed us all down equally; it was just a question of cracking on with the bearings, having confidence in the map and compass. Every day I felt better, and my confidence grew.

Snow fell heavily for much of the second and third weeks. We were given a six-figure grid that was accurate to within 100 metres, which is a big area when all you're looking for is a bivvi bag in a snowdrift.

Visibility was down to 20 metres one day. I got to the vicinity of my next checkpoint and was running around for valuable minutes trying to find a hint of green GoreTex. Eventually I found it, tapped on the bag, and the zip came down. I was a sweaty, dirty mess, starting to shiver because I'd stopped moving. Even in the very cold weather I wore just a pair of trousers, boots, and a T-shirt with a water-proof over the top.

I was hit by the waft of coffee fumes and a cloud of steam from the boy in his sleeping bag. He was probably blowing the vents because he was so hot.

I wanted to be out of there as quickly as possible, number one because of the timings, and number two because I was starting to freeze. I was dripping all over him.

He looked up, took a sip of coffee, and said, 'Stop fucking sweating on me.'

As he gave me my next grid reference, he said, 'See you,' and did up the zip.

I turned to face into the blizzard again and trudged on.

I arrived at one checkpoint at the same time as two ruperts who'd tabbed in together from a different direction.

'This checkpoint is not where it should be,' one of them said to the DS.

The bivvi bag was in a snowdrift on a piece of ground called a spot height. The DS, who happened to be Peter, the chief instructor, said, 'Well where do you think it should be then?'

The rupert pointed on the map, then the two officers started to argue between themselves. There was only a

difference of 100 or 200 hundred metres, it wasn't as if we were in different valleys.

The DS said to me, 'Where are we?'

I pointed to the spot height on the map and he said, 'Correct.' I wasn't going to argue.

Then he turned to the two ruperts and said, 'Wherever you think you are, here is your next grid.'

Off they went, and as he gave me my grid he shook his head and said, 'I can't understand what's the matter with these guys. They're here to become part of something that I'm already a member of. I'm the chief instructor, and they're arguing with me. Even if I'm wrong, what's the point in arguing with me?'

I didn't see them again. Next time, if there was a next time for them, perhaps they wouldn't approach Selection with their rupert's head on. At that stage, the DS couldn't even be arsed to know our names unless we'd done something wrong. All they were trying to confirm was that we had endurance, stamina, and determination. They couldn't give a monkey's about our skills and aptitudes.

A character called Jock was in the next bed to me. Every night, when we got back from another shattering day on the hill, he'd say, 'Och, I think I'll just nip down the town and have a drink.' He'd get all dressed up and go down to one of the discos, rolling back at three o'clock in the morning, stinking. He'd fall into bed, curl up and fall asleep.

Next morning I'd give him a nudge and say, 'Jock, it's scoff.'

'Och aye.'

He'd get up, right as rain, put his kit back on, make loads of toast and carry it to the wagon in his hands. The most I could manage, and it certainly wasn't every night, was a trip to the local chip shop and a couple of pints of Guinness on the way.

At the end of the first two weeks the really serious stuff started, revisiting the Elan valley. I used to like the drive up there because we had to start really early in the morning. I

95

could get my head down in my sleeping bag and drink loads of tea. All good things come to an end, however, and the truck would eventually stop, the engine would be switched off, and there would be silence. Time to get out.

The cold air always attacked my ears first, then my feet started to go numb. I'd be torn between wanting to get moving to get warm, and knowing that it was going to entail a fearsome tab of eight or ten hours.

The Elan valley was as I remembered it, a godforsaken, daunting place, full of reservoirs and big stumps of elephant grass, ranging from knee to chest height. The area was very boggy, and because of the reservoirs we could only move on the top half of the hills. We did a lot of night marches there as well and I spent a lot of time falling over. I hated the Elan valley.

By now we were carrying a rifle as well as a bergen, and it always had to be in our hands. They were only drill SLRs, but it was a bit of extra weight I could have done without. The carrying handles had been removed; there was no putting it over the shoulder or strapping it into the bergen. I found the SLRs made life much more difficult, because I couldn't swing my arms to pump uphill. We had to cross a lot of fences, and if you were seen resting the weapon on the other side before you clambered over you got a fine – and mentally they'd got you.

Some of the tabs went on and on. Sometimes I could see the checkpoint about ten kilometres away; I'd come off the high ground on that bearing, so I knew it was at the end of that delta, but then I'd just seem to be going on and on and on. The Elan valley took a hell of a lot of people out. It wore them down. And because it was further away, it meant we got back later, and we had to start earlier.

As the week went on, Jock carried on pissing it up. He explained to me that he'd just got over a bad dose of penile warts. For eighteen months he had been 'off games', and he wasn't going to let a little thing like Selection get in the way of his rehabilitation. He opened his flies one day and

showed me the damage. The end of his cock looked like the moon.

Day after day we'd be humping over hills. The weather was horrendous. On one of the tabs the snow came up to my waist. It was quite a long one – 35 kilometres – and it was scary stuff. The mist was in, visibility was down to about ten metres and we all failed to find a checkpoint. Eventually about six of us all bumped into each other, flapping about our timings. At long last one of the blokes found the DS's bivvi bag, and we were all busy making our excuses about the weather. No need. They'd already accounted for all this. They made the decision that we'd carry on, but in a group until we got to the next checkpoint.

Timings-wise I was in the middle of the order of march. I was on my chinstrap after wading through the snow for so many kilometres, but I got lucky. There was a Canadian jock who wanted to lead from the front, and I tucked in behind him. He was forging through the snowdrifts like an icebreaker and we were tabbing in his wake, grinning our faces off.

The Endurance phase culminated with Test Week. The routes were a selection of everywhere we'd been, and ranged from 20 to 64 kilometres. This was where all the injuries began to play on people. There were only about forty of us left, which I thought was great: less of a wait for food. Each day now I was feeling stronger, because I knew the ground and what to expect.

I hadn't had a gypsy's, so I reckoned I could even screw up on one of them and I'd be all right. Best of all, I had no blisters, which I was really impressed with, but I was still strapping up my feet because the ankles were taking a fearsome pummelling.

By now, I was always landing up in the same wagon as another fellow, George. I discovered that we'd both been in Crossmaglen at the same time. He was in an engineer unit that was building the submarines; he then transferred, and was now in 59 Engineers, the Royal Engineers attached to

the Commando Brigade. He was into mountain climbing and had all the kit. He really annoyed me because every time I'd get there, he would already be in, lying in his sleeping bag, eating oranges. We'd sit together in companionable silence and wait for the wagon to fill up. George was tall and lean, with varicose veins behind one of his legs. It looked like a relief map of the Pyrenees.

The day came when it was time for Sketch Map. There was no way I was going to cock up this time, and I didn't. We got back to camp at about three o'clock in the afternoon after a 4 a.m. start. At ten o'clock that same night we'd be setting out for Endurance, so it was straight in, sort the kit out, and have a bath. I'd always been a shower man, until I'd seen all the boys going in with boxes of Radox and I thought, right, I'll have some of that for Endurance. But I put far too much in. It was like floating in the Dead Sea. I didn't know if it did me any physical good, but in my mind I felt that it did.

We drove to Talybont, one of the reservoirs. When I got off the wagon and put the bergen on, I started getting pins and needles in my hands because the weight on my shoulders was restricting the flow of blood. I had that initial pain of getting it on, then even more pain as welts broke out where it was rubbing. And then after about ten minutes, as soon as I got moving, my skin started to tingle because I was starting to leak. I got the wetness around my neck, and it started to get at the base of my hair. That was always quite an uncomfortable time, that very first ten minutes or quarter of an hour, because my legs were really stiff. Then I started to get my second breath and everything started to loosen up. After about twenty minutes I was into the swing of it again. My mind was switched off; I was listening to jingles in my head. It was bitterly cold and the wind was getting in all the little gaps. Until I got a good sweat on, it was a horrible feeling, especially after getting out of the cosy sleeping bag I'd been lying in for the hour-and-a-half drive.

Most of Endurance was in darkness, and because it was wintertime there was even less daylight. Everybody looked quite excited, but apprehensive. I was feeling confident and fit. I had no bad injuries, just bergen sores.

They called out the names and off we went. The bergen was the heaviest it had ever been, about 55–60lbs, because of the extra food and water. I always took water from the camp because I knew it wasn't contaminated. I didn't fancy drinking water from a stream, even with sterilizing tablets, only to see a minging dead sheep upstream: if you start getting gut aches, it's going to slow you down. The extra weight was worth it.

We were not allowed on roads. If the checkpoint was on one, we had to hit at an angle, not aim off and then move along it. We couldn't use tracks or pathways either; everything had to be cross-country. We'd get to the checkpoint, where sometimes they had water. If there were other people coming in they might hold us for five minutes, and that was the time to fill up from the jerrycans if there were any. If they weren't going to hold us, I wouldn't waste time filling up.

If I met other people on the route there was never time to say more than 'All right?' before shooting off again. All I wanted to hear them say was that they were late, and I'd think, 'That's good.' If it was so bad that they said, 'Fuck!' I was even more pleased. It didn't make me go faster, but it made me feel better.

I was just bumping along, my head full of jingles, thinking about the route ahead, trying to remember what was on the map so I didn't have to stop. 'If you stop every five minutes for thirty seconds,' Max had said, 'that's minutes taken up every hour.' I did my map checks on the move.

I had an extra pouch on my belt that was full of aniseed twists and Yorkie bars which I had stocked up on just for Endurance. I didn't use them on other tabs, but for some reason I just went downtown and bought them for this one. Now I was digging in and eating, and wondering why I'd never done it before.

I tabbed through the second night. On the last five or six kilometres the batteries went in my torch. I knew because of the lie of the ground that I had to go downhill, hit the reservoir, chuck a right, and then head for the bridge, which was the final checkpoint.

Unable to use my map, I was cursing the gods at the top of my voice. On the side of the reservoir was a big forestry block. I searched for a firebreak to get through, honking to myself and remembering why I failed last time.

I found a firebreak, a good wide one. No problem. I was moving along, but then I hit fallen trees. Extra sweat, extra cuts. Every few metres I'd have to get the bergen off, throw it over a horizontal trunk, roll over it myself, find the bergen in the pitch blackness, put it back on. I was flapping; I couldn't believe my future was in danger through making the same mistake twice.

I was relieved to see the first rays of moonlight and made my way down to the bottom of the reservoir. I knew I had to turn right, and off I trogged, dragging along.

I reached the last checkpoint after a tab of twenty-one and a half hours. I was pretty chuffed with myself, but George had got in before me. So what was new?

I noticed a distinct change in the attitude of the DS. It was as if we'd turned a corner, as if a phase was over and done with. There was no praise or anything, but they said, 'All right, are you? Right, dump your kit down, and there's some brew by the wagons.'

The medic was there for any problems, but everybody was too elated to notice if they had any.

The QMS (*quartermaster sergeant*) on training wing turned up with big slabs of bread pudding and tea, which he laced with rum. I discovered there was a big tradition with the Regiment that when on arduous duties they got this G10 rum, called 'gun-fire'. They saved up the rum ration and served it up on big occasions. I hated rum but this didn't seem the time to say so. I didn't like bread pudding either, but I threw a lot of that down my neck as well.

One of the ruperts came up to me and said, 'Bloody hell, were you having some problems down by the reservoir?'

I explained what was going on and he said, 'I could hear you. All I could hear was this "Fucking fuck, fuck ya!"' He had been caught up in another firebreak, having the same problem.

We climbed into the wagons for the last time. Everybody was happy but subdued. Nobody was sleeping, we were all too deep in thought.

I had the big Radox bath, and tried to get all the strapping off my legs. It was 2″ tape which like a dickhead I'd put on the sticky way round. All I'd needed it for was support, so it could have been the other way round. I was in the bath, talking to George, and effing and blinding as I ripped the tape off. By the time I had finished, half of my leg hairs had disappeared.

One of the DS came around and said, 'Everybody be in the training wing lecture room for eight o'clock in the morning.'

I was feeling confident. There were some who were on a dodgy wicket who weren't too sure, but they were soon going to be finding out.

As soon as the DS said, 'The following people go and see the training major,' I knew that they were binned. If they didn't call my name out, I'd know that I'd passed.

He called out ten names. No McNab.

'The rest of you, are there any injuries? The medical centre's open now, go and get them sorted out.'

There was one little job I had to do first. One of the blokes who had failed needed driving to the station, and I had offered. There had been an unfortunate incident on the hill – at least according to his version of it. He was doing well and had got to a checkpoint at night where he was held because a rupert had arrived in shit state and binned it. He was told, 'Go with this officer, make sure he's all right.' He got the man safely down to the next checkpoint, but by now was very late.

'I was told to wait,' he told the DS.

The DS just said, 'Tough shit.'

He was held because of the rupert, and quite rightly so; his job was to make sure the rupert got down to the next checkpoint that had a vehicle; he would then carry on. But he was late because of it, and they didn't seem to take it into account. Maybe there was a cock-up in the administration. Whatever, this boy was stuffed. As I drove him to the station, he was crying. This had been his second attempt; for him there were no more tomorrows. I could imagine how he felt.

We had the weekend off, and it was very much needed. My feet swelled up as if I had elephantiasis and I couldn't put my shoes on. I had to cut holes in my trainers with a pair of scissors.

I wanted to tell everyone that I'd passed Selection, that I was a big boy now. But it meant jack shit to the blokes in the camp. Apparently a lot of them did Endurance once or twice a year anyway. It was good for them to get up on the hill – it showed example, and also meant there were more people in the area for safety reasons. Some people slipped through the safety net. Two weeks later, a fellow from R Squadron was missing after a tab, and the standby squadron was called out to search for him. They found him in his sleeping bag, half in, half out, with biscuits in one hand and a hexy burner in the other. He must have died in that position.

10

I had passed Selection, the only phase that we had a certain amount of control over. Now, as we entered the lecture room on Monday morning, we were going into the unknown.

The training sergeant major stood up and said, 'You are starting Continuation training now. There's going to be a lot of work involved. Just switch on, and listen to what's being said. Remember, you might have passed the Selection phase, but you're not in yet.'

From the original intake of 180, we were now down to just 24. Sitting around me were people from many different organizations – blokes from the Signals and Royal Engineers, infantry, artillery, and a Marine. It was accepted that everybody would have different levels of expertise and different levels of experience. In terms of training, it was back to the drawing-board.

The first step was to train us in the use of the Regiment's weapons. 'If you finally do get to the squadrons,' the DS said, 'you might find yourself arriving and going straight on jobs. They won't have time to train you; you've got to go there with a working knowledge of all the weapons.'

The standard expected of us would depend on our previous experience. I was a sergeant in the infantry, weapons were my business. But the last time a lance corporal in the Catering Corps had touched a weapon might have been a year ago, and even then it would

probably just have been a rifle – he'd know nothing about the GPMG, sustained fire, or any of the technical stuff. He'd find it more difficult than me, but wouldn't necessarily be doing any worse. The DS said that to their way of thinking, if one person hadn't got the same experience as another but was learning, and was getting to a good standard compared with the more experienced bloke, then in essence he was learning more.

It was very much like a Bible story I remembered, when the rich man turned up at the church and dumped off six bags of gold and everybody was thinking how wonderful he was. Then an old woman came in and she had two coins, her whole wealth, and she gave one of them to the church. The fact was, this woman gave more to the church than the rich man did, because the six bags of gold was jack shit to him. The instructors were looking at us in the same light. They were looking at what we were, and what they expected us to become. It was during this stage that we lost the Marine corporal, who as far as they were concerned had a standard of weapon handling which wasn't as good as it should have been for a corporal in the Royal Marines.

I suspected that our personalities were also under the microscope. From the way the DS looked at us I could almost hear the cogs turning: is the experienced soldier helping the less-experienced corporal in the Catering Corps to get on, or is he just saying, 'Well hey, I'm looking good'? Was a bloke maybe such a dickhead that he spent his time joking away with the DS? They'd joke back with him, but at the end of the day they'd probably think, what a big-timer. It was their job to make sure that people who were going to the squadrons were the best that they could provide. They had to go back to the squadrons themselves; they might be in command of us. They took the responsibility very seriously.

We trained with the personal weapons that were available to the squadrons. First was the 5.56 M16 and the 203, the grenade launching attachment that most people went

for, apparently, because of its increased firepower. Some people, however, still liked carrying the SLR, which fired a 7.62 round. They were in a minority, because it meant that the patrol had to carry two types of small arms ammunition.

Another weapon at patrol level was the Minimi – again, firing 5.56 rounds. The Regiment also still used the GPMG, the standard army section machine-gun. I knew it to be an excellent weapon at section level, and we were told that a lot of people preferred it to the Minimi. There were quite a few jobs where people would insist on taking a GPMG: it was reliable, and very powerful.

We worked with Browning pistols, Colt 45s, and a number of different semi-automatic weapons. For some jobs people might prefer a certain type of pistol, but the majority would go for the Browning.

Then there were shotguns – the Federal riot gun, a pump-action shotgun which had a folding stock and was an excellent weapon. Each squadron had its own assortment of mortars – 81mm, 60mm and 40mm – and the Milan anti-tank weapons. There was also the LAW 90, an 84mm rocket, the standard rifle company anti-tank missile. Then there was the Stinger, an American-made, anti-aircraft fire-and-forget missile.

'Stingers turned up in the Falklands and nobody really knew how to use them or what to do with them,' the DS said. 'It was just a case of, "Here they are, get to grips with them." So the boys were sitting around on the grass one day, reading the instructions and having a brew, when over the horizon came a flight of Pucaras. A D Squadron member stood up and put the Stinger on his shoulder. It was like the kid in the old Fisher Price ad: "How's this work then? What does this do?" The bloke was pressing all the buttons to make it fire, and it did. It took down a Pucara. So the first time the Stinger was used in anger was by a Brit firing at an Argentinian aircraft.'

The story didn't end there. About two years later

apparently, D Squadron went over to Germany to the Stinger training centre run by the Americans. The training was in simulators because the weapon was so expensive. The American instructors only got to fire one a year, and had certainly never used it in war.

'We've got this wonderful weapon,' beamed one of the instructors. 'Any of you guys seen it before?'

The bloke put his hand up and the instructor smirked. 'In a simulator?'

'No, I shot down a jet with it.'

Besides the British and American hardware, we were trained with all the Eastern bloc weapons: AK47s – the Russian, Czech and Chinese ones – all the mortars, their medium anti-tank weapons, and masses of different pistols, such as the Austrian Steyr. We were told that a lot of times we'd be on tasks where we wouldn't be using our own weapons; we'd have to go to a country and use what we could find.

The AK family were excellent weapons. They fired 7.62 short, which meant you could carry more 7.62 than our 7.62 for the same weight. They were good reliable weapons because they were so simple. The only drawback was the big, 30-round magazines; when you lay down, you couldn't actually get the weapon in the shoulder to fire because the magazine hit the floor. A lot of the Eastern bloc policy on attack showed in the AK; with the safety catch, the first click down was automatic, then the second click down was single shot, so the mentality was clearly: give it loads. On western weapons it was the other way round – single shot first, then on to automatic.

We did live firing down at Sennybridge, practising live attacks. Sometimes they'd tell us things on the range, such as how to hold our weapon, that were contrary to what some of us had been taught. We were doing standing targets at 100 metres; the way I fired was to put the butt into my shoulder, and have my hand underneath the magazine, resting my elbow on the magazine pouch. It seemed to

work for me. One of the DS came over and said, 'What are you doing? Put your hand on the stock, lean forward, and fire it properly.' There was no way I was going to say, 'Actually, I shoot better like this, and this is the way I've been doing it for years.' I just nodded and agreed, put my hand on the stock and carried on firing.

Some of the blokes would actually say, 'No, that's wrong,' but what was the point of arguing? We wanted to be with them, not the other way round.

People had weird and wonderful qualifications which they thought were going to be an asset, but the DS soon put them straight. 'If the squadrons need specific skills, they'll send their own people off for training. The most important thing is that we send them somebody with the aptitude to do a certain type of work and the personality to get on with other people in closed and stressful environments. Then they have the base line. Then they can send you out to become the mortar fire controller or whatever.'

I heard a story about a fellow from a Scottish regiment on a previous Selection. When they started training on the weapons, he sat muttering in the class, 'I don't want to be doing this shit. This is what I do in the battalion. I want to get onto the Heckler & Koch and all the black kit.' The instructors heard it, didn't say anything, they just got on with the lesson. But they'd pinged him as a big time Walter Mitty; they took him quietly to one side afterwards and gave him directions to Platform 4.

I was phoning up Debbie once a week and occasionally I'd write her a letter, but she was second in my list of priorities; I wanted to crack on and get into the jungle. As far as I was concerned she was fine; she was still working, she was having a good time with her friends. The telephone conversations were tense and stilted.

I'd say, 'Is everything all right?'

'Yeah, fine,' she'd say, offhand. 'What changes here? Still going to work, still bored, still nothing to do.'

Never mind, I thought, at the end of the day everything

will be sorted out. We'd get the quarter, the problems would disappear.

We started to learn the techniques we'd be using in the jungle, and why they were used – the way to LUP (*lying-up point*), the daily routine, hard routine, how to ambush, how to cross rivers. We'd go down to the training area and walk around in plain fields and forestry blocks as if we were in the jungle. Anybody looking at us would have thought we were a bunch of dickheads, prowling around right up close to the trees.

'When you get into your tactical LUP,' the DS said, 'you put up a hammock – as low as possible, so your arse is just a couple of inches off the ground – and fix up a poncho above you. If you've got to sleep on the floor, you've got to sleep on the floor – but why do that if you've got the means not to? When you do get up in the morning, you're more effective if you haven't been bitten to bits during the night and you've had a good chance to get some sleep. You're more refreshed and better able to go and do the task.'

Some people took bivvi bags with them, he said. As well as keeping the rain off, it kept the dry clothing dry – the wet clothing would just stay outside and get soaking wet anyway, that was no problem. If we could keep ourselves well maintained and free of embuggerances, the better tactically we would be. There was nothing soft about it. We were told it was far more sensible than playing the he-man and ending up being effective for about two and a half minutes.

'People live in the jungle for months at a time like this, with no adverse effects at all. In fact it's a wonderful environment – it's far better than any other environment you've got to operate in, because you've got everything there. You've got food if you need it, you've got continuous supplies of water, you've got cover, the weather's good, you don't have to worry about the elements – everything you need is there. So why go against it? Just switch on, and keep as comfortable as you can when you can.'

We got all our injections done and filled in more

documentation. I was delighted; I felt it somehow meant we were starting to get further into the system.

The atmosphere was changing slightly, becoming slowly more sociable. I was careful it didn't give me a false sense of security, however. It was easy to forget that I could still be binned, that they were still seeing if they wanted me in their gang or not. There were months and months to go, and trying to make an impression on a DS over a cup of tea wasn't going to get anyone anywhere.

All the drills we were learning, we were told, were based on actual experience, things that had gone right, things that had gone wrong.

We practised contact drills. The task of the Regiment in the jungle was not to go out and start shooting people, it was to go out to get information, come back, then go back again with other people or a bigger force.

'During the Malayan days,' said one of the DS, a veteran himself, 'a lot of the four-man patrols got through enemy ambushes without the ambush being initiated – simply because the people manning the ambush thought, there's the recce group, let's wait for the main group to come through.'

There was still lots of physical training. They'd beast us about in the gym but I found it enjoyable because there was no discipline. There didn't need to be: if we didn't want to be there, we were at liberty to walk. Nobody hassled us about the rooms, but we kept them clean anyway, because that was what was expected of us. I loved it, it was a really wonderful atmosphere.

At this stage, the only areas we were allowed into were the training section and training-wing accommodation, but I still felt part of the organization. We were no longer segregated from the other blokes in the cookhouse now, and I bumped into one or two people I'd met in the battalion or on courses. They were happy to chat over a cup of tea. One day I saw Jeff, who was now on the

counter-terrorist team. He still looked younger than Donny Osmond.

'Still here then?' he grinned. 'When do you go to the jungle?'

'In about two or three weeks.'

'Know who your DS is yet?'

'No idea. They're going to start putting us in patrols very soon.'

The next morning we were given batteries of tests. First was language aptitude. I looked around the training-wing theatre, trying to work out who would be the most intelligent at this sort of stuff. Jake, the American, was a main man. I knew that he spoke Farsi and could write the script, so I thought, there's the brainy fucker, I'd better start edging my way next to him. I went for a piss with the idea of sitting as near to him as I could when I came back. I found that twenty-two other blokes had had exactly the same idea. Like a lot of other people in the vicinity I cheated, copying off Jake.

Next was the pilots' quick-reaction test. We were handed a list of calculations and given a minute and a half to do each one in. They were weird and wonderful things like mean averages and square roots, concepts way beyond the basic maths I'd taught myself with the Janet and John book from Peckham library. Then there were lots of items like the Mensa tests they had in newspapers. I doubt my results would have got me into the Noddy Club, let alone Mensa.

I kept thinking, if we fail these are we binned, or what? Have we got to be brain surgeons or are we going to be soldiers? It went on all morning and it became a bit of farce, with everybody cheating off everybody else. The DS must have known what was going on.

One thing they had been teaching us from the very first day was decision-making. In the training-wing corridor there was a big picture of a load of sheep in a pen, and underneath was the message: Either lead, follow, or get out of the way.

It was a big thing: don't dilly-dally, make a decision. If it was wrong it was wrong, if it was right it was right. One of my new decision processes was to think: what's done is done; if I've failed I've failed.

When we went into the cookhouse at lunchtime we were like kids walking out of an exam room.

'What did you reckon to number sixteen?'

'I made the answer two hundred and fifty.'

'Oh fuck.'

Whatever the results were, we were issued with our jungle kit the next day – jungle fatigues, mosquito nets, bergens, different types of ponchos. I was like a pig in sugar.

The same afternoon, we were going to be told what patrols we were in, and who our DS was going to be. Everybody wanted to get together with the people who'd been in the jungle before, because in theory they were going to have an edge and be able to help.

I was made a patrol commander because I was an infantry sergeant. In the patrol we had a bloke, Raymond, a Falklands veteran, who'd done a six-month tour in Belize as a lance corporal with 2 Para. He was very thick-set with jet black hair; if he had a shave at six o'clock, by eight o'clock he'd need another one. Raymond knew all about pole beds and the routine of living in the jungle; the closest I'd been was a school trip to Kew Gardens when I was seven years old – and my only memory of that was of the other kids having ice creams afterwards and me not having enough money to buy one.

Another member of the patrol was Mal, a corporal in the Royal Anglians. He came from London and was about the same size and height as me, but with the world's biggest teeth. A couple of them were missing, and he always had a smile on his face and a fag in his mouth. He reminded me of the Tommy Atkins character from the First World War. He didn't seem to give a stuff about anything, but was very confident in what he did. If he hadn't been in

the army he would have been a market trader down Portobello Road. He was the scruffiest person I'd ever seen. He looked as if he'd been dipped in glue and thrown through the window of an Oxfam shop. He was a good soldier, without a doubt, but he was so laid back he was almost lying down. Because he found things very easy, it looked as if he had no commitment.

Tom was a corporal from 29 Commando, part of the Royal Artillery attached to the Royal Marines, and he was completely the opposite, hyped up about everything. He was the funniest bloke I'd met since Dave left. He had a sag-eye: if he was looking at his shoelaces, one eye would be looking at the moon. He was also the tallest of us, just on 6', and athletically built. He was very loud; I suspected he was deaf after a lifetime of artillery pieces banging off in his ear.

I was still phoning up Debbie, writing her letters and telling her how exciting it was. When she wrote or spoke, I didn't listen or read between the lines. It didn't occur to me that she might be bored shitless. I was in the UK doing something I wanted to do, and she was in Germany just plodding on, not really doing that much. I couldn't have cared less; me, I was off to Brunei.

11

In March we flew to Hong Kong, en route to Brunei. We came into Kaitak Airport at night, and I couldn't believe what I saw. The aircraft did a steep turn then flew in really low. I could see people walking in the street and pottering around in their apartments.

We stayed at a camp near the airport. It was the first experience I'd had of somebody in authority in the army giving me money, a ration allowance because they wouldn't be feeding us. It was supposed to be money for food, but of course it paid for a night on the town, with just enough left over to buy a bag of chips on the way home. I thought, hell, yes – I need to keep in here, they give you money!

Hong Kong was one of the places I'd always heard about, but never thought I'd see. Now I just wanted to take as much of it in as I could in case I never came back. The city was packed and never seemed to stop. It was full of neon, food shops open everywhere, dense traffic, and this was at ten o'clock at night. We could sleep on the plane to Brunei in the morning; tonight was ours to enjoy.

Raymond had been to Hong Kong before when he did an emergency tour with the Parachute Regiment in the New Territories. 'No problems,' he declared, 'I know all the good places. Let's get in there and have a good old time.' We dutifully followed him around all the tourist attractions that appealed to visiting British soldiers – mostly bars with

names like the John Bull and Ned Kelly's Last Stand. I bought some tapes and shirts, and generally had a good old spend, wandering around in a bit of a daze. I couldn't get enough of the bamboo scaffolding and fearsome modern buildings right next to a little shanty with a family in it. Before long we were half-pissed and sitting on the pavement, eating some of the local fry-ups from the boy on the street corner. I felt I was living in a James Bond film.

Next morning we all had the shits, but dragged ourselves to the airport to get away on a scheduled flight to Brunei, home of the British Army jungle training school. There wasn't a cloud in the sky as we flew over little islands scattered in the see-through water of the China Sea. I was looking through the window taking everything in. I watched the sea become land and soon I could see nothing but miles and miles of green canopy.

As soon as I stepped from the aircraft I got my first insect bite. The heat and humidity knocked me sideways. We were all sweating buckets in our jeans, shirts and trainers as we drove to the camp past primitive-looking houses on stilts, many with a TV aerial sticking out of the roof and a shiny Mazda parked underneath. The canopy was everywhere, creeping into the gardens, trying to reclaim its territory.

We had a day to draw our weapons and pack our kit. Half the stuff we'd brought with us from the UK had to be left at the camp: everything we took into the jungle the next morning, we were told, we would take in on our backs.

We were advised to eat as much fresh food as we could, and I stuffed myself with melon and salads. The lecture room was an old tin hut with a fan in the ceiling; one of the instructors gave us a safety brief about snakes and how to treat a bite. Basically, there didn't seem much that could be done, apart from trying to restrict the flow of blood. 'And try to kill the snake,' he added. 'Then we know what antidote to get in. Otherwise, you're in the shit.'

I wandered around the camp, stopping from time to time

to listen to the night. The jungle sounded more or less as I'd expected it to, with insects chirping and monkeys screeching, and the occasional scream or squeal of some other animal. I was quite apprehensive; in twelve hours' time we would be going in there for the big test.

It was a beautiful morning, really hot, not a cloud in the sky. We lined up with all our beltkit and bergens and clambered aboard the Hueys that were going to take us in. We flew for about three quarters of an hour in a brilliant blue sky, over a vivid green canopy. I could see nothing but miles and miles of treetops and hills, with mist rising above. It was absolutely beautiful. I thought: even if I fail, I've had this view.

We started to lose height and I heard the rotor blades strain as the aircraft started to slow down. We were going to land on a spur where the trees had been blasted to make a helipad. As I looked down I saw blokes running around with the world's biggest beards; as the helicopter came lower their hair was blown back by the rotor wash and dust, leaves and twigs exploded into the air.

The doors opened and I was hit by exhaust fumes and heat. One of the blokes who had been there for three weeks preparing the base camp said he would take us down to the admin area. We gathered our gear and followed him. The spur, being high up, was in blinding sunlight; as we came down off it, we entered the rainforest. It was like walking into a greenhouse without ventilation on a baking hot day and closing the door behind us. The noise and direct heat of the landing site gave way to semi-gloom and comparative silence, apart from birdsong and the odd word from our guide. I broke into a horrendous sweat, and found it hard to get my breath.

We had to cross a river. Logs had been positioned over it to make a small bridge and as we started to cross I caught my first glimpse of a palm-leaf shelter and, nearby, a group of tribesmen. The Regiment had enjoyed a long association with the Ibans, dating back to the Borneo conflict.

'They're good blokes,' the DS said. 'We employ some of them to help build all the atap [*foliage-covered*] huts for the admin area, including what is going to be your school-house. They also help with a lot of the survival training.'

As we went past these boys, squatting on their haunches and smoking away, it hit me that we really had come into a totally different culture in a totally different part of the world. We were going to be self-contained in our own little world, miles and miles from civilization, for at least a month – whether we liked it or not. This was exciting stuff.

Looking at the rainforest around and above me, I couldn't help wondering how people survived in the claustrophobic, green-tinged semi-darkness. The tall trees of the primary jungle, profusely leaved, blocked out the sun. Humidity must have been running at close to 90 per cent. I was hot, I was short of breath, I was sweating, I was getting bitten to bits. It seemed every animal there wanted to have a munch out of me. I looked at the Ibans, relaxing against the shelters with just a pair of shorts on, as happy as sandboys.

We got into the 'schoolhouse', which was in fact little more than a roof over two rows of log benches. We put down our bergens and the DS came around for a brew and a chat.

Each patrol's DS would stay with it all the time, we were told, though he lived in the admin area rather than with the patrol. Every time we were out on the ground, he'd be there as well.

They spelled out a few golden rules.

'Never go anywhere without your golock [*machete*]. Never go anywhere without your beltkit and your weapon. Even if you take your beltkit off to sit on during a lesson, the golock stays attached to you by a length of paracord. It's your most essential item of survival kit – it gets you food, it builds you traps, it gives you protection.

'You never go anywhere in the jungle on your own, you always go in pairs. It's incredibly easy to get lost. You can

walk five or ten metres away from the camp area and there's a possibility of getting disorientated. So even if it's going down to the river to fill up for water, go in pairs. You might be relaxing, sorting your shit out, but if somebody's got to go down and collect the water, somebody else has got to go with them. The only place you don't have to go to in pairs is the shit pit, which is just off to the side of the patrol area.'

We had all arrived with as much extra kit as we could cram into our bergens – extra water bottles, loads of spare socks, all sorts of crap. Now we found out that we needed very little.

The DS explained: 'To live in the jungle, all you need is two sets of clothes: one wet and one dry. Sleep in the dry, and always have your wet ones on. Even if you stand still all day, you're going to be soaking wet. There are no seasons in the rain forest: it's just wet and hot. You get two rains a day. Especially if you're on a spur, you can feel the wind coming, and then it will rain. If the rain doesn't get you, the humidity will.

'The important thing is to keep your dry kit dry – we're a bit short on tumble driers around here. So put it in a dry wrapper, then put that in another dry wrapper. Once you're wet, you're fucking wet, and that's it.'

The DS then gave us a practical demonstration of how to build an A-frame.

'You start with the two end pieces in the shape of an A. These don't need to be more than two or three inches in diameter, just strong enough to support your weight. Then you get two more lengths of wood, again no more than two or three inches in diameter, to support your hammock. You slip the two poles through the holes in the hammock and push them down over the apex of the As and tie them on. All being well, what you've created is a bed that's a couple of feet off the floor.

'Once that's done, you then put a poncho over the top and then just bungee it off onto the trees. Now you're

protected from the rain, and then underneath that you can put your mozzie net. There's nothing macho about sleeping in your A-frame without a mozzie net; getting bitten means that you're more uncomfortable the next day, and that means you're less able to operate. If you take the time, sort yourself out, you're a much better commodity the next day. It's not wimpy kit, it's sensible. There's times when you've got to be in the shit and then OK, you do that, but there's a lot of times when you don't have to be. If you're back in a base area you make yourself as comfortable as possible.'

Some people, apparently, built another platform under the bed level, to store their bergen and other kit. The ground was soaking wet and teeming with ants, scorpions and other beasts that would end up biting if they got close enough. The more kit we could keep off the ground, the more comfortable we were going to be when we put it on.

The DS took us to our patrol area and said, 'Sort your-selves out. I'll be back later; any problems, come and get me.'

'Sorting ourselves out' meant building ourselves an A-frame. Raymond got his up in less than an hour, and then chopped more wood to make himself a platform to stand on.

'This'll last about two days before it sinks into the mud,' he said. 'So then you just bung another load on top.'

'I see,' I said, still only a quarter of the way through building my rickety bag of shit.

Once we had all finished, we sat down and got a hexy burner going for a brew. We'd brought an empty grenade tin to cook with, which held about five pints of liquid. We filled it with water from our bottles and brewed our first mug of tea in the jungle. I was starting to feel a little more at home.

We talked about how we were going to crack the jungle phase. Everybody knew what the DS were looking for: people with aptitude, who could blend in.

I said, 'What we must do all the time is back each other up, and not get the hump with each other.'

Mal, leaning back with a fag in his mouth, said, 'Well, our leader, you'd better be doing all the work then, and don't fuck up.' Then he lay on his back and blew out a long trail of smoke.

It was time to go back down to the schoolhouse. We put on our beltkit and picked up our golocks and weapons. All the DS were there. We sat on the log benches in the schoolhouse and they were outside, facing us.

The training-wing sergeant major said, 'This is the routine within the admin area. Every morning and every night, you stand to – half an hour before first light, half an hour after first light, and the same at last light, around your own basha [*shelter*] area.

'You can send out letters once a week. There will be fresh [*fresh food*] once a week. The area where the DS live is strictly out of bounds. If you need to go through, you have to stop and call for somebody to give you permission. Right, go back to your areas. I want you back here at eight o'clock tomorrow morning.'

We packed everything away in our bergens and sat on them for an hour for the stand to, weapon butt in the shoulder, covering our arcs. As I watched the daylight fade, there was a sudden burst of high-pitched, purring bleeps all around us.

'Basher-out beetles,' Raymond said. 'That's your indication that it's going to be last light very soon.'

The darkness buzzed with airborne raiders; most of them seemed to be heading in my direction. I put more cam cream and mozzie rep (*mosquito repellent*) on my face and hands, but it made no difference. They still hovered and swooped like miniature Stukas, biting and stinging. Above the steady buzz and hum of insects came the occasional rustling in the undergrowth and canopy. Apart from the bites, I loved it.

When the hour was up we picked up our bergens and walked into the admin area. Torch batteries had to be conserved, so we lit candles. I lit a hexy burner, put the

grenade box on top, and the blokes tipped in their sachets of beef stew and rice for a communal scoff.

Mal was quite confident about things, stretched out in the mud with a fag in his mouth. Tom was asking questions or worrying about something every five minutes in his usual hyper fashion: 'We must get up tomorrow morning for stand to, we mustn't forget,' he ranted, with one eye on the food and the other on his boots as he laced them up furiously.

Everybody was still pretty tired after the rigours of Hong Kong and feeling drained by our new environment. We weren't acclimatized yet, and were covered in lumps and bumps where the beasties had got in. I was looking forward to getting on my pole bed.

I took my wet clothing off, rolled it up and put it on the shelf under my A-frame. I put my dry clothes on, and a pair of trainers: we didn't know what surprises the DS might have in store, so even if they bumped us during the night at least I knew I could just jump out and start functioning. I got my head down under the mozzie net and listened to the jungle conducting its life around me – crickets, beetles and other insects clicking and buzzing, unknown things scratching around in the undergrowth.

It started to rain, and it was the most wonderful feeling in the world to be snug under my basha, listening to the water splash onto the roof.

I didn't sleep too well, tossing and turning, thinking about everything that lay ahead. Let's just get the month over and done with, I said to myself, and hope that you pass. At times I looked over and I could see that everybody was having the same problem. In the darkness around Mal's pole bed I saw the glow of a cigarette end as he inhaled. I slowly started to drift off.

All of a sudden, Tom leapt up.

'We're late! We're late! It's half six! Stand to!'

Bodies tumbled from pole beds into the mud as we scrabbled for our kit. I pulled on my wet clothes, keeping

an eye out for the DS. If they came round now and caught us still in our beds we'd be in severe shit. It would be seen as incredibly bad self-discipline.

Mal was trying to put his boots on while standing up and fell over. I heard a soft *fizz* as his fag hit the mud.

Tom was still ranting loudly when Raymond said, 'Stop, stop, stop. It's fucking midnight, you dickhead. It's not half six.'

Tom had woken up in the middle of the night, looked at his watch, and misread the hands. He wasn't exactly flavour of the month as we sorted ourselves out again and got back into our beds.

Our first lesson was in how to administer ourselves in the field.

'First thing in the morning,' the DS said, 'slap loads of mozzie rep all over your clothes, face and arms. As you will soon find out, it's so strong it melts plastic.'

He passed around his compass. He'd been there three weeks and it had started to lose all its lettering, and the roamers which measured the grid references. Mozzie rep melted through plastic, and there was us slopping it on our skin.

As soon as we'd done that, we had to take our Paludrine anti-malarial drug.

We learned more or less straightaway how to blow landing-sites and winch holes, because we might have to do it. If somebody broke his leg, we'd have to stabilize him, cut a winch hole and wait for the helicopter.

'When blowing an LS for a long-term base, you can put direction on the way the tree falls,' the DS said. 'The higher the ground the better, because as the taller ones fall they'll take the smaller ones with them. The explosive pack is called "packet echo" – ask for it and a big wad of chainsaws and explosives and augers will be dropped, enough to blow a site.'

We went out one day with explosives to practise blowing

trees. Tom was flapping as we studied the massive buttress tree we'd just packed with PE4.

'Do you reckon that's enough? I don't, I think we need more.'

'I quite agree,' I said. 'P for Plenty.'

We wadded another pound or two of explosive into the holes. In theory we should have been using as little as possible, but it did look a very big tree.

'Sure this will be all right?'

'Yeah, no problems.'

We moved back with our firing cable. Everybody else was doing the same; we were going to fire them all off one by one and see what happened.

Raymond and Mal were by their tree. Keith, our DS, said, 'Put your cable into the initiator, and fire.'

They fired the electric current into the det, which detonated some det cord and blew up the plastic explosive.

There was a boom and we all looked up to make sure nothing was going to fall on our heads. The tree fell perfectly.

'Good stuff, well done. Next one.'

Tom and I put our firing cable in.

'Standby. Firing!'

There was a massive explosion that shook the ground. The tree went straight up in the air and disappeared from sight.

'How much fucking PE did you put in that?' the DS raged.

'The correct amount,' I said. 'We did the formula, honest.'

'Bollocks!' Keith stormed over to where the PE was stored. There was almost none left.

'That's tearing the arse out of it,' he said, and I waited for the bollocking that I thought would follow. But instead he said, 'Oh well, at least it ignited, I'll give you credit for that much.' It was the first time I'd seen a DS smile.

The next day, I took my patrol up to an area where we were going to blow more trees. When we arrived we found

that the explosives, which were the responsibility of the DS, hadn't been delivered.

'We'll have to go back down to the camp and find somebody,' I said. 'Otherwise we'll screw up our timings.'

I knew the area where the DS lived was out of bounds. We got to the edge of it, called, and didn't hear anything, so I decided to take a chance and go through. After all, it wasn't our fault that the explosives weren't where they should have been.

Bad mistake. The sergeant major caught us and started to rip into me.

'Why are you doing this? We've told you not to come through here.'

'Well, the explosives weren't there and the timings are crucial,' I said. 'We're not going to get everything done unless we get hold of them. I called, and I know it's got to be there on time, so I made the decision to come through.'

I thought I was in the right, and possibly I was. However, I was on Continuation. I should have just shut up and taken the bollocking and let it go. But like an idiot I didn't. I just hoped that he hadn't marked my card.

One of the major components of our training was jungle navigation. The first time I looked at a map of the jungle, all I could see was contour lines and rivers. We had to learn how to travel with these limitations, but more importantly, simply how to recognize where we were on the ground.

'A lot of people within the squadrons use different aids,' said the DS. 'You can get a rough idea of where you are on some high feature by using an altimeter, for example, but at the end of the day, it all boils down to a map, a compass, and pacing.'

We did a lot of live firing drills in what were called 'jungle lanes'. The DS would pick an area along a river and turn it into a range. We would then practise patrolling along, as individuals to start with, looking for the targets. We'd be moving along tactically; all of a sudden

the DS would pull a wire and a target would go up.

'You're there for a task,' they said, 'the majority of time as a small group of men. If you bump into something, you don't know what it is. For all you know, it could be the forward recce of a much larger group. If you're not there to fight, the idea is to put a maximum amount of fire down and get the hell out, so you can carry on with your job.'

The ranges were great. I'd never done anything like it before in the infantry. It wouldn't be allowed in the normal army; it would be seen as too dangerous. Yet the only way to get the proper level of realism and test people in this close environment was to use live ammunition.

We did single-man jungle lanes, where we'd be patrolling as if we were the lead scout. When it was my turn I found my body was all tensed up; I walked with the butt in the shoulder, trying so hard to look for the target, picking my feet up to make sure I didn't trip over.

Suddenly I heard, 'Stop!'

What have I done now?

'Look right.'

I looked right, and found I'd just walked past the target. I hadn't seen it. Tuning in was so important.

'Right, come back and start again.'

Next time, when I saw it I reacted.

Then we did it in pairs. We lay in a dip in the ground with the DS while he gave us a scenario. 'You are part of a ten-man fighting patrol. You got bumped in an ambush and everybody split up. Now you're trying to make it back to your own area. You're moving along the line of this river. Any questions? Carry on in your own time.'

'I'll go lead scout first,' I said to Mal.

We moved along, me playing the lead scout, Mal playing the man behind. It was really hard to see these targets. Sometimes they'd be ones that popped up, sometimes they were just sitting there. I stopped by a tree, got down, had a look forward as far as I could, then I moved again. Mal was behind me, doing his own thing.

I went along the track and spotted a small bit of dead ground about ten metres ahead. As I approached it, I just saw the top of a small target. Straightaway I got the rounds down.

'Contact front! Contact front!'

I kept on firing; Mal stepped off to the right and opened up. As soon as I heard him I turned round, saw him to my left-hand side, and screamed past him. A couple of metres on I turned again and fired. He then turned and ran, stopped, and fired. I turned and went off to the right-hand side and down to the river bank.

'Rally! Rally! Rally! Rally! Rally!'

Running over logs, jumping behind trees, it was all over within fifteen seconds. Then the DS shouted, 'Stop!'

After each contact the DS would debrief us. We'd be panting away, trying to catch our breath; it was only a short, sharp burst of activity, but even patrolling I'd get out of breath – the body was tensed up, the brain was concentrating, it was live ammunition, and we were being tested.

I was already finding the jungle as physically hard as Selection, because the pressure was unrelenting. I assumed that all the time they were asking themselves the questions: would I want him in my patrol? Has he got the personality? Has he got the aptitude? The closed, harsh environment of the jungle, where everybody depended on everybody else, would show us in our true light.

'Why did you take that bit of cover there? Look over there – the world's biggest tree. That'll stop 7.62.'

The DS, Keith, walked us back to the static target. The canopy had retained the pall of smoke and the smell of cordite from the contact. I took a swig of water from my bottle as I listened.

'When you saw that, you were right on top of it. Walk back five metres, turn around, and now look. You can see it now, can't you? The reason you can see it is that you know that it's there. You've got to be good enough to notice it

before you get there – and the only way you're going to do that is getting up and down here, and watching, and practising.

'Let's now go and see if you hit what you saw.'

There wasn't a scratch on the target Mal and I had been firing at.

'What's the point of firing if you're not going to kill him?' Keith said. 'It's all well and good getting that constant fire down to get away, but what you're trying to do is kill them so they don't follow you up and kill you.'

We built up to four-man contact drills. The lead scout would be moving very slowly, stop, observe the area, start moving. If we had a rise to go over and the other side was dead ground, he would tell the patrol to stop, and go over, butt in the shoulder, using the cover of the trees. If that was OK, he'd just wave everybody on. The rest of us would be covering our arcs as we walked. The lead scout might have missed something; we might end up with a contact right or a contact rear.

The one piece of advice I'd got from Jeff in D Squadron was: 'Butt in your shoulder, sights up.' It was tiring to move so slowly and deliberately. I was breathing really hard and deeply, concentrating so much on what I was doing.

In any slack time, we were expected to mug up on what we had been taught the day before. Mal was so good at everything that he didn't need to. He'd just lie there with a fag and a brew. It was impressive. I was jealous; I would have done the same, only I was way behind because my Morse was shit. Any spare time I had, I cracked on.

The jungle canalizes movement. The dense vegetation, deep gullies, steep hills and ravines, and wide, fast rivers are obstacles which make cross-country movement very difficult. However, it's got to be done. High ground and tracks are where every Tom, Dick and Harry moves, and where ambushes are laid.

126

We navigated across country, using a technique called cross graining. Up and down, up and down, not keeping to the high ground. It took us much longer to travel a small distance, but tactically it was better: we weren't getting ambushed, we weren't leaving sign, we weren't going to bump into any opposition.

The DS said, 'You never cut wood: you move it out of the way, patrol through, and move it back. If somebody's tracking you, they're looking for two types of ground sign – footprints and top sign. If you see cobwebs, you don't touch them, you go around them. If a tracker isn't getting cobwebs over his face, it's another good indication that somebody has walked past.'

People were getting severely on each other's tits now, especially during the navigation phases. The navigation was not just a matter of taking a bearing and off you go. We had to confirm regularly where we actually were; we could not see any lower or higher ground at any distance because of the vegetation and canopy. It was pointless going down from a high feature if we'd gone down the wrong spur. That would mean that we'd have to come all the way back up again and start again. So we had to stop, sit down, work out where we were – where we thought we were – and then send out recce patrols. Two blokes would go out and confirm that at the bottom of this spur there was, for example, a river that ran left to right. If that was happening a couple of times an hour, people were getting hot, pissed off, knackered, and frustrated. It started to grate. I calmed myself by thinking: take it slowly and send out your navigation patrols, you'll do it, there's no problem.

The physical exertion of being on the range or patrolling on two- or three-day exercises was very debilitating. Then we had written tests, or had to plan and prepare for a scenario. We were under constant pressure. There was never enough time. The DS would always be behind us saying, 'We've got five more minutes. Let's get this done.'

At the debriefings, they would dish out fearsome

criticism. 'You fucked up! You didn't see the target! Why didn't you look right? As lead scout, that's your job.'

I was on my chinstrap one day. We'd probably covered twice the distance we should have done because of the amount of recces we were doing, going up and down; we were all over the fucking place.

It was my turn to map read and as I started to go down from what I thought was the highest ground, to the right of me I saw higher ground. That was wrong; I'd cocked up. We stopped; Raymond and Mal were the next two to go on a recce patrol and I could see in their eyes that they were not impressed. I said, 'At the bottom of this spur there should be water running left to right. If not, I've severely fucked up.'

They were gone for about an hour and a half. When we got back that night I said, 'Fuck, that was a long recce you guys did.'

Raymond said, 'Yeah, well, we just got to the bottom, had a drink, and sat in the river for half an hour to cool down and get all the shit off.'

I was hot and sweaty all the time, stinking and out of breath. As I sweated, the mozzie rep I'd put on my face would run into my eyes and sting severely. It didn't seem to matter what amount of mozzie rep I put on, I still got bitten. And I was covered in painful webbing sores. And all the time, the DS were watching. They seemed so calm and casual about it, there seemed to be nothing embuggering them. Nothing seemed to fuss them, and we were standing there like a bunch of rain-drenched refugees. We would be soaking wet, all bogged down, and we'd have to go on yet another navigation patrol.

I asked myself, how do you survive here? How do you get comfy? The only enjoyable experience about the place was sitting and having a communal brew and scoff at the end of the day – if it wasn't raining. Then I loved getting into my A-frame, revising by candlelight and listening to the rain on the poncho.

I was really missing Debbie. I felt vulnerable in the jungle; there was no-one to vent out to my personal anxieties and fears of failing, and I wanted to feel attached to something beyond my immediate environment. I wrote to her regularly, trying to tell her what was happening. 'I really hope I pass, because it will be great. We'll get to Hereford, we'll be able to afford a house, and everything will be fine.'

I found the jungle harder than Test Week – much harder. All we had to do in Selection was switch off and get over those hills. Here, it was just as physical, but we had the mental pressure as well, of learning, of having to perform and take in all this information.

We were tested to the extremes, mentally as well as physically. They took us right up to the edge, and then they brought us back. Then they took us up there again.

We got better and better, but always at the back of my mind was the thought that the DS were looking at every-thing – not just tactical skills or practical skills, but my personality, whether I would blend in with a closed environment like jungle, whether I'd blend in within the squadron. I could see it in their eyes; I could see their minds ticking over. Does he take criticism well? Does he want to learn, does he ask relevant questions or does he ask questions just for the sake of asking questions, to look good?

The jungle, Peter the chief instructor said, was absolutely full of food – from beetles and spiders down to the bark on a tree.

'If you've got something but you're not too sure whether you can eat it, you rub it on your skin and see if there is a reaction. Then you wait, and a couple of hours later rub it on your lips and see if there's a reaction – then on the tip of your tongue, then around your gums. Then you just taste a little bit, then eat a little bit, and if there's no reaction, you take the chance and eat it.'

We were sitting by the Iban huts down near the river, quite a pleasant, flat area. The helipad was on the spur on the other side of the stream, and I could see shafts of sunlight streaming down.

Fish under four inches long didn't have to be gutted, the instructor said, you just cooked them. There was a plant called the jungle cabbage which was like a small tree. You split the bark and inside was a pulp that was absolutely beautiful. It tasted like a soft cabbage. You could also make tea with the bark.

'On operations, you don't eat lizards and snakes and all that sort of stuff unless you absolutely have to. It's pointless. If you've got to, that's fine, but why not take in food that is going to give you the nutrition so you can do the job? Also you've got less chance of getting disease or gut aches. Can you imagine having the shits and being totally out of it on operations for two days? You've gone into an area, you've got no support, you've got no way of coming back, and you're eating lizard heads, and then you get gut ache. You can't do your job – at least, not a hundred per cent. Anyway, the amount of energy and time it takes to collect food, you wouldn't have any time to do anything else, so you take the food and water with you.'

We were sitting on our beltkit along the river bank, cradling our weapons. The Ibans were with us; they had a few little fires going and were smoking their huge roll-ups as they showed us various fishing nets and traps that they'd made. We had a go ourselves and everything we made fell to pieces.

One of the Ibans held a small termite nest over the water with a stick. The termites tumbled into the water and the fish rose to eat them.

'We also have the red buttress tree,' Peter said. 'It holds a natural source of fluid.'

We thought this was all rather interesting, especially when he went around the back and pulled out several six-

packs of beer. It was the first time we'd got anything overtly friendly from the training team.

Once a week we had 'fresh'. We were given an egg, a couple of sausages. One particular afternoon, they said, 'Go away, eat the fresh, and then come back, we've got a lecture two hours before last light.'

It was lovely to be able to cook in daylight, and afterwards, as we came back at the appointed hour with just our beltkit, golock and weapon, everybody was full and content. I settled down for the lecture, thinking about what I'd do afterwards – which was to sort out my webbing sores, and the sores inside my thighs. I was looking forward to getting some army issue talcum powder between my legs, lying on my bed and going through my notes.

No sooner had the DS started than the ground was rocked by explosions. Rounds whistled through the air and thumped into the ground.

'Camp attack! Camp attack! RV, RV, RV!'

We bomb-burst out of the schoolhouse. There was smoke everywhere and bits and pieces of shit flying through the air.

It was a complete pain in the arse. It was week three, we were starting to get fairly comfortable, starting to adjust to life in the jungle, so all of a sudden they had hit us with 'night out on beltkit'.

I made my way to the troop RV. We all had emergency rations in our beltkit, but no hammocks. We had to sleep on the floor. A lot of armies think it's dead hard to lie on the ground in the jungle; but there are so many other factors to fuck you up in that environment, without having to lie in the mud getting bitten and stung, and being so wary of scorpions and snakes that it's impossible to sleep. It's not macho, it's stupid, and the idea of 'night out on beltkit' was to treat us to that little experience. We got it in spades, because it poured with rain all night.

* * *

During one five-day exercise I was moving into a troop RV (*rendezvous point*) one evening. We were patrolling tactically, moving really slowly, to get into an area from where we could send out our sitrep. It had been a long day, I was tired, and it was raining heavily.

As I sat down to encrypt the message to be Morsed out, my hand started to shake. Seconds later, my head was spinning. My eyes couldn't focus. I took a deep breath and told myself to get a grip.

It got worse, and within a minute the shaking was uncontrollable. I tried to write but my hand was all over the place. My vision was getting more and more blurred.

I knew what was happening.

We were doing a lot of physical work in the jungle. We had heavy loads on, we were under mental pressure, yet the body was still trying to defend its core temperature. To maintain a constant temperature, the heat loss must equal heat production. But if the heat production is more than the heat loss, the temperature's going to rise. When the core temperature rises, more blood reaches the skin, where the heat is then released. This works fine as long as the skin temperature is higher than the air temperature. But in the heat of the jungle, the body absorbs heat, and the body counters that by sweating. This has limits. An adult can only sweat about a litre per hour. You can't keep it up for more than a few hours at a time unless you get replacement fluids, and the sweat is only effective if the outside air is not saturated with moisture. If the humidity is more than 75 per cent, as it is in the jungle, the sweat evaporation isn't going to work.

We were sweating loads but the sweat wasn't evaporating. So the body heat was rising, and we were sweating even more. The way the body tries to get rid of that is by sending blood to the skin, so therefore the vessels have to increase in size. The heart rate increases, and sometimes it gets to a rate where its automotive function loses control and it starts to go all over the place. Less and less blood

flows to the internal organs. It's shunted away from the brain, so the blood that goes there is going to be hot anyway. The brain doesn't like hot blood going to it, so it responds with headaches, dizziness, impaired thinking, and emotional instability. Because we were sweating so much, we were losing loads of electrolytes, sodium and chlorides – and the result was dehydration. We were losing non-circulating body fluids.

The problem is that just a few sips of liquid might quench somebody's thirst, without improving their internal water deficit. You might not even notice your thirst because there is too much else going on, and that was what was happening to me. I was mooching through the jungle, the patrol commander, under pressure to perform, trying to make decisions. The last thing I was thinking about, like a dickhead, was getting the fluids down my neck.

'When you have a piss,' the DS had said, 'you look at it. If it's yellow and smelly, you're starting to dehydrate. If it's clear and you're pissing every five minutes, that's excellent, because the body always gets rid of excess water. You can't overload with water because the body will just get rid of it. So as long as you've got good clear piss, you know that everything's all right.'

I turned round to Raymond and said, 'Fucking hell, I'm going down here.'

Everything stopped; the whole effort switched to making sure I was all right. Raymond got some rehydrates and boiled sweets down me, put a brew on and gave me lots of sweet tea. Fortunately the DS didn't see what was going on; it was my fault I was dehydrating. Within half an hour I was right as rain again, but I had learned my lesson.

We came back in off the exercise and they checked our bergens for plastic bags of shit. We weren't allowed to leave any sign, and that included body effluents. We had to shit into plastic bags, and collect our piss in plastic petrol cans.

They checked another patrol as we came in. 'You've not

got much shit there,' the DS said. 'You constipated or something? Where's all your shit?'

The fellow made an excuse and the DS just said, 'OK.'

Sometimes I wished they would just give us a bollocking, to get it out of the way. They'd told us why not to shit in the field – because the enemy would know people were there. They had even shown us how to shit into a plastic bag by getting somebody to do it. If we weren't doing it, it was bad discipline.

Sometimes we'd go back to an area we'd used that day to look at some of the problems we had created. They might say, 'See the marks on the trees? Soft bark is easily marked, hard isn't so you leave no sign.'

Because they'd shown us that, they didn't expect it to happen again. If we didn't learn it must mean we didn't want to learn, or didn't have the aptitude.

The jungle phase ended with a week-long exercise that was a culmination of everything we'd learned, involving patrolling, hard routine, CTRs (*close target recce*), bringing everybody together at a troop RV, preparing to do an ambush, springing the ambush, the withdrawal, going to caches for more stores for the exfil (*exfiltration*). At some time in the future, we might go into a country before an operation and cache food, ammunition and explosives. We could then infil (*infiltrate*) later without the bulk kit, because it was already cached. We had learned how to conceal it, and how to give information to other patrols so that it would be easy to find.

By now, physically, we were not exactly as hale and hearty as when we first went in. We were incredibly dirty, our faces ingrained with camouflage cream. Everybody had a month's beard, and we had been wearing the same clothes all the time.

One thing I had never got used to was getting out of my A-frame or hammock and putting my wet kit on. It was always full of bits and pieces that gathered as we were patrolling along, and it was cold and clammy. It grated

against my skin for the ten minutes or so until it had got warm.

We had our beltkit on all the time and some of the pouches would be rubbing on the sides and producing sores. I went through a phase of not wearing any pants, to try to keep the sores from between my legs. I tried little things that I thought might help, such as undoing my trousers, tucking everything in, and doing them up again. I came to the conclusion that nothing worked. I was in shit state, and in shit state I would stay.

Once the exercise had finished we all RV'd at a bend in the river; that night we went non-tactical, waiting to get picked up the following day by the Ibans in their dug-out canoes with little outboard engines on the back. They took us downstream to a village, where we were going to get picked up because there were no landing sites in the area.

It was like a scene out of a film. There was all the jungle, and then there was a clearing, with grass, chickens running around, little pigs and goats and all sorts, in the middle of nowhere. There were no roads, just a river. They had a schoolhouse, with a generator chugging away. There were TV aerials sticking up out of these Iban huts made out of wood, atap and mud. All the kids were going to school in just shorts and the teacher was dressed as any other schoolteacher would be.

The DS said, 'When you come into these places you've got to introduce yourself to the head boy. Show him respect; then the next time you come in he won't fuck you off.'

For the first time in days, people were allowed to smoke. Blokes were sitting on the river bank, sharing their fags with the DS. The training major got his out and offered one to Mal. There was a mutual understanding between them; it made me envious not to be a smoker, joining in the camaraderie.

I just sat there, drinking in the scene. As far as I was concerned, it was done now. I'd passed or I'd failed; I was just pleased that it was over.

The rest of the day was spent cleaning weapons, cleaning kit, eating scoff. In the evening, there was a barbecue for everybody who had anything to do with the jungle school. The DS produced crates of two-pint bottles of Heineken and the cooks sorted out the steaks and sausages.

'Might be the last time you ever come here lads,' the DS said. 'Get on the piss!'

We did. I was drunk on three bottles of the Heineken, threw up at about midnight, and went to bed with the jungle spinning.

There was a day off in the capital but it was a Muslim country so there was only drinking in one hotel. Everybody felt so sick anyway they didn't bother. I went shopping with Mal, Tom and Raymond, buying armfuls of bootleg tapes, Walkmans, cameras and watches. All the traders seemed to be wearing David Cassidy T-shirts.

I had lost a stone. One of the blokes, the Canadian jock who had been our snowplough during Selection, came out looking like a Biafran. Like a dickhead, he hadn't even been cooking scoff for himself at night because he wanted to go hard routine all the time.

We'd been under the canopy and not seen daylight for a month. I came out looking like an uncooked chip. I was all pasty, full of zits and big lumps. No matter how many showers I had, I still had grime under my nails and big blackheads on my skin. Some of the mozzie bites had scarred up a bit from where I'd scratched them and they'd welted up. Basically, I looked minging.

We had a few hours in Hong Kong and then flew back on a British Caledonian charter. Four long-haired blokes who were sitting near us looked the typical 'Here we go, here we go' lads, wearing hideous orange and purple flowery Hawaiian shirts, jeans and flip-flops. I sat there wondering if they'd had a slightly more enjoyable time in the Far East than we had, frolicking on a sex holiday in Thailand or smuggling drugs.

I felt quite subdued and started to get my head down.

One of the DS, a fellow called Dave, was in the seat in front of me. The four drug smugglers got out of their seats and gave him a cuff on the head. I was just wondering what I was supposed to do about it when Dave turned round and grinned, 'All right, mate?'

It was four blokes coming back from a team job, routed through Hong Kong.

'Good shirts!' Dave said. 'Good job?'

'Yep.'

They'd obviously done their job somewhere in the Far East and now they were settling down with their gin and tonics for a nice flight home. I thought again, I really hope I get in. I need to be here!

'Any chance of a lift back?' they asked the DS. 'You got your wagon there?'

'Yeah, we can sort that out.'

Then they chatted away to us, which was wonderful. It was my first real contact with strangers from the squadrons.

'How did you find it?'

'Oh, it was good.' I didn't know what to say. I just sat there smiling, not wanting to commit myself.

'Have they told you if you've passed yet or not? Go on, Dave, tell them, don't be a wanker!'

But he didn't.

We arrived back in Hereford on a Friday morning and were given the rest of the day off.

'Be back in the training-wing eight o'clock tomorrow morning,' the training-wing sergeant major said.

That night everybody went out on the piss and had a really good night – again, for all any of us knew, it might be the last time we'd ever be there. We turned up on Saturday morning with bad heads, stinking of beer and curries.

The sergeant major said, 'Right, combat survival, Monday morning, half eight. All the details are on the

board. However ... the following people, go and see the training major.'

We were sitting in the training-wing lecture room, in three rows. I was at the end of one of them.

He started reading out the names. He called out Mal's first. I couldn't believe it. Mal was good; as far as I was concerned, he was really switched on. I had to stand up to let him pass, and we exchanged a knowing glance. He shrugged his shoulders and smiled. While I was still standing, the sergeant major called Raymond's name. Then Tom's. That was that, then: everybody from my patrol was getting binned. I just stayed standing up. There didn't seem much point in sitting down.

My name wasn't called. Then I realized maybe these were the people that had passed. Maybe it was the knobbers like me left behind that were going to be binned.

Out of twenty-four who went to the jungle, there were eight of us left on the benches. The sergeant major made eye contact with each of us, then said, 'Well done, that's another bit over with. Next is combat survival. Monday morning, half eight. Anybody got any medical problems? No, OK. Remember – you're not in yet.'

I thought, I've passed! There was no way I was going to fail combat survival.

'Right then, fuck off. Everybody except McNab and Forbes. The training major wants you to stay behind.'

What was this about?

Everybody else left, and the training major spoke to Forbes, the rupert, about officers' responsibilities and the extra duties he'd have to do.

Then he said, 'Right, McNab, do you know why I've got you here?'

'No, I haven't got a clue.'

'You've passed. The only problem is, you've got to fucking watch yourself.'

'Why's that?'

'We've got you down as gobby. Just listen to what people have got to say and take it in. Don't gob off.'

As I walked from the lecture room I couldn't work it out; I'd tried so hard to be the grey man. Then I remembered the incident with the explosives. I should have just shut up and taken the bollocking and let it go. But like an idiot I hadn't. Luckily, the training team had obviously made the decision that although I was a gobby git, I'd got what they wanted, and just needed to be told to wind my neck in.

Which I did. Fucking right I did.

12

I telephoned Debbie as soon as I found out I'd passed. She was excited, I was excited. The only obstacle now, I said, was three weeks of combat survival, and there was no way I was going to fail that.

The feelings and thoughts I'd had about her in the jungle had evaporated as soon as I was back in the UK; I was firmly back in selfish mode. She'd kept her job because, if I failed, I'd be going back to Germany for a while, but I didn't ask her how she was getting on – it was all me, me, me.

By now there were eight of us left – myself, George the Royal Engineer, a Household Cavalry officer, a Para, two Signallers, a gunner from the Royal Artillery, and Jake, a member of the US Special Forces. He had come over with a colleague on a three-year secondment, but they still had to pass Selection first. Jake did; the other fellow failed the first month.

All prone-to-capture units, from all three services, send their people on the combat survival course – aircrew, helicopter crew, Pathfinders from the Parachute Regiment, elements of the Royal Marines, and elements of the Royal Artillery, which has forward observation officers.

After the jungle it was more like a holiday for the first couple of weeks, but we were warned that we could still be failed – an external agency, JSIW (*Joint Services Interrogation Wing*), had the power to bin us. As the training-wing

sergeant major never stopped telling us, 'You ain't in yet!'

I was starting to talk to Johnny Two-Combs, who was already in. He was telling us about his Selection, for which he had done the winter combat survival course. 'Two of the blokes landed up in hospital with trench foot,' he said. 'I got frost nip around my fingers and toes. You'll crack it in the good weather – it's a piece of piss. Just keep your head down, find the biggest bush to hide in and you'll be all right.'

It was the Regiment's responsibility to teach the survival phases. We learned how to tell the time by the sun, gather water, and forage for food – the most important aspect, I reckoned, being the equation between the energy spent finding something to eat and the energy to be got from eating it. We went to one of the training areas and learned how to build shelters. There was a permanent stand with shelters made out of leaves, branches, turf and bin liners. It looked as though Wimpey's had won the contract. With my experience of making an A-frame, I knew there was no way I'd be making anything that looked remotely as professional.

This stuff was all very interesting, but as far as I was concerned I only wanted to learn it so that I could pass. I looked at it as an embuggerance.

Then people who had been prisoners came and spoke to us about their experiences, ranging from those who were in Colditz during the Second World War and prisoner-of-war camps in the Far East, to the Korean and Vietnam wars and the indoctrination of Allied soldiers by the communists. It was a humbling experience to hear about some of the women from SOE (*Special Operations Executive*) who were parachuted into Holland and France after minimal training, captured and subjected to horrendous and prolonged torture. Jaws dropped all round the room. I couldn't believe the outrageous inhumanity. 'When I got captured,' one woman said, 'they took out a lot of frustrations on me. I was raped and burned.' She had been kept in solitary

141

confinement in freezing cold conditions and was continually abused, yet she was speaking as if she was talking about a shopping trip to Tesco's. I supposed it showed that the human body and mind could put up with a lot more than might be expected, but I couldn't help wondering how I would bear up under the hammer.

We listened to an American pilot who had got shot down near the Choisin reservoir. He was still very much the all-American boy, dressed in a green bomber jacket with Missing In Action memorial badges and various flashes. It was easy to imagine his freckly face and light blond hair as a young man. He had landed up in a model prison that was used for propaganda purposes. He was held in a cell, but at least he was fed. He went through the mental problems of being incarcerated, but survived and came back to his family, going straight back into the air force. The biggest problem he'd had, he said, was guilt. 'I walked around with my head down for a long time,' he said. 'I couldn't handle being treated so well when so many others had suffered.'

The next speaker, a British infantry corporal in his late fifties, jumped to his feet. 'There's no way you should feel guilty,' he said. 'I positively wish I'd been in your camp!' A soldier in the Glorious Glosters, he had been through a fearsome amount of indoctrination, on starvation rations. He caught dysentery and had to bung himself up with charcoal from the fire. Eventually he had been force marched across North Korea in winter, without shoes. He saw many of his friends die on the march. He came home in shit state, having been beaten continually and lost all his teeth. He was so psychologically damaged by it all that he alienated himself from his family and ended up alone. 'I've got over it all now,' he said, 'but I still don't buy anything Korean.'

That struck a chord with me; my dad's brother had been killed by the Japanese in a prisoner-of-war camp, and even forty years later Dad wouldn't buy anything made in Japan.

'How did you cope?' somebody asked.

'I don't know. All I knew was that I didn't want to die.'

'Would you have signed all the confessions and so on if they'd asked you?'

'Bloody right I would have. If it had meant getting food or getting shoes, I'd have confessed to being Jack the Ripper. We sat there getting indoctrinated and we nodded and agreed – of course we did, it meant we got food.'

One speaker told us what a large part religion now played in his life, having found God during his time of capture. Another fellow had been a prisoner of the Viet Cong for four years; when we asked him, 'Did God play a part in your life?' he replied, 'Yeah, it played a big part. Because when we had dysentery and I was shitting myself, the Bible was something that I could clean my arse with.'

We started going out on trips and visits. We went to see an old woman near Ross-on-Wye, a country person all her life, who knew every plant in creation. She had a beautiful garden, and had tables covered with trays and trays of different flora. It was a funny scene, this frail old lady running around the fields and forests with a big bunch of boys towering over her and hanging on her every word.

We were sent out on two- or three-day exercises to make our shelters, light a fire, forage about, put a few snares out. The non-Regiment characters were well into it; for some of them it was the biggest course they'd ever be on. Once they had passed they'd be qualified as combat survival instructors and could go back to their own units and train people in the techniques. All I wanted to do was get through it.

One of the instructors, a massive old country boy with big red cheeks and hands the size of shovels, had been on the training team for years. He did the fire-lighting demonstrations, and got to the one where he was rubbing two bits of wood together to start the fire. It was quite a big thing for him; he obviously prided himself on his skill. So he's there and he's rubbing away, and nothing is happening.

'Any minute now, lads, just you wait.'

Nothing.

'Right, we'll give it another five minutes.'

He rubbed furiously, but still he couldn't do it. We had to move off to the next lecture, but about ten minutes into it he came running down the field shouting, 'It's started! Come and see!' We all had to troop back up the hill to save his pride.

During these periods when we'd be going out and building shelters and living in them for two or three days at a time, we started producing the stuff that we were going to use on the last week of combat survival. They'd taught us how to make clothes out of animal skins, and weapons out of sticks and stones. People were spending hours making jackets out of bin liners and rabbit fur hats that would have passed muster at Ascot. I did the minimum I thought I needed to pass.

On one of the exercises a large crate turned up. 'Right, lads,' the sergeant major said. 'Chicken time. The only problem is, there's only one chicken between every six of you. If you don't get one, you'll have to go to somebody who has one and hope he'll share it.'

We were sent to the bottom of the hill, the chickens were released, and on the command it was every man for himself. The Worzel Gummidge convention raced up the hill; I pulled off my combat jacket as I ran, and threw it over the first hen within range. That night it was cooked in the fire and shared with three others.

The old poachers came in and gobbed off about how to catch a salmon. We had one weird lecturer who worked for the Water Board, in charge of all the lakes. He was a real Herefordshire boy with a craggy old face and greasy blue nylon Parka, and a checked cap that was probably older than he was. He was in a world of his own as he passed on his expertise.

'When you put your net out here, don't 'ee worry about that,' he'd say mystifyingly, chuckling to himself on the

The square of Crossmaglen with Baruki sangar, 'can', and Green Jacket.
Pacemaker Press

Puma on helipad, being covered by sangar,
outside Crossmaglen security base, 1977.

McNab with M79 grenade launcher, South
Armagh 1979.

With GPMG, South Armagh 1978.

Preparing for Selection, top of Pen-y-Fan
1983. From left to right: Dave, McNab,
Johnny Two-Combs, Bob, Kev and Max.

Preparing for a river crossing,
Belize 1985.

Christmas in the jungle. Sandy
and A-Frame, Belize 1985.

B Squadron at a roadhead in
Malaya 1984.

Abseiling into the jungle, Malaya 1984.

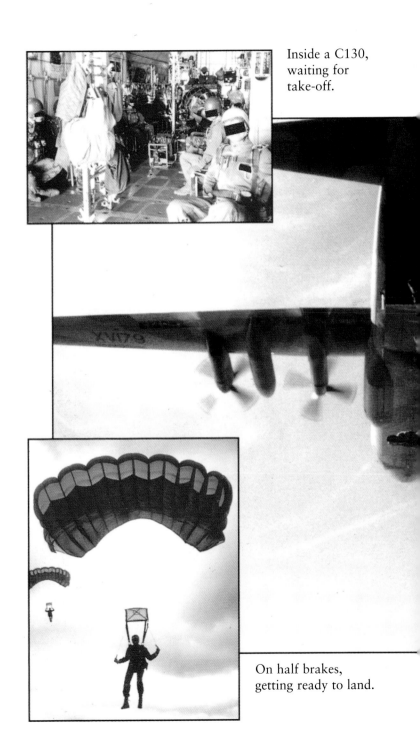

Inside a C130, waiting for take-off.

On half brakes, getting ready to land.

'Six-way' exiting from a C130.

Dive exit with GPMG
and bergen.

C130 landing on desert airstrip.

7 Troop LUP in dead ground.

7 Troop mortar crew. McNab is nearer the camera.

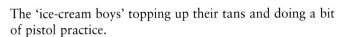

The 'ice-cream boys' topping up their tans and doing a bit of pistol practice.

river bank as he seemed to remember old stories that he then didn't share with us. Then suddenly he was telling us, 'When you go into a pub, lads, make sure you've got your back to the wall.' We were rolling up.

The DS said to us afterwards, 'We let him get on with it because we don't want to upset him. He's so good at what he does.'

After the first two weeks we'd had all the theory, we'd had all the practice, it was time to go and do it for real.

We were put into groups of four. The scheme was that we were going to navigate for seven days from point to point as if we were on a 'rat run', the system of passing escaped POWs from agent to agent in an occupied or enemy country. It was down to us to move from RV to RV; the only navigation kit we were allowed was the button compass we'd have around our necks and the escape map that we'd made ourselves – the whole of Wales on a piece of parachute silk the size of a handkerchief. We were told that sometimes on operations we'd be given a ready-printed one, but more often we would make our own.

We were told that in the areas where we'd be operating, the Regiment invited in all the farmers and householders for a big barbecue. They were told that combat survival was on again, that it would be very much appreciated if their land could be used, and that if they were approached by any people wearing bin liners and rabbit fur hats they were to turn them away and report it. It was emphasized that they had to be cruel to be kind; feeding us wouldn't help us, because we wouldn't be learning.

A Guards rifle company would be the hunter force out to capture us. They would be in vehicles and helicopters, and would be using dogs. As a performance incentive, each soldier was told that if he made a capture he would be given two weeks' leave and money.

We turned up in the training-wing with all our survival equipment, including a small tobacco tin of bits and pieces that would be all we could take apart from what we had

made. The contents included a razor blade, spare compass, water sterilizing tablets, matches and bits of magnesium block to start fires with, a magnifying glass, a heliograph and a condom. This last piece of kit wasn't in case we got lucky on the top of the Black Mountains; a condom can be used to make a catapult, collect water in, or even as an emergency flotation device.

All our kit was searched and checked, and put into the toilets which were going to be the changing room.

Each of us in turn was sent in to see the doctor.

'Strip off your tracksuit and put it in that bin liner,' he said. 'Then sign this.'

Bollock naked, I signed a bit of paper to say that I didn't mind being internally checked. As I signed, I could hear the rubber gloves going on.

Then it was a quick squirt of KY jelly and, 'Right, touch your toes.' With a swift, practised movement the doctor plunged his finger up my arse as far as it would go, presumably to check that I hadn't cached a box of Milk Tray.

The MoD police were mooching around outside with their dogs, making sure no-one was going to try and do a runner, and sniffing for hidden food. I had it all squared away; I'd known that the toilets would be used as changing rooms and had wrapped chocolate, peanuts and raisins in polythene bags and hidden them in all the cisterns. When I went back to the toilet block to change, I said to one of the police, 'Just going to have a quick dump.'

I went into the toilet, smiling all over my face, and lifted up the cistern.

Empty.

A week before that, George and I had also put out caches of food all around South Wales. We had no idea of exactly where we would be going to go, but made an educated guess. For most of a weekend we were running around buying cans of tuna and hiding them at prominent points. Tesco's made a fortune out of us.

We were issued with a set of battledress from the Second World War, a pair of boots and a greatcoat, and that was it – onto a vehicle and off we went. We were driven at night to a drop-off point, and from there we were then told where our next RV was going to be the following night. The idea was to move during the night, as tactically as we could in groups of four.

My group included a fellow from the PT corps, and two Navy aircrew, one of whom had terrible flatulence. All the Selection people had been split up. I took one look at my teammates and decided to detach myself from them at the earliest opportunity; nothing personal, but I didn't want to get caught, and I thought I'd be better off on my own. The first time we got bumped by the Guards I would do a runner.

We moved tactically at night, and in the daytime it was just a matter of finding the world's biggest, prickliest, most antisocial bush, getting right in the middle of it, and hiding. At last light, we would start moving again into the area of the RV, to meet up with the agent who was going to put us further onto this rat run. In real life the agents would want as little to do with us as possible because they wouldn't want to compromise themselves; to add realism, therefore, the DS, who were the agents, were being hunted by the ARF (*Airborne Reaction Force*) as well.

At the RV one of us would go forward and make contact, while the other three stood back; I always held back and made sure somebody else went forward, because they had a better chance of being caught. The bloke who had gone forward would get the information, come back and brief us, and off we'd trog.

We had our little tins and were supposed to be trying to catch rabbits, but we had too much distance to cover for any of that nonsense. For security, we were never going to put a fire on, we were never going to have flame. We went hungry, apart from at one checkpoint where the PTI fellow came back with a dark plastic carrier bag with a knot at the top.

'They gave me some scoff!' he beamed. He undid the knot and looked inside. His face fell. 'What the fuck's this?'

I looked. 'Tripe,' I said. 'My grandad used to live on the stuff. It's heaving.'

We ate it raw, and within an hour the Navy character was piping us aboard.

I had a premonition that things were going to go wrong. The PTI fellow was jumping clumsily over fences, which would then twang for about another fifty metres down the line. He was going at obstacles like a bull in a china shop; he'd obviously never been taught that you take your time, take it nice and gently. Every time I heard a twang I was flapping; I had it in my mind that to be captured was to be binned.

The two Navy guys had no sort of tactical sense whatsoever. They weren't to blame; it wasn't their job – and passing the course didn't matter for them, it was just a three-week embuggerance before they went back to the wardroom for a few pink gins. So they were wanging over fences as well, and all of them, even the PT instructor, were knackered.

'Don't forget,' I said, 'the drill is that as soon as we get bumped we split up to make it harder for all of us to get captured. Then we regroup at the last emergency RV.'

We were waiting at one particular RV which was a rise of ground overlooking a small roadbridge over a river in the middle of nowhere. It was cold just sitting still in the shadows. We were sitting within a metre of each other in cover in a dip, and had agreed that two of us would stay awake and the other two would get some sleep. It was just a matter of getting the collar up and retreating inside the greatcoat and dozing off.

I heard helicopters running around but that was no problem, as long as we stayed still.

I was in a semi-daze when I heard a voice bark: 'Stand still! Don't move!'

The two on stag had fallen asleep.

As I looked up I saw a semicircle of Guardsmen closing in on us with pick handles. I thought, fuck! I was really annoyed. I put my hands in the air, yawned with exhaustion, got slowly to my feet and bolted.

I ran and ran, but only as far as the cut-offs they'd put in. I was brought to the ground by a rugby tackle and four of them piled on top. I struggled, but one of them rammed a pick handle down on my neck and shouted, 'Stay still! Stay still!' That was me caught. They turned me over and kept their feet on my neck while they tied me up with plasticuffs. They prodded me and said, 'What's your name? What's your name?'

I gave my name and number.

'What rank are you?'

I told them, and gave my date of birth for good measure. They dragged me away to their helicopter.

'Fucking good news!' one of them shouted. 'We've got one of the fuckers – we've got our leave!'

No sooner had the Puma taken off than it seemed to be landing again, in what I took to be their holding area.

They stripped me of my clothing so I was there in just my skiddies, and put on blindfolds. I was made to stand a pace or two from a wall, then lean forwards so my hands touched the bricks and I was standing at forty-five degrees. It wasn't too difficult, but my shoulders ached badly.

Then I had to kneel down on the ground, keeping my back straight and my hands on my head. That was a bit worse. The one I liked least was sitting on my arse, cross-legged, with my back straight and my hands behind my neck.

At some stage, when I was back on my knees, my blindfold was removed and I found myself looking up at the training sergeant-major.

'Am I binned?' I said pitifully, remembering how I'd cocked up in the jungle with him.

'No, you nugget. Get back on the helicopter and don't fuck up.'

I'd caught him in a good mood. An ex-Household Division man himself, he was delighted to see the Guards doing so well.

I was put back out in another group, consisting of three Navy aircrew. Again, not one iota of tactical awareness. I was desperate: I couldn't afford to get caught again.

We were going along the side of a forestry block one night when we heard shouting just forward and left of us. We bomb-burst away from the area; in theory we should have made our separate ways back to an ERV (*emergency rendezvous*) but I thought sod that, and cracked on alone.

During the daytime it was quite good. I was hiding up, and sometimes I could hear the ARF in their helicopters. Sometimes I'd hear dogs; it was quite exciting stuff. These boys were really close but I was getting away with it. I now knew that if they caught me they weren't going to muck about, because they didn't know my reactions. They would hit me hard, tie me up, and take me in.

I saw the sun occasionally but most of the time I was freezing. No matter how well insulated I was, after days and days in the field my body was cold and damp.

I tried to sleep, but it was scattered sleep. I might doze for twenty minutes, wake up, nod off for another ten minutes, acutely aware of any noises.

It came to the last scheduled night of the exercise and I knew that at some point very soon one of the DS would compromise me so that I was captured and put through the interrogation phase. I knew it would be quite a lengthy time, no scoff, and it would be a pain in the arse – especially if I was going in hungry. I decided to do something about that.

I did a recce on a farmhouse, which seemed to be occupied by an old couple and a daughter in her early twenties. Seemed all right. I banged on the door.

'Hello, you haven't got any bread, have you?'

They knew at once who I was.

'You want something to eat? Come in.'

Decision. Do I go in? Are they going to get on the phone?

I went in. It was a beautiful old place, oak beams and a log fire, and a wonderful smell of something or other bubbling away on the Aga. I sat down and the woman brought me a saucepan of mincemeat stew. As she sat there smiling, I helped myself to three or four bowlsful, washed down with gallons of hot, sweet tea. For pudding, I was presented with a plate of Christmas cake with inch-thick marzipan. I ate my fill, and stuffed a couple of extra doorsteps in my pocket. I'd have given anything for a few minutes by the log fire and maybe a hot bath, but it was time to go. I'd pushed my luck far enough as it was. I thanked my hosts profusely, offering to do the same for them one day if I could, and was off.

Later that night, approaching a checkpoint, I was still full. I tried to eat more of the cake but felt sick. Very reluctantly, I had to throw it all away in case I was caught.

I met up with the DS, who said, 'Wait over there. We've got a cattle truck that's going to pick you up and take you to the next RV.'

Oh yes, I thought, and I suppose Hereford will win the next FA Cup. Knowing what was coming, I climbed into the cattle truck and joined the others who had got their heads down on the straw. Nobody spoke; we knew what was going on. I knew where I was going, and there was nothing I could do about it. As far as I was concerned that was the first phase of the test over with; let's now get on with the second.

A couple of hours later we landed up in Hereford, in a part of the camp that I hadn't seen before.

As soon as we arrived they banged into us. The tailgate came down and they shouted really aggressively, 'Everybody now, turn round, lie down, put your hands on your heads!'

I could hear people getting picked up and dragged away. Eventually somebody put his hand on my head, pushed it down, tied my hands up and put a blindfold on. Two

people picked me up and started to drag me out. They were people who did this for a living; straight in, no words, nothing. I felt myself go down the ramp, walk over some tarmac, and go into a building.

The handcuffs were taken off, I was stripped of my clothing and left sitting on gravel in what had the feeling of being a very big squash court. I could hear what I thought at first was an attempt at white noise, then I worked out it was air being pumped into the place. There couldn't have been any windows.

I started to shiver. Two blokes came in with a set of coveralls, which they helped me get into. Then it was back on the floor, cross-legged and straight-backed, my hands behind my head. I concentrated on making my neck relax, and left it at that.

I could hear other people in the room getting moved around. From time to time they moaned and groaned; perhaps they were being put into different stress positions, or lifted for interrogations. Nobody was talking.

After about half an hour the footsteps came up to me. Two boys grabbed hold of me, picked me up, and then walked me. I thought I was going for an interrogation, but they got me to a place where they threw one of my hands against the wall, then the other, and then started to kick my feet back so I was at an angle, resting against the wall. Very soon, I started to get pins and needles in my hands and then they went numb. I tried gently banging them against the wall; the guards came over, got hold of my hands and threw them against the wall again, and kicked my legs out even more.

The hands really started to hurt. I had to push against them to keep the tension in my body so I didn't collapse. Fuck this, I thought. I was in pain, I was cold, soon I would be hungry. The only consolation was the thought that this was the last major step. If I passed this, I was in; if I got binned, it would be my own fault. It was just a matter of sticking in there. At the end of the day it was an

exercise, they weren't going to kill me, it was just a big test.

They grabbed me, took me somewhere else, and made me sit cross-legged with my hands behind my head and my back straight. Every time I bent my back to release the stress, they'd be in, grab hold of me, move me, and put me down again.

There was no noise; nobody said a word. All I heard was the two sets of footsteps walking along, picking me up. Sometimes they'd put me back against the wall in another stress position. After a few hours I told myself that I needed to switch on here. Just keep your head, I said to myself, and you'll be all right. I told myself that it was more about giving us an experience than anything else. They would hardly be putting us through it just for the sake of fucking us about and giving us a good beasting. It was probably as much an experience for the people who were doing the interrogating as it was for us. They needed training also. They needed to get the experience of reacting to people who had been under pressure for seven days on the run, not somebody who was just coming in from the canteen and play-acting the part.

As the hours ticked by in my head there were some people who by the sounds of things believed it was for real. I heard two or three get into such a state that they started blattering off and wanted no more of it.

'I've had enough,' somebody shouted, and it echoed around the room. I recognized the voice. It belonged to a Signals captain in his forties who'd come up through the ranks and had been giving little bits of advice to all the lads on the course. He'd had his toothbrush with him all the time: 'You don't need toothpaste,' he said. 'I always keep my teeth clean. Look at these teeth. Twenty-four years in the army, out in the field all the time – good teeth. And that's because I keep my toothbrush with me.'

'I don't want this no more! I don't want this no more!' He screamed and hollered and I heard several sets of footsteps going up and dragging him away. He was spaced out, he

was gone. It made me feel really good. Number one because he was gobby all the time, giving us the benefit of all his advice, and Number two, because somebody had been taken off. It made me feel better that I was still hanging on in there.

Maybe he didn't have the same incentive as the Selection blokes. Yet, very occasionally, I had been told, Selection blokes did fail at this late stage as well.

This was extremely demanding, physically and mentally. So it should be: what they were doing was training prone-to-capture troops for a real possibility. They couldn't go round beating us up, of course, or breaking our arms and giving us electric shocks, but they could take us to such a point that we didn't know whether we were going to be able to survive or not.

I was placed back in the stress position against the wall, and this time not even the first half hour was bearable. I had to keep the position; as soon as I went down they came in and forced me up. I tried to grin and bear it.

I heard some footsteps go past me to move some other people around. Then the footsteps came back and this time they stopped, grabbed hold of me, and I could smell the coffee on their breath. I thought I was going to be moved to another stress area, but I was off, walking carefully in my bare feet, mincing around when we hit shingle. We went into a building and along corridors. We went into a room, I was put down on a chair, and I heard a voice saying: 'Close your eyes.'

The blindfold came off and I looked down at the ground. The people walked out and the door was closed.

'Open your eyes.'

I looked up, opened my eyes, and there were two boys sitting there at a desk. It was a small room, white walls, an empty desk, them and me.

Both men were in their mid-forties. One of them was wearing a black polo-neck jumper. He had grey hair and was very stern looking. They both just looked at me, with obvious disdain.

154

'What's your name?'

'McNab.'

'What's your full name?'

'Andrew McNab.'

'What's your number?'

'24408888.'

'Rank?'

'Sergeant.'

'What's your regiment?'

'I can't answer that question.'

'What's your regiment?'

'I can't answer that question.'

'What do you fucking mean, you can't answer that question?' he exploded. 'We just caught you. We know what your fucking regiment is. But we want you to tell us. You're not helping us at all, are you? What's your number?'

I went through it again.

'What's your rank?'

'Sergeant.'

'What were you doing when you were captured?'

'I can't answer that question.'

'Well if you don't fucking answer that question you'll be in the shit. Do you understand me?'

'I can't answer that question.'

'What – were – you – doing – down – in – that – area?'

'I can't answer that question.'

'Are you in the army?'

'I can't answer that question.'

'Well you must be in the army because you've got a regimental number. What's your regimental number?'

'24408888.'

'So you're in the fucking army then, aren't you?'

'I can't answer that question.'

'Look here, sonny – if you don't fucking answer the questions you're in a lot of trouble. Do you understand that?'

'I can't answer that question.'

'OK, this is the score. This is what you're going to do. You're going to sign that bit of paper for the Red Cross and tell them that you're OK. Then, you might be getting some food. Do you understand?'

'I can't answer that question.'

They leapt up, hollering and shouting. 'Stand up! Stand to attention! Who the fuck do you think you are?'

They walked around me, saying, 'Are you thick or something? Are you fucking thick? I'm asking you questions and you're not answering. Do you understand?'

'I can't answer that question.'

I knew that as long as I stuck to the Big Four – name, number, rank and date of birth – and 'I can't answer that question' I'd cracked it.

The one in the black polo-neck turned to his mate. 'Do you think he's thick? Yeah, he's got to be fucking thick, look at him. Why doesn't he talk to us? He's thick. Do you have a mother?'

'I can't answer that question.'

'I bet you don't know your mother, do you?'

'I can't answer that question.'

'I bet your mother's a fucking stinking whore, isn't she? That's why you don't know your mother, isn't it?'

'I can't answer that question.'

I didn't mind any of it. In fact, compared to the stress positions, I actually rather liked it. The room was warm and I could sit down. I wasn't in a stress position and the blindfold was off. I just kept saying to myself: don't deviate from number, name, rank, date of birth and you're home and dry.

They went through the good guy, bad guy routine and I got the pieces of paper that they wanted me to sign.

'I'm sorry,' I said, 'I cannot do that.'

'What's your number?'

'24408888.'

The session must have lasted about an hour.

Finally they said, 'Right, sit down there, and close your eyes.'

I was blindfolded again and just sat there. I heard scribbling, but no talking. Then the door opened, and I was picked up and dragged out again. As I went down the corridor I could hear, on the left-hand side, another interrogation going on.

'What the fucking hell do you mean?' somebody was shouting.

Then I felt the air being pumped in and felt the gravel, and knew I was back in the holding area. Straight back up against the wall, hands up high, and the legs kicked back.

I could hear lots of movement. Like me, everybody was obviously starting to feel the effects of the stress positions. The boys were walking around more, moving people more because they weren't holding the positions.

I heard people falling and hitting the floor.

The cycle of interrogations and stress positions went on over a period of about twenty-four hours. The interrogators were brilliant actors. They'd start with a nice friendly approach, then suddenly throw the switch and hurl a frenzy of abuse.

I was sitting in a stress position, my legs crossed, back straight and hands behind my head, trying to find a comfortable position without moving too obviously. I had pins and needles in my head, my back and neck were strained, every time my elbows came forward to rest someone would yank them right the way back.

I was picked up and taken for another interrogation. I tried to lift my legs up to keep them from dragging on the gravel. I heard the boys straining to carry my weight and felt quite pleased to be getting my own back.

One boy held my head, grabbed hold of my hair to point me forward. They undid the blindfold and straightaway I closed my eyes.

A young cockney voice said, 'Look forward, mate, that's all right.'

He was all ginger hair and freckles, the first younger man

157

that I'd seen. 'Sorry to mess you about, mate,' he said. 'Let's just go all over it again, if you don't mind. We're getting all cocked up here. Let's just get your details right. What's your number again?'

I said.

'Name?'

I said.

'All right, that's fine. Now, is that an Mc or an Mac?'

That put me in a bit of a dilemma. What do I say?

'I can't answer that question.'

'Ah, come on, mate. I'm trying to do my job here. We've got to sort all this out. Is it a small N or a big N?'

'I can't answer that question.'

'Oh, all right then. What's your date of birth?'

I gave it.

'OK, don't worry about the difference in the spelling then. We'll sort that out later. But what exactly were you doing? I'm totally confused – I've got all these notes and bits of paper all over the place from these people you've been talking to. What were you doing?'

I saw through it: the friend, the same age group.

I couldn't help noticing that he had half a cheese sandwich and a cup of coffee in front of him.

'Can we just sort this out?' he said. 'What's your number again?'

I remembered a Green Jackets officer who took over A Company, who had been the ops officer for the Regiment. When he rejoined the battalion he started doing little interrogation exercises, and something he had once said stuck in my memory: 'If you get the chance of food, take it. Once it's inside you, what can they do?'

I looked at the cheese sandwich. They could hardly punish me by putting me in a worse stress position than they had already. They might drag me out and be a bit rough with me, but so what? At least I'd have a cheese sandwich and a mug of coffee down my neck.

I couldn't see any steam coming off the coffee, so I

knew it was fairly warm and I'd be able to gulp it down. Anyway, it was in a metal mug, and they tend to cool it down quicker. So I thought: fucking right.

I lunged forward and grabbed the food and drink. The boy recoiled. Guards came bursting in but they were too late to stop my feast. They blindfolded me and held me down.

The young guy, still being my mate, said, 'Did you enjoy that?'

'I cannot answer that question.'

I went into the next interrogation. It was the same routine, being picked up from the stress position, and by now I was really looking forward to interrogations because it was so painful against the wall or on the floor. It was the same two interrogators I had the very first time.

'You're a dickhead,' they said. 'We gave you the chance to help us, now you're going to pay for it. Get your clothes off.'

I undressed.

'What's your number?'

'24408888.'

'Right, now say it slowly.'

I did, and I had to do it again. Because of the training I knew to play on the injuries, looking like I was knackered, all that sort of stuff. I repeated my number for what seemed like hours, really slowly. Great, I thought; it took up more time, I was in a better atmosphere, rather than being in a stress position in the holding area, and I wasn't being moved around every five minutes by the guards.

Then I was told to jump up and down on my toes, which was even better, because I started to get warm.

They said, 'We've had enough of you, you fucking idiot.'

They walked out and two women walked in. One was in her late twenties and looked very prim and proper in glasses. The other, who was in her forties, was wearing jeans.

'Take off your pants,' they said.

I took them off.

159

'That's a bit small, isn't it?' the older woman laughed. 'What are you going to do with that? Is that why you're a big, rough tough soldier, to cover up your inadequacies? My little finger's bigger than that. Not going to impress many girls with that, are you?'

She turned to the younger one and said, 'Would you do anything with that?'

'With what? I can't even see anything.'

They were trying to find a chink in my personal armour, but as far as I was concerned everything they were saying was fair comment. After all, it was freezing cold in the room: in the circumstances, even Errol Flynn wouldn't have been looking his best.

I guessed everybody was learning about their own personalities, their own strengths, their own weaknesses. I was certainly learning about mine. I had no trouble with the insults and abuse, but some people were starting to trip. When I was in the stress positions, I heard people shouting, 'Fuck this! I've had enough of this shit!' Realistically, we were having a rather nice capture, but physically doing it still wasn't nice at all. I clung to the fact that this was an exercise and it would end.

I was taken for yet another interrogation. I was sat in a chair, and the blindfold came off. There in front of me was a cup of soup, and the training-wing sergeant-major.

He said, 'Do you recognize me?'

I didn't say anything.

'Do you recognize me?'

I said jack shit. I wasn't too sure if this was a ploy.

'Right, I'm telling you that now's the end of the exercise. Do you recognize me? If you say yes, that's fine, if you say no, we can just stay here until you do.'

He was wearing a white arm band; I remembered that we'd been briefed that that would signify the end.

'Yes, I recognize you.'

'Drink the soup.'

* * *

We had a debrief with the interrogators.

When it came to my turn, they said that I'd stuck to the Big Four, which was good. It had been a bad move, however, to make a grab for the coffee and the cheese sandwich.

'If it hadn't been an exercise I wouldn't have done it,' I said. 'I know that in real life there would have been repercussions. But this was an exercise and I was hungry, so why not?'

'How were you feeling physically? Were you as exhausted as you gave the impression of being?'

'No, I was playing on the physical side.'

'How many interrogations did you have?'

'Six.'

Wrong. This was interesting. I was one interrogation out. And I had been held for thirty hours, not the forty that I'd thought.

'What about the interrogators? Was it obvious what they were trying to do? Were there any stages when you were worried about it?'

I gave it to them straight. Some of these people had been right fuckers. They'd done their job very well.

They were aggressive, there was aggressive handling, but we'd had to expect that. We were cold, but so what? It was very demanding, physically and mentally, but at least we knew there was an ending. I'd have hated for it to have been real, or to have gone on for very much longer.

The last big hurdle was over. We looked a state. We'd been out in the field for a week, and we had a week's growth. Everybody's hair was sticking up, and tangled with twigs and straw. We had those really big, wide, bloodshot eyes; we were stinking. Nobody in the camp gave us as much as a second look.

I had a shower and headed for the cookhouse and a great big plate of steak and chips. A couple of blokes were already back, and the others trickled in over the next twenty-four hours. All the stories were coming out, including one or two with unhappy endings. One bloke

had been in a stress position when he felt his blindfold slipping down. He knew that he stood a chance of getting fucked off, purely because they would think he was actively pulling the blindfold down himself, so he put his hand up. Nothing happened. He stood up and sort of semi-turned, and by now the mask was down. They binned him on the spot. The argument was that he'd pulled his mask and broken the rules. They fucked up and it was unfair. But then, no-one said it would be easy.

In the pub the following night, the Selection blokes compared notes. Everybody had been of the same opinion about the others in their team and had wanted to spread out and get away.

Dave, one of the Paras, said, 'I got to a farmhouse, put an OP [*observation post*] on it, had a look around. Everything seemed OK, so I went up under the window and I thought I'd just listen. The TV was on and it sounded all rather nice, then I could hear loads of people talking. I got up and had a look through the curtains and it was the whole training team sitting there. I said to myself, I think we'll give this one a miss.'

There was a long weekend off; on Monday morning we would carry on with our Continuation training. By now the training team had more or less got what they needed. We were starting to get a relationship, we were starting to talk about squadrons and things in general. They opened up a bit more, but we still had to call everybody 'Staff' apart from the Squadron SM, whom we called 'Sir'. We weren't in yet.

There was a pub that used to put trays of sausages and French bread out on the bar on Sundays, so George and I went and had a few pints of Guinness and filled our faces out. We were walking down the road afterwards, bored out of our heads, and decided to go round to see an ex-Green Jacket who was in D Squadron. His wife used to work for Bulmer's, distributors of Red Stripe lager, and the four of

us sat there all afternoon, chatting away, slowly getting pissed.

After a few hours I announced that I was going to the toilet. I got to the top of the stairs and felt an ominous urge in the pit of my stomach. I ran into the toilet, and projectile vomited all over the floor and walls.

Panic. I cleaned up as best I could, then fell down the stairs and into the front room.

'Well,' I beamed, 'must be going.'

In the morning I was in shit state. I went round to D Squadron lines to see what had happened.

'Bloody hell!' he said. 'She's gone ballistic!'

I thought I was severely in the shit. I ran off and bought her a bunch of flowers and a box of chocolates. I went around to the house, hoping against hope that she wouldn't be in. I knocked on the door. There was nobody at home.

I propped the gifts on the doorstep and pulled out a card from my pocket.

'So sorry about my terrible behaviour and all the inconvenience I must have caused you,' I wrote. 'I hope that one day you will forgive me, and certainly promise that it will never happen again.' Then I signed it, 'With all best wishes, George.'

13

I telephoned Debbie and said, 'I'm in! I reckon I've passed!'

She was really pleased, I was really pleased. But the sad thing was that I was so engrossed in what I'd been doing that I didn't stop to think about what she'd been going through. She'd been stuck in Germany, unsure of whether I was going to pass or what the future might hold; she hadn't seen me for months, and all I'm doing is phoning her up and telling her how great I am. I was so selfish; she was getting two letters a month from me and maybe a phone call a week, and it was never to say: 'How are you?' Maybe I didn't ask because I didn't want to hear the answer.

The idea of continuation training was to give us an introduction to the skills that would be needed once we got into our squadrons.

Our first introduction was to be to the CT (*counter-terrorist*) team. We sat in the classroom on the first day, dressed in civvies. It was the first time I'd ever done a soldier's work in civilian clothes, and it felt a bit strange. The training team weren't going to be teaching us for this phase, we'd been told; it would be members of CRW, the counter-revolutionary warfare wing.

In came a bloke called Ted I knew from the Green Jackets. We'd always known him as Ted Belly because of the losing battle he fought in the inch war; now he was on the CRW.

Ted was a tall, approachable cockney with hair like straw. No matter what he did with it, his head looked like a bird's nest in a gale.

'Today we're going to learn all about the nine millimetre,' he said. 'Anything you don't know, just ask and Uncle Ted'll tell you. We'll have a day down here, and the rest of the week we'll be on the ranges. Maybe we'll have a few wagers – all right?'

The 9mm Browning pistol was extremely important to the Regiment and underestimated by many outside, Ted said. It was an extremely effective and powerful weapon, easy to conceal, yet hitting at a surprisingly long range. The Regiment used them for VIP protection, counter-terrorist and covert operations. On the counter-terrorist team, everybody's secondary weapon was the pistol.

We had to learn every bit of theory there was to know about the Browning – as well as the stripping and assembling, all the technical details on what happened if a pin was filed this way, what happened if the trigger mechanism was slightly adjusted.

We learned how to hold the weapon correctly, and how to stand correctly. The method the Regiment used was totally different from the army's. It was based on combat experience, which the army hadn't got much of with pistols – I had fired one twice in my career. Ted taught us how to draw the pistol from various types of holster, how to draw it covertly when we had our jackets on, and even what sort of jacket to wear and how to wear it.

From different firing positions, we practised until we could hit the target with both eyes open from 35 metres – then 50 metres, while pushing people out of the way in a crowd. We practised from seven-thirty each morning until dark o'clock. We'd get a tea urn in the morning, pick up loads of scoff, and scream down to the range, eight of us having a really good time with the pistol.

I thought that as a sergeant in the infantry I'd know lots, but found it was a vastly different world here. I guessed I

was near the bottom of what would turn out to be a very steep learning curve.

'When you get back to the block,' the instructor said, 'practise your drawings in front of the mirror. Don't worry, nobody will laugh – we all do it.'

We were there for an hour after dinner, practising in front of the mirrors in the toilets. Finally Ted came by with loads of boys and said, 'What the hell are you doing, you dickheads?'

We looked sheepishly at the imaginary pistols in our hands while they took the piss mercilessly.

On the final day Ted said, 'Right, let's have a bit of fun then.'

He got all the targets in and marked one of them with a circle the size of a 10p, another with one the size of a Coke can, then a larger one still. We had to fire at different timings: firing three rounds into the 10p piece in five seconds at 5 metres, then back to 10 metres, going back and back. We all put a fiver in at a time and the winner took all.

Next we did some demolitions training with basic charges, saw some more of the squadron kit, and did a bit of signals work with the squadron radios.

'Wherever you are operating in the world, you will send directly back to Hereford,' the instructor said. 'You'll have to learn a lot of antenna theory; it's not like in the films where they've got a radio the size of a cigarette pack with a little antenna and they start sending signals off to Katmandu. It doesn't work like that at all. Depending on the frequencies and the time of day, you'll have to calculate the size of the antenna.'

We had introductions to all the different departments, from the education centre to the Regimental Association; the only ones we didn't see were the 'grey' ones tucked away that we were told we would only find out about later.

After three weeks, it was time to go to Brize Norton to be para-trained. It was one of those things that had to be done but that I couldn't really be arsed about; I was itching to go

straight to the squadron. The one consolation was the thought that the only way I was not going to get in now was if I broke my neck – or blotted my copybook.

I found out what squadron I was going to go to. If I'd wanted a particular squadron, and there'd been a reason, maybe I'd have got in. If you wanted G Squadron and you were a Guardsman, for example, you would definitely get it. Otherwise, it all depended on the manpower requirements. I wanted to go to D Squadron because Jeff was in it and they were the current counter-terrorist team, based in Hereford. Things with Debbie were not exactly brilliant. I was paying a bit more attention now to what she said in her letters from Germany, so I knew she was severely pissed off. In reply, I kept telling her that as soon as I'd passed I would organize a quarter. However, D Squadron wasn't to be; four of us were off to B Squadron, though we wouldn't be allowed anywhere near them yet.

Blokes who were already para-trained were badged now and went to their squadrons. The rest of us went to Brize Norton, into the RAF's hands and out of the Regiment's system. It was like a holiday – but one of those holidays that went on too long.

For a month we were taught a lot of drills which we later found out were crap – but they had to teach hundreds of people a year, so everybody was pushed in together and round went the handle. Brize Norton was a sausage factory.

The upside was that the RAF always tended to have superior recreational facilities. Here, the NAAFI disco was called the Starlight Club. Every night the baby Paras on our course turned up, all crew cuts and Brutus jeans, desert boots and maroon sweatshirts, as hard as nails. Two of them were pissed and dancing together one night. The next morning, they were all out on parade, helmets on and ready to go. Their corporals came out and said, 'Oi, Smith and Brown, come here. Smith, were you dancing last night?'

'Yes, Corporal.'

'Who with?'

'Him, Corporal.'

'And Brown, you was dancing last night. Who with?'

'Him, Corporal.'

The full screw went inside and came back out with an ironing board under his arm. With the two baby Paras standing at attention, he banged them rhythmically on the head: 'We–don't–dance–together–in–the–Airborne.'

'Yes, Corporal.'

And off they went. All the other recruits were rolling up. It was a fun thing; they obviously had the same relationship with their recruits as my team had had at Winchester.

We got our parachute wings and went back to Hereford to be badged.

We turned up with our normal regimental kit on and hung around in the 'Kremlin' (*head shed building*). I had a fantastic feeling of achievement. Everybody seemed pleased for us; probably there wasn't a single person in the Regiment who couldn't remember how they felt when they got badged.

The RSM came out, shook our hands, and said, 'Well done, congratulations. What you're going to do in a minute is go in and see the colonel. He's going to badge you, and then you start moving off to your squadrons. I'll give you one piece of advice. When you get to your squadron, look at somebody you think is "the" Regimental soldier, and copy him. Take example from him, learn from him. Don't start going off thinking that you rule the world, because you don't. Just keep your gob shut, look and listen.'

The CO had a pile of sand-coloured berets on the table in front of him and flipped one at each of us. No formalities, no handshakes. Then he said, 'Just remember, it's harder to keep than it was to get. Right, good luck to you.'

The army doled out a horrible beret called a Kangoule. Within the army there was a definite fashion about such things; you could always tell a person by his headgear.

We'd all sent away for the much smarter Victor beret.

And that was it. George and I trooped off to B Squadron office, almost six months to the day since we'd done the Fan Dance. The first fellow we met was Danny the clerk – skinny, no face hair, and looking sixteen. He was in fact in his early twenties, and was, we were told, the person who really knew what was going on. The squadrons were all over the place, doing ten things at once, little gangs here, little gangs there, and the only one who had any continuity was the clerk, always there with the HQ element of the squadron. If we needed anything or wanted to know what was going on, Danny the clerk was the man.

'Nice to meet you,' he said. 'Everybody's away at the moment, but there's one or two people bumming around. Just go and sit in the Interest Room and we'll sort you all out.'

George and I spent a lot of time that day just hanging around. We couldn't contribute anything, the whole squadron was away, and everybody was busy. We were feeling rather helpless, sticking out like sore thumbs in our uniforms. The few blokes who were around were in track-suits or jeans.

The walls of the 'interest room' were covered with plaques, photographs, AK47s from Borneo days to the present – all sorts of bits and pieces that people had brought back from all over the world. It was a history of the squadron written in bric-a-brac.

Blokes came in and said, 'You just joined the squadron? My name's Chas. Nice to see you. You coming on the trip?'

They seemed genuinely pleased for us that we'd passed. There was no feeling of us being the nigs, as we would have got in the battalions. They knew what we'd done to get this far.

'I don't know,' I said. 'Are we going on a trip?'

Danny said he didn't have a clue yet. I was hoping in a way that we weren't. I'd now got everything I'd wanted, but I very much needed to get things sorted out with

Debbie. Our conversations on the telephone were still a little strained. The relationship seemed fine on the surface, but underneath I wasn't sure what her feelings were. She seemed to understand how important it had been to me to get into the Regiment, but I knew she was fed up with taking second place: when she arrived from Germany I wanted the quarter to be ready. In the meantime, I didn't know how she'd take the news that I was going away with my squadron for a couple of months.

We bummed around to the stores, handed in all the equipment from training wing, and drew out our squadron equipment. Unfortunately, everything we drew out was brand new. We looked as if we'd just stepped out of a catalogue.

'Turn up tomorrow,' Danny said, 'and we'll see what's going on.'

This was at ten o'clock in the morning.

'What do we do in the meantime?' I asked.

'Nothing. Go down town if you like.'

This was so different from the battalion, where we'd have had to stay, even if there was nothing to do.

When we did go back the next morning we were told: 'Malaya, Thursday.'

We packed all the brand new kit and drew out shiny new jungle boots. There wouldn't be time to break them in. On Thursday we boarded the aircraft. I still hadn't organized the quarter for Debbie; I only hoped that things would be sorted while I was away.

Some of the blokes had already been in the jungle for quite a while by the time we turned up at the base camp, two hours' drive from Kuala Lumpur. We drew some more kit and the next morning we were choppered in to join them: four new blokes, every bit of kit shiny and squeaking. I felt like a nun in a whorehouse, knowing none of the jargon and none of the people using it. Nobody wore rank, everybody was on first name terms; it was impossible to make

out who was who. Best, I reckoned, to follow the RSM's advice. I shut up and listened.

The squadron set-up in the jungle was very much as it had been on Selection. There was the squadron HQ element, then the troops positioned satelliting it. People had set up home in the admin areas; A-frames were dotted around, many of them sprouting extensions. Figure 11 targets had been made into sit-up angle boards as a makeshift gym. Tables and chairs had been made out of crates. Here and there, two or three ponchos had gone up to join A-frames and make what looked like mini-communes.

Everybody in sight had beards and long, greasy hair. Some blokes were lying in their A-frames reading books, others were bumming around in shorts or squatting over hexy burners, brewing up. But whatever he was doing, every bloke had his beltkit on, as well as his golock and weapon.

The medic came up to us and said, 'Most people are out at the moment. When they come back everything will be sorted. Do you want a brew?'

While we were drinking tea the squadron OC came over with all his entourage.

'Good to see you! Right, we need a bloke for each troop.' He looked at each of us in turn, then said, 'You look like a diver . . .'

George was a mountain climber, so he said, 'I'd like Mountain Troop.'

'OK, you can go to Mountain Troop. You, go to Mobility, and you look like a freefaller.'

The last bloke he was pointing at was me, and that was me in Air Troop. 'Wait here,' he added, 'and somebody will be along to pick you up.'

Blokes from different troops came down to pick up their new boys. The OC and his party disappeared. I was sitting there on my own, taking in a bit of the set-up, watching the signallers and medics at work at makeshift tables under

ponchos. People were coming up and saying, 'All right? How you going? What troop you going to?'

'Air Troop.'

'Bloody hell, you'll have fun – the fucking ice-cream boys! Got your sunglasses with you, I hope?'

I didn't have time to ask what they meant. A fellow who was 6' plus and 4' wide appeared, walking on the balls of his feet. His hands were so big his M16 looked like a toy.

'Your name Andy? I'm Tiny, Seven Troop. We'll sort out some bits and pieces and then we'll go back up to the troop area.'

I was smelling all nice, got my new boots on, and feeling like it was my first day at big school. Off we went, my eyes scanning the ground for a patch of mud to dunk my boots in.

As we walked up the hill he said, 'What battalion are you from then?'

'Two.'

'Great! I'm Two Para myself.'

'No, Two RGJ. I was a Green Jacket.'

Tiny stopped in his tracks, turned, and said, 'Well what the fuck are you doing here?'

'I don't know – they just told me to come.'

'Fucking hell, we haven't had anybody here for eighteen months, and now they're sending you.'

I'd never felt such a dickhead in my life.

We went into the troop area, which was on a small spur occupied by A-frames. In the middle was a large fire. All eight members of 7 Troop were sitting around, having a kefuddle and brewing up.

As we walked in, Tiny said, 'We've got this fellow here turned up, his name's Andy McNab and he's a Green Jacket. What the fuck's he doing here?'

He started having a go at a guy called Colin, who I assumed was the senior bloke present.

Colin was about 5'6", very quietly spoken but extremely blunt in his replies to Tiny. He sounded as if he was from Yorkshire.

'I'm a Para, too,' he said as he shook my hand.

Christ, was anybody in 7 Troop not from Para Reg?

They introduced themselves.

'Nosh.'

'Frank.'

'Eddie.'

'Mat.'

'Steve.'

'Al.'

'Get yourself over there,' Colin said, 'and bung a pole bed up.'

I went to the edge of the clearing, dropped my bergen, and got out my golock.

I'd only ever made one A-frame, and now everybody who was sitting around brewing up was able to watch me make a bollocks of the second. Brunei seemed a long time ago as I thrashed at the trees and tried to chop branches to required lengths. Every time I pulled up one bit the next would fall down. God knows what they must have been thinking. I wanted to make a good impression, and was flailing away like a man possessed, but my pole bed was all over the place. And they were sitting there, chatting away and smoking, watching me and scratching their heads.

I finally sorted it all out, just as it started to come to last light. They didn't stand to. I thought, well what goes on now? I didn't want to intrude on their session so I did a few exaggerated yawns and stretches and got my head down. They carried on the fuddle all night, probably thinking that I was a right antisocial prat.

In the morning I got a brew on and some food. Then I wandered over to Tiny and said, 'What happens now?'

'Just get ready and we'll go out, I suppose.'

'When do we go out?'

'Don't worry about it.'

Colin took me in his patrol. He seemed really switched on and I clung on to him. Colin was my role model.

We were going to do jungle lanes, very much as we'd

173

done on Selection. We patrolled along in a group of two, then in a group of four, practising contact drills.

The communist insurrection in Malaya had started in 1948, and 1,200 guerrillas, under the leadership of Chin Peng, still subsisted in the mountains along the Malay–Thai border. It had been one of the longest wars in Asia, but fairly inconsequential; however, hundreds of people had been killed during anti-Chinese riots in Kuala Lumpur in 1969.

The New Zealanders had a battalion stationed in Singapore. They operated in Malaya, but they couldn't commit the battalion to work in the north, for whatever political reason. We were there to demonstrate a presence.

As Colin and I were patrolling, we saw a target. I remembered my drills well; I got some rounds down, turned and ran back. Inexplicably, Colin gave it a full magazine, dropped in another one and kept going forward.

He turned and shouted, 'What the fuck are you doing?'

'We weren't taught to do it like that.'

'Oh for fuck's sake.'

Every squadron did it differently, I discovered, and so did every troop. For the rest of the day Colin had me running to and fro on the range until I was decimating targets with the best of them. When we finished that night, I felt quite good. I'd shown a shortcoming but I had done what was expected of me – I had learned. I felt a little bit accepted.

We were sitting round in a fuddle that night, and I sampled my first 'fruit cocktail', a unique B Squadron concoction made from rum and boiled sweets. I didn't have a clue what or who anybody was talking about. There were all these different terminologies and personalities and I had no idea. I had to ask for translations.

I gathered that Colin had been rebuilding his house. He was honking about the price of logs: 'Forty-five pounds a ton – it's a rip-off. If you go down Pontralis you can get

them for forty-three pounds.' I sat and listened, and over the next few days I pieced together what I could about all the characters.

Nosh was built like an athlete but apparently very rarely trained or ran, and was a thirty-a-day man. He was passionate about anything to do with the air and had logged in excess of 1,000 freefall jumps. He struck me as incredibly intelligent; he'd be sitting there, picking his nose, farting and burping, but chipping in with comments that sounded like paragraphs from *The Economist*.

Frank Collins had ginger hair, was about my height and weight and came from up North somewhere. He was fairly quietly spoken, and more forthright than blunt. It seemed that he was starting to get into born-again Christianity. Everybody was giving him a slagging about it. A copy of *Holy Blood, Holy Grail* was going the rounds, with people reading it avidly for ammunition to give Frank a hard time with. They had a copy of the Bible with them as well, as a cross-reference. It made an odd sight, all these rough, tough men in the middle of the jungle listening to people reading out passages from the Testaments and checking them against this book.

I'd seen Al Slater before. He was the training corporal giving recruits a hard time in the 1983 BBC series *The Paras*. He was about 6', lean, and he looked like an officer. I could still remember him shouting at the recruits: 'Getting noticed is absolutely the last thing you want to do.'

Al's special seat was a massive bag of rice. There had been a fresh day just before I arrived. Al had asked for a large bag of rice, thinking in terms of a two- or three-pound bag. To everybody's amazement, a fifty-pound bag had turned up. Al immediately adopted it as his chair. He used to sit on it, scoop out some rice now and then and throw it in a pot. Over the next few weeks we had rice pudding, fried rice, rice with onions, rice with dried meat, rice with fish, and Al's arse got lower and lower.

With the same drop, the mail had come through. Al was sitting on his bag of rice and put his book down to open his

letters. He looked inside one envelope and started rolling up. 'I think somebody's put a major hint in here,' he laughed, pulling out three sheets of paper, a self-addressed envelope with a stamp on, and a pencil.

Nosh was having a brew one day and said, 'We ought to have a seven Troop suntrap, somewhere we can wear our shades. We've got a reputation to keep up.'

I wondered what on earth he was on about.

A couple of days later we were mincing around in the base camp, cooking away and gobbing off, and Nosh decided that the time had come. He had a fag in his mouth and a golock in his hand, and was walking around a massive buttress tree right on the edge of our area. He didn't say anything, but we suddenly heard *ching, ching, ching.*

Colin walked over. 'What the fuck are you doing, Nosh?'

'Suntrap,' Nosh said, one hand down his trousers, scratching himself. 'If I do the cuts right it'll fall downhill towards the river.'

'You sure?'

'Trust me.'

If the tree fell the other way, it would come down right on top of our basha area. All day we heard *ching, ching, ching.* Finally, the noise became *ching, ching, creak.* The tree started to groan.

Nosh came over to Mat and said, 'I think you'd better move, mate. It might go your way as well. I'm not too sure, I think I might have fucked up here.'

People were running around with their weapons and beltkit, but nobody was too sure which way to run. In the end we stood and watched.

With an almighty scream and a screech the tree finally toppled, falling just inches from Mat's basha.

'There you go,' Nosh said. 'Very professional job.'

It was, too. A big beam of light suddenly appeared through the canopy and 7 Troop got its sunglasses out.

* * *

Food plays such an important part in anybody's life in the military – not so much for the calorific value and the fact that it keeps you warm as for the fact that it's one of the only areas where you're going to get variety and can spend time doing something entirely for yourself.

We talked a lot about what we were going to cook and how, and all the different mustards or spices we'd be using. It was a diversion from normal routine. Some people would go and catch fish to supplement the rations. Others would set a trap and see what they caught, then make a big stew out of it.

Al Slater was having a wash in the river one morning. We heard a couple of five-round bursts going down the river and rushed to see what was going on. It was Al with big Hissing Sid coming up to him, now deceased. We ate it that night. It tasted shit, but was fine after being marinaded in Tabasco.

Tiny and Eddie made a friend that they refused to eat. His name was Stan the Scorpion. He lived in a hole below Tiny's pole bed and seemed to like the Spam that was fed to him.

We were sitting on the floor in the middle of nowhere one day. It was pissing down with rain. I was drenched, rivulets of rainwater running through my matted hair and trickling from my chin. I put up a little shelter sheet to stop the embuggerance of everything dripping off my nose while I was trying to brew up.

As I stood up, trying to sort my beltkit out, I felt something drop down my leg. I didn't think much of it; there's always beasties making best friends with you in the jungle. Then I felt a warm and wet sensation around my bollocks and thought, right, I'll have a look and see what's going on. I pulled my trousers and pants down and found that the whole of my groin area was covered in blood. Fuck! It was capillary bleeding, exacerbated by the fact that the skin was so wet with all the rain and sweat.

I was flapping good style trying to see what was going on and pulled my trousers right off. Down by my boots was the world's fattest, happiest leech, as big as my thumb. It had got inside my clothing somehow, attached itself to my cock, and then drunk so much it fell off. When leeches bite they put in an anticoagulant and anaesthetic twistball, so you keep bleeding and you don't feel a thing. I had instant visions of other leeches crawling up my pride and joy, so one of the boys had to have a quick look inside to make sure everything was all right.

The leech was very proud of himself, very full up. I kept him to one side for ten minutes or so while I tried to decide what to do with him. Eventually I gave him a burst of mozzie rep, which really pissed him off. Then he died, poor soul.

It took ages for the bleeding to stop. Afterwards, I had a bite mark that looked like a cigarette burn, which would stay there for life. It was quite a shock, and the blokes were very solicitous. Then they spent the next week reminding me that the leech was considerably bigger than the morsel it had eaten for dinner.

We had an American with us called Dan Dan the Chainsaw Man. On secondment from Delta Force, the US equivalent of the Regiment, he was in his late thirties, and deeply macho. The problem with Dan was that he was running around too much, trying to impress everybody, when there was no need to. He'd brought a chainsaw with him and wanted to chop the whole forest down for everybody so they could build things.

Hammocks or A-frames were not for Dan. 'The jungle floor is good,' he drawled.

Within a week he was in shit state. He wouldn't use a poncho, he built a sort of tepee with leaves and branches. He would scream and shout 'Goddamn shit!' in the middle of the night as things bit him. He had lumps and bumps all over him, but there was no way he was going to submit.

178

One of squadron HQ came down and said, 'Look, here's a poncho.'

'Naw, don't need it.'

One of the blokes was down on his haunches making a brew one day. He looked up and could see into Dan's atap shelter. Dan had been using the poncho after all, but he'd covered it with leaves so he wouldn't lose face. Gotcha, Delta!

Dan lived in his own little world in more ways than one. One day Tiny, who was well into demolitions, was preparing a thing called an A-Type ambush. It was an explosive ambush, tripped by any patrol that walked into it. Dan had made a DIY claymore mine out of his little soapdish and he wanted Tiny to try it out. This A-Type ambush consisted of about 40lbs of PE (*plastic explosive*), plus about five or six 81mm mortar rounds, claymores, and home-made claymores. It was a massive accumulation of explosive, to which Dan insisted on adding his soapdish. The explosion took the top off the spur, flattening an area of about 20-metres square so it looked like a landing site.

Dan came up and said to Tiny, 'So, how did the soapdish do?'

Tiny said, 'Ever watched a mouse rape an elephant?'

We finished the trip and had six days off. A lot of blokes were going to go to Thailand and to see the Burma railway. The Kiwis were going to sponsor the rest of us in Singapore. Dan couldn't wait to get there.

When we reached the base area at Kluang, the SQMS (*squadron quartermaster sergeant*) had laid on tables of beers and food. But everybody knew they had to clean the weapons first. Well, everybody except Dan.

I had the GPMG at that stage. It was a section weapon, so everybody was responsible for cleaning it, not just the person who carried it. In my battalion days, a corporal had to dish out the weapons, because everyone selfishly just did his own. Tiny came over and started to help me, then

another bloke came over and took another bit, and somebody took another, which was all rather nice. It made me feel a bit more part of the group. We'd been together now for about two months, but I was still on probation. I could still be fucked off if these blokes didn't want me.

Meanwhile, Dan Dan the Chainsaw Man was nowhere to be seen. He was too busy throwing two-pint bottles of Heineken down his neck, and had gone on overload. Instead of sorting his kit out, he just went straight on the piss because he thought it was the manly thing to do. It was nice to have a party after work, get the barbecue going, have a few beers, but there were priorities. Everybody was looking forward to having a couple of beers, then going downtown and having a proper shave. Nobody, however, wanted to get stinking and out of his head; you just lose the day.

We got a wonderful picture of Dan to be put up in the squadron interest room when we got back to the UK. After an hour on the Heineken Dan was out on the floor. We heard later that about two weeks after he returned to the States, he shot his neighbour's son for jumping over his fence. Nothing about Dan would have surprised me.

We went down to the local town of Kluang. It was the first time I'd been to Malaya and I wanted a barber's shave and a look around. Three or four of us wandered around, bumping into some of the others from time to time. We went and had some fried chicken, visited a bar and listened to karaoke, hit another bar, had another bit of chicken and more beers. By the end of the night we were stinking, and soon only George and I were left. We were walking around the town at two o'clock in the morning, and we couldn't remember where the camp was.

'We'll get a taxi,' George said.

'What taxi?' I said.

We knew the camp was uphill, so we set off. After a few minutes George said, 'Let's nick a car.'

'We'll land up getting hung for this,' I said.

A few hundred yards further on we came across a large red tricycle with a trailer on the back.

'Perfect.'

We both jumped on it, George in the saddle, me in the trailer. We got to the steep uphill bit and George couldn't pedal, so we got off and pushed. When we got to the camp, it was such a large place we couldn't remember where we were supposed to be. The gate was closed.

'We'll leave the bike there and get over the fence,' I said.

Within minutes we were in our beds and fast asleep.

In the morning, we were lining up to get some money and the sergeant major was pacing up and down. 'Is George about anywhere?' he said.

'That's me,' George said.

'Did you have that bike away last night?'

'Er, I might have.'

'Well I think you ought to go and get it, cycle it back down to the town. That's probably someone's livelihood you've got there. Don't fuck these people about.'

George looked at me but I had developed sloping shoulders and a wide grin. The last I saw of him was a rear view as he wobbled off towards the town. When he eventually reappeared an hour or so later he was struggling with the world's biggest sheaf of long green vegetables on his shoulder.

'Mm, nice souvenirs,' I said.

'You owe me a fucking tenner,' George said. 'I was cycling down the hill when the owner spotted me going past his vegetable stall. The only way I could calm him down was to buy this lot.'

Off we went to Singapore, and the occasion was designated a bone-shirt night. We had to look like dick-heads, but not blatant anorak wearers: we had to do it in such a way that people thought, 'Hmm, strange!'

Everybody else had brought one with them; a few of us had to spend a day running around Singapore looking for a decent specimen.

I went into one shop, half-pissed, and said, 'I've come in for a bone shirt.'

'Ah, bone shirt! You know Tiny! Number one!'

I ended up with a rather sophisticated Hawaiian number, sunset orange with green palm trees and great big purple flowers.

It had been a really good trip for me. I was fortunate in joining the squadron when the majority of people were together. Sometimes, I heard, blokes could join a squadron and not see all the members for maybe a year or two because of all the different jobs.

True, I could hardly count myself as a mate, but at least I was aware of them and they were aware of me. I felt that in my own small way, I'd arrived – whether for good or bad, I didn't know. And the memories of Malaya wouldn't leave me for as long as I lived – or at least, not as long as I had a small, brown circular scar halfway down the leech's dinner.

14

We were on probation for our first year. After Selection, we lost our rank, but kept the same pay, since we hadn't qualified yet as Special Forces soldiers. I became a trooper, but was still receiving a sergeant's infantry pay, which was less than a trooper earned in the Special Air Service.

To qualify for SF pay I would have to get a patrol skill – either signals, demolitions, medical or a language. The first one everyone has to have is signals – if the shit hits the fan everybody's got to be able to shout 'Help!'

I would also need my entry skill. Mobility troop need to know how to drive a whole range of vehicles, divers need to be able to dive, mountain troop need to get themselves up and down hills, freefallers need to learn how to freefall into a location. No patrol skill, no extra pay, but it was a Catch 22: we were going away and doing the job, but we couldn't get paid unless we'd got the qualifications to do the job – but we couldn't get the qualifications because we were too busy doing it.

Soon after I came back from Malaya, we were going to start training for the counter-terrorist team. One troop from the squadron would go to Northern Ireland; the other three troops would then comprise the counter-terrorism team. Seven Troop had been designated for over the water.

There were no patrol skill courses running in my time slot, but there was one for my entry skill. It wouldn't qualify me for the pay on its own, but at least I would

understand what the other blokes in the troop were talking about when they mentioned riggers, risers, brake-lines, baselines or flare.

When people think about the 'SAS' their image is either of Land Rovers screaming around the desert, men in black kit abseiling down embassy walls, or freefallers with all the kit on, leaping into the night. Freefall, like the other entry skills, is in fact just a means of getting from A to B.

To count myself as proficient in the skill I would have to be able to jump as part of a patrol and keep together in the air at night on oxygen, with full equipment loads weighing in excess of 120lbs. I would have to be able to follow a 'bundle' (*container*) holding my own extra equipment or gear that we were delivering to other troops on the ground, and the patrol must have maintained its integrity. If the entry phase went wrong, there would be a snowball effect and big cock-ups.

For all that, it was obviously addictive. There were world-class freefall jumpers in the Regiment, people who had represented the UK in international competition.

The freefall course was about six weeks long, and by the end of it I would be able to jump confidently. It would provide a baseline; from there the troop would bring me on.

My particular course entailed two weeks in the UK, two weeks in Pau, a French military base in the Pyrenees, and then two more back in the UK. If the weather was bad, some courses would take place entirely in the United States, with RAF instructors. It's no good having an expensive aircraft sitting down doing nothing because the weather's shit; it's cheaper and better to go to somewhere with a guarantee of sunny skies, so the job can get done.

The way of life in Brize Norton was even easier than it had been on the basic parachuting course. The intake consisted of just me and four SBS (*Special Boat Service*) blokes, and we had an excellent relationship with the instructors. The majority of them were in the Falcons

display team; they knew that a lot of the stuff they were teaching us was outdated, but that was what the manual said. I found it strange to be learning for the sake of learning again; I thought I'd left 'bullshit baffles brains' behind me at the basic parachuting phase. It was only later that I found out that freefall manuals were obsolete almost before they were printed. Sport techniques were changing at a weekly rate; the Regiment monitored them constantly to see how it could adapt their equipment and methods to a military context.

We had about two days of ground training, learning how to put on the basic freefall kit. Our first jump would be with a PB6, round-canopy parachute. We would then go on to a TAP, which was much like the sports rig, a Para Commander. Even that was an antiquated bit of kit; all it could do was turn left, turn right, and go with the wind.

On day three I sat there in the C130 (*Hercules transport aircraft*) thinking, whatever happens, I don't want to look a dickhead. I was going to jump, there were no problems with that, but I just didn't want to cock it up. I was mentally going through my drills.

'Even professional jumpers who've been jumping for years and years do the same,' the instructors had told us. 'As they go up in the aircraft they're mentally and physically dry-drilling, simulating pulling their emergency cut-away, then deploying their reserve.' It didn't mean they were scared, it meant they were thinking about their future.

I closed my eyes and went through the exit drill – 'One thousand, two thousand, three thousand, check canopy.'

No canopy? Cut away from the main chute, then pull the reserve.

Once we got above 6,000 feet it turned quite cold. I started to feel a bit light-headed as the oxygen got thinner. If we'd wanted to talk we'd have needed to shout; the noise of the aircraft was deafening, even from inside our helmets.

There was one instructor per student and we jumped together. When my time came I was called up onto the

tailgate. I stood on the edge, on the balls of my feet, facing back down the aircraft. My instructor was looking at me and holding me steady with one hand. Our eyes were locked together as I waited for the signal. A gale was thrashing at my jumpsuit; 12,000 feet below us was Oxfordshire.

'Ready!'

This was it. On the next two commands he would pull me towards him slightly in a rocking motion, and then away – and down.

'Set!'

I rocked forward.

'Go!'

I launched myself back.

I kept my eyes fixed on the tailgate and watched the instructor exit a split second behind me. A gap of one second between jumpers equated to in excess of sixty feet, so he was jumping virtually on top of me. The slipstream created a natural gap.

For the first couple of jumps we had to be 'stable on heading': as we jumped, we didn't turn left or right, or tumble.

I came out, I didn't tumble.

I kept looking ahead. We were supposed to pick a point on the ground and make sure that we were not moving left or right of it, or going forwards or back – just stable on heading, falling straight until the altimeter read 3,500 feet and it was time to pull the cord. I was moving slowly around to the left and I didn't correct it. The altimeter reached 3,500 feet and I pulled. There was a rumbling sensation as the chute unfurled, then flapping and a fearsome jerk. I felt as if I had come to a complete stop.

I looked up, checking the canopy. Everything was where it should have been. I reached for the steering toggles and looked down and around to make sure there were no other canopies near me.

I watched the main dual carriageway going into Oxford,

then the vehicles, huts and people at the DZ (*drop zone*). There was total silence. It felt as if I was suspended in the sky, but before I knew it the ground was rushing up to meet me. I hit, rolled, and controlled the canopy. And that was it; straight into a vehicle for the half-hour drive back to the airfield and the waiting C130.

The first couple of jumps were rather cumbersome, just thinking about how to move and control ourselves in the sky. We were in 'clean fatigue' – just the parachute, no equipment, no weapons, no oxygen kit. Once we could fall stable on heading, we then had to turn left and right through 360 degrees, then do a somersault. To get used to handling an unstable exit, we next had to force ourselves to fall out unstable. It was quite strange; only a week before we hadn't had to practise at all, it just happened.

If we got unstable, we 'banged ourselves out', stretching our limbs out into a big star. Like the concave surface of a saucer falling towards the earth, you instantly level out. It was no big problem at all – until we jumped with our kit on.

We learned how to prepare and pack our equipment, and to rig it onto our parachutes. We would only find out a bit later, when we got to the squadrons, that what they were teaching us on the course wasn't that realistic; they were teaching us to release our equipment once we were under the canopy and let it dangle on a 9-foot rope. If we had sensitive equipment in the bergen, this method would damage it. So what we would eventually learn to do was release it and then gradually bring it down our legs so that the shoulder straps were on our toes and we were holding it. Just as we landed, we'd gently let it tap onto the ground and we'd flare the canopy.

We then started learning about the oxygen equipment that we would be jumping with. When we went onto an aircraft, we had our oxygen bottle on but we didn't use it. There was only a certain amount of gas in the bottle so we went onto the main console instead, linking us to the

aircraft's supply. When we jumped, we switched onto our own. There were drills that we had to learn, and it was all done with big flashcards held up by the oxygen NCO. It was serious stuff, learning how to rig onto one console, then come off that and go onto your own.

The next jumps were called 'simulated oxygen'. We'd go up in the aircraft, go through all the drills, and jump with our equipment but without weapons. We weren't doing any jumps higher than twelve grand, the maximum height we could go to without oxygen.

Our first lot of night jumps started, and they were wonderful – absolutely splendid. I was standing on the tailgate and could see nothing but the lights of Oxford twinkling away below me.

Soon we were doing night jumps with oxygen *and* kit. Whenever we 'jumped kit' and whenever we jumped at night, we would have an automatic opening device attached to the parachute. This worked by barometric pressure; every day a reading had to be taken so we knew the pressure at 3,500 feet. I'd make the necessary adjustment so I knew that at 3,500 feet the AOD (*automatic opening device*) was going to kick in; if I got into a spin or had a mid-air collision and knocked myself out, nothing was going to open; this device was there to at least get the rig up.

Within the squadrons there were horrendous stories of people going into spins, especially with heavy kit. If the kit wasn't packed or balanced right, then as they jumped and the wind hit them, it did its own thing. You'd have to adjust your position to fly correctly with it. If you had to fly to somebody and dock with all your equipment on and one of the straps wasn't done up tight, or one of the pouches on the side was catching air, that might lift up your left-hand side and you'd have to compensate with your right; you could end up flying in some really weird positions. But most dangerously, it could put you into a spin, and once that starts, it just gets faster and faster.

One fellow in D Squadron got into a spin and the only way he could get out of it was to try and track to get away. He did, but all the capillaries in his eyes exploded. He looked like Christopher Lee for months afterwards.

We reached the point where we were simulating oxygen jumps, doing all the drills but not going high: we were doing it at night, with equipment, and as individuals. That was us ready to go to France.

The French DZ had a quick turnaround because the site we jumped onto was also where the aircraft landed. In the UK, we had to jump on a DZ and from there get transport back to Brize Norton; the turnaround was inefficiently long. In Pau we could jump, the aircraft could land, get us back on, and throw us back out again.

We were starting now to do day jumps in teams of four, practising keeping together, then night jumps with equipment. We started to learn how to put weapons on the equipment, first so that they were good and secure whilst we were in freefall, and second, so we could get them off as soon as we landed.

The rule within the RAF was that we only did three jumps a day. There was a big fear of hypoxia if we were going up to 12,000 feet continuously; one symptom was rapid tiredness, which could lead to mistakes. Hypoxia didn't affect anybody in the sports world because they took a little oxygen bottle up with them, but it was the RAF's ball and we had to play by their rules.

We went afterwards to RAF Luffingham, the RAF medical centre, for chest X-rays and lectures about the signs and symptoms of hypoxia and what would happen if our teeth were not in good condition. A small air pocket in a filling would expand with altitude, until finally the tooth exploded. I saw it happen twice to other people and it was nasty. Stomach gases also expanded as we climbed in an unpressurized aircraft, so we farted continuously. I'd have taken the exploding tooth any day.

We then spent time in a decompression chamber, doing

189

exactly the opposite of what divers do, gradually being starved of oxygen. We sat there chatting away and were asked to do our ten times table and draw pictures of pigs and elephants. My elephants were outrageous, with disproportionately big eyes. Then, as the chamber drained of oxygen my ten times table went to ratshit; I felt myself getting slow and lethargic. The moment I was allowed to put my mask back on and take a breath, it all came good again. Apart from the elephant; the monster with big eyes was the best I could do under any conditions.

We would have to go to RAF Luffingham once a year for the rest of our careers in order to keep our freefall qualification. Every year we would have to go through the same lecture, have another set of chest X-rays, and have our ears checked; if we couldn't clear the pressure in our ears we'd be heading for major dramas.

The culmination of the course was everybody leaping out at night, with full equipment, from over 25 grand. We jumped together and landed together, and that was us qualified as freefallers – until we got to the squadrons, and had to completely retrain with square rigs.

It was madness not to be training with the equipment we were going to use. Crazier still that in a few days with my troop I was to learn more than I had in six weeks with the RAF: you learn what life's all about when you have oxygen equipment, radios, and a GPMG strapped to your bergen, packed out to the brim with in excess of 100lbs of kit. You might also be bringing in ammunition for the squadron; there might be mortar bombs strapped onto you, a mortar baseplate, all sorts wrapped all over you. Basically, you can't move for the amount of equipment that you have on, and you can't do much in the air. You fall, try to keep yourself stable, and work like a man possessed to keep in a group.

Members of Air Troop were starting to practise HAHO (*high altitude, high opening*) instead of HALO (*high altitude, low opening*). Freefalling at night was dangerous and required

190

an aircraft to fly near the target. When parachutes are deployed close to the ground, the loud, tell-tale crack of an opening canopy can alert the very people you're trying to jump on. Using this new technique they could land accurately from an aircraft flying at high altitude anything up to fifty miles from the target. Jumping from a commercial airliner at 40,000 feet and immediately opening their rigs, they could use a square canopy fitted with an electronic device to guide them to within fifty metres of a beacon placed on target, even in bad weather or at night. The first man, however, still had to map-read himself in with a compass and sat nav.

The blokes had to wear special oxygen equipment and astronaut-type heated suits to survive temperatures of minus 40°C – especially as a 50-mile cross-ground descent could take over an hour.

HAHO was soon replacing more traditional freefall infils. By being dropped many miles away from recognized civil air routes as a deception, a freefall troop could fly under the canopy to a target undetected by radar. A counter-terrorist team could land close to a hijacked airliner and put in an assault with total surprise. Instead of freefalling towards the ground with the possibility of no real idea of where they were heading or where the other blokes were once they were on the ground, they could be guided gently onto the target on the end of a comfortable parachute. Madness not to, quite frankly.

Towards the end of the course I got a letter from Debbie. She had by now already moved into a quarter in Hereford on her own. 'I'm by myself,' she wrote, 'and spending most of my time alone.' Like a dickhead, I took it at face value. I was too busy having fun without her.

15

I was told I was going over the water with my troop, but first I had to do a 'build-up' – the training beforehand.

A build-up could last anything from a couple of days to six months, depending on the task. For Northern Ireland, the main component was the CQB (*close-quarter battle*) training.

The DS said, 'The aim is to familiarize you with all the small weapons that the Regiment use over the water, especially covert operations with the pistol. On the Continuation phase of Selection you learned all the basics of the pistol, how to fire it, how to carry it, how to draw it, but now you're going to put in so many man-hours that the weapon becomes part of your body.'

In conjunction with the pistol, we learned unarmed combat – or, as some called it, jap-slapping. I was half expecting to come out the other side as a black belt in karate, but karate is a sport in which one man is pitted against another, both using the same techniques and adhering to certain rules. The basis of CQB was learning how to drop the boys as quickly and efficiently as possible so that we could get away. The Regiment was not in the province as a belligerent force; the object was to conduct covert operations. If there was ever a problem, we were going to do one of two things to the enemy – either drop him and run away, or kill him. It would all depend on the circumstances.

The instructor said, 'You need to know how to control a

threat within closed environments – down alleyways, in pubs, while you're in your cars, while you're getting out of your cars.'

More importantly, we needed to know how to recognize a threat in the first place. It was all well and good having weapons and the skills to drop people, but unless we knew when and where to use them we were in trouble.

We couldn't automatically use our weapons to protect ourselves: that might compromise an operation that had been running for two or three months, and therefore put other people needlessly at risk. If we could get out of a tight corner by using just our hands, head, knees and feet, so much the better, but if we couldn't do that, we had to start using our pistols.

The instructor carried on, 'There's a big difference between firing at a static target on a range and being in a situation where people are trying to push and shove or get in the way, and the targets can fire back.'

Mick had been in charge of jap-slapping in the Regiment for years. He was about 5'6" and wiry, slightly cross-eyed, and with only about two inches between his chin and his nose. He reminded me of Punch, but I wouldn't have mentioned it to him – we'd been told he came from the world's most aggressive family of Taffs. Apparently his old man still walked into pubs and tried to start fights, and he was in his eighties. As a schoolboy Mick had been picked for the Welsh gymnastics team, but couldn't take part because his old man wouldn't give him the fare to go training. He then got seriously into the jap-slapping and fought for the UK. Mick had become a millionaire in his youth with a shop-fitting business, but got ripped off by his partner and ended up in a council flat on social security.

We'd driven to the training area in the civilian cars that we were going to be trained in. We were sitting in a big, long concrete shelter in our jeans and T-shirts and long hair, pistols in our belts. It was a dusty, musty building with gym mats on the floor, punch-bags hanging from the

girders and targets on the walls – all the equipment we'd need to go around beating each other up.

'What I'm going to teach you is from twenty-seven years of experience,' he said. 'However, the first twenty-five years of it, the martial arts, have been a waste of time. If you're my height and ten stone, and he's six foot six and sixteen stone, knowing a few chops and flying kicks isn't going to do you much good.

'If a sixteen-stone monster hits you in the face you're going to go down, no two ways about it. When you have a slight knock from a cupboard drawer, it hurts – so if you get a fist with sixteen stone behind it coming down at you, you're going to go down like a bag of shit, no matter who you are.'

What was called for was a combination of street-fighting and certain skills from the jap-slapping catalogue, together with the controlled use of weapons. If we got involved in a scuffle outside a Belfast pub, the other person wasn't going to bow politely from the waist and stick to the rules. It would be arms and legs everywhere, head-butts, biting and gouging. In other words, we had to learn to fight dirty. If we got cornered in Northern Ireland and did a Bruce Lee, they were going to say, 'He knew what he was doing. It looked too clear and precise – there's something wrong.' But if it just looked like a good old scrap with ears torn and noses bitten off, they'd think it was a run-of-the-mill street-fight and nothing to do with the security forces.

'And when it's done,' Mick said, 'the idea is not to stand over them, cross your arms and wait for the applause. The idea is to fuck off as fast as you can.'

What we needed was, as always, speed, aggression and surprise. 'Once you've committed yourself to go for it, you must crack into it as hard as you can, apply maximum aggression and get it done. If you dilly-dally you'll go down, and once you're down, and somebody's on top of you, it's very difficult to turn things around. If the sixteen-stone monster gets you on the floor and is lying on top of

you, it's going to be very difficult to get up again.' He pointed at Tiny and said, 'If he's on top of me, all I'm going to do is bite his nose off, and run like fuck.'

We learned how to use our weapons while being pushed against a wall or into a corner, or in a lift, or closed in on by a group of people. We learned how to use the weapon just as it came out of the holster: you don't need to be in a full on-the-range shooting position, just close enough to know you're going to hit what you're firing at. It has to be well-practised, however, if you don't want to land up shooting yourself. By the end of the session we were wet with sweat and covered with dirt and dust. For the others it was revision, but I was learning all this for the first time and really enjoying it.

We learned how to get out of situations where people were aiming a pistol at us at close quarters. In the films, I was used to seeing people with a pistol about a foot away from somebody, and they're saying, 'If you move I'm going to shoot you.' In fact it's very simple: you just slap it out of the way and drop them. It's only got to move six inches and you're out of the line of aim. Even if they fire, it's going to miss. 'Bang it out of the way,' Mick said, 'then use speed and aggression to get him down, get hold of the pistol, and decide whether you're going to shoot him with it, or run.'

This phase included a lot of jap-slapping live on the range, where somebody would come up behind us, say, 'Get your hands up!' and we had to fight our way out of it to a position where we were using them as cover and we were doing the firing.

After a few days everybody was covered in bruises, lumps and bumps. We moved on to the next stage, which was learning how to fight and shoot at the same time. We might be in a very closed environment, but want to shoot some of the people around us. We might be in a shopping area, so we'd have to push people out of the way, manoeuvring our way around them. We had to be looking for our targets, holding people down, yet still be firing.

It might be that we were getting pushed around by a group of blokes. They're not exactly sure who we are at the moment, but we've decided we're not going to fight and go. This would be a terrorist situation, not just a couple of piss-heads coming out of the pub looking for trouble. We'd have to decide when to draw our pistols and take these people down.

'People who flap get killed,' Mick said. 'Make a decision about what you're going to do, every time. If you don't, you're going to die.'

He told us about a member of the Regiment who was operating in Londonderry. He had a job on where he had to go into a place called the Shantello, a large housing estate. He was on his own, wearing his pistol in the front of his trousers. As he was walking along, three players came out and began to follow him – not because they knew what he was, but simply because he was somebody strange they had seen getting out of a car and walking down one of the alleyways.

As he neared the end of the alleyway, they came up behind him and gave him a push. The moment he felt it, he started to roll: 'If you get pushed, you don't fall down on your knees; as soon as you feel that push you know there's something wrong, so you're going to try and roll out of that and get into a position where you can fire.'

As the bloke rolled on his shoulder, he could see the problem behind – two boys with pistols. Still in the roll, he pulled his weapon out and shot two of them; the third one ran. The whole thing had taken no more than three seconds. The combination of jap-slapping – going with the shove – and the pistol drills, saved his life. He had a successful night.

'You've got to remember what these people are going to do to you,' Mick said. 'If you look at the victims of the Shankill Butchers, you'll know that these people don't mess about. They start playing with you with electric drills and lumps of steel and rock.'

We were told that a lot of people in Northern Ireland had guns and were all macho with them, but it was the intention to use them that counted. Sometimes blokes had walked straight up to people with guns and disarmed them because they didn't know when to fire.

We knew that every time we drew a pistol we must have the intention to use it: we were never to make a threat that we weren't going to carry out.

Mick said, 'It isn't enough to know how – you have to know when. The intention to use the skills is as important as the skills themselves. Otherwise, in a place like Northern Ireland, you'd be drawing your pistol every five minutes – and that's just going to get you killed and compromise your operation.

'Sometimes people will come up and say, "Who the fuck are you?" Or people will stare at you the whole length of a street. You've got to have that Colgate air of confidence; it's your most important weapon.'

Walking through any of the housing estates over the water we'd get the boys coming up. They might be coming out of their houses or just mincing around having a fag by the car. They'd look at us with their eyes, saying, 'Who the fuck are you?' If we looked at the floor and thought, oh dear, I'd better get out of here, that would alert them: they wouldn't know who we were, or what we were, but they'd sense there was something wrong. 'You don't draw your pistol,' Mick said, rounding off the lesson. 'You use your secret weapon – a good, loud Irish: "Fuck off!" – and nine times out of ten they'll take you as one of their own.'

Nosh said, 'It's OK for you, you already have a bone accent.'

The training went on for weeks. We did everything from CTR skills to fast driving drills, shooting out of cars and shooting into cars, and I loved every minute of it.

16

I was picked up at Belfast airport and driven to our location. The smells and sounds inside the building took me straight back to Crossmaglen: fried eggs and talcum powder, music and shouting. Four or five dogs mooched around the place, looking as if they got fed no end.

'Finished your leave have you?' said a familiar voice behind me, followed by a resounding fart. 'About fucking time. They said they were sending some wanker from the Green Jackets.'

'Hello, Nosh,' I grinned.

He'd just come out of his room and was wearing a pair of jeans, flip-flops and an old minging T-shirt. His hair was sticking up and there was a cigarette in the corner of his mouth. At least he had his teeth in. 'Brew?'

I followed him over to the brew area just outside the living accommodation. The Burco boiler looked as if it was kept going twenty-four hours a day; next to it was a big box of NAAFI biscuits and jars of coffee and sugar.

'How's the ice-cream boys then?' I said.

I'd eventually solved the mystery of that nickname, discovering that the Air Troops had always had the piss taken out of them. Wherever there was a camera, said everybody else in the squadrons, the Air Troop would be posing in front of it – usually with shades and a deep tan. It stemmed from the way we had to operate. When there was troop

training or squadron exercises, Mountain Troop would go and live on a mountain, Boat Troop might go down to the dark and murky waters of Poole Harbour and paddle about in the freezing cold, but we'd have to go where the clear skies were, and that happened to be where the sun and Cornettos were too – so, a few jumps, then rig and jump-suit off, get an ice cream and walk around in shorts and flip-flops, looking good. No-one said it would be easy. There was one exception, and that was G Squadron Air Troop, who were known as the Lonsdale Troop because they were forever fighting each other. They even fought a pitched battle on a petrol station forecourt one day because they couldn't agree about who should get out of the minibus and do the filling up.

'Seen anybody yet?' Nosh said. 'The ops room is up the top there. Just leave your kit here. Fuck knows where you're sleeping. I think you're going in Steve's room. But if you go upstairs and see who's up there they'll be able to sort you out. Tiny got his bike nicked in London, so he's really fucking pleased about that – make sure you ask him about it because he gets all bitter and twisted. What's even worse, I'm living with him now, and he hates it. Got to go now – *Blockbusters* is on.'

Nosh, I discovered that evening, after finding myself a bed space in Steve's room, was still a nose-picking ex-member of the civilized human race, living in a disgusting world of gunge. If he didn't like something on the tele-vision, he picked his nose and flicked the bogey at the screen. The glass was covered with the things.

'He's decided he wants to learn the guitar,' said Frank. 'He spends all his free time knocking out "Duelling Banjos". Not that you'll be able to tell. It sounds like "Colonel Bogey" to me.'

'Talking of which,' Steve said to me, 'don't look inside the guitar.'

'Why not?'

'Just don't.'

I did. Judging by the volume of the crop, it was a miracle Nosh's head hadn't caved in.

Besides farting, picking his nose and strumming, his other passion in life was eggy-weggies and Marmite soldiers. Every night he'd go to the cookhouse to get his boiled eggs and Marmite toast, then he'd come back, do the crossword, watch the telly, have a fag and a fart, and go to sleep.

Johnny Two-Combs was also with us, from Boat Troop. There still wasn't a hair out of place. The last time I'd seen him was in a bar in Hereford. He was wearing a black polo-neck jumper, a yellow shirt over that, and black trousers. He went up to a girl and said, eyes half closed and half flickering, doing his best Robert de Niro, 'I just want to tell you that you have the most beautiful eyes.'

It was the most ridiculous chat-up line I'd ever heard. Half an hour later he was escorting her into a cab.

Colin had been in charge of the troop when I went to Malaya. Getting words out of him was still like drawing teeth; it would just be a sniff and, 'That was good,' or a sniff and, 'That was shit.'

Eno had been on my first Selection and passed, getting in six months before me. He was from the Queen's Regiment, a rarity in the Regiment. Predictably, everybody spoke to him in camp voices, but for some inexplicable reason also shouted, 'Three queens, three queens,' whenever they saw him. A thin little midget, Eno was a tremendous racing snake, heavily into triathlons. He smoked twenty a day but was so fit that at one championship he stood at the start line with a fag in his mouth. 'Got to spark myself up, ain't I?' he said. Eno was very much like Colin, never flapped, never got excited, and you had to beat him up to have a conversation.

Jock was there too, whom I'd met on Selection. There seemed to be no compromise with him. He had a policy of working really hard, being incredibly serious at work, then when it was fun time, it was outrageous fun time. We were

at a squadron party once; he went up to the colonel's wife and he said, 'Do you fancy a dance?' She said, 'Yes, that would be lovely,' so Jock walked her onto the middle of the dance floor, pulled out a Michael Jackson mask, and taught her to moonwalk.

Frank Collins was still Mr Calm and Casual. He never shouted, never got annoyed. Steve told me he had been one of the youngest soldiers in the Regiment when he did the Embassy in 1980. From the first night of the siege, he and the rest of the assault team were ready on the roof, dressed in full black kit and expecting the order to go in at any moment. It must have been tense stuff – but not for Frank. Apparently he was so relaxed he took a pillow with him to snooze away an hour or two. I knew he was into climbing, canoeing, freefall and religion, and I found out he was being called Joseph at this stage because he was into carpentry as well.

'You'll never see Frank when there's nothing going on,' Nosh said. 'He'll be doing the family business.'

He was going down to one of the local timber yards and making tables and cupboards and things that he was going to be taking back to the UK for his house. In fact they were quite good – big kitchen tables and things.

I was lying on my bed one day, scratching my arse and drinking tea, when Frank came in and said, 'You bored, or what?'

'Yeah, I'm doing nothing, just hanging around.'

'Do you want something to read?'

'Yeah, what you got?'

'I've got something with sex, violence, intrigue, you name it, it's got it.'

'OK, yeah, I'll have a read of it.'

So Frank went to his room, fetched the book and tossed it onto my bed. It was the Bible.

I'd turned up with big wide eyes. One of the first things I had to do was familiarize myself with the various weapons.

Over the water at that time they were using the Heckler & Koch family and the LMG – the old Bren gun, converted to 7.62 – as well as GPMGs.

Pistols were 9mm Brownings and the Walther PPK, known as the 'disco gun' because it was nice and small, and therefore easy to conceal. If I didn't want to carry my Browning when I was out and about but not working, I could slip the disco gun into my belt.

Most people would have an M16 or 203, an HK53 5.56mm or MP5, so that whatever job we were doing we could take the relevant weapon – whatever gave the right balance between concealment and firepower.

I was talking to Tiny in the armoury. Every day, the weapons had to be checked, and Tiny, the armourer for that day, was showing me the ropes.

'What's the score on this shoot-to-kill policy I keep on hearing about?' I said, half expecting him to say, 'Hose the lot down.'

'Is there fuck such a thing,' he said. 'If there was, we wouldn't still be here – we'd be back home and they'd be dead. We know where they all are – if someone was giving the green light we'd just go in and take them out.'

'Very clear-cut,' I said.

'And totally counterproductive. It's little things like that that bring down governments. Of course at the same time, there can't be a shoot-to-wound policy either,' Tiny went on. 'It would take a laser gun that was self-guiding to the shoulder to do that shit. People's perceptions of what goes on are so wrong. I remember after the Embassy, when we were making our statements, there were all these questions coming up, commentators on the TV saying, "Why didn't they just shoot him in the leg?" How the fuck can you shoot to wound somebody? It's impossible. You can't say, if somebody's a hundred metres away, "Right, I'm going to shoot him in the legs." You just see a mass of body and if he's shooting at you, you're going to shoot back at him. It's not a shoot-to-kill policy, it's just reacting to the threat. The

problem is, the people who make these sort of comments have never had a gun pointed at them.'

I knew that if I was staring down a barrel, I wasn't going to be firing at their legs. If they ended up just wounded, they'd be lucky. That wasn't a shoot-to-kill policy, that was reacting to a perceived threat and saving your own life and the lives of those around you that you had a responsibility for.

My room-mate Steve, also an Embassy and Falklands veteran, was originally from the airborne Ordnance Corps, heavy drop, who were based in Aldershot. Married with a couple of kids, he was a local lad from Gloucester; the first words I'd hear every morning were, 'All roight, boy?' Steve was slightly shorter than me but much stockier, and played rugby for the army; as a result, all his front teeth were false. He was one of the original bone-shirt people, one of the four drug smugglers who'd come back with us on the British Caledonian flight from Hong Kong. He shared the passion of most of the troop for watching *Blockbusters*, but had one annoying habit that was all his own. Every time he saw an aircraft he'd say, 'See that aircraft? The distance we're going to walk today, he's just travelled with one sip of his gin and tonic.'

Clive was a singley who'd been a Royal Engineer, and was another old Embassy and Falklands hand. He kept himself to himself, but was very much into cycling and running; he had all the cycling stuff and bone T-shirts. Clive's nightly ritual was a pint of beer and a cigar. He was an excellent long-distance runner, despite his height; he looked too tall and gangly to move fast. It was very annoying; he looked this uncoordinated mess on the run, but he really motored. One New Year's Day, Bulmer's had organized a 10-kilometre race. Clive turned up with a couple of runners from A Squadron and I thought, it would be really good to beat him, just for once. I'd been doing a lot of training and was feeling really fit; off we went, and for the whole race there was no sign of Clive. I was chuffed to

bits that he was behind me, and was looking forward to slagging him when he got in. Then, as I was running down the hill towards the finish line, I spotted him. He was on his bike, all wrapped up in his Helly Hansen, having finished the race and already on his way home.

Ken was the staff sergeant, the troop head boy, and had been away during Malaya. A southerner from the Intelligence Corps, he was a fellow jap-slapper of Mick's. The two of them had known each other for donkey's years, even when Mick was a civvy; when Mick was shivering in his council flat in Wales when everything had gone bust, half a ton of coal had turned up. Mick had run outside shouting, 'No, no, no, don't deliver – I can't afford this!' but the driver had shown him the chit, paid for by a 'Ken' in Hereford. It was something that Mick had never forgotten, and he still talked about Ken as the one who had saved him.

Ken was an excellent troop head shed, always very honest about his capabilities; rather than bluff he wouldn't be afraid to say, 'I don't know about this. Anybody got any ideas?' He was tall and toothless, having lost his front teeth while jap-slapping for Britain; you'd know when Ken was pissed because his jaw would sag and his falsies would clatter out onto the table. He talked very rapidly and aggressively; somebody would ask, 'Hey, Ken, give us that newspaper a minute,' and he'd say, 'Fight you for it.' Joking, but meaning it. Sade was doing well in the charts and he drooled over her. We used to slag her down all the time and call her Sadie, then wonder why we were walking around with black eyes.

Ken had brought his dog over with him, a big Dobermann. When he went away on operations he'd say, 'Don't over-feed this dog. It gets one scoff a day and that's it.' Tiny used to get trays of sausages and feed this dog stupid until it couldn't move – it would be splayed out all over the place. It would get so exhausted with the amount of food it had eaten that we'd get it into Ken's bed and tuck it in. Ken

would come back to find the dog fast asleep in his bed, farting and severely overweight.

Fraser was the troop sergeant and very experienced, which was good when it came to working with other organizations – communicating with helicopters, for example, if they were going to come in. It was his job to have the overall picture. He had been part of the training-wing when I did my first Selection; then he went back to the Squadron and I caught sight of him again in Malaya.

Everybody was after stitching Fraser up. Like Steve he had been in heavy drop before transferring to Para Reg, and the easiest way to spark him up was to say, 'Fraser, when you were in the Ordnance Corps . . .'

It started with putting a kipper in the little portable radiator in his room so it was stinking for weeks, and got worse from there. He was a big-time boxer with a broken nose and cauliflower ears, spending hours in the gym punching the bag. He used to love watching bouts on the TV. A fight that he particularly wanted to watch was coming up one evening, so to stop himself getting stitched up he locked himself in his room with a six-pack of beer and a pile of sandwiches. Poor bloke, he spent the whole fight wondering why the channels kept hopping. He got more and more irate. He didn't cotton on to the fact that all the television sets in the building were exactly the same, and each one had an identical remote control. We'd spent the evening outside his window, flicking the channel button and tittering like schoolgirls.

Purple in the face, he was so angry, Fraser decided to salvage a bit of the evening by going out for a pint. He went to have a shave, only to discover that as he was lathering his face with his shaving stick, a prawn gradually materialized. Somebody had cut the stick in half, grooved out the centre, inserted an old prawn, and then soaped it all up again. Fraser stormed around the compound throwing a major eppie scoppie, while even the innocent hid behind locked doors, giggling.

'Solid Shot' was there from the Signals. He came from somewhere up north and annoyed the hell out of all of us, being a big old boy and one of life's natural good lookers. He had all his own teeth, and they were white; he did the weights and a bit of running, and his only physical imperfection was that he sometimes found it hard to walk because there were so many women hanging round his feet. He had also got in on the Selection before me. He was very experienced, having done the Falklands and been over the water before; he was also very funny and confident. His nickname had come about because his favourite weapon was a Remington pump-action shotgun. There were different kinds of ammunition that we used for shotguns, including a round called solid shot – basically a big lump of lead. He was always running around with his favourite Remington pump-action, so he came to be called Solid Shot. But really it had a secret meaning; it also meant that he was thick as shit. And he must have been, because he never switched on to it.

Eddie's motto was: All work and no play, keeps you alive to fight another day. He was ex-Para Reg, ex-Embassy, ex-Falklands. He shared a room with Al Slater, who was still as I remembered him from the jungle – very straightforward and very serious about everything. His nickname was Mr Grumpy, and somebody managed to find the appropriate Mister Men sticker to put on his door.

Jock and Johnny Two-Combs shared a room. Somebody had had a notice printed and put up on their door that said: 'Johnny and Jock's Hairdressing Saloon – Mince and a rinse, £2.50 – Johnny's famous blue rinse, £1.50,' and so on, complete with two bone hair models from the Sixties with styles like Englebert Humperdinck. Boredom's a terrible thing.

That was the troop, apart from the Boss. His job was not so much on the ground but liaison between us and all the other organizations that we dealt with. He left quite early during the tour; we didn't know if it was a new job,

promotion, or the number of times he found prawns in his shaving kit.

A job came up. We took mugs of tea with us to the briefing room, Nosh still honking because Solid Shot had solved the conundrum on *Countdown*. We sat on a mixture of plastic chairs and armchairs; on the walls were maps of the province, close-up maps of different areas, blackboards, magic marker boards.

Nosh and Eno filled the place with smoke. Ken walked in with the Boss, carrying armfuls of paper.

'It looks like there's a job on,' Ken said. 'It's going to be a hit, just outside of Portadown, on a UDR major. As far as he's concerned, the players are on to him and are going to take him down. From what he says he's seen, it's going to be on the way to work. TCG obviously want to confirm this; he's being debriefed at the moment to confirm what he's seen and to make sure he isn't just flapping.

'If the job goes down, what we're looking at is having someone in the car with him. Al, do you fancy it? Have a think about it, it's up to you.'

We all looked at Mr Grumpy. Without batting an eyelid he said, 'Yeah, that's all right, I'll do that.'

'We're going to be covering him from midnight tomorrow. What I want you to do is get down there tomorrow morning, have a look around, get yourself familiarized, and be back here for two o'clock. Liaise with Fraser, he'll sort it out, stagger you down there. Hopefully by two o'clock we'll have some more information, and a set of orders before we shoot off.'

Back in our room, Steve said, in a serious voice, 'As soon as the boys start hosing those two down Al and his mate are going to be severely in the shit. We'll have to be right up Grumpy's arse on this one.'

Ken, Fraser and the Boss would be going through the options. There were many considerations when providing protection. To start with, what sort of threat was it? Did it

mean that somebody was going to blow the boy up? Did it mean a close-quarter shoot? Were they likely to threaten his family? Then, how much cover did the man want? Did he want to cut himself totally away from everyday life, or did he want to carry on as if nothing had happened? A lot of people choose just to carry on; they might have kids, and want them to have a normal existence.

Fraser got us together the next morning and we left in pairs, driving around the area. We drove past the UDR man's house, then took the route that he normally took to work, which was downhill from the house, down what was known as the old Dungannon road. There wasn't that much to look at; we just orientated ourselves to the area, turning down all the roads. Fraser had it staggered so there weren't loads of cars screaming around the place at the same time.

At two o'clock we arrived for another briefing. Ken and the Boss came in, straight from TCG (*Tasking and Co-ordination Group*) in Armagh. Ken said, 'Right, it's on. The boy's no hyper dickhead, he's switched on and he knows what he's seen. As far as TCG is concerned the boys are going to hit him on the way to work, just as he reckoned. So the plan still stands – Al, you still on for it?'

'No problems.'

'Good news. OK, we're going to insert at about four o'clock in the morning. Al's going to go to the house and sort all the shit out for the drive to work. We're going to have three groups. I want one group that's going to be on the roundabout on the old Dungannon road. They'll be dropped off by a two-man car team, who'll then stay out of the area backing up the two blokes on the roundabout. Your names are up on the board with the vehicles.

'Then there's going to be two cars to back Al in the Saab. There's going to be my car, the Lancia, callsign Bravo, and we'll take the maroon Renault, callsign India. My car will be three up, including me; the Renault's going to be four up.'

As I looked on the board I could see my name down as the driver of the Renault.

'Bravo and India are going to move down to the area, and I'll drop off Al. Al will go into the house and stay. We'll then support Al from the outside. About an hour later, I want the ground callsign to insert. I reckon that the hit's got to be around that area anyway, because once he gets on the old Dungannon road it's quite a good run all the way to work. The dodgy area is the slow patch where there's all the junctions going up to Henderson's.

I knew the roundabout he was talking about. It was where the M1 met the Coalisland and Dungannon road. The UDR major was always running down the old road, which was smaller and with less traffic. Everything converged at this roundabout. From there it became a faster road.

'Ground callsign, you will be in uniform. Your job is to give us early warning of anything that you see. If we're really going for it, your job is to get out on the road and act as a cut-off. India, when Al starts moving in the Saab, I want you to back him. Al will give a running commentary of what's going on. I'm going to be floating around. I just want you to stay static, backing up Al all the time. If there's any hijackings in the area, hopefully we'll know straight-away and we should get a list of recent stolen vehicles as well.'

It would have to be a van or truck, so they could get in a good fire position to take out the Saab. Even if they were looking at ramming it, the Saab was a big heavy machine so they'd need something really big.

'It's a matter of keeping flexible,' Ken said, 'and keeping on Al's arse, making sure you back him up.'

If nothing happened on the way down, we'd then cover him on the way back. All he was going to do was drive the route to work, turn around and drive back to the house.

'Any questions?'

Eno said, 'Do we know how many players are involved?'

'Not a clue. It's got to be at least three men – two firing, one driving. It might be a hit as soon as he comes out of the

209

house, but it's our job to make sure that doesn't happen.' He turned to Al and said, 'If you want to try some body armour on it's up to you, mate. You can wear it or not. Make sure the UDR boy's got so much body armour on the fucker can only just about get in the car!'

Al said, 'I'll try it on and see what it looks like. If it looks shit, I'll take it off.'

'I want you with comms and I want you to give us a running commentary as you're going along the road. You can hear what we're doing, so if we say to get out of the way, just fuck off out of it and we'll take over. If the van comes up in front of you, act on it – just ram the fucker, and we'll be straight in and climbing aboard them.'

That was it; there wasn't much else to say. 'There'll be no move before two o'clock.'

This was where, as much as the training and the skills that we'd learned, the relationships between people came into the equation: Al had to have total and utter trust in the people who were covering him. He also had to make sure the UDR man was calm and feeling secure, because he might have to control him if the shit hit the fan. Al's job was twice as hard as ours: not only would he have to react to the incident, but he'd also have to get to grips with the man he was protecting.

During all the planning and preparation, the head shed and the troop worked out together the way we could best protect these two. We worked through our 'actions on' for all the possibilities – whether they were going to come and ram the car, or come up behind it, overtake and then start shooting at him as they drove past and got in front of him; whether they were going to force his vehicle to stop and then shoot him, or wait until he got out of his house and into the car, or vice versa.

Ken said to Al, 'When you come out of the house we'll have you covered, so don't worry about that. Let him do the normal checks that he does under the vehicle, get in, and away you go.'

'No drama.'

We all knew that the highest risk times of any hit were a) when coming out of the house, b) driving to and from work, and c) coming out of the place of work. Terrorists studied routines. There was nearly always a time-frame, say between eight or eight-thirty, when the target would go out, kiss his wife and kids goodbye, get in the car, and go – people always drove set routes if they were unaware. At the other end of the day, they'd always leave work at the same time. A professional terrorist would always go for the most predictable timings. That's when kidnappers struck, too.

Al tried on some of the different body armours, but he just didn't look right. He decided to bin it. It was a personal choice; had he wanted to look like the Michelin man, that would have been his prerogative: he was the boy who was going to get shot at.

At two o'clock we were ready to go. All the weapons were loaded and in the cars. I took an HK53, the 5.56 assault rifle. Most people were taking 9mm MP5s or 5.56 to give a combination of concealment in the car and a good amount of firepower. The other weapon I had was the car itself: I could use it to ram.

Fraser was going to be running the desk with a couple of the scaleys. We had the two boys in uniform, who had M16s. The cars were loaded up with flasks, pies and sandwiches; it looked like it could be a long night and a long day.

We sat in the briefing room again, our 9mm pistols in holsters on our belts. We had magazines strapped all around us, we had body comms, and each man had a pair of thin leather gloves and industrial glasses, so that if the windows went in, at least we could still drive and protect ourselves.

Ken said, 'Before we go, any questions? No – right, let's crack on and get it done.'

I got into the driver's seat and put my HK53 across the

bottom of the footwell with the muzzle sticking up by the gearstick. I checked the comms: 'Bravo, India, check?'

'India, OK.'

From the ground callsign drop-off car we heard: 'Delta, check?'

'Bravo, OK.'

We drove along and kept Fraser informed of our location. We were the first ones in position; I drove past the house and got on the net: 'Bravo, India – that's the house clear.'

Ken came on the net: 'Bravo, roger that – going for the drop now.'

The car pulled up and Al got out casually and walked to the door. The door opened and he walked in. As the car drove away Ken said: 'Bravo, that's drop-off complete.'

'Delta, roger that.'

'India, roger.'

It was just a matter of hanging around now. After about five minutes we heard Al doing his radio check on his personal comms. We were ready to go.

We were parked up in a little alleyway about 300 metres from the house, drinking coffee and eating biscuits. There was a pocket scope NVA (*night viewing aid*) in the car and occasionally somebody would pick it up and have a look around. Everything was fine. We sat in darkness.

Every half hour Ken came on the net. 'Hello, all stations, this is Bravo, radio check.'

'Delta.'

'India.'

'Bravo, roger that.'

It was quite chilly. My feet were cold and I started to shiver. I did my coat up a bit more, and then I became conscious of the wind on my face from the half-open window. I was starting to get a bit tired. I wanted morning to come so we could get the job over and done with.

It started to get light at about half past seven, and we heard Ken on the net: 'That's Bravo going mobile.'

He was going to have a cruise around the area to see if

there was anything outrageous going on. We knew that Al would soon be coming out.

A couple of minutes later Al came up: 'Radio check.'

'Bravo, roger that.'

'Another five minutes and I'll be going.'

'Bravo, roger that.'

The Lancia, callsign Bravo, was cruising around but didn't see anything. The plan was that Ken was going to be in front, clearing the area as we moved; Al was going to be in the centre, and we'd be backing him from the rear.

'That's me moving out of the house now,' Al said.

'Bravo, roger that. India and Delta, acknowledge.'

I switched the engine on. Everybody picked up their weapon and held it between their legs, ready to go. All the banter stopped now; this was serious time.

'That's me now at the door.'

'Bravo, roger that. Callsigns acknowledge.'

'Delta.'

'India.'

'Walking towards the car.'

'Bravo.'

'That's garage doors open.'

'Bravo.'

'He's checking the car.'

'That's me now in the car.'

'Bravo.'

'Engine on.'

'Bravo.'

'Standby, standby. That's me now mobile.'

'Bravo, roger that.'

We came up: 'That's India mobile.'

'Bravo, roger that.'

Al drove past us in the car, a top-of-the-range Saab. I fell in behind him, covering his moves from positions where we knew we would be able to get to him as soon as the shoot took place.

Al was giving a running commentary as he was moving

along – what cars were coming up, their registrations, how many people were inside, what he could see ahead, what he could see behind him, what speed he was travelling at, whereabouts he was on the road. I had a mental picture of exactly where he was and what was going on around him.

Ken came on the net from his vehicle: 'That's a yellow van moving around in the area. It just doesn't look right, it's hanging around the junction for too long. It's a yellow Enterprise Ulster van. It's gone towards the old Dungannon road and I can't see it now. It's out of sight. Callsigns acknowledge.'

Everybody acknowledged. We were all sparked up; it looked as if it might be on.

Ken drove up towards the roundabout and parked up. He was going to let the Saab and us go past. All of us were looking for this yellow van. It sounded right.

Al, still very calm, was talking into his covert comms. There's quite a skill in talking while people are looking at you, without them realizing what you're doing.

Even if this van came up in front of him he would still have to drive up naturally to it, for a number of reasons. The first was that if he started to slow down and move back, they'd be aware that something was wrong. The second was that if he stayed up close – not exactly nose-to-tail but almost – then as soon as he saw the barrels come out of the back of the van he could put his foot down and ram the back of the wagon with three quarters of a ton of Saab. If that stopped it, all well and good – we could all get out and start shooting. If not, he could either back off, get out and start firing, or get out and start running. Al was only armed with a pistol. If there were a couple of boys in the back of the van pointing G3s at him, he wasn't going to be able to do much in return – unless they were off balance after being rammed. But if he rammed the vehicle at full pelt, there was a possibility that he might damage himself.

'That's a Renault Five coming towards me now. That's now past. My Sierra (*speed*) thirty to thirty-five mph.'

I adjusted my speed to maintain distance.

'Bravo, roger that – Sierra thirty to thirty-five.'

'That's now approaching Venners Bridge.'

'Roger that.'

'That's at the bridge, and still towards Henderson's.'

'Roger that.'

If there is a calm net, there are calm reactions. If there's hollering and shouting on the net it sparks everybody up; either calmness or tension will radiate to everybody else.

By now Al had passed the roundabout that was manned by the troop, concealed and acting as a cut-off. We were still backing him – close enough to give protection but far enough away not to stand out.

Everything was still under control except that we didn't know what had happened to the van. The one thing we did know was that Al was there on his own. By now we had passed the roundabout and were well on the way to Dungannon.

Bravo came up: 'That's me static at Henderson's.'

The Saab passed, and then we passed. If it didn't happen at the roundabout it was going to be really difficult for them to do anything. I was slightly pissed off that there was nothing happening. We did so many jobs where we got really revved up, only for nothing to happen.

Al got some speed on and headed down the old Dungannon road. We were still behind him.

Suddenly we heard from the ground callsign: 'Stand by, stand by – the van's coming back towards the roundabout! They've missed him, they've missed him! The back windows are out. It's on. He's coming back to you, Bravo.'

'Roger that, we will take it, wait out.'

Ken and his group were still the other side of the roundabout and the van was coming towards them at full speed. It seemed that the players had missed Al and didn't realize that he was well down the road to Dungannon. They were probably panicking; if they fucked this up they'd be in the shit.

Ken could see the van now coming towards them. As far as he was concerned he was going to take it. He shouted, 'Ram it! Take it!'

Ken put his seat belt on and he was ready to go. Everyone just hung on and waited for the bang.

As the van came towards him there was a boy on the front seat firing through the windscreen. Both vehicles swerved and Ken came to a screeching halt.

The only bangs that happened were the gunfire from the van. The boy was firing at the car as it approached. They started to take rounds into the windscreen; everyone ducked down as both vehicles missed each other by inches. As the van passed, firing came from the back.

All three Regiment blokes went to roll out of their vehicle and start firing. They wouldn't have enough time to turn it around. They were taking incoming; it took the back window out and the boys were now firing out of the hole. The best thing was to get out of the way of the vehicle, because that was going to take the majority of the shots.

Ken shouted: 'Get out! Get out!'

Eno was in the back, firing away, waiting for the others to get out so he could follow.

Ken had put on his seat-belt as the intention had been to have a major crash and take these boys on. In fact it still saved his life. Eno the unflappable was putting rounds through the back window. He fired nice, three-round bursts; all he needed was one of the twenty cigarettes that he smoked every day and he'd have looked like he was having a day out on the range. Ken opened his door and started to get out but was restrained by his belt. In that instant, the door took three or four rounds, just where he would have been standing.

All three were out now and Ken was on the net giving directions to the rest of the troop. The other two were still firing at the van.

'Contact, contact, contact! That's the van still going straight, that's at the crossroads – India acknowledge.'

'India, we have it, wait out.'

As soon as we heard that the van was racing down, we screamed around and started driving fast towards the roundabout. Everybody already had their gloves on; now they started putting their goggles on too: they knew we were going to start firing through the car.

We could see Ken's car, Bravo, facing us. The boys were starting to sort themselves out and get back in the car. The yellow van was moving off fast. Ken was going to turn around and back us. I put my foot down hard on the floor.

We got in range of the van and opened up on it.

The front passenger used his legs to push himself back against his seat for support as he fired. One of the back men leant between him and the driver and fired through the windscreen.

One boy was firing from the front seat, another from the back. The barrel of his HK53 was right next to me. As the 5.56 Armalite rounds went off my whole body shuddered. There was a fearsome burst of flame from the muzzle each time and it was scorching me. My eyes clenched up involuntarily with each round.

Our windscreen had crazed with the first round but being safety glass it didn't cave in. I had to lean over to the right-hand side so I could see through a good patch. We drove towards the van.

There was glass everywhere, my hands were bleeding, everyone was shouting to be heard above the wind rush. I was trying to keep the car as stable as possible as it sped along so that the fire could be accurate.

'Faster, faster, we're going to lose him!'

We were gagging on cordite flames. The wind howled through gaps in the glass with weird whistling noises. Everybody was shouting.

By now Ken and his gang had got back into their wreck of a car and were moving towards the contact.

'Bravo is trying to back you, India.'

We were starting to lose him.

'He's going left, he's going left!'

I could see the turning and had to slow down to make sure I could get round. By now we had Bravo backing us. We screamed left on the wrong side of the road that went under the motorway. Suddenly there were roads leading everywhere. We drove down a steep right-hand bend shouting, 'Where the fuck are they?'

Ken got on the net. 'You take the first option right; I'll take the second option left. Let's sort this out!'

We started turning into the little roads. Every time we saw somebody we stopped and shouted, 'Where's the van? Have you seen the van?'

'That's first option right cleared.'

'Roger that.'

'Check the next option left.'

'Roger that.'

In my mind I knew we'd lost them now, but we had to go through the motions. They could be anywhere. Al was halfway to Dungannon; he'd pulled off the road and was waiting.

By now the whole community was out looking to see what was happening. All they saw was two cars screaming around with no windows and weapons sticking out of them.

Everyone was severely pissed off. Bravo had taken hits; we had fired back without results, apart from the fact that none of us was dead. Al and the target weren't shot, and there were no injuries. A success is doing the job, and everybody coming back alive. If a task was technically a success but we had a man down, then to me that would be a failure.

Al Slater did his job well that day. He knew that he was going to be part of the target and that to survive he'd have to take on the threat on his own, as well as look after the UDR man. And all the time he'd have to stick with the attackers, until everybody else could get up with him and take them on.

'You're all wankers,' he said to us that night. 'I can't see what the problem was. I had a lovely drive into Dungannon.'

What Al did showed a lot of bottle and he got the MM for it, but he was doing it because it was his job. It had nothing to do with Queen and country. He wouldn't have looked at it and said, 'Hell, this is exciting.' He would just have thought, I need to sort my shit out for this one. The fact that there was a possibility of dying wouldn't have particularly worried him. If it had, he'd have been in a different line of work.

Everybody took a job like this extremely seriously. We were talking about people's lives, and we all knew the value of life because we'd all had our Nicky Smiths. True, we might make light of it and have a laugh at the dead man's auction, when all the man's kit was sold off and the proceeds sent to the next of kin. But bravery didn't come into it; if anyone was doing it for heroics, they'd soon get kicked out. The Regiment didn't want heroes; heroic blokes do things that are unpredictable and put other lives in danger. The idea was always to let the enemy die for his country, not you for yours.

The op had failed but that was just one of those things. I wasn't pissed off long term about it. No problem; it would be a long war.

Sadly, later in the day, we discovered there had been a casualty, Frederick Jackson. An innocent victim of the fight against terrorism, he'd been hit with a round from one of our weapons during the firefight.

The van was later found abandoned in one of the cul-de-sacs. The boys had legged it cross-country before hijacking another car for their getaway. Inside the van were a shot-gun, a radio and empty cases from an automatic weapon. The players had been there to kill – at long range with the automatic, or if they had the chance, close up with the shotgun.

Some lessons were learned. We had been needing a large-

calibre weapon that could be easily concealed for our type of work; the SLR was too big and bulky for use in cars, and in any case 5.56 didn't give us enough stopping power if we were firing out of one car into another. The short-term answer, until the 7.62 G3s arrived from Heckler & Koch, was to acquire some Argentinian folding stock FNs that the Regiment had brought back from the Falklands. They did the business very nicely.

Later on that tour we had a 'fast ball'.

There were a lot of close-quarter shoots going on at the time in County Fermanagh. The players would come up to a front door, knock, and just barge in and shoot as soon as somebody answered. The targets were mostly RUC or UDR people; whether on foot or by vehicle, the players would get back to safety. What we planned to do was split ourselves up over a period of a few nights to cover a number of main targets, but this time we'd be waiting on the premises.

The tactic might involve a combination of being in the house and being the one that opened the door, or being outside and watching them make their approach. It all depended on the terrain and the make-up of the house, garden and outbuildings.

There were four of us in one house, sitting with the main target. Of all the possible targets we could think of, this one was the most likely to be hit. It was a large bungalow in the middle of nowhere, the nearest neighbour being over a quarter of a mile away.

Frank was in charge. The rest of the team was me, Eno and a rupert called Boss 'S'. To avoid suspicion, we had decided to make it look as if we were a vanload of friends turning up with six-packs of beer and big bags of fun-size Mars bars.

He was a great old boy in his forties, full of jokes and totally nonchalant about the situation. This might have had something to do with the fact that everywhere we went in

the house there seemed to be a shotgun hanging off a wall ready to give somebody the good news. 'Let's get the kettle on, boys, and we'll sit down and watch some television. I've had this for years and years – they say there's a threat on me, and all you lads come down and look after us for a couple of days. I wouldn't take it too seriously if I were you. But it'll be interesting to see what happens. It's a cold night, I can't see them coming out in this.'

It was a beautiful house. The kitchen was boiling hot, with a Rayburn going full tilt on one side and a huge kettle steaming away on one of the hotplates. He shooed away the flask and sandwiches he saw me bring in. 'Forget that horrible stuff,' he said. 'I'll do us a decent cup of tea, and there's pies and things cooking in the Rayburn.'

It was a still and icy cold night. I was so glad to be inside, stuffing my face with pies and tea, instead of lying in an OP in a bush. Frank and Boss 'S' were watching the telly with him in the front room. Eno and I were in the kitchen, sitting in armchairs that we'd pulled up near the large, double-glazed back door. All the lights were off; nobody would be able to see us. We sat with our feet up on pouffes, our weapons resting across the arms of the chairs. It was a brilliant way to go to war.

There was no way the players would come to the front of the house; it was one of those places where the front door had never been used. From our armchairs we had a grand-stand view of the approach that we reckoned they'd use. They were very unlikely to drive in; they'd be coming across country and entering via the back. If they did, they wouldn't be exiting.

Eno whispered, 'I'm gagging for a fag.'

'Why the fuck do you smoke?' I said. 'It costs too much, and you stink.'

'Yeah, but it's good for the training. The old kickstart. I'll give it up one of these days.'

The still of the night was shattered by Fraser coming on the net to us: 'Everybody, sort your shit out, TCG wants

you down at the Drumrush Lodge now. Nobody knows what's going on, but everyone needs to get down there. I'll give you sitreps if anything comes in. Get down there – now!'

Frank said, 'Roger that. We're on our way.'

We got our kit together and went to the van.

Frank said, 'Boss, you map read, I'll drive. Andy and Eno, in the back.'

The UDR boy waved us off and said, 'Don't worry about me. I've got more shotguns and Mars bars than you can shake a stick at. See you later.'

Fraser came back on the net: 'A few minutes ago a woman phoned the RUC station at Kesh. She said, "Listen carefully, this is the Fermanagh Brigade of the IRA. There are a number of blast incendiaries in the Drumrush Lodge Hotel. The reason for this is that the Drumrush Lodge serves the bastards of the security forces."'

The weather was horrendous. The mist was heavy, with visibility down to no more than twenty to thirty metres, and ice on the road was slowing everybody down. As soon as we went over about 30mph we started skidding. It was better just to slow down, take the vehicle to a maximum speed of about 25mph; at least we would get there, not crash and lose 25 per cent of the troop's effectiveness.

We could hear on the net that the other two cars were now in the area of the hotel and starting to search. One of the suspicious vehicles in that area that we knew to look out for was a blue van, possibly of foreign make.

Eno said, 'I bet it's a fucking come-on.' Maybe the boys wanted us in the area because they had planned a party.

The Boss was map reading with a small Maglite torch: 'Down here, turn left.'

The car slithered round the bend. Frank said, 'No point rushing. Let's just trog on, we'll get there eventually.'

Then we heard: 'Stand by, we have a possible here, wait out.' Everybody shut up now, waiting to hear what happened next.

Al, Eddie and Clive were in one of the cars and drove past a blue Toyota van parked up on another road just off the Drumrush Lodge. Everyone apart from the driver was keeping right down; they didn't want to put anyone off their work. They came back on the net: 'It's parked up, no lights, no movement but the door is slightly open. It looks like something's going down.'

Ken was on the net: 'Block the road. We'll stake it out and see what turns up.'

His team were now at the other end of the road. The van wasn't going to go anywhere; hopefully the area was contained. However, we still didn't know what was going on.

Clive's team were out of their car and Al put out the caltrops, spiked chains that would stop a vehicle by blowing the tyres out.

Ken was on the net to Fraser: 'Is there any area that I've left?'

He obviously wanted to know if there was any road or track between the two cars that they hadn't seen.

'No, that's OK, everything's covered.'

They stopped and listened. Sound travels much more at night, and even further on cold ones.

As we slithered along as fast as we could on the ice, I pictured Eddie listening in the fog as he tried to learn what was happening around the car. He'd be opening his jaw to take out any noises of swallowing that he made with his mouth, and leaning his ear to the area.

Eddie could hear something but he needed it confirmed: 'Clive, listen to this.' He came to Eddie and turned his radio off so that there was no interference from his earpiece.

Someone was walking down the road. In the freezing fog, this was wrong.

'Stand still and put up your hands where I can see them!' Eddie shouted. 'This is the security forces!'

The walker was about ten metres away and Eddie had decided that that was close enough. He called out just loud

enough for this walker to hear, not loud enough, he hoped, to alert anyone else further afield.

'It's OK, it's only me!' The boy sounded as if he was flapping good style; he was hoping no doubt that his challengers were just a local army patrol so he'd have time to think of something or get some back-up.

'Shut up, stand still or I will fire – do you understand?' By now Clive had his HK53 in his shoulder and was starting to move forward.

The boy ran.

Al moved to the back of the car to get a Schermuly flare from the boot. He fired it into the air and night turned into foggy day.

Clive and Eddie fired to the side of the boy as he ran over a ditch and fence and into a field. Night viewing aids were of limited value in fog. They were going to lose him; they had to do something.

From Ken we heard: 'Contact, contact, wait out.'

We started to get sparked up. The Boss said, 'Fucking hell, it's on! We need to get there as fast as we can.'

Frank said, 'It's pointless rushing. We'll get there.'

I knew Frank was right but I felt helpless in the back seat.

Ken's team didn't know any more than we did; they would not move forward in case of a blue-on-blue (*friendly fire*). If Clive and Eddie needed any help they would call for it.

All this time, two other members of the PIRA gang had been no more than 5 metres away from Clive's team in the car. They must have heard it stop, and remained hidden. As the Schermuly went up and Clive and Eddie started to fire, so did they – at Al.

Clive and Eddie had got the runner. He quite sensibly stopped as the Schermuly was doing its job and he knew that he was in the shit.

'Bring your hands up and turn towards me. Now walk towards me.'

Clive was giving commands but the boy wasn't

listening. He got dragged onto the road and put face down.

'I am going to search you,' Clive said. 'If you move you will be shot, do you understand?' Eddie shouted for Al to bring some plasticuffs so they could immobilize him until the RUC arrived.

We were nearly there now and telling Ken the direction of our approach so he could put us in where he wanted. The area was in darkness again.

Al hadn't responded to their request so both men dragged the prisoner to the car.

Eddie said to Clive: 'Take my weapon, I'll get in the back for the cuffs.'

He handed it over to Clive, who covered the boy on the ground. There wasn't a sling on Eddie's weapon so Clive was holding it in his hand.

Next person we heard on the net was Eddie: 'Hello, all callsigns, we have a man down. It's Al – we need a heli. Get a helicopter in now!'

Fraser came back: 'Roger that, confirm it's Al. Confirm it's Al, over.'

He needed to make sure so that the blood type could be matched.

Eddie came back: 'Yep, it's Al. Get it in now! We need it in now!'

We heard Ken say, 'Get it in now! Fuck the weather, I want a heli in there now!'

The scaleys were on other frequencies now, trying to get a heli up. But there was no way a helicopter could fly in freezing fog. The boss down at TCG was trying to organize to get an ambulance in.

Fraser came back to Clive and Eddie a few minutes later, 'We can't get a heli in, the fog's down too much. We're trying for an ambulance, we're going to get something in for you, wait out, wait out.'

Al had taken rounds in the arm and chest. Eddie got the trauma pack out of the boot to stop the bleeding and get some fluid into him.

This wasn't looking good: as well as Al being down there were more players around in the darkness.

Ken's team were out in the fields following up, and by now so were we.

The boy on the floor must have heard everything and considered himself deeply in the shit, because he decided to go for it. He lunged at Clive in an attempt to get past him; Clive dropped Eddie's HK53 so he could use his arm to drop him.

He was too late. The boy was gone, and so was the weapon.

'He's got a fifty-three!' Clive shouted. 'He's got a fifty-three!'

They went after him.

Eddie had drawn his pistol; they both fired and the boy dropped. They ran forward and checked his body, but there was no pulse. They went back to Al, but it was too late. Al Slater was dead.

Ken came over the net, 'Contact, wait out.'

Frank replied, 'We're about two minutes away, I'm stopping anything moving out.'

We stopped any vehicles we saw coming from that direction. I was glad we were in uniform: there was a security base nearby and now the shit had hit the fan I wouldn't have wanted to be in civvies.

We saw lights coming along the road and put in an instant VCP.

Frank went to the car as any normal soldier would, so as to not arouse any suspicion: 'Hello, could I see your driving licence please? Where are you going? Thank you, good night.'

What they didn't know was that I had an M16 pointing at the head of the driver and Eno had an LMG ready to stop the car and its passengers if there was any threat to this local army VCP.

We started to follow up in the area but it was going to be more luck than anything if we bumped into them. We had to cover as much ground as possible as quickly as possible.

On the net we heard the local unit's QRF being called forward by Fraser to cordon off the area, hoping that the players from the bomb team were still in the area feeling like trapped rabbits.

We could tell by the radio traffic that there were far more chiefs than Indians. Some of their Land Rovers were in ditches because of the ice. All they knew was that there were casualties and terrorists in the area. Every time a tree moved it was reported. There was a danger of us being shot by our own QRF.

There were short bursts of gunfire in the distance. Every time, we got on the net: 'What is it? What is it?' We wanted to react. Fraser came back each time, 'Stand down, stand down.' It was the QRF, firing at shadows. There was a good chance that the boys could still be in the area, but the QRF were multiplying the problems and if any more time was wasted we might lose them.

Ken was severely pissed off and got on the net: 'Get this to the QRF – we will contain this area. They are to stay where they are. They are not to fire at anything unless one of us tells them to or they are being fired at. No patrols, no movement; stay in the vehicles. Tell them not to react to anything until they're told.'

We were well insulated, but my feet and hands were stiff with cold. Every few steps I was slipping on the ice.

Fraser said, 'The QRF have reported movement in some hedgerows by the river. Are there any of our callsigns down by the river, over?'

Silence.

Frank said: 'Me and Andy will take that.'

'Roger that. Frank's going down to the river. Ken, acknowledge.'

'Ken, roger that.'

Frank said, 'Andy, what I want you to do is just keep moving forward and scanning the hedgerow with your night sight. I'll be behind you with mine and we'll get these boys out.'

I switched my sight back on, took a deep breath, and started moving.

It was eerily quiet. I could hear the ice cracking on the grass. I was in a semi-crouched position, safety-catch off, butt in the shoulder, picking my feet up really high, trying not to breathe too hard, trying to keep the noise down, trying to keep as small as possible. Frank was about five to seven metres behind, aiming just to my right so he could take anybody on. Because he was detached, it would be easier for him to react.

I was listening in on the radio, making sure I knew where everybody was.

By now an ambulance had turned up and he had his blue light flashing. It was a fair way away from us, but as the light spun round it was catching us like dancers in a disco strobe. I thought, fucking hell, this is a good day out this is.

I took two or three steps, stopped, ran my night sight up and down. We moved on, stopped, moved on. At any moment I was expecting to hear a burst of gunfire and to feel the rounds thud into my body. It wasn't a nice feeling at all.

Big drainage ditches ran alongside the hedgerows. It was pitch black, visibility was shit, there was lots of commotion, lots of noise in the distance. Running around in there somewhere were terrorists who'd just had a contact. They would be flapping, they would want to get out of it, and they would be armed.

It was only after about twenty minutes that I thought to myself: shit, I've drawn the short straw here, haven't I? I'll take all the rounds and Frank lands up shooting them.

We found nothing.

After a few days pieces of the puzzle started to come together.

Antoin Mac Giolla Bride was an ex-Southern Irish soldier and a well-known terrorist since he was first arrested with a rifle in 1979. His ASU (*active service unit*) had planned to

lay a land mine, consisting of beer kegs crammed with low explosive, in a culvert at the entrance to the hotel. By the time we got the call the bomb was in place.

As Al's car drove past they must have heard it and hidden. Unfortunately, the car stopped just feet from two of the boys. As he sent the Schermuly up they must have seen his silhouette and opened up.

Al took rounds but managed to turn and fire back. Then he fell.

They moved off and got to the banks of the Bannagh River. One of them jumped into the water to cross to the other side. The river was only about twenty feet wide but it was in flood and there were deep pools. When he got over, he couldn't find his companion. He'd drowned further downstream.

The troop was a close-knit group and Al Slater's death put all of us on a downer. It's never easy losing somebody you know, but there's not a lot you can do about it, you've got to get on with it. Within about two days the jokes were being cracked.

We were going to have a Christmas piss-up. The troop invited all the different personalities from the police force and other organizations that we had dealings with.

One of the policemen there, a fellow called Freddie, had lost his left hand in an accident and had a Gucci replacement strapped onto his stump. It worked on electrodes, and gave him the capability to flex his fingers to grasp things, but unfortunately the arm occasionally developed a mind of its own. It would be all right when he put it on, but then all of a sudden the electrodes would short-circuit and the fingers would be flexing all over the place like something out of an old B movie. We all used to think it was great.

We were thinking about getting him a present, and there was much humming and hawing about what it should be. The best we could come up with was a regimental plaque, but Ken said, 'That's crap. Don't worry, I'll sort it out.'

Freddie turned up at the do, and there must have been 150 or so people present.

Ken got up with a small parcel in his hand, wrapped in fancy paper and ribbons.

'Well, Fred,' he said, 'this is just a little something to say thanks very much for all the help and support this past year. We hope this will come in handy, and rather than giving you something really bone like a plaque to hang on a wall, we thought we'd give you something much more practical.'

'Thanks very much,' said Fred. He started to undo the ribbons and paper, which took him ages because Ken had used four layers of wrapping just to fuck him up. At last, after Fred had got a decent sweat on wrestling with ribbons and sellotape, our gift was finally revealed in all its glory – a can of WD4O.

Freddie took it really well, rolled up his sleeve and had a little squirt.

I bought Al's Barbour jacket at the auction; it would have been cheaper to have bought a brand new one, but that's how it goes.

Nobody was worse affected by Al's death than Frank Collins.

'I've seen a lot of mates die during my seven years in the Regiment,' he said, 'but this has hit me the hardest.'

Maybe Al's death was the first big test of his Christian faith. Frank left the Regiment soon afterwards and decided to train to be the ayatollah. However, he wanted to pay off his mortgage before he enrolled at Bible college, and his first freelance job took him to Sri Lanka.

Frank lasted two weeks. When I saw him much later in Hereford he said, 'They had no understanding of right or wrong and thought nothing of wiping out Tamils. Some of the people we trained committed atrocities. It was well-paid, but I came straight home.'

He then got a BG (*bodyguard*) job in Athens, and worked

230

for Burton chief Sir Ralph Halpern and Harrods boss Mohammed Al-Fayed. Finally, when he'd saved up enough, he did the Church's version of Selection and passed. After two years of studying he was badged as a fully fledged vicar, and an excellent one he was, too.

Debbie had a job and I assumed she was enjoying it. I didn't know for sure, because I was never there.

I phoned her whenever I could, but every time I'd tell her how I was and never really listened when she told me how she was. I still wasn't getting my priorities right. Everything was the Regiment; I loved what I was doing. But I was being selfish; I was sacrificing the marriage, and it was my fault. If I came back for R&R, all I wanted to do was go downtown and see all my mates again. Everything I did revolved around them; she was secondary. It must have been outrageous for her. I was even stupid enough to start talking about kids, when I wasn't even responsible enough to look after my wife. But I didn't realize, because I was a dickhead. I didn't know that the marriage was going down; I was too busy wanting to get the skills in, and the big one I wanted was demolitions.

17

'One of the aims of this twelve-week course is to teach industrial sabotage, strategic tasks and strikes on defined targets,' the instructor said to us. 'A typical Regiment task might be to render useless the industrial base of a nation we're fighting against. Their army might be at the front line, but at the end of the day an army's no good if it can't get supplies. Attacks on the industrial base also lower the population's morale, which is all good for the general war effort.'

It was gripping stuff and I couldn't wait to get stuck in. Even as a kid, I'd been fascinated by television pictures of steeplejacks dropping power station chimneys and tower blocks collapsing within their own perimeter. I had a little basic knowledge from Selection, and I wanted more.

Training-wing, as well as taking Selection, was also responsible for teaching demolitions and all the patrol skills. Joe, the dems instructor, was coming up to the end of his two years in the job, and really knew his stuff. Demolitions would also be used within other jobs, he said, as a surgical strike: we might want to drop a bridge, railway line, hydroelectric power station or crude oil refinery; or render docks useless, open floodgates, destroy military or civilian aircraft.

We learned how to disrupt microwave and landline communications within military and civilian environments. 'So much damage can be done with just two pounds

of PE,' Joe said. 'Why send in an air force to destroy a big industrial complex when the same result could be achieved by taking out its power source?'

If we were going in covertly, we had to know and practise our trade craft – including surveillance and anti-surveillance.

For the first couple of weeks we learned parrot-fashion all the rules, the dos and don'ts, and all the formulae. We weren't going to have our little reference books with us when we were on ops. Joe banged the rules into our heads from day one, and tested us every day. Every spare moment we had was taken up with learning it all by heart; to a scholar like me, it felt like trying to pour 10lbs of shit into a 2lb bag.

We learned about all the explosives used by the British Army and others, what explosives were commercially available, and where and how we could get our hands on them.

Having obtained them, we had to know how to use the stuff. Industrial sabotage nearly always involves cutting steel. However, the explosions are not Hollywood classics – a big blast, a massive fireball, and the bridge comes tumbling down. The hallmark of a Regiment strike would be the minimum amount of explosives to create the maximum damage – unlike my effort with the buttress tree on Selection – because then there's less to carry or make, and less to conceal.

Depending on the type of bridge, the aim was to do specific cuts so that the bridge would collapse under its own weight. To demolish a building, all you do is initiate the momentum of the building falling, and the building itself does the rest.

We learned how to blow up everything from tele-communications lines to power stations, trains to planes. Everything had to be destroyed in such a manner that it couldn't be repaired or replaced – or if it could, then it must take the maximum amount of time. Destroying something did not necessarily involve taking it off the face of the earth.

It might just mean making a small penetration of about half an inch with explosives into a certain piece of machinery. That might be all that's needed to disturb the momentum of the turning parts inside. The machine then destroys itself. The skill is in identifying where the weak part is, getting in there to do it, and getting away again.

A lot of motorways and structures are built with concrete, so we learned how to destroy it – and that did take a lot of explosives. Sometimes it wasn't enough just to take down the spans of bridges: the piers had to be cut as well to maximize the damage. Gaps could be repaired; whole elevated sections of motorway could be replaced in a fortnight, as the Californians prove every time they have an earthquake.

A large factory or even small town can be immobilized just by taking out an electricity substation. Obviously there are all sorts of countermeasures, and in times of conflict key points will be protected. Much of the time, however, the Regiment would not be doing this in a theatre of major conflict; we'd be doing it in a small guerrilla war or revolutionary scenario. If the target was protected, that would be just another problem we'd have to get over. We might be putting charges in to go off the following month. In theory, a charge could be placed to blow up in five years' time. There are plenty of ways to initiate an explosion, from anywhere in the world.

We went down to one of the local bridges around Hereford, and each did a recce report in slow time (*not covertly*). We had a good look at the bridge, measured it out and did whatever we needed to produce the mechanics of a recce report, wandering around the structure with tape measures and cameras as we worked out how to destroy it. While all the rest of us were doing this technical stuff, Bob, one of the world's most confident men, the sort who not only knows where he's going but also how he's going to get there and what time he's going to arrive, was doing pin-steps along the footrail, whistling away as he counted them out.

Bob always spoke at Mach 2. 'You don't need all this technical stuff, all these fucking tape measures,' he scoffed. 'If you were doing it for real, you'd just be pacing it out. Twenty feet, twenty-one feet . . .'

When he got to the far end of the bridge he sat down and did a film director's square on it, took a couple of snapshots, and relaxed in the sun.

The instructor came over and said, 'You all sorted then, Bob?'

'Yeah, no problems. I'm happier doing it this way.'

Bob sat there for the rest of the afternoon, enjoying the sunshine and having the occasional brew while everybody else was running around like idiots. I was then up until two o'clock in the morning getting my recce report just right, but not Bob. He bounced into the classroom the next day as fresh as a daisy and said, 'Piece of piss.'

The instructor assessed our efforts and passed comments. Most reports were competent, but Bob's, he announced, was outstanding.

'Enjoy yourself yesterday, did you?' he asked Bob. 'Lovely sunny day, wasn't it? I'm surprised you didn't get sunburnt, all the lying around you did.'

'Did my report though, didn't I?' Bob smiled. 'And you reckon it's a blinder.'

'In every respect,' the instructor said. 'Except one.'

'What's that?'

'All your photographs show a bridge in the pissing rain!'

'That's extraordinary,' Bob said. 'Camera must be a bit damp.'

Bob had spent the whole of the previous weekend doing all the photography and technical measurements on the bridge so that on the day he could piss us off by appearing to do nothing. It would have gone down as one of the great stitches if only he'd remembered that it had poured with rain the whole weekend.

The dems course taught us how to use the equipment, but it also taught us how to translate that information for

other people to use. Part of that involved covert photography and infrared photography. We might be a businessman with a view from his hotel room, or a hiker. The stills or video camera might be concealed about our person or in a bag, or we'd be tucked a couple of kilometres back and using large mirror lenses in a covert OP.

As well as all the technical bits and pieces for the demolitions, we'd be looking at all the defences. How many guards are at the gate? Do they look alert? Are they slouched in a heap with fags in their mouths? What is the best way in and the best way out? We could be planning and preparing for another group – telling them what charges were required and sorting out the RVs and exfil from the target. We might be required to stay in the area afterwards to confirm damage and reassess. It was all part of demolitions; there was much more to it than Clint Eastwood on his horse, lighting a stick of gelignite and lobbing it over a wall.

We had all been trained in trauma management, dealing with gunshot wounds and fractures, stabilizing injuries, and intravenously administering fluids; everybody had the skill to keep a person alive if they'd been hit by a bomb blast or rounds. But the kind of work that the Regiment is involved in calls for somebody who has taken it a stage further; the patrol medic must be able to carry out surgical procedures in the field, to recognize illnesses, and prescribe and administer drugs. The result then is a patrol that can stay longer out in the field if it has a major problem; helicopters don't have to be called in to extract a casualty, with the risk of compromise.

The Regiment operated a 'hearts and minds' policy in the Third World countries where it worked. In Oman in the Seventies, for example, a lot of the Regiment's time was taken up with looking after the Baluch and the Firqat, prescribing drugs and looking after their welfare. There were case notes that covered everything from assisting with a

birth to operating on a villager who'd had half his head blown off. Sometimes the medic pack contained more drugs and equipment than some of their hospitals. The problem was that as soon as the medics started administering medical aid for major injuries and illnesses, there'd be a mile-long queue outside their A-frame of people with warts and ingrown toenails.

One of them told me: 'We looked after a couple of blokes in the jungle who had problems with their feet. Suddenly every man and his dog is on the case, turning up with little cuts and bruises on their tootsies. The next bloke that pestered us, we made it look as if we were going to amputate his foot. We went through all the procedures of making sure the table was clear. We had the knives out and all sorts.'

Apparently they explained to the man that the only way to deal with such a troublesome foot was to take it off altogether, so if he'd just lie down on the table they'd have it squared away in no time. The cut suddenly wasn't such a problem and the character ran away. He spread the good news about, and not many others turned up with bad feet.

Meeting up in Hereford with blokes who had been doing the medics course while I was doing dems, I heard some wonderful stories.

They had done about six weeks in Hereford starting from the basics, learning how to put in IVs (*intravenous drips*), administer drugs through injection, prescribe and use drugs. All the drugs had to be learned by their universal, Latin names, which was enjoyed no end.

They then had to go away and do a couple of weeks at the London School of Tropical Medicine. Because a lot of the work was in tropical climates, they had to know about tropical diseases, how to prevent them, and the way of treating them when they did take hold.

It was then back to Hereford for a bit more time in the lecture room, and eventually they got their hospital attachments, all around the country. Most of their time was spent

in Casualty, getting hands-on experience: they could learn all the theory they liked, they were told, but there was nothing like a bit of hands-on with a road traffic accident casualty, or the Saturday night people getting filled in and cut.

They had also spent a lot of time learning how to become hypochondriacs. A fellow called Rod, who spoke with a thick Yorkshire accent and lots of thee and nowt, spent the first two weeks of his month's hospital attachment working in the casualty ward. The next two weeks were taken up purely on his own body MOT. He'd be using all the machines that went ping, having his heart looked at, convinced that there had to be something wrong.

Charlie was another hypochondriac. He'd left the Regiment in his thirties, gone to work overseas, and then come back and done Selection again. He passed, and was the world's oldest corporal. We were doing some troop training and were on the ranges one day, sharing mugs. Charlie hated us doing that.

'You don't know what you could pick up,' he said.

'Too true,' somebody said. 'I was in the Far East, and contracted leptospirosis. I lost about two stone.'

'That was bad luck,' Charlie said. 'When did it happen?'

'Last month.'

'You dirty fucking thing!' Charlie screamed. We all started to laugh, because we knew how much it pissed him off. He honked for days about drinking out of the same mug as someone who'd had leptospirosis. He made his own tea after that.

At the end of the week's training we said, 'You ain't caught leptospirosis yet then, Charlie?'

'No,' he said, 'but I'm not too sure what all you people are going to catch.'

'Why's that then?'

'Because I've been pissing in the tea urn every day.'

The placement system worked really well, both for the Regiment and for the hospitals. The blokes gained

experience, and the casualty ward got another pair of willing hands.

A fellow called Pat had been on hospital attachment at Birmingham General. All the drunks were coming in with bottles sticking out of their foreheads, and gangs of young lads who had been fighting and thought they were as hard as nails because they had a cut on their face. The staff did their best to help them out, but the lads were drunk and full of bravado, getting aggressive with the nurses, pushing them away. Nurses got attacked by these sorts of people all the time. They're trying to do their job and look after them, and the boys are getting gobby and trying to fill them in.

Pat was on a refresher course after spending a couple of years away. It used to piss him off severely to see the abuse these girls had to take. The trouble was, there was seldom much that the blokes could do, because they were supposed to be keeping a low profile.

One night, however, one of the nurses came screaming out of a cubicle. Pat walked in to see what was happening.

A character came up straightaway and started finger-poking him. 'Yeah, that's right,' he gobbed, 'fucking sort me out now!'

Pat looked at him for a second, and said, 'Yes, OK, if that's what you want.'

And he head-butted him and dropped him.

The lad burst into tears and said, 'What's going on?' as if it was all Pat's fault. He then started shouting for the police. Two officers happened to be on the ward after bringing in a drunk; they stuck their heads around the curtain, sussed out immediately what had happened, and said, 'Sorry, sir, we didn't see anything.'

The bloke with the sore forehead had a badly injured mate outside on a trolley. Pat and a nurse were asked to get him into a lift and take him up to have surgery. While the boy was lying on the stretcher he was giving the nurse a hard time, calling her a slag and yelling that everyone was a wanker. So Pat put the lift on hold and said, 'Look,

sunshine, let me read your horoscope. You're dying. If we don't get you up the top there, you'll check out for sure. The lift's stopped. If you don't shut your gob I'll just keep you here. So can I take it that we have *détente*?'

Members of the Regiment hold life as dear as anybody else. During one operation, a team had been off somewhere doing their stuff. They stopped after a firefight and were clearing the area when they came across a young member of the opposition. He was shot in the legs and in a bad way. Rather than bugging out, they stopped, used their own medical equipment, which they might be needing themselves the next day, to stabilize him and got him onto their vehicle. Then they went out of the area of the task to reach an LS (*landing site*) where a helicopter could come in and casevac him.

A fellow called Billy was watching Hereford play football one Saturday when one of the players swallowed his own tongue. Billy saw what was going on, jumped onto the pitch and did the necessary and saved the player's life – and then ran off pretty sharpish to avoid attention. He was very annoyed afterwards about missing the match.

I found people were extremely careful to preserve life and limb, perhaps because they understood the dangers more. It was a wonder to me the kids of some Regiment blokes could go anywhere, their dads were so protective. But then, maybe they understood dangers that other people didn't, because they'd seen the consequences. When a person is hit by a car at 30mph they get thrown in the air, their body gets shattered; chances were the dad had seen some of that, and it made him more aware of everyday dangers, not just danger in the military context.

18

It seemed that as soon as I got back from somewhere I was getting ready to go away again. To all intents and purposes Debbie and I were living separate existences.

She said to me, 'What exactly are we doing with our lives? Even when you come back, you disappear straight down town.'

I said, 'It'll be all right – it's just a busy time. Look, I'm going away for another three months soon – when I get back we'll sort ourselves out.' There was nothing those Relate people could have taught me about running a marriage.

The three-month trip to Oman was a whole squadron effort to practise desert warfare. I was really excited; there were strong regiment links with the area, and because most of the squadron had been to the Middle East before, I felt that at least when this one was over we'd be speaking the same language.

The Regiment was founded in the desert in the Second World War and had operated in Oman for many years. The principles hadn't changed – moving with vehicles, navigating, using special tactics and fieldcraft for that type of terrain. It was still all about using the weapons we had to their maximum ability, operating at night, moving tactically during the day. The idea behind the squadron trip was that if there ever was a conflict again in that theatre, at least new members like me would have a foundation and not be stumbling into a new environment.

Initially it turned out to be a major anticlimax. We were in a tented camp in the middle of the desert, protected by fences and all kinds of elaborate security devices. We weren't allowed out. For the first three days the most interesting thing that happened was Tiny sitting up in his sleeping bag every morning and shouting, 'I'm bored!'

We'd saunter over to the cook tent where some of the locals were making pitta bread and chapatis. Then we'd go around nicking chairs and putting up washing lines made of paracord, until we got fed up. By Day Three hints were being dropped to the hierarchy. A few blokes put a sign up saying '8 Troop's escape tunnel', with a pair of upside-down boots poking out of the top. Some others put in a requisition chit for a gym horse, and specified that it must be wooden and have room inside for at least three men. Mountain Troop put up a sign on the gate that said 'Stalag 13' and spent hours standing looking wistfully towards the west.

It was warm, but one fellow called Gibbo, who'd fought in the Oman war and had spent so much time in the Middle East he might as well have had an Arab passport, would be walking around with a duvet jacket on in the morning, honking about the cold weather. We were on a beautiful desert plain with sheer mountains in the distance. Sitting on the thunderbox one night I looked up at the stars. There wasn't a cloud in the sky and the inky blackness was chock full of twinkling lights. It was absolutely stunning.

Eventually things livened up. John organized a Huey and we spent three or four days doing freefall in perfect blue skies. It was the first time I had jumped out of a helicopter; instead of the deafening, buffeting windrush of a jump from an aircraft there was only a weird feeling of acceleration and silence, apart from the whistle of the wind in my ears.

We started roaring around in the new 110s (*long-wheel-base Land Rover*) with 50mm machine-guns dangling off the back that were replacing the old 'pinkies'. I was in a mortar

team. Nosh was No. 1, who laid all the aiming devices, Steve was No. 2, who put it down the tube, and I was No. 3 – basically, the boy who sorted out the ammunition and stuck his fingers in his ears. Colin was the MFC (*mortar fire controller*).

We went to a training area a couple of kilometres away, armed with more ammunition than a battalion got through in about ten years – hundreds and hundreds of rounds.

My vision of the Regiment and the squadron was still nice and fluffy, but now I started to hear various honkings. The main one was about the squadron sergeant major and something to do with 'cabbage'. It took me a little while to find out that this meant money, and that what they were moaning about was squadron funds. The SSM was awarding VCs (*voluntary contributions – i.e. fines*) all over the place to boost the fund. There was a fridge full of soft drinks running on a generator; every time you took one you signed your NAAFI number and got a bill at the end of the week. We found the SSM had loaded the prices by 200 per cent.

The four MFCs came down with us in the wagons and set themselves up with Martini parasols, iceboxes and masses of food amongst the mortars and the piles of ammunition. We learned how to cover a whole area with pinpoint accuracy, co-ordinating illuminating mortars with high explosive so that at night the MFC could see what was going on. It took a lot of co-ordination; the fuses had to be set so that as one was going out the other was blowing up. By the end of two weeks we were the Eric Bristows of the mortar world.

John announced a five-day squadron exercise with the 110 and mortars to practise live firing 'advance to contact'. The Mobility Troop drove forward with their 110s and motor bikes, moving tactically across the ground. The procedure was basically the same as rifle company firing and manoeuvring, but without the firing. A couple of vehicles moved up into the high ground and got into a position

from where they could use their guns to cover the next lot moving on the low ground. Everything was co-ordinated by the squadron commander.

We came into an area where we couldn't be seen and there was lots of dead ground. The squadron waited and sent out a couple of motorbikes on recces. They moved around trying to find routes, trying to find possible attack points – and the enemy. Vehicles stopped and sent foot patrols into the high ground. It was all about dominating the ground.

Behind the squadron commander were the mortar crews; while all this activity was going on we were just sitting in the back of the wagon drinking tea and in Nosh's case picking his nose. The mortar fire controllers were up front with the lead elements of the squadron; as soon as any attack came, they could start calling down the mortar fire and we would swing into action. As they moved forward, they were doing their own tactical appreciation and giving prominent areas identification marks.

The forward elements were bang onto the enemy. I heard firing, then on the net came, 'Contact, contact. Wait out.'

As soon as we heard it we jumped out of our vehicles and started getting the mortars rigged up. We knew the direction of advance, we knew where the troops were. We pointed the mortars in that general direction, waiting for precise co-ordinates.

Our job was to get the maximum amount of fire down on the enemy, to suppress their fire, make sure they didn't go anywhere, and kill as many as possible. Then, when the rest fought through the position there'd be hardly anybody left to resist.

The vehicles were manoeuvring, trying to get their heavy machine-guns to bear on the enemy position. Not everybody was engaged in the firefight; some were held back in reserve in case we started losing people at the front. The squadron commander was giving orders on the net, telling

different troops what he wanted them to do. The principles hadn't changed since the Charge of the Light Brigade.

While the firefight was going on, people were manoeuvring, under cover from our fire and the physical terrain, into positions close to the enemy. Some movement was on foot, some was a combination of foot and vehicle, it all depended on the terrain. Whatever, we had to get that fire down.

Mortars work by the angle of the barrel and the amount of energy supplied by the explosive charge on the mortar round. There are seven bands of propellant. If the mortar fire controller says 'Charge three', that means there's three bags of propellant, which, with the angle of the barrel, provides its range. What it does at the other end depends on what fuse is set – airburst, delayed, instantaneous, or it might be smoke.

The MFC reported that the enemy were troops in buildings: that meant I had to put a delay fuse on the rounds. They would go into the building then explode: the earth would be churned up and their defences would collapse, hopefully taking them out in the process.

As I looked up to the high ground I could see the squadron commander getting people into position, but it was no good them attacking until the firefight had been won and all enemy fire was suppressed – as we were about to do.

The troops who were going to attack got into the FAP (*final assault position*). The suppressing fire would be 'switched', which meant that it still went down, but was moved along, so that as our blokes were advancing towards the target we weren't firing on them. All this had to be co-ordinated by the squadron commander, who could either see things visually for himself or was getting the information on the radio. We couldn't see jack shit, we would just fire on command.

Nosh and Steve were getting the mortar sorted out and waiting for direction and elevation. The MFC, working on

a small, handheld computer, shouted: 'Immediate action! Direction 164!'

Nosh shouted: 'Direction 164!'

From the No. 2 came the confirmation, 'Direction 164!'

The MFC called: 'Elevation 1228!'

Nosh: 'Elevation 1228!'

Next mortar: 'Elevation 1228!'

As soon as all the bearings were done on the sight, Nosh shouted, 'Number One ready!'

Then we heard, 'Number Two ready!'

They were set commands and standard actions, though slightly different from the rest of the army's. I was listening for a command about charges.

'Two rounds, charge three! Standby!'

I shouted, 'Two rounds, charge three!'

I prepared the ammunition, and Steve took it and waited for the command to throw it down the tube.

Everything was going incredibly smoothly on our tube. We had the elevation and the bearing, we had the lot. We were all ready.

'Number one, fire!'

We threw two rounds each down the tube to 'bed in' the weapon. When a mortar goes off, it starts burying itself in the ground. We all stand on the plate at this stage to help it bed in. If the baseplate isn't correctly set, the mortar bounces around and the ammunition goes off-target. The next rounds, once the baseplate was buried into the ground, would be on target.

We got another fire order, and complied.

Then we saw the mortar fire controller running and shouting out.

I said, 'What the fuck's the matter with him?'

Nosh said, 'Who gives a fuck – let's just go with him.'

I didn't have a clue what was happening, but if he was running, I was running. Then I realized: he must be running away from the line of the mortar. I looked up and saw the mortar round, going straight up in the air and then

disappearing from view – so chances were it was going to come straight down.

Everybody's feet sprouted wings. I could see the squadron head shed on the high ground. They, too, started to leg it. The motorbikes roared away. None of them knew what was happening, but they all knew there was a problem. When there are problems with live ammunition, you get out of the way.

We were still running when the mortars landed about 100 metres behind us. They exploded, but nobody was hurt.

The mortar fire controller had a severe voluntary contribution – which the SSM loved because it boosted up the cabbage – and an even more severe hard time from us for the rest of the trip.

We did some more jumping. By now I was really getting into the swing of the ice-cream troop business, ripping off my jumpsuit as soon as I landed, putting on shorts and walking around eating crisps, waiting for the next jump.

Then we had to start the serious stuff. We were sitting on the desert airstrip one morning, waiting for the C130 to fly up from Muscat.

The terrain was totally different from the original camp; gentle, undulating dunes that were nice and fluffy to land on. Little forts and watchtowers sat on the hilltops; villages looked like something out of the Crusades. History was all around me. I thought, this is the life, this is what I've been after all these years.

John said: 'We're going to get a bundle ready. What we want to do tonight is a full troop night jump from twenty-five grand.'

We were sitting around the tailgate; it was six o'clock and the sun was setting.

'On the bundle I want Steve, Andy and Mat.'

This was good. It was the first time that I'd ever jumped with a bundle; I'd followed them before, but I'd never jumped with one.

There were three of us on the bundle, which was on a trolley. As soon as the green light showed, everybody would pile out on top of each other, really close. The container would go just slightly before the team.

We sat facing the oxygen consoles, in full kit, bergens between our legs, ready to attach behind our arse when we jumped. The aircraft took off and circled the DZ, gaining height.

I checked the altimeter on my arm: 20,000 feet. We got the command to rig our kit up. I pushed the bergen behind me and attached it by hooks to my harness. Now we were waiting for the command to go up towards the tailgate. When it was time to jump we took the oxygen off the main console and put it onto our own bottle. All the commands were on flash cards; nobody could speak because we were on oxygen. I watched the ramp start to come down.

On the command, we moved to the rear like a line of ducks, shuffling from foot to foot, weighed down by the parachute, oxygen kit and bergen – well in excess of 150lbs. The GPMG I was carrying added another 24lbs. I was on the left-hand side of the bundle. Steve was on the other side and Mat was at the back. We pushed it on its trolley towards the tailgate; about six inches from the edge of the tailgate there were chocks which stopped it falling over the edge. We stood there holding it in position. The rest of the troop moved right up onto the tailgate itself. The front people had their toes on the edge; everybody was bunched up, really close to each other, because we all had to get out at the same time. With us were three blokes from A Squadron who'd finished a team job in the Middle East, heard we were getting in some freefall, and gave up their free time to come and join in.

Steve was bent over, ready to push out the container. We were waiting for the two-minute warning, which would signal that we were on the run-in.

All of a sudden the load-master held up two fingers and everybody was banging the next man and showing two

fingers. I tapped Steve and he nodded his head. The loadie was holding the paracord that was retaining the two chocks, ready to pull when it was time for the bundle to go. Everybody was tensed up on the tailgate, looking at the red lights either side. As soon as they went green everybody would shout, 'Ready, set, go!' It had to be as loud as you could yell to get above the noise of the aircraft, wind and the oxygen mask.

The aircraft started doing corrections, jocking us around. We had to hold on to keep standing. The loadie gave the cutthroat sign and did a circle in the air, which meant he'd got the wrong track, so we were going to go around and try again.

I tapped Steve again and gave him the cutthroat sign; he nodded. Then he put his head back down and I put my head back down. We were bracing ourselves; we knew the aircraft would have to do some quite steep turns.

The wind was rushing in and it was cold. I saw lights now and again from distant towns.

Steve was resting his helmet on the bundle; everybody was tired because we had all our kit on and it was a pain in the arse, holding on to each other for balance as the aircraft moved position. Then the two-minute warning came again and everybody sorted themselves out, getting ready to go.

I tapped Steve but got no reaction. I gave him a shake and nothing happened. I couldn't figure it out – then I thought: shit! I lunged across the bundle, grabbed hold of his oxygen bottle and checked the reservoir gauge. It was showing red.

I grabbed hold of the loadie, shook him, and started pointing at the reservoir gauge on my bottle and pointing at Steve. He got on the net and straightaway the aircraft went into a steep nosedive.

The tailgate was coming up. The troop was looking around and within seconds everybody realized what was going on. The oxygen NCO came screaming up, dragging him back to the main console. Steve was lying on the floor,

on just about his last breath. The NCO pulled the tube from Steve's reservoir and put it into the main console. He was flapping good style, his eyes like goldfish bowls; the oxygen bottles were his responsibility.

The aircraft came down below 12,000 feet and we were out of the danger zone. The jump was aborted, but the aircraft couldn't land in the dark at the airstrip we should have been dropping onto, so we had to go and stay in a smart hotel in Muscat, which was a blow.

The hotel had a wonderful restaurant with indoor palm trees, a pianist tinkling away in the corner and nice crisp tablecloths. All the diners were dressed up in suits and ties, and long evening dresses. Enter Air Troop in their flying suits, hair sweaty and sticking up after being under a helmet all night.

We ate in sombre mood, until Mat said, 'Don't worry, it won't have affected Steve – he was brain damaged anyway.'

It turned out Steve had been issued with a defective bottle. He obviously got a slagging the next day, and was branded a big-time wanker for trying to get out of the jump.

I was fascinated by the local customs, and wondered if what I thought I was seeing was necessarily what was happening. They might be drinking Coca-Cola, chewing Wrigley's gum and driving air-conditioned Land Cruisers, but their whole way of thinking was very different. We sat down and drank tea with these people. The Regiment was the least racist group of people in the British Army I had ever met, no doubt because they came from so many different backgrounds, religions, classes and nationalities. Nobody was ever derogatory about indigenous populations. How could we be running around with local guerrillas, for example, if we were thinking, what a bunch of dickhead hillbillies? Nine times out of ten, their cultures are much more established than ours, and they're more true

to their origins. We're just slags compared with a lot of the people that westerners consider backward, Third World and dirty. We're putting our Pepsi and Levi culture in comparison with theirs, which might be older and wiser. At least when it comes to holding beliefs they're not like us, as flexible as Access cards.

The Omanis had feasts called *haflas* where they'd bring a goat in and cook it in the fire. It was always a fantastic gathering. They'd turn up in their Land Cruisers in the middle of nowhere, put the carpets out, and start a fire up. Sometimes they'd tow in a small water bowser as well. There was a huge amount of ritual involved; the animal was treated with immense respect before it was killed, in accordance with Islam.

I really used to enjoy sitting there and pigging out. Western protocol didn't exist; everybody sat down, ate, then just stood up and walked away. Once you were finished, you were finished.

We had a whip-round one day to buy some meat. Everybody chipped in three rials and off the boys went to market. We were sitting on the carpets in the late afternoon, building up the fire, when we heard a familiar chug and a Toyota pick-up appeared in a cloud of dust. Roped down in the back was our meal for the night, a young and very pissed-off-looking camel.

The rituals were observed and the meat was chopped up. Some was hung up to dry in the sun to make camel jerky, and the rest was soon in the pot. Within an hour, out came the camel and rice. There were a hundred of us, sitting under the stars on ten carpets joined together; each of us had a huge plateful, and just sat around and spun the shit for the rest of the night.

The Omanis, like all locals everywhere, wanted to show us their culture; they wanted us to see that there was a bit of finesse about what they were doing. It might have looked basic, but it wasn't. There was an art in how to squeeze the rice, and how to choose the best bits of meat. In

some of the old villages down in the south they had their own culinary delight; sausages made in goat's gut. The meat was prepared in a very interesting way. Basically, the old girls took mouthfuls of goat meat and chewed it until it was soft and gooey, then spat it into the sausage skins. They twisted them into sections just like British bangers, and then cooked them. When I was offered one, I wished I hadn't seen the old girls in action. But I had to take it, there was no way I could turn it down.

By the end of the trip the SSM had made a fortune out of everybody, and now it was time to spend it. 'We'll have a big barbecue down at the beach club in Muscat,' he announced.

The local expats' rugby team was invited to have a game with us and we all moved down to Muscat for the last few days. We won the match and as it came to last light we hit the beach club. There were fridges full of beer, and five or six big barbecues burning away. Everybody was determined to spend all the cabbage that had been extorted from us.

We heard a few local stories. Down at Seeb there was a military base, with an old Arab storeman who'd lost an eye and a leg. He was retired from the army but ran the blanket stores to keep his interest in life. The camp was full of young recruits, and what they tended to do at weekends was roll up their mattresses and hitch a lift back up into the hills where they'd come from, near Niswa.

One day the storeman offered a young lad a lift. The recruit staggered back to the camp a few hours later and alleged that the old boy had raped him.

A British company commander was taking orders that day. He called the lad in and listened to his story, then got the old storeman in for his version of events. Then he called both of them back in and passed sentence.

The storeman was sent to military prison for a long term.

Then the officer turned to the young lad and said, 'Look at the state of the man who attacked you: he's old, he's

knackered, he's got one eye and one leg, and you're a young, strong man. Basically you didn't put up enough of a struggle.' And he sentenced him to six weeks in jail as well.

Towards the end of the night the SM was running around again. 'Slow down on the drink, we'll take some of this back to the UK!'

He was told: 'Fuck off! We're going to drink it.'

Things were starting to get out of control. The civvy rugby team started a fight with our team, so there was fisticuffs all over the beach. Then the nurses arrived. An invitation had gone out to all the European nurses who worked in the city; as they started coming down the steps towards the beach club there were shouts of, 'Piss off!' They walked off in disgust, as one would.

The SM closed down the barbecues and bars and everybody got their head down on the beach. Tiny woke up on the sand in the morning and said, 'I'm bored.'

The squadron were assembled and the SM said, 'That's the last time we have a squadron do when we leave anywhere. It got totally out of control.'

Some of the senior blokes stood up and said, 'What do you fucking expect? You tear the arse out of the VCs, you tear the arse out of the cost of the drinks, then we're told it's for a party, and when we have the party, you're running around trying to stop us enjoying ourselves.'

We came back to the UK and were told we had the weekend off, but were to be in the squadron interest room for eight o'clock on the Tuesday morning because the CO wanted to talk to us. We thought he was going to say, 'Well done, lads, good trip.'

The colonel walked in, followed by the SM and squadron OC. 'I've got a letter here that I want you to listen to,' he said. He read it; it came from Cabinet level, and it was complaining about noisy and unruly behaviour at the beach club in Muscat. There must have been some very well-connected expats there that night.

When he had finished, the colonel turned to the SM and said, 'Right, you've got the sack.'

He turned to the OC and said, 'The only reason you're being left here is because I've got nobody to replace you.'

Then he turned to us and said, 'They're looking at disbanding B Squadron. If that happens, you're all in the shit.' Then he walked off. Fuck, I thought, I've only been in twelve months and I'm out on my ear.

19

I went home and told Debbie all about it. By now we had a quarter and she had settled in well. She had a job in Hereford and was enjoying being back in the UK. I, however, was still busy messing up the marriage. I couldn't see past the end of my own selfish nose; my priority was finding out what time the singlies were going down town for a night out. I had everything I could have asked for – the Regiment and a partner to share the benefits of that with – and I was screwing it up.

'It's outrageous, ' I said to her, describing the CO's threat. 'It could all be over.'

'Oh, that was interesting,' she said, miles away. 'I'm off to work now.'

As I watched her drive away it dawned on me that she had her own life now. Maybe, by being back, I was an embuggerance to her. But there was no time to dwell on such thoughts or try to sort anything out: there were phone calls to be made, a night on the town to be organized.

We went to her sister's flat for the weekend, staying in the spare bedroom. The flat was above her mum's greengrocer's shop, and to get in or out we had to go through the shop and up two flights of stairs. At night, the door was locked and her sister kept the keys. All day Saturday I had a strong sense of unease, a feeling of something not being right. I couldn't work it out, but that night, as we were getting ready for bed and I heard her sister locking up, I

thought: it's because I'm being locked in. I don't want that door to be locked and somebody else to have the key. And then it hit me: it wasn't the door, it was me. I was in a marriage that was going nowhere, because I had never given it a chance – and I didn't feel any inclination to start now. But if I carried on, all I'd be doing was screwing about with her life. The instant I'd had the thought, I said, 'Debbie, I've got something to tell you. I don't really want to be here.'

She looked up from the dressing table and smiled. 'OK, we'll leave in the morning then. We can't really leave tonight, it's too late.'

'No, no. You don't understand. I want to *go*. I want to leave everything.'

'What?' The smile slipped from her face as she realized what I was saying. She started to cry. It made me feel even more of a shit, but I thought, if it's got to be done, let's get it done before we get into the realms of children.

I left there and then. I threw a few things in a bag, went downstairs to the first floor window, and jumped. I only ever saw her once again after that.

I moved into the block, and started to save money to put a deposit on a house. It was hard going as I was not yet getting Special Forces pay. Not many people lived in; most who did were like me, or had their families elsewhere, or were simply new members of the squadron looking for somewhere to live. The room was small and my kit was everywhere. A friend gave me a kettle; with a pack of tea bags and a pint of milk on the window ledge, that was me sorted. I was running a Renault 5, no MOT and no dashboard. I'd had to take it off to sort out the wiring one day and had never really got round to putting it back on.

In late 1985, I heard that I was going away. In one way this was helpful. It meant I'd be away from the situation, and therefore, to my immature way of thinking, that meant the situation would go away. On the other hand, I was

severely pissed off about where I was going. From what I'd heard, it was the absolute pits.

Belize, we were told at the briefing, was formerly the colony of British Honduras and lay on the Caribbean coast of Central America. About the size of Wales, it had a population of 170,000 – mostly black English speakers – but there was also a growing number of Spanish-speaking refugees from El Salvador.

In the eighteenth century, the British in Jamaica had begun logging hardwood on the mainland. By 1840, the territory had become a colony. Guatemala claimed that it had inherited the territory from Spain, but nevertheless signed a treaty with Britain in 1859, recognizing British sovereignty and agreeing on the border. However, a clause in the treaty stated that the parties had to build a road through the jungle from Guatemala to the Caribbean coast. The road had never happened, and on that basis Guatemala claimed that the 1859 treaty was invalid. The government even inserted a clause into the 1945 constitution stating that British Honduras was in fact part of Guatemala, much as the Argentinians had with the Falklands.

In the 1960s, as other British colonies in the Caribbean moved towards independence, Guatemala turned up the heat. In 1963, they massed troops along the border and Britain sent forces to repel any invasion. British troops had been there ever since.

In 1972, Guatemala had again assembled troops along the border, and this time Britain sent the *Ark Royal* and several thousand men. In 1975, after yet another threat, we installed a squadron of RAF Harriers.

Finally, in 1980, Guatemala agreed to recognize Belize, but only if the famous road was built. There were riots in Belize; people were killed. The treaty wasn't ratified and Guatemala went back to refusing to recognize its neighbour. Britain had kept a small garrison in Belize ever since as a permanent deterrent against incursions,

and we were going there as part of that force.

The maps consisted of vast areas of closely packed contour lines, which were hills, covered in green, which was jungle. There were no proper roads, and very few tracks. As I was to discover for myself, there were still open sewers in the towns, and a lot of the locals were none too friendly. One of the lads in the unit before us had got his arm chopped off in a mugging.

The British presence amounted to something like an infantry battalion plus all the support – Harrier jump jets, artillery, the lot. And part of that was an outfit called F Company, basically a dozen Regiment and SBS blokes. It had quickly been renamed F Troop after the comedy series about a US cavalry unit in the Wild West, manned by a load of bumbling old idiots.

I turned up in July. There were people there that I already knew, like Solid Shot, Jock, and Johnny Two-Combs, though Two-Combs was due to return to the UK soon.

'You'll hate this place,' were his words of welcome.

He was right. To a man, we loathed the garrison on sight. Our rooms were in semicircular tin huts with no air-conditioning, a really good idea in Central America. The first thing we did was go and buy fans that then stayed on for the whole tour. In the rooms there were two metal lockers and two beds, and that was it. I shared a room with Solid Shot. The first evening there we lay on our beds putting the world to rights and thinking of ways to make our fortunes. Outside we could hear 'Des Doom' hammering the 'face of the day' on the punch-bag. Des's arms and chest were covered with tattoos. 'When I was single,' he said, 'my chat-up line was: "If you don't find me interesting, you can always read me." ' He was due to get out; he'd decided he wanted to pursue other things after only four years in the Regiment. This was deemed to be disloyal and he'd been sent to Belize for the whole duration of B Squadron's tour. He was severely bitter and twisted about it and forever on the bag; he always had many faces to 'talk to'.

There was a swimming-pool but that was put out of bounds because someone had shit in it one night in protest about the timings that favoured the 'families of' not the rest of the garrison. Apart from the punch-bag, the only training facilities consisted of some catering-size baked-bean cans, filled with concrete with an iron bar stuck into each of them to form makeshift weights.

F Troop was part of a garrison and all the bullshit that that entailed. Our hut was part of the sergeants' mess, but unless we were a Regiment corporal or above we couldn't use it, even though we were still expected to pay the monthly fee the mess claimed.

The team were therefore split into two groups, those who could go in the mess and those that couldn't, and I hadn't joined the Regiment for that sort of bullshit. Tiny was with us for three weeks, filling in space between changeovers. Being a regimental corporal, he could have gone in the sergeants' mess but chose to come down to the cookhouse with us low life – but then that was stopped. In the end, just four of us lepers would walk down to the cookhouse; in fact it turned out for the best as they used to put on a great Gurkha curry.

Part of F Troop's job was to be first response unit if a commercial or military aircraft went down in the jungle. We would be the ambulance brigade, steaming in with all the emergency equipment and medical aid kit in a Puma. Having stabilized any casualties, we would then establish a base and try to enable other helis to get in, which might entail anything from blowing winch holes to creating full-size landing sites.

Our entry into the crash site would not necessarily be straightforward. We would hope to get in where the aircraft had crashed as the ground might now be flattened, but what if it was still a ball of flame, or just a light aircraft? We therefore had to practise abseiling into the jungle and getting in all the emergency equipment that would be needed.

There were four of us on standby at any given time; the rest went patrolling in the jungle for a week or two. I hated being in the camp almost as much as I loved being in the jungle. There was nothing to do in the camp apart from going for a run, then waiting for the most exciting event of the day, tea and toast at 11 a.m.

I had a definite feeling of: what have I done wrong to be here for the next five months? We felt like social outcasts. I'd wondered why people tried to avoid being sent here at all costs; I now knew the reason.

One of the small reliefs from the boredom was practising entry into a crash site. It required enough kit to fill two Land Rovers: five-gallon jerrycans of water, medical equipment, a generator, lights, food, shelters – everything we would need to get on site and start to sort these people out – plus our own bergens.

On practice days we drove down and met the pilots by the Puma. At this time of the year the main topic of conversation was what crews were going to be on standby over Christmas, as they wanted to book a car and drive to Cancun for the holiday.

The pilot would say to me, the sucker with the kit, 'Same place?'

'Why not,' I'd reply, 'we have to keep the troops entertained.'

They would stand there drinking a Coke and watch us load all the equipment, rig up the ropes, put our harnesses on and sit in the heli; we'd then wait for the rotors to wind up and cool us down. The weather only ever did one of two things: it was either pissing down with rain, or scorching hot. The Royal Engineers would be coming out of their own little camp they had made for themselves; using all their skills they had constructed a bar and barbecue area with chairs and benches, and without a doubt it was the most organized area on the camp. I wished at times like this that I'd stayed at school and got some O levels.

Off we went flying around Belize for a while, doors open

and enjoying the view and the cool wind. The heli came to a hover at 150 feet above the football pitch, and the Engineers, dressed in shorts and flip-flops, and by now on their second bottle of ice-cold Coke, had their scorecards ready.

The first two at the door got ready and I threw the jungle penetrators out. One of the blokes was Terry, an ex-Royal Marine now in Mountain Troop, and known among other things as Fat Boy. Not because he was, but he had the largest chest I'd ever seen. He was about 5'10" and built like a brick shithouse. One of the downsides of working with the SBS – come to that, all Royal Marines – was that they seemed always to be tall and good looking. This made us come across like a bag of shit. We decided that Fat Boy had come to the Regiment instead of the SBS because he would have failed their Good Looks Selection; his face looked as if life had been chewing on it.

The other man, in the opposite door, was the troop senior, Joe Ferragher. Joe was a monster of a man, 16 stone, and over 6'. He was very quiet; it was like getting blood out of a stone to get him to talk sometimes, but when he did there was no stopping him. He was the gentle giant, except for one occasion when travellers took over his house while he was away. Joe went to visit them on his return, and after ten minutes they decided that they didn't want to exercise their squatters' rights after all. To show that there were no hard feelings, Joe sent flowers to all of them in hospital.

A 'jungle penetrator' is basically a heavy sack containing a rope inserted in such a way that it doesn't tangle. Because it has a weighted bottom, it smashes into the canopy and allows you to work your way to the ground. Once the 200-foot abseiling rope was on the ground, Joe and Fat Boy would start to ease themselves out of the heli so that their feet were on the deck and their bodies were at 45 degrees to the ground.

The abseiler is attached to the rope by a figure-of-eight device. He remains locked in position until he pulls up

some slack from beneath him and feeds it into the figure-of-eight; the best position is one that gives least resistance to the rope as it travels through, and that is a crucifix position with the body parallel to the ground and arms running along the rope, hopefully controlling it. If there is a drama the man on the ground pulls down on the rope, locking the figure-of-eight.

The first two down did not have that luxury. Out they went, the weight of the rope making it extremely hard to pull up enough slack. The effect was the same as if someone was on the ground pulling the rope, which was why Fat Boy and Joe went first: it took a lot of aggression. Sometimes it all went to ratshit and people landed up banging into the heli and getting caught up. This was a quite funny sight, especially if they then started to lose control of the rope and got to the ground with lumps all over their heads and hands that looked as if they'd been in a toaster.

The Engineers were by now giving points for style.

'Not as good as the team last month, but the heli has stayed in the hover better,' they were probably saying as they went for their third Coke and changed position for a better tan.

Once the boys were down they would man the ropes and control the kit that was to follow. We would rig it the same as if it was a body and then heave it out one at a time after the count of three. We tried a different method every time but it was just reinventing the wheel; we decided the best way was to grab it and just throw it out. Once all that was done we followed; the heli would then leave and get back to base as soon as possible – like us the pilots were hoping to get back for 4 p.m. tea and toast, the second most exciting thing to happen in camp. The Land Rovers would come and pick us up; the Royal Engineers would drag their chairs back to their lair.

'Not as fast as D Squadron when they were here, but there you go. Shall we have another Coke?'

The rest of the time, we'd go out and patrol, gathering

information and basically preparing for if the Guats invaded. We'd go as maybe a four- or six-man patrol, dropped in by helicopter, and spend ten to fourteen days on different tasks in and around the border. I loved it.

The only local industries seemed to be grapefruit, marijuana, whoring, and supplying and working for the British Army. I was told that a third of Belize's income came from cannabis. Apparently there used to be big frenzies where the police would go over and burn a couple of fields just so that the government could say, 'That's it, we're fighting the drug problem.' But for every field they burned, there were another twenty left. It brought in revenue, so there was no way they were going to destroy it. We had nothing to do with countering the drugs problem in Central America; everybody just accepted it as part of business that went on in that part of the world.

About an hour away from our camp on a dirt road lived Gilbert. He was an Indian with a smallholding that fed his large family. To help him make ends meet he would come into the jungle with us and help build shelters and teach helicopter crews and Harrier pilots jungle survival; if they were still living once they'd creamed in, they could keep themselves ticking over until we got there. He would also come with us when we trained NCOs of the new battalion manning the garrison in jungle tactics so that they could teach their men. Belize was an operational posting and the battalion had a hard job ahead of them. This was the good part of the tour for us as at least we did achieve something.

Gilbert's house was built from breeze-blocks, corrugated iron, and noise. Inside was just one very big room, with a curtain dividing off his bedroom from the two double beds that housed his eight children. The running water was a hosepipe connected to a main; the outside toilet was a pit. He always made us welcome with coffee and some food; we would take a bottle of Famous Grouse to return the hospitality. He had lived in and around the jungle all of his life and there were always new things that he could show

us. We drove up to see him about a course that was going to be happening and started talking about the amount of drugs that seemed to leave Belize for the US.

He said, 'People do not see it as a problem here. If they want to use it, fine – people here are more than happy to make money from it. If you go thirty minutes further along this road it becomes very good, no potholes and each side is cleared of trees and bush. This is where the drugs are picked up. They mark the road with cars and it's used as a runway. At night you can hear the planes coming in to pick it up. Who cares? If America wants to use drugs, let them.'

It was a relief to get away from that sort of stuff. In the bergen we'd carry just enough food for the duration of the patrol. We had just one main scoff a day, which normally consisted of rice or pasta, something that was dehydrated that we'd add water to – as in all jungles, there was no problem here with water.

As my dry clothing, I took a pair of trainers, a pair of socks, a camouflage T-shirt and a pair of OG (*olive green*) shorts – Fifties khaki National Service Far East shorts that look like something out of *It Ain't Half Hot Mum*. I had a space blanket to wrap around me at night, a poncho and hammock, and that was it. The less I had to carry, the less knackered I would get.

Beltkit consisted of spare magazines, a TACBE (*tactical beacon radio*) per man, water, first-aid kit, and emergency rations. On my beltkit I used to carry three water bottles – six pints of water – but would continually fill them up anyway, always adding Steritabs for decontamination. The water tasted shit and tea made with it tasted no better. Part of the SOPs (*Standard Operating Procedures*) was that every man carried a 15-metre loopline (*inch-thick nylon webbing strap*) and carabiner. We had to cross a lot of rivers; the first man put the snap-link around him with the loopline and swam like a man possessed over to the other side. He rigged up the loopline and everybody else came over with

their kit attached to it. The rivers were incredibly swollen and screamed along.

On my body all the time were my two syrettes of morphine, my golock, my watch, my Silva compass, and my map. My golock hung on a bit of paracord around my waist, and was now a Gurkha khukri rather than the British army issue, known as a tree-beater, which was no good to man nor beast; all it did was beat the tree up, it didn't really cut it. Indigenous people in the jungle use a golock where the top of the blade is heavier, so that the momentum of the blade does the cutting. Most people tended to use the old Iban-type of golock, or, like me, a khukri. They had a nice heavy bit at the top, and could slice through trees like a chainsaw.

Kit-for-task included the patrol radio and medical pack. If we were doing anything around the border – putting an observation post in, say – all the materials for that would have to be taken in as well.

High humidity combined with sweltering heat meant that in theory there was a definite limit to how much kit a man could carry; the maximum should have been around fifteen kilograms, but it could be much more. Mess tins were thrown away, because they were pretty useless things anyway. All that was needed was a metal mug, and a small non-stick frying pan, ideal for boiling rice.

The most popular weapon to take into the jungle was the M16 or 203. They rarely needed cleaning, so we didn't have to waste time and energy trying to keep our weapon in good condition.

One bloke never used to touch his M16 at all, out of principle. He said, 'I know that it's going to work, I know that the weapon's reliable, so I don't need to clean it.' And the fact is, if you squeeze the trigger and it goes bang and a round comes out of the end, that's all you want.

There were some practices in the jungle which new-comers perceived as bone, when in fact they weren't. One of them concerned headbands; in the normal army such

fashion accessories were perceived as lairy – big-time and Rambo-ish. But moving through the jungle meant losing a lot of body fluids. Your face was covered with cam cream and mozzie rep, and if it ran into your eyes it stung fearsomely and attacked your vision: not advisable if you're out there as scout. Hence the headbands.

Every time we walked into a village near the border the locals would scatter. The Guats used to come over the river and steal their women at gunpoint, and to the villagers one set of jungle camouflage looked very like another because they couldn't see the pattern for mud and wet.

The villages were little more than a collection of wooden huts. Pigs wallowed in puddles of mud, chickens and children ran between the huts or on the small football pitch that every village had. The kids didn't care if we were Guats or Brits; they always came up, hoping we were going to give them something. I loved them; they didn't understand us and we didn't understand them, but we had some good fun. Some villages were just starting to get electricity on a generator, and visits from American Peace Corps volunteers. Like modern-day missionaries, these fresh-faced twenty-year-olds were bringing in hygiene and preventive medicine, and the lot of the villagers was improving – or so the volunteers said. The fact was, these people had lived like this for hundreds of years. They now had new illnesses, a new culture and religion. The soul of these villages had been dragged away to the town. The kids now wanted to wear Levis and smoke American cigarettes. As soon as they were old enough, they left.

First stop on our visit was always the headman. We'd go up, shake his hand, and say, 'Hello, mate, all right then? How's it going? Any chance of using your hut, or what?' He, too, would start gobbing off, probably taking the piss. His hut would also be the local town hall, and we were usually welcome to put up there for the night – in exchange for a magazine or something from the rations. Using that as

a base, we'd do our little hearts and minds bit. As soon as the villagers realized we weren't Guats but friendly Brits with a party-size medical pack, they'd be turning up with babies and young kids with coughs and runny noses, and old men with sores and cuts. Although we were carrying loads of medical equipment, we had to be careful in what we dispensed. These people were not used to western drugs yet; give a bloke two aspirins and he'd be flat on his back. Half of what we gave them was placebo, a spoonful of water that we pretended was a magic concoction. Throw it down the baby's neck and the mother was happy.

The long wooden hut with a grass roof would house a whole family, from grandparents to babies. In one corner there would be a mud cooker and a sheet of metal that was used as the grill. This was where the tortillas were cooked; the basic food was corn that they grew by burning down the jungle and spending weeks clearing. Coming in and out would be small pigs, chickens and more kids. The hut would be thick with smoke, both wood and cigarette.

The villagers lived an incredibly basic lifestyle, but I enjoyed being allowed to share a little of it. I got a buzz out of going back to a village six weeks later and seeing that an injury I'd sutured up had healed, or that a kid who had been on her back with croup was running around on the football pitch again.

We weren't there entirely to patch up their injuries and illnesses, of course. While I was treating them I'd be asking about the Guats and whether any of them had been over. We slowly built up relationships, and over the period of a tour we would come to recognize each other. Besides giving us information, they'd give us useful tips about the jungle, such as where the fish were hiding, and which were the best plants to boil up and eat.

We did a lot of liaison work with the Harriers. Part of our job in the event of hostilities would have been calling in air strikes on predesignated targets on the other side of the border, such as power stations and desalination plants. We

would go in, mark the targets, and talk the Harriers in. We spent a lot of time practising on the net with the pilots, because it was quite difficult to bring an aircraft in over the canopy. We used air-marker balloons, which penetrate the canopy and leave an orange balloon stuck up above the tree line as an identification marker, and would then talk them on from that.

Being an idle fucker, I liked jungle living. There were only two bits of kit to look after – wet and dry. Most of the time we were sitting down, brewing up and drinking tea with the locals. But best of all, we weren't spending money. I still didn't have enough money to put a deposit on the house, so I was using this trip to save up every penny I could. To save on stamps I wasn't writing home to anybody, and there were no letters coming back.

Sandy had come into the Regiment a year after me. He was a public schoolboy who went wrong somewhere and joined the army as a tom. I knew he was clever because he used a fountain pen to write letters with. He was about my age and height, and was very into the weights. He wasn't massive but he had a male model's physique, which annoyed me. Luckily he had really horrible hair, like a mass of rusty wire wool. He was having déjà vu, having just spent six months in Belize with his battalion before going for Selection, and was mightily pissed off. He said it was even more boring for him than last time round.

I'd first met him when we were freefalling at Brize Norton. He had a mid-air collision with one of the instructors; as they both fell to earth with their canopies like a bag of washing, I saw Sandy start kicking to get out of the tangle. As he landed and sorted himself out he said, 'Fair one,' and left it at that. He knew he couldn't put the blame on the instructor as they would close ranks. He had only been 200 feet from creaming in.

Sandy and I came in off a two-week patrol around the border and after sorting our weapons out we headed straight for the shower rooms for the big degunging

process. You take everything in with you – all your clothes, all the kit that you've used, your webbing, your beltkit, and you just dump it in the shower and scrub it all clean. When that's done you get yourself sorted out; the priority, as always, is your weapon, your kit, yourself.

There was Sandy and me standing under the cold shower, fully clothed, cleaning our frying pans and other bits and pieces.

'Are we going to sort this wagon for Cancun at Christmas?' I said.

'We'll have to get hold of Joe and find out who's going to be on standby. We can hire a Land Rover and get down there.'

After the kit we showered ourselves with our uniform and boots on, washing our clothing with soap as if we were washing our bodies. Then we took it off, rinsed out our boots, and finally washed ourselves.

Once that was done, the real business started. In the jungle, you get infested with little tics, and you've got big zits on your back and all this sort of shit. Most of them are in places that you can't reach yourself, so your mate has to oblige.

Sandy came out of the shower and said, 'I've got some tics in my back, are you going to get them out for us?'

He bent over the sink while I got up behind him and busied myself with grooming his back, and that's how we were, both in the nude, when an RAF officer came in to use the urinal. He sort of trumpeted like a rogue elephant, did a smart about turn, and marched off to report two homosexuals in the shower block. It was quite funny after the fuss had died down and our explanation had been accepted, and whenever I saw the officer after that I always made a point of blowing him a kiss.

There was a delightful place towards Belize City called Raoul's Rose Garden. The first time I was taken there I was expecting some sort of elegant colonial tearoom with a

pianist and little cucumber sandwiches, but it turned out to be a run-down breeze-block building with rickety tables and chairs and even more rickety whores. It was a typically minging Central American setting. I got bitten by more mozzies inside than outside, and the band played non-stop Central American classics. The one good thing about the Rose Garden was that it was out of bounds to all the squaddies. The young lads would always be trying to get in there or the other whorehouses, and coming back with horrendous syphilis. Sometimes I'd see them coming back from the town, arm in arm with a whore they had fallen in love with – girls who were basically after a quick marriage and a passport to the UK when the unit left.

The Royal Marines were the resident battalion at the time. Every morning at six-thirty, their HQ and support companies would be lined up and doing a 3-mile circuit of the camp. Wandering up the road towards the guardroom would be one of the garrison personnel, like an Ordnance Corps bloke or a REME fitter, hand in hand with some hooker, and the 200 bootnecks would run past and give their marks out of ten.

One young bloke from the Catering Corps married a Central American Indian. She was five feet nothing and stunningly beautiful; in her mind she wasn't a whore, she was just earning money. She went back to the UK as a wife, spent a year in Catterick, and was getting shagged fearsomely by anyone in uniform. Every man and his dog was roaring up this bloke's wife, and she was getting paid for it as well. Obviously the marriage went to ratshit and she came back, resuming her place on the career ladder at Raoul's and passing round the photographs: 'That's me outside the NAAFI in Catterick, and there's me on a day's shopping trip in York.'

Every Friday night, the sergeants' mess of the garrison had a do – an open invite occasion, basically trying to get all the local women to come into the camp. They came in their droves, but it wasn't the music and conversation that

attracted them, it was the offer of chicken and chips at ten o'clock. The local girls dolled themselves up to the nines and tried to look their best for the occasion.

We were lying on our beds, watching the fan go round and round. One of the blokes had got a letter from his kids. They'd done a drawing of them taking the dog for a walk, but it looked more like a man in a noose. 'I need that picture,' I said. 'I want to stick it on the wall, because that's what I'm going to do if I have to stay in Belize any longer – I'm going to fucking hang myself.'

Jock had got a letter from his future wife, telling him that their marriage had been placed on the back burner. He was severely down because there was nothing he could do about it from that distance, so we decided to give him a night out. We made a punch from a couple of bottles of rum and a tin of pineapple chunks, and sat in his room for an hour or two, listening to the party that we were not allowed to go to and putting the world to rights. By about half past eleven everybody was revved up and I suddenly heard myself saying, 'Right, we'll go down to Raoul's.'

We got the admin corporal out of bed and told him to organize a Land Rover. By the time we got there, some people from the sergeants' mess had also turned up, senior ranks with their shirts and ties hanging off, chasing the working girls around the tables.

One of the senior ranks joined in with the band and tried to teach them a Mungo Jerry number. Things got out of hand and the management – Raoul – phoned up the Military Police.

Two young lance corporals arrived and told us we all had to leave. We knew that recruits to the Military Police were immediately given a rank to give them some authority, and we didn't take kindly to these lads of nineteen or twenty saying, 'Can you switch on? Get in the wagon, we'll drive you back to camp.' It was the sensible thing to do, but fuck them.

They knew the sergeants would go, because they weren't

going to risk being gobby to a lance jack who was only doing his job. However, there was no way they were going to take us – we had nothing to do with the garrison people and were not causing any trouble. There was a little bit of a to-do and after about half an hour of listening to the MPs pleading, we relented. They dropped us off outside F Troop lines: the officers' and sergeants' messes were more or less adjacent to each other, and in between was F Troop.

It was incredibly hot this particular night and as soon as we got in we took our clothes off and hung around in our skiddies and flip-flops. My head was spinning. Everybody was sitting on the beds honking about all and sundry, and we finally decided to have a scoff.

I got the hexy burner out on the step, frying up bits of Spam. There was stuff strewn all over the place because everybody was pissed, and by now even the skiddies had come off.

Unfortunately, just as our barbecue party was in full swing, all the officers and their wives started to come out of the mess. The ruperts had an instant monk on because there were these naked squaddies lying on the grass in star shapes, farting and shouting at each other, giggling, pissed, and falling over. Spam was flying everywhere and in places the grass was on fire.

One of the officers came over and said, 'I think you ought to pack this in now.'

Sandy replied, 'I think you ought to fuck off.'

The officer went storming off, and even in my state I had a funny feeling it wasn't the last we'd hear of this.

I woke up in the morning and the place was in shit state. Holding a wet towel around my head I thought, right, we'd better police the joint. Everybody dragged themselves outside with buckets and mops and we transformed the area. Then we had to go and see the bloke who was running F Troop at the time, who just happened to be B Squadron's SM, in Belize for three weeks.

'The shit's hit the fan about this,' he shouted, 'and the fan is not amused.'

It was suggested we make a voluntary contribution to squadron funds. VCs could be anything from a fiver up to hundreds of pounds, depending on how much shit had hit what particular fan. Three of us were awarded £300, two others £250. It was a severe blow, considering that Sandy and I were saving so hard that we were even going around collecting rejected soap fragments out of the washrooms and pressing them all together to make a bar, using other people's razor-blades despite the risk of hepatitis, and salvaging 'stims' – empty bottles from gassy drinks like Coca-Cola or Cherryade – and taking them down to the choggy shop for a refund of two cents a bottle.

I was devastated at the loss of so much money, but as one door closed another door opened. Two weeks later, a money-making opportunity presented itself.

A scaley attached to the Regiment during the time they were operating in the jungles of Borneo now owned a hotel on San Pedro, an island far out in the Keys. He had kept in contact with F Troop, and telephoned one day to say that although San Pedro was a very beautiful place, what was holding the place back as a tourist trap was the fact that the water was sulphurous. However, it had just been discovered that under the layer of lime was the world's supply of fresh water.

'I can't afford to get outside contractors to bore down to it because of the expense of bringing all the machinery over,' the ex-scaley said. 'You don't know anybody handy with explosives, do you?'

Just possibly.

Des, Solid Shot and I went down to the stores and found some old-fashioned engineer's beehive charges, used to make craters in runways. They were rusting and flaking but hopefully would do the business, penetrate the lime, expose the fresh water, and give us all a pay day. One Friday night the three of us boarded a Gemini inflatable

with a Yamaha engine on the back, laden with explosives and fuel: a floating bomb. We got on the river by the airport camp and then navigated down to the coast.

San Pedro was so far away it wasn't visible from the mainland. For navigation we had just an ordinary 1 in 50,000 tourist map; there was this little speck in the middle of the Caribbean which was San Pedro, and we just took a bearing and off we went.

After a few hours we passed a ship en route to Belize City. The captain hailed us and asked if we were all right. 'No problems,' we waved and smiled, trying to cover the beehives and firing cable. We must have looked like terrorists.

'Where are you going?'

'San Pedro.'

He threw his hands in the air and went back into the wheelhouse.

The first place we were trying to find with our map and Silva compass was called Hick's Island. From there we took another bearing, and four hours later, with just one fuel bladder left, we motored into San Pedro. We spotted a body lying in a hammock and said we wanted to find the main quay, which was near the airstrip.

'Well, man,' she said, 'it's like further up there. Nice to see you guys, you know, like – wow.' She had a lovely tattoo of a butterfly on her ankle; pity she was in her late fifties and beaten half to death by the sun.

It was a beautiful island; most of the inhabitants were Americans seeking an alternative lifestyle. The scaley was a little jock with a big white bushy beard. He looked really excited to see us – or maybe it was the two bottles of Famous Grouse we handed over.

We started digging the next day. We had to go down about twelve to fifteen feet to reach the lime layer, but raw materials were at a premium on the island – there weren't any boards or corrugated iron sheets to put up around the sand, and every time we dug down, it caved in. We finally

got down to about two foot above the lime, rigged up the beehive charge, and Des initiated it.

It was a big occasion. All the hippies had gathered around to watch the clever Brits reach down to the first fresh water they'd ever seen on the island. That only made it even more embarrassing when the charge didn't penetrate. We tried again, and then we ran out of explosives.

'I've heard sulphurous water is good for you,' I beamed at the ex-scaley. 'Maybe you could market the place as a spa?'

We had three days walking around the hotel making excuses, then we headed back to the mainland with our tails between our legs. No water, no money.

In the jungle, even a simple cut can become a serious problem. Fungi, parasites and exotic diseases battle to prevent your body from healing. Fat Boy went out on a patrol and came back in shit state. He'd gone down with bilharzia and a liver infection, and looked like a ghost. He was in the military hospital for a long time.

Soon after the San Pedro trip I went back on the border and got an injury on my knee; within days the joint had swollen up like a football covered in scabby zits. When I bent my knee pus oozed out, and I could hear the joints creak.

Before long I had trouble moving at all, and had to be casevac'd out. It was nearly Christmas and I thought, this is all rather nice, I'll be home in time for the Morecambe and Wise show. Casualties had to be escorted back, and I was told that a nurse was being sent over from Woolwich hospital to come and get me. In my mind, I had a vision of a Bo Derek lookalike holding my hand and soothing my brow all the way to Washington, and then on to the UK. By the time we got to Woolwich, I had us practically engaged.

I packed my kit and was all ready to go on the Wednesday night flight. I was lying on my bed when

the nurse arrived and was introduced to me. Bo had aged a lot – and lost a lot of hair and grown a big moustache and beer belly. There wasn't much of a sense of humour about Nigel, either. I got the feeling he belonged to one of those end-of-the-world-is-nigh sects and would retire to San Pedro.

I spent two or three days at Woolwich hospital, but was back in Hereford in time for turkey and Christmas pud. Not long after that, I heard that my offer had been accepted on a house in Hereford: at last, I was a fully fledged, home-owning yuppie. All I needed now was 10,000 more empty Coke bottles and I'd be able to buy something to sit on.

20

It was a two-up, two-down thing, one of those new Westbury-type houses. The asking price was twenty-five grand, but I was feeling really good because, the big-time negotiator, I'd got it down to twenty-four and a half.

The place was very basic and I didn't have the time or money to do anything about it. To save on bills I didn't have the gas reconnected, and boiled water for food with a hexy burner sitting in the stainless steel sink. The kettle came from my room in the block.

Next pay day I got a microwave, so anything that went ping after forty-five seconds, I'd be eating it. I got a telly, then a small stereo, and that was about it, the ultimate singley's place – bare walls, a chair, a bed, and a china ornament of a cat the previous owner had left on the mantelpiece.

The garden was overgrown, and I didn't have a lawn-mower or tools; I had to borrow them from a friend who lived around the corner. I bunged all my washing in the laundry at camp. I had my Sunday dinners at work as well, or I'd go down to the pub that put out trays of sausages, and clear them out. Otherwise, it was Chinese takeaways all the way, collected from the town in my decrepit Renault 5. However, I was happy. I was one of Thatcher's children.

Roundabout Christmas time I got talking in a bar one night with a girl called Fiona. The conversation came round to where we both lived.

'I've bought a house near the camp,' I said, naming the road. 'Number four.'

'I don't believe it!' she laughed. 'I live at number two. You must be my next door neighbour!'

She told me that she came from Hampshire. She'd moved up to Hereford to be with her partner, but the relationship hadn't worked out. She didn't want to go home, so she rented the house and was working in the town.

She was tall, with long brown hair, and very confident. We really enjoyed each other's company and started going out. I thought, this is good news – a new house, a microwave, and now a new girlfriend. What more could I need? But no sooner had we got together than it was announced that the squadron was going to Africa.

The chief opposition force to the apartheid regime in South Africa was the ANC. It had been crippled by the arrest of Nelson Mandela and his colleagues in the early Sixties, but revived after the Soweto riots in 1976. Each time the government banned a moderate black opposition group, the ANC's membership swelled. In 1980, it began a successful bombing campaign, attacking plants manufacturing oil from coal.

In December 1982, the South African military raided Lesotho and killed forty-two members of the ANC in Maseru. In May 1983, a car bomb outside the Ministry of Defence in Pretoria killed nineteen people and injured over 200, including many black civilians. The bombing campaign increased after the 1984–6 riots. There were scores of attacks throughout South Africa, killing many people.

Then, in June 1985, South African forces carried out a raid on Gaborone, the capital of Botswana. Several homes were raided and twelve men, allegedly ANC members, were killed in their sleep. The South African government alleged that Botswana territory was used by ANC guerrillas to launch attacks inside South Africa, including recent mine blasts which had killed white

farmers near the border. Botswana rejected the claims, arguing that it did its utmost to prevent ANC military activities inside its territory.

Botswana appealed to the British for help; the appeal was approved by Foreign Secretary Sir Geoffrey Howe and a Regiment squadron of eighty men was to be sent to train Botswana's soldiers to defend their country against border raids by Big Brother. Selected soldiers from the BDF (*Botswana Defence Force*) would be given special training, including techniques of aggressive counter-attack to neutralize South African raiding parties. We were told the training would take place in the north of the country, well away from the South African border. We would not be involved in any contact with the SADF (*South African Defence Force*).

The Botswana Defence Force's mobility was shortly to be enhanced by the arrival of a number of helicopters to be provided by the US under a $10 million military aid programme. The US was also providing special training in counter-intelligence techniques to the Botswana security forces to offset penetration by South African agents; the skills we taught them would also make it easier for the BDF to detect any counter-infiltration by ANC guerrillas.

We finished our planning and preparation for the job. Everything, we were told, was 'TS' (*top secret*). The squadron would be flying from Brize Norton to Kenya, because that was not an unusual troop movement. From there we'd all be splitting off into little groups, making our way into Botswana by different timings and routes.

We got to Kenya and split up. Six of us stayed in the country for a while; others were going off to other African countries for a few days, before starting to filter into Botswana to our squadron RV. Some of the blokes went off on safaris while they were biding their time; I mooched around with Ben, a Jock who'd just joined the squadron. We went to a place called the Carnivore, a big meat-eating

place where you could eat as much meat as you wanted for about tuppence. I stuffed myself and got food poisoning, and had to spend the next two days in bed.

The six of us finally got on a plane to Zaire. We spent a little time mooching around there, then flew to Zambia. The country was chock-a-block with Russians. They all looked like bad Elvis impersonators from the Seventies, with greased-back hair, sideburns three-quarters of the way down the face, and unfashionable suits and plastic shoes.

We wandered around Zambia departures looking at the Russians, and the Russians were looking at us. They knew who we were, and we knew who they were. The official cover story for us was that we were a seven-a-side rugby team on tour. Nobody questioned us about it, which was probably just as well. I could have been hit over the head with a rugby ball at that time and I wouldn't have had a clue what it was. And the seven-a-side story was a bit dodgy as well, seeing as there were only six of us.

We ended up sharing a small propellered aircraft with three or four Russian 'officials', and a Russian pop music band that was ostensibly travelling around all the military units. The drummer had fallen straight off the cover of the Woodstock album, dressed in flared loons, a headband and a Cat Stevens T-shirt. Judging by the way he was air-drumming on the magazine on his lap, he was no more a drummer than I was JPR Williams.

We eventually got to a small metal airstrip in the middle of Botswana. A few blokes from the squadron were already there; some of them, I could see, were nursing injuries. The squadron OC and Fraser turned up; Fraser had broken his collarbone and was walking around with his arm in a sling. We got in some vehicles and went off to the squadron RV which – inevitably – was an aircraft hangar.

Over the next couple of days the rest of the blokes trickled in from all over the place. Some came in from Zimbabwe, and were in a right state. They'd had a day out in the sun and Toby, better known as Slaphead, having been

bald since he was aged about nine, had gone up on the roof of the hotel and fallen asleep. The front half of his body was totally burnt, and his face and forehead were already starting to peel.

While we were waiting, the ice-cream boys organized an Islander turbo aircraft that could take seven of us at a squeeze, and off we went jumping. We wanted to learn infiltration techniques in that part of the world, going in against not too sophisticated radars. I jumped my arse off over the next three or four days, getting back into the swing of freefall, going up to twelve grand, leaping out and just basically having fun.

On one particular jump I was going out as a 'floater'. An Islander only has small doors, which meant that everybody couldn't exit at the same time. We were only jumping at twelve grand, so it was important to get all seven of us going off at the same time. The technique was for various floaters to climb outside the aircraft and hold on to whatever bits and pieces they could.

I was rear floater, which should have entailed putting my left hand onto the left-hand side of the door, wedging my left foot against the bottom corner of the doorframe and then swinging out and holding on with my right hand to a bit of fuselage. However, I screwed up. As I swung out I lost my footing and fell, going straight into freefall long before the planned exit. To make matters worse, I was over the town.

There was no way I was going to be able to track to get the distance to reach the DZ, so I pulled quite high, hoping I'd be able to use the canopy to go in. With the wind behind me the canopy gave about twenty-five knots, but I was losing too much elevation. Soon I would have to turn back into wind to land. I scanned the ground, trying to sort myself out. There seemed to be nothing below but high-voltage pylons and cars speeding along the roads, then masses of people running out of buildings to look at this little thing dangling from a big blue canopy.

I just managed to clear a line of pylons and hit the street, landing between cars. It was a really bad landing; I hit my arse hard, and the canopy enveloped me. Immediately, hundreds of little hands started tugging at the fabric, shouting and laughing joyously. I had visions of my parachute being ripped to shreds and shouted the first thing that came into my head.

'Okey dokey!'

A hundred voices replied, 'Okey dokey! Okey dokey!'

I rolled the canopy up and sat at the roadside chatting to all my new friends while I waited for a wagon to come and pick me up.

'Okey dokey?'

'Okey dokey!'

The conversation was still going when the vehicle arrived, and for days after that all anybody would say to me was, 'Okey dokey!'

We moved to the camp where we were going to be based. We got our campbeds or airbeds out, spread out our sleeping bags and made our own little world. The camp was an old, run-down group of buildings. Very much like everything else in Africa, the walls had holes in them and the plaster was coming away. We rigged up some lights to the generator and that meant we could read. Fiona had bought me a book called *The Grail Romances*; I'd read *Holy Blood, Holy Grail* just to give me enough information to give Frank Collins a hard time about the religion, and had ended up really gripped by medieval history. Poor Fiona had trooped around hundreds of churches, forts and motte-and-bailey castles with me.

They'd been used to a lot of South African incursions in the area. Basically, the SADF would come out of South Africa, chuck a left, and go up into Angola along the Caprivi strip. There was quite a lot of attention initially when we arrived; people were unsure of what we were and who we were. To these villagers, if there was a white eye and a gun, it meant a South African.

After a while, we'd wake up in the mornings and there'd be hundreds and hundreds of villagers along the fenceline. They'd turned up for freebies. Now and again I gave them the sweets out of the compo rations and a can of tuna or something. They seemed quite desperate, as if it was starvation stakes; there were lots of shiny cans everywhere, and they wanted them.

Then, of all things, an ice-cream van turned up one day. It was just like Blackpool, with the old ding-dong chimes. He must have travelled at least 100 miles to get there; perhaps he'd heard that 7 Troop were in town.

We spent a week planning and preparing. A character called Gilbert the snake man was brought in to show us all the different types of snakes – the ones that were poisonous and the ones that weren't.

'There are two ways of dealing with a bite,' he said. 'The first is to dress the wound and try to get an antidote. The second is to lie very still in your sleeping bag and wait for death.'

We were standing around in a circle while this boy brought different snakes out of their bags. All of a sudden a particularly mean-looking fucker with a deep hatred of men in shorts and flip-flops hurled itself out of Gilbert's hands and was off, spitting venom in all directions. Within seconds all the rough-tough SAS men were hanging off trees and vehicles or sprinting towards the perimeter fence. This was one very pissed-off snake; when it couldn't find a man to attack it started to eat one of the vehicles, trying to sink its fangs into the tyres. I had no idea how it was recaptured and put back in its bag – my view was a bit restricted from the roof of the ice-cream van 100 metres away.

The locals were starting to pester us good style now. It happened almost every time we went into a place where Westerners had been working: people would be expecting us to give them stuff, and if we didn't they hassled and poked. They were given so much aid from so many sources

that in the end it wasn't something that they were grateful for, it was just something that they expected as of right. The best aid foreign nations could have been giving them was education, to show them how to be productive themselves. Instead, all we did was give them 600 tons of wheat to salve our consciences. But in doing so we created a nation of takers, who were not contributing to their own country, their own economy.

We decided one day that we'd all had enough of being hassled and told, 'Give me, give me, give me.' Out came the hexy blocks, which we cut into little cubes. These were then smeared with jam and arranged on plates. Then, every time we were crowded, we fucked them off with our confections. They grabbed the stuff greedily and threw it down their necks. After about three crunches the taste of the hexy got to them and they spat it out with much gagging and choking. Nobody came back for seconds.

Being freefall troop, and waiting to get into our stage of the game and try and defeat all these radars, we were very much left to our own devices. We spent our days doing our own weapon training and just generally mincing around. When a squadron went away like this, weights turned up, punchbags started hanging from trees. People would do a run around the compound, and then a routine with the apparatus – a circuit might be two minutes on the bag, two minutes' skipping, two minutes' rest, then two minutes on the weights, two minutes' skipping, two minutes' rest. You'd do maybe ten circuits and then warm down with another run.

The other troops started to disappear off to do their tasks, and then it was decided that we should go with 9 Troop, who were up in a hill range called the Tsodilo Hills. We set off in vehicles for the two- or three-day mooch across the Kalahari Desert. Tracks ran across vast empty flat plains of scrub and dust.

On the second day we came to a crossroads of tracks in the middle of thousands of acres of sandy scrubland. A

little mud hut had a sign up saying it was a café. The proprietor, an old fellow in his eighties, was mincing around on a hammock. We went in, but there were no tables or chairs, nor, come to that, electricity. Just a few bottles of Fanta on a shelf, and a sign, that must have been at least twenty years old, advertising Bulmer's cider from Hereford. Once we'd felt the temperature of the Fanta bottles we left them where they were, but negotiated with the old boy for the sale of the sign, which we mounted on the dashboard of the 110.

We got to 9 Troop's position on the afternoon of the third day. It was weird terrain, totally flat and then these mountains that rose abruptly out of the ground. I wasn't the only one to notice that they had an eerie air about them.

'I did this area for geography A level,' Tiny said. 'There are thousands of rock paintings in and around the hills, scenes of eland and giraffes painted by desert-dwelling Bushmen hundreds, maybe thousands, of years ago.'

When we arrived most of the troop were out on the mountain. There was a bit of a flap on as someone had injured his back and was being carried down to the camp. It was Toby. Slaphead was a veteran of the Falklands, Northern Ireland and countless fights up north as a policeman, all without injury; now he had jumped 18 inches off a rock and damaged his back so badly he was on a stretcher.

He was in fearsome pain and had to have more morphine.

Tiny yelled, 'Not yet, wait!' to the medic and went running to his bergen. He came back with a camera and said, 'OK, you can do it now.' Slaphead's face was screwed up in pain as he got the good news. The picture would go into B Squadron's interest room as soon as we got back.

Eno by now was on the radio sending the Morse message that we needed a helicopter. As usual he was Mr Casual about the whole affair. He had been told one day by the police that his sister had been murdered; he just said, 'I

think I'd better go to London then.' It wasn't that he didn't care, he just didn't get excited about anything.

The weather started to change. The sky was thickening with dark clouds and the wind was getting up; there was a smell of rain-wet earth. A storm was coming – this was worrying as it could affect a heli's chances of getting in. Slaphead had been stabilized, but he needed to be taken to a good hospital.

His new KSBs (*boots*) had been taken off and were by the side of the stretcher. I knew he took the same boot size as me so I went up and said, 'You won't be needing these any more on this trip, will you?'

Slaphead told me where to put the boots, and it wasn't on my feet.

Things started to settle down, a heli was being arranged and Eno was still on the radio standing by. Then another drama started.

It was about two hours before last light and there was no sign of Joe Ferragher and Alan, the new troop officer. The troop were just starting to mutter dark thoughts about the incompetence of new ruperts when somebody spotted a flashing light on the mountain. We got our binos out and could just see somebody on a ledge. No-one knew for sure what it was but everybody knew something was wrong.

Eno was back on the radio again, leaning back on a canvas chair, cigarette in one hand, Morse key in the other. Three or four of Mountain Troop got radios and their kit and drove over to the mountain.

As all this was happening the heli turned up. He couldn't do anything about the blokes on the mountain; he couldn't get that far in.

The weather was still threatening to give us a storm and the sides of the tents were blowing out. Most of 7 Troop felt quite helpless as we didn't have the skill to climb; we just waited to see if any more help was needed.

'Might as well have a brew and sort our kit out,' was Charlie's answer to the problem. We had been there for

about three hours by now and hadn't even got our kit off the wagons due to all the excitement.

We could hear on the radio that Ivor was now with them on the mountain and needed everyone's help. About 5'7" and wiry, Ivor was a mountain goat from somewhere up north. He came from an armoured regiment and had been at the Embassy and in the Falklands. He wasn't one to mince his words on the net.

'Joe is dead,' he said. 'The boss is going to be taken down by Harry and George. This is what I want to happen.'

He wanted everyone to get as far up the mountain as possible and meet him coming down. How he was going to do it we had no idea, but we started up towards him.

The storm now looked as if it was just teasing us. There was a little rain but nothing to worry about, apart from time. The heli didn't want to leave at night; we had to get a move on or it would leave without Joe, Slaphead being the main priority now.

It was about two hours before Ivor got to us. He was in shit state; he was sweating heavily and covered in grime, he had cuts on his elbows and knees, and his face and arms were bruised from the effort of moving a very heavy Joe off the mountain. He had put Joe into a mountain stretcher and then started to abseil down. It was a major feat of strength to kick himself and Joe over the overhangs. He should have got a medal that day. We took the body the rest of the way down. The heli then had two bodies on board instead of the one they had expected.

We learned that a device used to attach a person to the rock face had given way, and Joe had gone bouncing down the hill until he got stopped by his next 'safety'. The Boss had climbed down to Joe and tried to save him but it was too late. However a casualty is not dead until he is confirmed dead, so he tried anyway.

Charlie had got hold of the troop's rum that Joe was in charge of and said, 'He isn't going to need this now. Let's have a drink on the old fucker.'

So we had a drink on him and hoped that the rupert was OK. He was quite shaken up. It is not the best of introductions to have your troop senior die on you and then maybe think that everyone blames you – which they didn't. It seemed that life on a mountain didn't suit him; about three months later he moved to our troop. Maybe it was the thought of all that ice cream.

We were sitting under a baobab tree – a weird, muscled sculpture with branches like roots sprouting white, starlike flowers – drinking the rum and talking about the locals. 'The Bushmen have great respect for the baobab,' Tiny said. 'Pick its flower, they say, and a lion will eat you. These hills are sacred to them, too. It's taboo to kill an animal that lives here.'

One of 9 Troop said, 'Joe was out in a one-ten yesterday and shot an antelope for us to eat. Apparently his death came as no surprise to the locals.'

As I lay in my bivvi bag that night, looking past a bright moon to a gleaming Milky Way, I was a believer. I had never been particularly worried about dying. We all had to die at some stage; I just wanted it to be nice and quick, I didn't want it to be painful. I didn't have any big religious notions about death. I liked to think there was something after it, a place or dimension where I'd find all the information I'd ever wanted to know, such as what a Love Heart tasted like and all the other great secrets of life. That was the only advantage that I could see.

I'd always been sure that I was going to die early in life anyway. I'd always had that feeling, ever since I was a kid – I'd always thought, I'm going to live till I'm about fifty-five, and that will be it. Didn't stop me being a sucker when the pension salesman came round, though.

When mates died I was upset initially, but after that it was OK. It was more upsetting if they died in a drastic way, but the fact that they were dead, there were no problems with that. What was horrible and a real pisser was if people died or got severely injured and impaired for the rest of

their lives for no reason. It was always unfortunate when people died during training. We'd lost quite a lot of people through drowning in the jungle; river crossings were the number one killer in the Regiment. Sometimes I thought, hell, we're practising things that are going to be dangerous enough on the day, so why tempt Providence? But if that attitude was allowed to prevail, we would lose all the advantages of realistic training.

Joe had to be taken into South Africa to get a British Airways flight out and this would unfortunately entail a delay. Barry the storeman at Squadron HQ hosed down one of the six-foot tables, sorted Joe out on it and cleaned him up, then got all the meat out of the freezer and stored him inside it instead; he then organized a huge feast to eat all the meat before it spoiled. When all the arrangements had been made, they got Joe in a motor and drove him into South Africa. From there he was put in a coffin and flown home.

Meanwhile, we had work to do. We were flown in a shuttle service of little Islander aircraft up to the Okavango, a vast expanse of lakes and river systems that borders the Caprivi strip, the area of drama with South African forces. The plan was for us to join forces with 6 Troop, who'd been up there for weeks.

The average contact in that sort of bush, even though it looked pretty sparse, was about five metres. Everybody was carrying their personal choice of weapon that they considered would be good at such close ranges – SLRs, 203s and M16s, and shotguns. Mine was a 203.

The BDF were armed with the Galil, Israel's answer to the AK47. It was a very good weapon, simple to use and to clean, and with a simple and reliable action. People could learn it quickly, but its one drawback was its weight – it was a bit heavy for the troops of many of the countries that used it.

The other equipment that we'd taken with us was

minimal – as ever, only as much as we could get into a bergen. As in the jungle, we'd need just two sets of clothes – a dry set and a wet set. As well as that I took a poncho, in my case an Australian shelter sheet which crumpled up really small, a hammock and an American poncho liner, an excellent bit of kit similar to a very thin nylon duvet. The rest was food, water, bullets and a bit of first-aid kit.

We were there to practise a two-troop camp attack in the swamps. The camp we were training on was an alligator farm in the middle of nowhere.

Members of 6 Troop went out and did the recces, spent a couple of days putting OPs on it, and got all the information back.

We were living on a little spit of land within the swamps, amongst beds of fast-growing papyrus. Over the years, as the hippos had come up onto these little islands they had obligingly created perfect landing slips for our Geminis. We could drag the inflatables onto the spit and conceal ourselves and our equipment in the reeds, and operate from there. There was no way anyone would find us.

Everybody was cam'd up and carrying beltkit and weapons as we climbed into the boats and set off into the darkness. One boat was up ahead as lead scout. Aboard were two people – one driving, one navigating. The cox was Solid Shot. As a member of Boat Troop he knew what he was doing. He would just let the motor run on its own revs and guide it through the reeds and obstructions. It was amazing how little noise was made by the motors.

The other member was the Boat Troop boss, the rupert who passed in my Selection. He was from some armoured recce unit and was quite funny and likeable. He would be checking with Solid Shot on navigation. Solid Shot was soon to be a fellow officer. When we got back from this trip he was going to be commissioned as Captain Solid Shot – so he wasn't so thick after all. We were all very happy for him.

We were moving along at little more than tick-over pace;

the Yamaha is remarkably quiet if you're just trogging along without revving it up. As we got closer to the target, the engines were cut off and we started paddling.

Sandy and I were up at the front of the second boat. With his blond Brillo pad hair under a very large bush hat he looked like one of the Flowerpot Men. Our job was to cover the first boat, which we could just about see up ahead in the darkness. We wanted lots of distance between boats in case of a contact, but at the same time we had to keep in visual touch. If we started losing contact, it would all go to a gang fuck.

We were mooching along, no sound except for the occasional slurp of a paddle in the water, when suddenly, from near the lead boat, we heard what sounded like an explosion. It was followed by another, and another, and then we could see the foaming white of violently disturbed water.

The lead Gemini stopped and so did we. The whole two troops were now just floating in the water and being taken slowly downstream. We then heard what sounded like the roar of a steam engine.

We heard the sound again, and this time it was getting closer, a deep, outraged bellow that told us we were about to be thrown out of the party.

Next thing we heard was 'Fuck, fuck, fuck!' from the lead boat as a massive head and shoulders reared out of the water and took a bite into the rubber. Luckily the inflatables were constructed in sections, so that if one did get a puncture, it was only that section that went down.

There was an ominous sound of rushing water and my eyes strained in the darkness to see the threat. An ugly head arrowed towards us, erupting into an explosion of foam and jaws the size of a Mini.

Sandy said, 'Fucking hell!' and everybody in the boat paddled so fast a man could have waterskied behind us. As the deep, honking voices receded behind us, I realized I was drenched – whether from swamp water, exertion or sheer terror I didn't know.

The snorting and thrashing of the hippos would have compromised us, so we had no alternative but to turn back and try to find another route in. Our time on the target would be severely cut as a result, because we had to be in and away again before first light, needing darkness to get back to our hide position, the troop LUP.

We eventually got to the area of the attack. The blokes from the lead boat jumped on others and we dragged the bitten vessel along behind. It was the first time I'd been in an attack where people couldn't stop laughing. It had been a ridiculous scenario: two troops of the world's finest, screaming along the Okavango waterways armed to the teeth, going in to do an aggressive act, stopped in their tracks by a hippo that had the hump.

We had a very interesting few more weeks in Botswana, during which I learned the Afrikaans for, 'Let's get the hell out of here!' and the Botswanan for, 'Look at that springbok run.'

At the end, we had a big barbecue back at the squadron RV. It was as much a drink for Joe as anything else, and during the course of the night things were getting out of hand. A thunderflash (*training grenade*) came over the roof, then another. The locals were still shitting themselves about SADF incursions and the explosions did not go down well.

The SSM shouted, 'That's enough, the next one who throws one gets RTU'd [*returned to unit*].'

Two minutes later, *BANG!*

The SSM went running around the area looking for the flash-banger, but no-one could be found. A few of us saw who he was but said nothing.

The following morning the squadron OC got everyone together. 'You have until midday to come forward,' he said. 'If not, there will be no R&R and from now on you will provide security with the Botswanans.'

We all knew who it was but no-one said a word.

The OC finished with the words: 'He has to make up his mind if he is a man or a mouse.'

The Botswanan Mouse was born. We got pissed off with the restrictions that were imposed on us as a result of this bloke's irresponsible behaviour, and even more pissed off with him. He deserved to be RTU'd, but everyone had a strange and probably mistaken sense of loyalty. He was flapping good style, however, and quite rightly so.

No-one ever exposed the identity of the mouse. Every group of people has someone they don't like or want to work with. When we returned to Hereford, as well as Slaphead's pictures in the interest room, there were several cartoons of the mouse, and he continued to reap what he had sown.

21

An entire squadron of the Special Air Service was 'on the team' in the UK for six to nine months, on permanent standby. After a build-up of four to six weeks, which included training with the squadron still on, the commitment was handed over; it might have been only eighteen months since the blokes were last on the team, but there was always something new to learn.

The team consisted of two sub-teams, Red and Blue, each with an assault group and sniper group. Having two teams meant that two incidents could be covered at once; there were also contingency plans for other squadrons to produce teams if there were more than two incidents that had to be covered.

The assaulters were the people with all the black kit on who go jumping out of helicopters and banging down doors; they tended to work in four-man teams, but this was flexible depending on the target. One of the assault groups was the MOE (*method of entry*) team, responsible for making up the explosive charges for the rest of the team to use.

There was also a signals set-up. As well as looking after the team's equipment they had to provide comms from anywhere in the world, as there were also commitments overseas. As some of them were required to enter a target with the team they trained alongside us.

The medic carried the world's biggest trauma pack. If there was a man down the firefight still had to go on; it was

the medic's job to get in there and start getting some fluid into him and managing the trauma.

Until everything went bang and an attack went in, the sniper group were the most important people. They were on the target giving the rest of us real time information. They, too, were trained as assaulters.

The squadron HQ comprised the OC, a major, and the SSM, a warrant officer, who were responsible for both teams.

I found being on constant standby no more of a problem than it must be for a doctor – we were on call and we lived with it. We each had a bleeper and didn't go anywhere without it.

Seven Troop was always part of the Red team, which was wonderful because the squadron HQ was next to the Blue. If there were any bone jobs to be done the head shed would just nip next door; we were 50 metres away in our own hangar.

First thing in the morning we'd meet up in the crew room. Some would have run in, or have already done their training in the gym. It was a personal thing; no-one ever told us to do it; however, the day we couldn't do our job because we had lacked the self-discipline to go and train, we'd be standing on Platform 4.

Cycling was very popular at one stage and some mornings it looked like the Tour de France coming into the main gate. I preferred to run in from my house, have a shower, then go and have a brew in the crew room. It had the look of a Seventies-built school staff room, with a TV and magazines that were six months out of date, army soft chairs with horrible coloured nylon covers, and mugs that were badly stained by coffee. It stank of stale tea, coffee and cigarettes.

One of us would go to the cookhouse in a Range Rover and pick up some tea in Norwegians and the packed lunches – brown paper bags that contained a typical school lunch of soggy rolls, Yorkie bar and crisps. By eight

o'clock we'd have eaten everything and would start discussing the day's training.

'What are we doing today then, Gaz?'

Gaz was in his mid-thirties, an ex-Green Jacket, and had been in the Regiment for years. He was very experienced over the water, and really switched on. Recently divorced, he was reliving his youth; he was immensely sociable, tailormade for B Squadron. He wore Armani suits and Jermyn Street shirts; even the sergeant major called him Champagne Charlie. At the same time, however, he was very sensible, and not the right bloke to get on the wrong side of. Everybody tried to be best mates with Gaz; get in his bad books and you were in trouble. There was no messing about, he'd just sort you out on the spot.

On 5 September 1972, eight men belonging to the Palestinian terrorist group Black September burst into a room in Munich housing eleven Israeli athletes. They shot two of them and held the others hostage, demanding the release of PLO prisoners held in Israel and members of the German Red Army Faction held in West Germany. They also wanted a plane to fly them to Cairo.

The West German government, who had no specially trained counter-terrorist forces, gave in to the terrorists' demands after a day of negotiations. They were flown in two helicopters to a military airbase, and as they prepared to board the aircraft army snipers opened fire. Visibility was bad, and the snipers were positioned too far away. The terrorists had time to blow up both helicopters, killing the nine Israelis.

In order to avoid such a débâcle in the UK, the British Government turned to the Regiment. A CRW (*Counter-Revolutionary Warfare*) wing was set up that would be responsible for training every member of the Regiment in counter-terrorism techniques – amongst other things.

CRW were still the continuity of the CT team, providing new equipment, training and buildings. If there was no

training requirement coming from CRW on a particular day – for example, going to see the London Underground, visiting an airport or looking at major venues where heads of state were likely to meet – we would conduct our own.

Instead of the head shed running things one of the team would be put in charge: 'Right, Harry B, you organize a day in the CQB house.' The head shed could then spend time working alongside us.

The sniper team would go to the ranges or train with the assaulters. I loved the ranges, especially in the summer. We used the PM, a 7.62 sniper rifle, and Lapua ammunition, made in Finland. The targets were 'Hun heads' – just a picture of a head. We always went for head shots, for two reasons: any terrorist with more than two brain cells would wear body armour if they had the opportunity, and there was always a chance that the players would be on drugs and therefore more pumped up. If they were shot in the body they could be so wired to the moon that they would still come forward, or start to kill the hostages. If they had their heads taken off they'd drop.

Within the Hun head targets was a circle, centred on the area of the nose. We'd start the session by firing just one round, at 200 metres, as a confidence shot. Some would do it standing, some lying, but we'd all have to hit the circle, dead centre. It made us more confident to know that the weapon kept its zero, even when it had been packed and put in the wagon: at an incident we wouldn't be able to test fire our weapons, so we had to be sure.

There would then be lots of moving target shoots as far away as 600 metres, and a lot of OP training and urban sniper work.

The development of a counter-terrorist role led to a number of changes at Stirling Lines. The CQB building or 'killing house' was constructed to enable us to train in hostage rescue and covert entry with live ammunition, and make entry at any level – anything from a four-man assault group to a complete team with vehicles and helicopters. It

was a single-storey building with a centre corridor and rooms leading off – large rooms, small rooms, connected rooms – with movable partitions and a whole range of furniture. It was up to the individual to arrange the furniture the way he wanted it, and then put up any barricades.

The smell of lead and gunfire seemed to cling to the walls. There were extractor fans, but they couldn't keep up with the amount of rounds fired. Even with the lights in the rooms fully on it was still fairly gloomy. Some rooms had bulletproof glass with little portholes so people could look in from outside or videotape us.

It was my turn to organize a day in the CQB house. My team consisted of me, Dave, Fat Boy, and a new boy, straight from Selection, called Tim.

'Let's do a three-man snatch,' I said. 'Fat Boy, go and sort the room out – I don't want you working up a sweat, do I?'

He went off to arrange the furniture in the room and put up barricades for us to fight through, and change the lighting in the room so we wouldn't know what to expect as we entered. He then went and sat down in the room as the hostage; the terrorists were simulated by Hun heads.

We started to move to the door. It was always a difficult time, because there must be absolutely no noise: the object of the three-man snatch is to get so much surprise and speed onto the target that they're totally overwhelmed. Once we reached the door Dave and Tim placed the door charge; we were right up next to it to maintain the element of surprise when it went off. It was something that we practised time and time again until we were used to being next to charges as they exploded.

Everyone was right on top of each other, really tight up, weapon leaning over the shoulder of the next bloke, ready to burst in.

When everything's quiet, the noise of the respirator sounds outrageous. I could hear my breath rasping in and out, and was trying to slow down and breathe rhythmically to cut down the noise.

I made sure my torch was working, my pistol wasn't going to fall out, and the weapons weren't banging together. As No. 1, once I was ready, I stood in position, safety-catch off; the moment the door opened I could see into it and start to fire. I had my weapon in the shoulder, ready to go. Tim and Dave were right up behind me.

Forward and peripheral vision from inside the respirator is good; all my concentration was focused forward, all I could hear was the noise of my breathing.

I could feel my face starting to get wet with sweat.

The command was given on the net: 'Hello, all stations, I have control. Standby, standby, go!'

As the second 'Standby' was given Tim took the door in. I was straight into the room to take on the first threat I saw. Reacting to the situation in a room is not so much a matter of drill as experience and training. The terrorists won't be sitting or standing where they ideally should be; they are not playing our game. It could mean going left or right, or I might have to fight through a barricade to get to a target. It could be dark; or the lights might go out just as I entered.

No more than a foot behind came Dave, the No. 2. He had to react to two different factors – me and the terrorists.

As we entered we were firing at the heads. Dave was on auto, I preferred to fire rapid single shots. It was a matter of personal choice.

We were firing on the move, and the name of the game was to shoot until the target was dead. Because we were training and not dropping live bodies, I personally would fire until I could see enough holes in the target, and then I'd know that it was dead. Each man might get through twenty-five rounds every time he went in, more than he probably would in a real rescue.

I moved closer to the target, still firing. I had both eyes open so I could see everything that was going on. The last thing any terrorist would see was my torch light blaring down on him.

Once Dave was in and firing he might have to move

around the room to protect the hostage and give cover for Tim to do his stuff. He came in with no weapons, apart from a pistol in a holster; he was shouting through his respirator at the hostage: 'Up, up, up! Move, move, move!' as he picked him off the floor by whatever he could get his hands on – collar, hair, head, anything – and very aggressively dragged him from the room. There was no time to mess around. For a snatch to succeed it has to be all over in a matter of seconds, and the only reason it is so quick is because of the months – and in most cases years – of practice.

All four of us came back into the room for a debrief.

'A bag of shite!' Fat Boy said, smoothing down his ruffled hair after being manhandled by Tim. 'Andy, the reason I put that target where I did was because I knew you'd go for the obvious, when in fact to the right of you was the real and immediate threat. As you came in, you should have seen that target straightaway. You fucked it up. Do it again.'

I was more than happy to practise it again. If I had missed the immediate threat in real life I would probably have been killed.

After practising the same snatch again we changed positions so that every time there was somebody in the room and three men outside. After each session we had another debrief, perhaps watching a videotape of the proceedings so there could be no bone excuses, and drinking tea that tasted of lead because of the 5,000 or more rounds that were fired in the building each day. The lead fumes get in the throat and nose and linger all day.

We trained for stoppages. It's not the most pleasant situation in the world for nothing to happen when you go to fire your weapon at a terrorist five metres away who's bringing his weapon up at you. There is no time to sort it out; you've just got to keep both eyes on the target and draw your pistol. You have to be quick or you are dead.

The reason we all went into the room as the hostage was so that we could give an honest account of what we heard

and saw from the other side, and gain confidence in the other team members. It takes total trust to sit there, sometimes in the dark, feeling the blast from the MP5s as these people burst in firing live ammunition all around you. Given the high number of rounds that are fired every day – more than by the rest of the British Army put together – casualties are very low. All training, however, must be as realistic as possible.

It got to the stage where we were so confident with each other that we did quite outrageous things while training. There was a fellow called Mel from B Squadron, at that time a member of CRW, who was so confident in the other blokes that he would stand between two targets in a dark room while they came in with pistols and torches and fired at the Hunheads beside him.

Mel was a bit of a fruit. He was trying to get us to wear a new type of body armour, but we were very sceptical about its effectiveness. In the end he said, 'Look, I'll prove it works.' He put the kit on, loaded a shotgun with solid shot and told one of the blokes to shoot him. It took him down, but he was alive. Mel felt he was vindicated. On another team, we were looking at some new Kevlar helmets. Mel was sure that they were a good bit of kit, but we were saying, 'We don't mind the extra weight and discomfort of having this Kevlar helmet on, but will it take the shot?'

Mel put the helmet on and said to Mick the jap-slapper, 'Listen, Kevlar's a wonderful material. Shoot me in the head with a nine millimetre.'

Mick said, 'Fuck off, behave yourself and have a brew.'

There were no other volunteers, so the event didn't happen. About three days later, the Regiment got a letter from the manufacturers asking what we'd thought of the dummy helmet. Apparently what they'd sent us was just a mock-up to demonstrate its weight and the shape. There wasn't an ounce of Kevlar in it. There was talk that a shot to the head wouldn't have made much difference to Mel anyway.

We'd practise procedures for Man Down. If one of our blokes was shot we couldn't do anything about it immediately; the only thing that was going to save him was us taking that room or area as quickly as we could. If we stopped to sort him out, we'd all die; we must still carry out the task and, now that he was down, also carry out his job as well.

We trained for every eventuality – and trained and trained and trained. There are so many different types of buildings, from high-rise blocks to caravans, and all sorts of scenarios in which people could be held. Getting into an aircraft, for example, is a lot different from getting into an embassy; clearing a ship is a lot different from clearing a hotel. For a start, the ammunition's got to be different. If we started firing ball ammunition – solid, full metal jacket rounds – it would be wanging around all over the place as it ricocheted off the metal structure; therefore it has to be able to fragment once it hits metal.

We looked at all sorts of vehicles, from coaches to jumbo jets. We practised getting up to an aircraft, then making an entry without anybody knowing. The counter-terrorist team has to know how an aircraft pressurizes, how it depressurizes, how the system can be overridden, how to open the escape chutes.

People came up with new ideas all the time. One of the team once said for a joke, 'How about trying to climb up the tail and somersault down into the cockpit?'

We did.

There was progression every time a team took over. The techniques never stayed the same, because what we were trying to get into and defeat never stayed the same – the technology always moved forward.

As well as the assault and sniper groups practising among themselves, the whole team would get together and train for the different 'options'. One of these was called the IA (*immediate action*), a plan that the 3 i/c had to organize. He had to get all the information available and be able to

give orders to one of the teams thirty minutes after they arrived; the OC, meanwhile, would be planning the deliberate options.

The IA was continually updated and changed as more information became available. If there was a drama and the terrorists started to massacre all the hostages, the IA would go in as prepared as it could be.

One of the teams was always on standby on the IA; within seconds it could be stood to, ready to go in on the target. Helicopters and Range Rovers were used to get the team on target as quickly as possible.

On days when we conducted our own training we would try to be finished by mid-afternoon. There were no breaks, we just cracked on until it was done. Then it would be back to the team hangar, clean the weapons, drink more tea, ensure everything was ready to go in case of a call-out, and close down. Some of the blokes would then go training, or go home and make an attempt at fixing their leaky guttering. Those of us with any sense would go downtown for a brew and talk about how close we were to our football pools syndicate winning on Saturday.

Another commitment for the team was to be ready at a moment's notice to go over the water to reinforce the Troop. I used to enjoy this; it got us away for a few days or even weeks.

Sometimes if there was only a small number required it was a case of first come, first served. There was a call-out on a Saturday morning; I jumped into my ageing Renault and screamed off to work; my foot was right down to the floorboards, gunning the vehicle at speeds of up to 50mph along the straight.

I knew the Puma would be flying in to RV with the team who were going, and within ninety minutes we'd be in the province – as long as I got to the camp in the first place. As I approached the main bridge in town that crosses the river Wye I had a bang, clipping a Mini Metro with my left-hand

wing. The other driver insisted on doing all the paperwork and there was no way I could run away or tell him who I was. Just as we had finished exchanging particulars, I saw the Puma lift off from the camp.

The CQB house was always on the list of tourist attractions at Stirling Lines and visiting VIPs were generally given a demonstration of firepower and entry techniques. All chief constables were given demos so that they understood the Regiment's capabilities, as were the many other organizations that needed to know the type of product we could supply.

Sometimes demos became a pain in the arse. It was OK doing things that needed to be done, but instead of being the counter-terrorist team we sometimes became the demo team.

The teams were becoming more and more fed up so that instead of training they were jumping through hoops for all and sundry during the demo season. We didn't mind doing it for Customs and Excise and police firearms teams – but teams of rugby players, or doctors and nurses? Even the fitters who were laying carpet in one of the messes had a morning out – the joke was that someone was obviously getting their front room done for nothing. It came to the point where the only people left in Hereford that we hadn't done a demo for were the Women's Institute.

The guests would ask some really daft questions.

'How much do your gloves cost?' I was once asked.

'One hundred and fourteen pounds,' I said, plucking a figure out of thin air. 'Give or take a few bob.'

It got to the stage where we started to stitch each other up to relieve the boredom. One of the better ones was during the pallet displays, for which all the vehicles were moved out of the hangar and the weapons and equipment laid out on show. A member of each part of the team would then talk about their kit and task.

I was doing the talk on the assaulters and had sorted out

my pallet. I had all the clothing, body armour, abseil kit, the lot, and the weapons that any member of the assault group would be taking, and there was Fat Boy, who was dressed up in the kit: as I talked about a weapon he would bring it to bear.

Everybody's looking, it's all rather impressive. Fat Boy drew his pistol, then the shotgun, and there were knives and all sorts coming out all over the place.

Earlier in the day I had gone over to the sniper team's pallet when they weren't around and had left a tennis ball on their display. When Eno started talking about the different ammunition, it would be good to see him get out of it. When I came back I didn't realize I'd been stitched up myself.

I carried on with the waffle and saw an old boot in the middle of my display. Everybody was rolling up on the other pallets. The Regiment head shed were giving me bad looks; they were not impressed.

I moved on to point out the weapons and there was a plastic water pistol. I couldn't do jack shit about it. Luckily, nobody asked what it was for, because I would have been obliged to pick it up and say, 'It's to shoot people with,' and give them a squirt.

One memorable day, the Prince and Princess of Wales and the Duchess of York came down to Hereford. The purpose of the visit was familiarization with the Regiment, so if the shit hit the fan for them they'd know what to expect when the boys came screaming through to rescue them. But also it was a fun thing, a good day out for us. A day like that was good for them, too – they could let their hair down away from the press, and without having to shake hands, pick up flowers or make small talk with Jonathan Dimbleby.

One of the demos that we gave them was how we could covertly enter a building and get to the hostages in total darkness.

They were sitting in one of the large CQB rooms listening

to an explanation of how we trained: 'As you can see we can control the light levels, from full to total darkness.'

The lights were now off.

'Sometimes the team has to operate in total darkness because there may be no power or the terrorists have control of the lighting.'

We were going in wearing NVGs. It was like looking at a negative with a green tinge. The goggles give a weird perspective; if you go to grab something, you might be out by an inch, so it takes constant practice. Going up a step, we'd have to exaggerate our movements to make sure we didn't trip up; to walk, we'd place a heel gently and run the outside of the heel all the way along the outside of the foot, then gently place the boot down, and then go with the next one.

Sometimes I couldn't hear what I was doing; I was trying to breathe shallowly; even the noise of the NVG, a tiny whine, sounded a fearsome noise because it was right next to me.

Nice and gently, taking our time, we slowly moved towards the table where they were sitting, all the time thinking, what if we screw up – we're supposed to be the smoothy clockwork operators.

The lights went on, and standing over the royal visitors were an assault group in full kit carrying MP5SDs, trying to breathe slowly and look casual. They particularly liked that one.

We staged mock sieges to rehearse the royals in the procedures we would go through in the event of a terrorist attack. The exercises were very realistic, and they didn't always go according to plan. During a demo of a building assault, the royal party were aboard Range Rovers as part of the attacking force, watching others who were fast-roping from a helicopter onto the roof. The Agustas were zooming in, lots of bangs, lots of firing, the big mass assault on the embassy. Suddenly, as the helicopter lifted away, a bloke in black kit tumbled out and fell 50 feet onto the

roof, his body being hidden from view by a 3-feet-high perimeter wall.

The blokes said they heard Prince Charles say, 'Oh my God – a man's been killed!'

Almost immediately what should have been a dead body jumped to his feet, dusted himself off, and continued with his task. Everybody looked at each other, open-mouthed.

Later that day the Regiment became trend-setters. Diana was going to be in a room where flashbangs were going to go off. Flashbangs are noisy things; they are designed to disorientate you and make you want to curl up in a ball and wait for your mum to come and get you. As it went off she turned and one of the maroons hit her in the head. There was the smell of burnt hair and lacquer, and our army pensions suddenly didn't look any too healthy.

The only lasting damage was to her hair, which was badly burned. Days later the press and royal fashion watchers noted that Diana was suddenly sporting a new, shorter hairdo. There could be no comeback. They had signed a disclaimer that was now in B Squadron's interest room: 'No member of B Squadron will be committed to the Tower if any of the demos go wrong.'

Nobody – least of all the other members of the Regiment – could believe what had happened to the bloke who fell from the helicopter, and it was only in the club later that we learned the truth about Superman. Unknown to anybody but the team in the heli, he had hidden himself behind the wall. Then, at the right moment, the lads in the heli had ejected a dummy dressed in black kit.

As well as all the training that was done for once we were on the target, we had to practise the call-out system and moving to an incident; we had frequent exercises enabling the different agencies and personalities involved in any hostage incident to practise their bit.

Mrs Thatcher had long been a fan of the Regiment. After refusing to allow the Government to give in to the terrorists'

demands during the Embassy siege, she had personally sent in the team to bring it to an end.

She might as well have had a bed space down in Hereford – she always seemed to be there. I respected her no-nonsense approach, and she laughed at the jokes. She might have been the only one walking around the camp with a handbag, but she was as tough as any man when it came to the crunch. She was in the CQB house once when we burst in and pumped live rounds into targets either side of her. One of her aides curled up into a ball. Maggie looked at him and snapped, 'Get up, you fool.'

There was a lot of liaison with different units of the police. We did major exercises where everybody was involved, from the Prime Minister down, because everybody had to be tested. It was no good having all the soldiers – the coalface workers – practising their techniques and practising co-operation with other organizations, if the people who were sitting up there in COBR (*Cabinet Office Briefing Room*) listening to all the information and making decisions weren't practised too. So we'd do exercises where COBR would take command and direct operations from a bunker under Whitehall, the idea being to put Mrs Thatcher and her team and everyone else down the chain under as much pressure as possible.

There had been a big exercise a couple of years before in the States, and some of the Regiment went over as guests to observe. The incident was of national importance involving the Security Council, the presidential committee that commits the troops. But the problem was, the Security Council didn't actually assemble to join in the exercise. There was a debrief afterwards, at which one of the Regiment blokes stood up and said, 'The exercise was excellent – all the different organizations worked together and any little problems are now ironed out. However, where was the President?' It was the President and his advisors that had to make the decisions, and they had to be

getting hit with the problems exactly the same as everybody else.

In the UK everybody from the Prime Minister down was hit with the problem at the same time as we were, and had to make decisions. So it wasn't just the SAS going in to kick ass, it was everybody working together towards the same aim – a negotiated surrender. The last thing any of us wanted was to start putting charges on buildings and go screaming through shooting people – or even worse, getting shot at. It's dangerous. Nobody's jumping up and down with excitement to go and do that sort of stuff; they might be killed. However, if it's got to be done, OK, that's a fair one, off you go, and if the people in command, up to government level, have practised alongside those at the sharp end, then at least the blokes are happy that the decision has been taken by people with experience.

During one tour I was on the thirty-minute team. I was in town shopping when I got a call on my bleeper. By now I had a 250cc Yamaha; I took it steady going over the bridge this time. As I rode in, all the hangar doors were open and vehicles were moving to the ammo bunker to load up. There would be maximum activity as blokes were loading their ops bags into the wagons, which held everything an assaulter could wish for.

Everything was laid out behind the wagons ready to go at any time. Once everyone had loaded up we moved into the crew room to find out what was going on. We were all eating our crisps apart from Slaphead, who saved his during the week for his kids. For some reason they always seemed to be the most horrible flavours like prawn cocktail. Maybe the army had a deal with Smiths or the head chef had a sense of humour.

The SSM came into the crew room and said, 'About an hour ago there was a call-out for four men, including the two i/c, to go over the water. We've just received another call, Andy. I want you to be three i/c on it.'

He gave us a brief.

'The Israeli trade commission was holding a conference at grid 632456, map sheet 135. This morning the Islamic Jihad got into the building and is holding hostages. We are stood to, waiting for the word to move. The OC and his group have already moved by 109 (*Agusta helicopter*). Steve is waiting with the second 109 for the two i/c and sniper commander. The rest of us will wait for the go.'

My chest felt tight as we were driven to the helipad; in the normal course of events I wouldn't have been tasked with the 3 i/c's job until at least my next tour. I felt honoured, but daunted. I didn't want to fuck up.

The second wave of slime (*Int Corps personnel*) were waiting for us by the 109. They were an integral part of any operation ever since the Prince's Gate siege had demonstrated the value of good and accurate intelligence. During the lead up to the actual assault, specialists from MI5 had been tasked with drilling holes in the walls and inserting tiny microphones and cameras to gain a detailed picture of who was where inside the building. But the information about the construction of the building was piss poor and the walls turned out to be too thick for the probes to penetrate. The result was that although the blokes had a model of the construction of the building, they did not know exactly where the terrorists were.

Since then, the Regiment had collated a massive database on computer that included such essential information as the thicknesses of walls and doors in buildings that were possible terrorist targets, and the designs of all military and civilian aircraft. The computer was portable, so wherever an incident occurred we could take it with us and access the information. If we called up a certain hotel, for example, we'd get a 3D image of the interior on the screen. Intelligence gathered on the numbers and location of people inside the building could then be added as it came to hand. Possible methods of entry could also be suggested to the computer, which would then plot the best method of

moving through the building. If the design of the building was not on the database, we could punch in details such as the construction of the outside walls, the number of windows and the location of various rooms. The computer would then 'design' the interior and provide a probability factor for accuracy, altering both as more information was added. It seemed the slime had every map, drawing and picture of every ship, aircraft and building in existence.

I liked going in the heli with Steve until he started to talk about squash. He was mad on the sport and to make it worse he was good at it. Squash was very popular in the Regiment; at lunchtime, the courts looked like the scene at a major tournament.

We arrived at the location just outside Liverpool, a large private park with its own massive mansion house; from the air I could see lakes and well-manicured lawns.

We landed alongside the other 109. One of the slime was there to take us to the holding area.

'It's not as good as we would want but it will do,' he said.

On the way there we passed scores of police, fire and ambulance crews, all with their vehicles and their own jobs to do. The holding area turned out to be two large rooms in an old outbuilding that had been taken over and used as incident control. The rooms were more or less derelict, with concrete floors and cobwebs at the joins of the walls and a damp, musty smell of cat's piss, but at least there was electricity. In one corner were a couple of bogs with high cisterns and rusty metal chains. The rooms must both have been about twenty-five metres by twenty; it was a building cut in half with a centre wall and two doors.

The first priority was to meet up with Jack, the squadron OC. He was easy to spot – very tall, very wide and with a nose that would have put General de Gaulle's in the shade.

'This is the briefing area,' he said. 'Next door will be the admin area. The IA vehicles will be placed on that hard standing to the right, everything else on that grass area there.'

Nobody else would be allowed to park near the ops vehicles, and the area would be kept clear of all clutter.

In the briefing area the slime and signals advance parties were sorting everything out. There was a long line of six-foot tables on which were boards that would soon have pictures of the target plus the X-rays (*terrorists*) and Yankees (*hostages*).

Plans of the building were being pinned up as more information was given by the police. Steve and Jerry, the other pilot, did the sensible thing – got some tea and talked squash while they waited for their support team to arrive.

'Let's go to the main incident room and get permission to go forward and see the target,' I said.

I took a walk to the main building with the OC and Bob, the sniper team commander. Bob was the first member of the Regiment I'd ever seen, in Crossmaglen. He had since become troop sergeant.

It seemed that the mansion had been renovated and turned into a conference centre much the same as the target, which was about a kilometre away. It was very plush with deep carpets, beautiful wood and leather furniture, and a fine central staircase. The scene put me in mind of a place that a film company had taken over: all the Gucci furniture had been moved to the side and there were wires fixed to the floor with masking tape and running up the staircases, telephones ringing, police men and women rushing around, and, like us, people in civilian clothes with ID cards pinned to their jackets.

Every sector had its own little cordon. To come out of our holding area cordon and into another we had to go through a police checkpoint. The slime had pinned ID cards to us. Within the main building there were other places that we needed other clearances to go into. It was chaos; everything was still getting jacked up.

The OC introduced us to a woman police officer who was one of the incident controllers. She called the forward control point and said, 'Our friends are on their way down to see you.'

312

I returned to the briefing area with Bob and Jack and saw the two pilots. Squash talk had finished now and they were looking at some air photography that had just come in. Steve had decided to get his pipe out and slowly kill everyone. Each time he left it the thing would go out, so he had to relight it, causing clouds of smoke to form above him.

The squadron OC and I got a radio each and did a quick roadie's sound check – 'One two, one two' – to each other and moved off towards the inner cordon. All the radios were secure comms so no-one else could listen on our net.

We must have been stopped and checked three times at different points along the route. Once there we wanted to get as close as possible to the target. The OC wanted to start thinking about the deliberate options, how he was going to get his teams on target and what he wanted to happen when they were there. On these phases we had the advantage over the terrorists.

Bob was looking for the best places to put his snipers. They needed to be as far away as possible for concealment but close enough to play the kind of detail that was going to be required. For my part, I was looking for the best way to get the team in and control the target thirty minutes after they arrived, which was the 3 i/c's job.

We got to the control point, a group of grey police Portakabins, each with a black-and-white checked line around it. It had been raining and our shoes were muddy. I tried to scrape most of it off as we entered. The Portakabin was pretty spartan inside and freezing cold, despite an electric two-bar fire – no taxpayers' money used extravagantly here. The place smelled of coffee, cigarettes and the stink of burnt dust when an electric fire is first turned on. The windows were steamed up; people were wiping them so they could see out. Every time somebody moved the Portakabin rocked backwards and forwards; it hadn't been stabilized yet.

Inside were the negotiators and the world's supply of policemen. The areas were pointed out to us on a sketch

map and then our escort turned up to take us as far as the nearest police sniper.

The boy was well and truly pissed off. It was cold and wet and he was lying in the mud with only a roll mat for insulation.

'I've been waiting to be stood down for the last hour,' he said.

'What have you seen?'

'Not a thing. When we arrived all the curtains were closed and there's been no movement anywhere.'

I said, 'If the curtains are the same as the ones in the main house we won't be able to see much tonight either.'

We stayed for about an hour, moving around the building as much as we could. I peered through my binos, having a good look at the target. It was a large, square, Georgian building, with very clean-cut lines, much like the main mansion house itself. At the front were large double doors and windows either side on the ground floor. Above that, there were three windows on each of the next two storeys. The roof was flat, with a little 2-foot wall around the edge, but I could see two large skylights. It had a gravel driveway coming up to it, which opened up either side; around the back were outhouses and garages.

A quick word with Steve and the slime and I would be ready. I walked back in the mud wishing that I had brought my wellies with me.

Standing near where the snipers would soon be positioned with a good view of the building, I did a quick appreciation of how I was going to implement the IA. We would have to travel up to the target by vehicles because of the distance from the holding area. Once we got there, did we then move on foot to get onto the target? No; there was too much open space between the cover and the target. There were some woods and little hedgerows dotted around in this vast park area, but the nearest lot of cover was a row of buildings down at the bottom of the driveway. A run up from there would take too long, expose

everybody, and possibly compromise the whole operation. So it would have to be one of two things: all in by helicopter, or all in by vehicle – or a combination of the two.

We had two 109s which could take a maximum of six blokes each, which meant they couldn't get everybody on target. I wanted to hit as many parts of the building as I could at the same time so there was no time for the people inside to react, so it was going to have to be a combination of vehicles and helicopters, depending on the latest information at the time.

The first wagons were now arriving after their Formula One race up the M6. As everybody came in they were told where the holding area was, and where they were to lay out their equipment. Soon there was a long row of blankets in a straight line; on top of all of them was all the equipment out of all the vehicles. The blokes unwrapped the MP5SDs and Welrods from their weapon bags, together with axes, crowbars, hammers, shields, half-shields, full body shields, ladder sections. The only wagon that was not emptied out was the MOE wagon, which was full of explosives and bits of wood and polystyrene for making up charges.

They knew where they were going to sleep – the holding area. All they wanted to know now was where the bogs were, and where they could get a brew.

With the arrival of the team the briefing area got busier. There seemed to be wires, radios and telephones being tested everywhere. I was sitting over the marker board, putting callsigns to vehicles and telling blokes where those vehicles were going and what would happen once they got there. The more I wrote down before I gave the formal set of orders, the easier it was for me, because then everybody already had an idea of what they needed to do.

As I was writing it down, people were coming in and leaning over my shoulder: 'How many vehicles needed?'

'I need two Range Rovers and two fast ropes.'

Bob took his first two snipers on the ground and showed them their positions; they would start to send information

as soon as they were on the ground. In contrast to the police, our snipers had some really good kit. Not just overalls and a roll mat for us; we had camouflage DPM coveralls made of GoreTex; inside was a complete body duvet, which was unbelievably comfortable. They only had to wear their tracksuits underneath, and could lie out in the mess all day if they had to. The only slight drawback was that the clothing was bulky; from behind, they looked like two Michelin men walking down the path. But they would be grateful for the warmth; the weather was still dull and overcast, a freezing, minging winter day that found its way into any little gaps in your clothing.

Now I'd had my chat with Steve and the slime I was ready to fill the board in and get changed myself.

The team now knew what time orders were and what those orders were likely to consist of, plus what vehicles they had to prepare.

As well as this, the MOE team were looking at the information that had been given by the police. They checked too with the scaleys, having a quick look at what measurements and plans they had. Then they started making charges to defeat the windows, which were plastic framed and double glazed.

The whole place was sparked up now, with everybody involved in their own little world. The team were sorting the equipment out, coming in and out, still in their jeans. The scaleys were sitting over their equipment, chatting away. They too were in jeans and rough wear.

On ops the assault teams wore three layers of clothing: flame-retardant underwear, very much like racing drivers wear, an NBC (*nuclear, biological and chemical*) suit to protect us from the gas we would use, then flame-retardant black coveralls. After that the boots – high-leg cross-trainers, which were also great for freefall. I put my beltkit on; this also carried my Sig 9mm pistol, which strapped on halfway down my right thigh. I just had to lower my arm and the pistol grip would meet my hand. On my left leg I

had my mags for the MP5 and Sig, again halfway down my thigh.

I had an instant sweat on; to make it hotter on came the body armour. By now I, too, looked like the Michelin man. To top it all there was the ops waistcoat: this carried my radio with its earpiece and throat mike – some blokes used a mike that went into their respirator, but I didn't like it – explosives, first field dressings, a knife, an axe, flashbangs, plus anything else that was task specific.

I carried a Heckler & Koch MP5, the high-powered, 9mm semi-automatic and automatic weapon. The reason it had become the basic assaulter's weapon was that it had a closed breech, which meant we could have a round up in the breech ready to fire, with the working parts forward – much like a self-loading rifle or an Armalite. Most small machine-guns work on the blow-back principle, where the working parts come forward to initiate a round, and the gases then push back the working parts, and they stay to the rear unless you pull the trigger again. The Heckler & Kochs are more reliable, and have an excellent rate of fire. And they're British of all things, Heckler & Koch being part of British Aerospace.

Another good feature of the MP5 is its three-round burst capability, so every time you squeeze the trigger, it just fires three rounds. Release the trigger, squeeze it again, it'll just fire three rounds. It's the first three to five rounds which are most effective on any automatic weapon.

The streamlight torch attached was zeroed to the weapon so we could use the beam for aiming as well as simply penetrating darkness or smoke. I used mine even in day-light because it was such a good aiming aid. There are little nuts and bolts to enable you to move the torch around; you zero it so you know that when the torchlight is on the target at so many metres, the rounds are going to go so high or so low from it. In a dark room, Maglites also have a good blinding effect on the people you're attacking.

I had two magazines attached to the weapon – one that

was in the weapon, and then a bracket with another magazine just to the side of it, so I didn't have to go to my main beltkit in a rush. The weapon was slung over the body on a chest sling so I could climb buildings, jump in and out of vehicles, and do all the business that I wanted, without having to worry about the weapon. It was one of the few times that the Regiment did actually sling weapons.

At the last moment I would put on my kid leather gloves and respirator; by then I would just be a big sweaty mess with a chest and shoulders like Arnie in a *Terminator* film. If I was really lucky I could also find myself carrying the 'Barclaycard', a sawn-off, pump-action shotgun with the butt taken off; it's used to take doors down by firing a 'Hatton round' which takes the hinges out without damaging the people in the room. It got its name from the advert – 'A Barclaycard gets you anywhere'. In the beginning it came with its own holster but that proved to be too cumbersome; most of the teams just put a bungee on it and had it hanging down at their side.

By the time of my orders group the briefing room was furnished with fold-up canvas army chairs from the wagons. Some blokes were sitting down, some were standing. People were coming in and out, I could hear all the people on the radios in the background.

They gathered around the board as I gave my IA orders, white paper cup in one hand and a soggy roll in the other. Before us were plans of the building from all elevations, plus air photos and floor plans.

This was one occasion when there was no time for anyone to voice an opinion. There was no Chinese parliament.

I said, 'These are orders for the IA that is in place directly after these orders.

'Ground. The building has three floors. At the front there are the main double doors; these are plate glass with a plastic frame. The doors have been covered over with tablecloths so we can't see in. On each side there is a

318

window, then a window above that per floor; these are all double glazed with plastic frames. All the windows in the whole building have their curtains closed. From the main door there is a central staircase that has two flights per floor. On the roof there are skylights that open up into the main corridor on the top floor. After these orders look at the plans and familiarize yourself with the rest of the outside – the front is all we are concerned with at the moment.

'Situation. Six hours ago members of Islamic Jihad took over the building that was the venue for a conference sponsored by the Israeli trade commission. They are demanding the release of five of their group being held in Parkhurst prison for the attempted bombing of the Israeli embassy. It seems that there are up to six X-rays and approximately twenty-seven Yankees.

'There are no pictures yet, or information, on anyone, except that one of the X-rays, X-ray One, is a woman. From her voice she appears to be in her mid-twenties with a strong northern Palestine accent. Her English/American is good. All indications show that the group have split the Yankees and spread them around the building. No weapons have been seen but it is a reasonable assumption that they have automatic weapons.

'Deadlines. Negotiations have been taking place since 1000 hours. The first deadline is in forty-five minutes' time, at 1600 hours. They want to talk with one of their group who is in Parkhurst.'

I then gave the mission statement, which is always said twice: 'Mission. To rescue the hostages, to rescue the hostages.

'Execution. Assault group. Red One and One Alpha, you are to fast-rope onto the roof and make an explosive entry though the skylight. Your LOE [*limit of exploitation*] is the top floor. I want a link man on the first landing to RV with Two and Two Alpha. Steve, which way are you both going to approach from?'

319

'From the north-west along the tree line, then low over the park.'

'OK, it will take twenty seconds for the wagons to be on target – if you give thirty seconds to target that will keep us together.

'Two and Two Alpha, you are to make an explosive entry into the two middle floor windows. Two, take the left window on callsign Tango One [*Range Rover*]. Two Alpha on the right on callsign Tango Two – your LOE is the middle floor. I want link men to RV with One Alpha and to move down to the first landing and RV with Three and Three Alpha.

'Three – that's me – and Three Alpha are to make an explosive entry into the front double doors. Three will go left on callsign Tango One and Three Alpha will take the right on callsign Tango Two. Your LOE is the ground floor. I want a link man to RV with Two.

'Sniper group. Sierra One and Two, you are to cover the callsigns as they move in from the inner cordon.

'Sierra Three and Four, you are to move forward from the inner cordon on the standby and cover both sides and rear with G3s.

'Hostage Reception. The reception area will be in the area of the main doors. Once entry has been effected you are to move forward.

'ATO [*Ammunition Technical Officer*] and Medic. You will be called forward on request. Callsign Three will RV with you at the main entrance.

'Tango One and Tango Two. I want you to drive head-on from the start line here,' I said, pointing at the map. 'Once you come around the corner you will come head-on to the building. The distance is approximately 150 metres. Once on target you will cover the teams in, become casualty replacement if called – if not, become part of hostage reception. If we get a stand down from the deadline I'll bring you forward so you can see the run in. Any questions?'

There weren't.

'Timings. After these orders I want the teams to look at the plans and sort themselves out. By 1535 hours the IA is ready. The first deadline is at 1600.

'Vehicle group, at 1550 everyone needs to be on the wagons, ready apart from respirators. We will then move in slow time to the start line. Tango One will lead and I'll show you the way. The team will be stood to at the start line at 1555hrs.

'Heli group, at 1555 you need to be on board, rotors turning. Steve, if you are not told otherwise, close down at 1610. Any questions? No? Right that's it.'

The formal stuff over with, I then talked with my team and mulled over the plans.

'Dave, you make entry, I'll go in Number One – Tim Two, Fat Boy Three and Dave Four. Once we clear the hallway we will go left and take the large room, then this one here by the stairwell. Once we are all clear I want you, Tim, to link up with Three Alpha at the bottom of the stairs, then clear to the first landing and RV with Two. Any questions? Good, let's sort our shit out and load up.'

That was all there was to say because everybody knew the rest.

We walked out of the briefing area to the two Range Rovers, Tango One and Tango Two, that were going to take us on to the target.

'Hello, Alpha, this is Three,' I said on the net. 'That's Tango One and Two moving to the start line. Over.'

'Alpha, roger that, moving to the start line.'

'Alpha' was the co-ordinating callsign for our base, which would be in the briefing area and manned by the scaley. 'Alpha One' was the commander.

The blokes were sitting all over the outside of the vehicles. All Don the driver could see was two pairs of black legs that belonged to my team, who were going to take the first floor. As we moved to the start line under police escort I could hear the Agustas' rotors starting to wind up.

I got out of the Range Rover at the corner of the row of buildings and watched as everyone put their respirators on and 'checked chamber' – pulling the working parts back slightly on their weapons so that they could see there was a round ready to fire.

The two drivers quickly turned up to the corner and got down on their stomachs. One of them peered around with just a quarter of his face and one eye so he could look up the drive and get a mental picture of the run-in. As soon as Tango One's driver had had a look, he got out of the way and the other fellow got down.

'Alpha, this is Three, that's Two and Three stood to, over.'

'Alpha, roger that, One acknowledge.'

'One stood to, out,' the pilot said.

In the background of his radio message I could hear the rotors turning.

The squadron OC would be with the senior policeman, listening on his radio and explaining everything that we were doing, and confirming that the IA was stood to. If the X-rays started killing the Yankees it was the police, not us, who would decide that we went in. We were there to supply military aid to the civil power, that was all.

All the team sat on the wagons and in the helicopters, listening on their radios and waiting for the deadline. Engines and rotors were running.

It was now approaching the deadline. The snipers were watching and listening intently.

'Alpha – Sierra One, that's shouting and movement on White One One,' came one.

Each window and door had a colour and number. I knew he was referring to the far left, bottom window.

'Alpha, roger that, shouting and movement on White One One.'

All the team could hear this on their own radios.

'Alpha, Sierra One, that's White One One opening, wait ... wait ... that's one X-ray, possible male, black ski mask with a green combat jacket carrying an AK ...

wait ... he's shouting and pointing to the control area, over.'

'Alpha, roger that, out to you. Tango One acknowledge.'

'Tango One.'

'Tango Two?'

'Tango Two.'

'One?'

'One, roger that,' Steve said. The rotors were still turning.

'Alpha One?'

'Alpha One, roger.'

It was the last chance for a check. Is my pistol held in correctly? Is the flap over the pistol so it's not going to fall out? Are the magazines secure?

The people with the window and door charges were checking them, starting with the clacker: is the clacker on correctly? Is it nice and secure? Then, all the way up, following that line. Is the det on securely? Is the det on securely to the det cord? Is the charge all complete?

Is the respirator on right? Is the seal tight between the respirator and the coveralls? You don't want to start getting gas down you, because it hurts. Gas doesn't only affect the breathing system and the eyes, it affects the skin, it stings severely. Are the gloves on tight? If they were baggy, I might have a problem as I went to draw my pistol or started manipulating my MP5 or pistol.

Everything was secure, I was holding on to the vehicle, waiting for that 'Standby!' to go.

We heard, 'Hello, One and One Alpha, move to your holding area, over.'

'One, One Alpha, roger that, out.'

The helicopters were starting to go up; within the forward control room the senior policeman must have been a bit concerned about what was going on. He hadn't handed over control, but he was saying: 'Get the helis up to save time, so at least once they're in the holding area we can start running them in.'

At the same time all the snipers were coming on the net.

'Hello, Alpha, this is Sierra One. That's still more shouting. Still more movement. It seems now there's movement on Two Two, the window above. Can't identify anyone, it's just movement. I can see the window and the curtains moving. There's a face at the window – can't identify it, over.'

'Yep, roger that.'

Blokes were pulling out flashbangs from their ops waistcoats; as we were going in, just as we were approaching the place, we'd start throwing them to produce distraction and confusion – the more the better. We wanted to disorientate and scare these guys.

All the engines were running. Everybody was just waiting for the go. And still we had more hollering and shouting; the snipers were bringing in more information.

The negotiators would be working really hard talking to the people inside the building – if they still had comms with them, that is, and these people wanted to talk. They'd be talking to them and at the same time they'd be giving messages in sign language to everybody around them in the main incident room.

For us on the Range Rovers, it was just a question of sitting there in the wagons twenty seconds away, out of sight. Nobody was doing anything; we weren't talking because we had our respirators on.

I sat back and put my head down, listening to what was going on. I didn't want to waste energy. I just slumped. I had my weapon strapped over me, I was weighed down with kit, it would have been pointless running around. We couldn't hear what the negotiators were saying but I knew they would have been trying to calm the situation down. There was no way that COBR were going to let them talk with their people in Parkhurst.

'Alpha, Sierra One, that's the X-ray back in White One One, window and curtains closed.'

'Alpha.'

The deadline had passed. The negotiators were doing

their bit; the chief constable must have been satisfied that the threat to kill two hostages at 3 p.m. had been successfully avoided.

'Hello, all callsigns, this is Alpha One – stand down the IA. Stand down the IA. All callsigns acknowledge.'

We all acknowledged the Boss and took our respirators off and made our weapons safe – an unload followed by a load, without putting a round in the chamber.

We drove back with the police escort and watched the heli teams walk back to the briefing room.

The place looked completely different. By now all the intelligence collation and signals equipment was on line. There were more pictures and plans of the building plus information on the wiring, sewage pipes, ventilation systems – more intelligence than you could shake a stick at.

Also there were a number of photos of one of the terrorists, taken by the technical teams of the Home Office. Now we had our second terrorist, called X-ray Two, and a picture.

There was nothing high-tech about the scene, just boards with things stuck on with pins, masking tape, magi-boards with magnets to hold bits up. It was a very fluid situation; we had to be able to pull information off and replace it quickly.

Each of us had a white paper cup of hot tea in our hands as we went over to the briefing area where the Blue team were waiting. The slime were going to give everyone an update.

'The situation so far is, the negotiators are trying to get three of the Yankees exchanged for food. These are one sixty-five-year-old employee, the gardener, and his two grandchildren, aged six and nine. Pictures are now starting to arrive of some of the Yankees; as soon as we get them I'll put them on the board with a description if possible.

'As you know we now have an X-ray Two. He is a male, approximately six foot two and fifteen stone. There is no

325

new deadline as yet and no more info apart from what is on the boards. Any questions?'

The squadron OC then took over.

'The Red team is to stay on standby for the IA until 0600 hours. Orders for the team changeover will be at 0530. Any questions?'

'What are the feeding arrangements?' Fat Boy asked.

I smiled. So what's new? I thought.

Everyone looked at the SQMS.

'There will be a container meal arriving at 1900hrs and from then on the police will take over. As soon as I know more I'll post it on the board. I will make sure the tea urns are filled. Try and save the paper cups – use your own mugs if you can.'

We filed out of the briefing room, throwing our paper cups into the black bin liners that the SQMS and his storeman had been putting up everywhere.

There was background noise of ringing phones and the amplified voices of the snipers sending back information, relayed through loudspeakers so that everyone could hear what was happening. There was a general buzz of people talking to each other and into phones and radios, and the noise and echo of others moving and setting up more equipment. It was still cold inside the building; there was localized heat as some heaters were now on, but I could still see my breath.

The admin area next door had changed also. The Red team had got their camp beds out and started to place their body armour and beltkit next to them, then the books and Walkmans were coming out. As we were the IA, no kit came off apart from our MP5s and respirators. I got a camp bed, unrolled my sleeping bag, but decided it was too early to sleep.

I went outside between the two rooms and saw a couple of the Blue team talking with two policemen who were part of a cordon to stop people coming into our area.

'It's great for the overtime,' one of the policemen was

saying. He started to talk about the miners' strike. 'There was one force that had their own T-shirts printed with the message: A.S.P.O.M. – Arthur Scargill Pays Our Mortgages.'

I went into the briefing area to see what was going on. The squadron OC was on the net to Sierra Two, who was tucked away in his OP, watching the front and right-hand side of the building.

'From your position could you get gas into White Three Two, over?'

Sierra Two said, 'Wait.' He'd want to take another look before committing himself.

'Alpha One, Sierra Two – yep, I can do that if I move twenty metres left before the standby, over.'

'Roger that, out to you. Hello, Sierra One, what's the cover like from you to the rear fire escape, over?'

'Sierra One, there is dead ground up to about sixty metres short of the fire escape – however, I haven't been there, over.'

'Alpha One, roger that. There will be someone down on your position soon and they will have a look. Out.'

He was busy planning a number of deliberate options covering day, night, covert and overt situation. These options would have to be ready for when COBR had had enough or the situation had deteriorated to the extent that the police handed the incident over. Planning for the deliberate attack could involve anything from an elaborate model being made up for us to look at, to just loads of floor plans and masking tape put out on the ground to represent the area. We would walk and talk through everything. Sitting in were both teams' 2 i/cs and their ruperts; they were all part of the planning process. The team 2 i/cs, the senior non-commissioned ranks, were there because of their experience; the team ruperts were there to suck them dry of information – to learn, as well as being part of an operational squadron. One day one of them would be in the squadron OC's seat – a fearsome responsibility.

The Regiment didn't need troop commanders; in 7 Troop we didn't have a troop commander for years. A troop ran itself under its senior NCO. However, what was needed was squadron commanders, a squadron HQ element. With troops dotted all around the world, somebody was needed who knew where they were and what they required. One of the troop commanders was one day going to be the squadron commander, so it was in everybody's interests to make sure we trained them up well. For them, it was another form of Selection; they did their three-year tour, and if they were any good they might get invited back to run a squadron. If they screwed up, it wasn't their fault but that of the troop senior, or the troop as a whole. It was our responsibility, not just to give the rupert a hard time – as you do – but to make sure that he was given all the opportunity in those three years to learn as much as possible. It was no different really from training recruits at Winchester. A bad product was down to us, not the recruit.

It was the senior NCO, the team senior, who really ran the show. He did the day-to-day planning and all the administration. And it was also his job to make sure that the officer knew what was going on, and we as a team needed to be teaching him as well.

I got bored and went back to my sleeping bag to read my book, *The Feudal Kingdom of England*.

Then it was time for the container meal. This was, as predicted, 'Airborne stew' – meat, potatoes, vegetables, all cooked up together. Sometimes there are paper plates on offer but most people bring and use their own – they hold more. For pudding, there were six rounds of bread each and a sticky bun.

One of the scaleys came in while I was still eating.

'Can we have both teams in the briefing room at 1930 for an update, I thank you!'

Some of the scaleys were the world's oldest corporals and sergeants. Because they don't want to leave 264

Squadron they forego any chance of promotion that would mean moving out of Hereford.

We sat down in front of the slime and finished off our stickies.

'We still have seen only X-ray Two. All the negotiations are still being conducted by the woman.'

We could hear her voice on the loudspeakers.

'Can you turn that up!' someone shouted from the back of the team.

Her words filled the room: 'If you do not put our state- ment on the BBC 9p.m. and ITN 10p.m. news we will start to kill people. We have shown you that we are not savages, you have your old man and children . . .'

'I want to help you,' said one of the negotiators. 'None of us want this to turn out a bloodbath, do we? I cannot make any promises, but I assure you that I am making all efforts to help you. Everything I said I would do has happened. We need to work together . . . you must understand I need time.'

'It is obvious you are not listening. We will start to kill if the broadcasts are . . .'

Somebody turned the volume down.

The slime continued: 'As you heard, the old man and two children have just been released. He is in shock and cannot give any information of any use apart from that he thinks there are four or five and only one of them a woman.'

One of the scaleys shouted out: 'Stand to the IA!'

We ran to the vehicles and turned our radios on. Weapons were made ready and respirators put on while we screamed off to the start line. The people with the entry charges were checking to ensure they were OK, and putting on the claymore clacker that would initiate the charge.

'Alpha, Tango One and Two at the start line, over.'

'Roger that, out to you. One, this is Alpha, over.'

'One, rotors turning and stood to, over.'

'Roger that, out.'

On the net, we could all hear the snipers giving

information on the target: 'More movement on White Two One and White One One. There is screaming coming from the ground floor, I can't tell what room.'

'Roger that, Sierra Two.'

I heard two bursts of automatic fire and knew it wouldn't be long before we went into action.

'Hello, One and One Alpha, this is Alpha One. Move to your holding area.'

'One, roger.'

We could not see them, but we knew that both helis would now be flying off to an area where they couldn't be heard by the terrorists, waiting for the order to move on target. It was dark by now and all lights were out. Steve and Jerry would be using their NVGs.

The chief constable now had to wait for confirmation that people had been killed. The sound of shots was not enough.

He was soon to have his confirmation: a body was dumped at the main door with the threat of another one in five minutes if the TV statement demand was not met.

The policeman spoke to COBR and the decision was made.

The squadron OC got on the net: 'Hello, all stations, this is Alpha One, radio check, over.'

We all answered.

'All stations, I have control, I have control. Callsigns One and One Alpha, commence your run in.'

'One and One Alpha, roger that, out.'

It was on.

The helis dropped low over the trees, still on their NVGs. The doors both sides of the Agusta 109s were open. Each helicopter had four men aboard. The No. 1, who was going to come down the fast rope, was looking out of the heli-copter as it screamed in, respirator on, looking at the approach. He had two hands on the fast rope, which was six inches in diameter. The rest of the rope dangled around his right foot ready for him to kick it out; he'd put two

hands around it, grip also with the sides of his assault boots, and slide down, very much like a fireman coming down a pole.

'That's thirty seconds, thirty seconds.'

This was the last chance to cancel. The OC would have looked at the policeman for confirmation.

'All stations, I have control. Stand by, stand by . . . go, go, go!'

The vehicles moved off with the teams holding on for grim death. As we turned the corner we could see the building; Tango Two came up level with us and I heard the helis making their approach. They were flying low towards the building; lower than the building itself.

A little arm sticks out from each side of the aircraft with the fast rope; as soon as the helicopter starts to hover over the target the No. 1 kicks out the rope. As soon as the rope goes out the No. 1 goes with it; he slides down the fast rope before it hits the bottom of the roof.

I looked up. The helicopters were coming in, lots of noise, lots of downblast, shit flying off the roof. They flared just ten feet above the roof. There were flashbangs exploding, and by now the pilots have taken their NVGs off. The instruments are on a swivel on their helmets; they just push them up above their helmets as NVGs are affected by flashbangs and would be whited out.

The helicopters were straining in a flare position, then started going backwards and forwards two or three feet in a hover. The blokes were streaming down the rope. The No. 3 on each team had quite a task, because as he fast-roped, as well as his equipment, he would be bringing down a rectangular charge over his shoulder. He'd have to be really careful with it so he didn't rip off the det or mess up the wiring.

At one time there were all four of them on the fast rope. As soon as each man's feet hit the bottom he moved out of the way. As they came down they were looking around, looking at the floor, making sure nobody was

coming out of the skylights to start taking a pop at them.

Seconds later, the helis were gone.

Someone put his head out of the top left-hand window; we knew Sierra One had him in his sights; there was no need for us to worry, that was his job. He didn't get on the radio, he just got his telescopic sight on him, covering the assault as it went in. If he was a threat he would soon have a 7.62 Lapua round in his head to make sure he stopped being one.

On the standby the other two snipers around the back, Sierra Three and Four, had gone running forward with G3s, choosing areas where they could cover two sides each. They didn't need telescopic sights because they were so close; their G3s had normal iron sights. They had the outside covered, they could take any runners that were coming out. If the X-rays ran out beyond the snipers they'd get caught in the police cordon, but that never came into the equation; as somebody in B Squadron once said, no-one runs faster than Mr Heckler & Koch.

As the Range Rover stopped, flashbangs were going off.

We jumped off and ran to the main doors. They were locked and still covered over with curtains. Dave secured the charge to the left-hand side door with double-sided tape; there was enough explosive to blow the whole thing in.

Everyone was back against the wall, looking up with weapons covering the windows. If anyone poked their head out with bad intentions they would not enjoy the view for long.

As he moved back, Dave checked with his hand the line of the det cord to the detonator, and then to the firing wire, a last check to make sure everything was right. By checking, he could say, 'Bin it,' if it was screwed up and we'd go straight in with the axes, just as Tiny had had to do at the Embassy. He was rushing, but he was still taking his time to make sure the charge was complete. The last thing he wanted to do was push that clacker and have nothing happen.

Both teams were ready. As Dave went past, Tim, the No. 2, was ready with another flashbang.

I had my weapon up in the aim, ready to go in. As I took off the safety, I shouted, 'Go!'

Our charge and one of the first-floor team's went off at the same time. I started to move. The flashbang flew past me and I followed it in: it would be no good going in after it had finished, I had to be there with it.

The hallway was dark and was starting to fill with smoke from the flashbangs. Another one exploded and I felt the effect of the blast. The noise jarred my whole body and I could feel the pressure on my eardrums. The flash was blinding but I had to work through that. We'd trained enough in these situations; my hands still carried burn marks from when one of the maroons had hit me.

The whole building was shaking with concussion and seared by sheets of blinding light.

On my right I could see the other team moving. I didn't look but I knew that my group would be heading for that first door.

The hallway was clear.

I turned and saw that I was No. 2 at the door. The last two of my lot had gone straight for it and were waiting. I heard flashbangs and firing from the other floors.

I ran over, pulling out a flashbang and getting right behind the first man. I put it over his shoulder so he knew that we were ready.

The No. 3 on the opposite side of us kicked the door open. As soon as four inches of gap appeared the flashbang was in and so were we.

Nobody was worried about what was inside or what would happen when the door was opened. We'd done it so many times. There was no time to think about danger or the possibility of cocking up.

The lights were on and the noise and flashes were doing their job well. Dave went left; as I came in I saw a group of

people huddled together in a corner but no people with masks or weapons.

I heard an MP5 fire. One of the group pulled an AK and was bringing it up.

I got my torch onto his head and gave him a quick burst.

The Yankees were screaming and crying and had to be controlled.

Tim, who was covering both of us as we took the room, shouted, 'Get down, get down!' He pointed his weapon at them to make them understand that he was serious – and because there could be terrorists in the group.

He was now dragging them down onto the floor if they weren't doing what they were told. This was no time to be sensitive and caring.

Dave moved forward at the same time to clear the room. Because he had to move a settee he let his weapon go on its sling and pulled his pistol.

At the same time Tim was shouting: 'Where are the terrorists, any more terrorists?'

Once we cleared the room we were going to the next one. As I came out Tim was pushing people onto the floor and shouting, 'Stay there, don't move!'

The other teams were still doing their stuff. I ran past our No. 4, who was covering the hallway. He was in a corner so that he dominated the whole area and at the same time could see up the staircase.

I got to the door and became No. 1. The bottom of my respirator had filled up with sweat and I was breathing so heavily under all the body armour that I could feel its diaphragm clanking up and down. Tim came up behind me and shoved a flashbang under my nose. Once we had a No. 3 we were ready and in we went.

The room was empty.

Shouts echoed from other rooms as the Yankees were controlled. My breathing was laboured, I was listening to the net, listening to two lots of people speaking at once. Oral commands were being shouted through respirators;

hand signals were flashing from man to man. Throughout the building there were weapons firing, maroons exploding, smoke and people everywhere.

It was very claustrophobic inside the respirator. I was a big sweaty mess, trying to do my job and think of about ten things at the same time.

We still had a problem. We didn't know if any X-rays had hidden among the Yankees – or maybe the Yankees were actively shielding some. The Stockholm Syndrome bonds victims to their captors; they had to be covered with weapons until we knew who was who.

Tim started to move up the stairs, covered by a member from the other team. He moved very slowly, his pistol out, ready. He was making sure there was no threat on the stairs, and ensuring that he didn't have a blue-on-blue with the other link man he was to RV with. They linked up and I got on the net.

It had been just over two minutes from the 'Go, go, go!' The firing had stopped but the shouting had not. Smoke was billowing everywhere and now all the callsigns were sending information back on the net that their areas were clear and what the casualty state was.

Fat Boy said, 'We have a wounded woman.'

I looked around and one of the Yankees was holding her leg.

I got onto the net: 'This is Three, we have a wounded Yankee, request medic back-up, over.'

'Roger that, Three. He is on his way, out.'

Dave went to the door to lead him to the casualty. I then got on the net and gave my sitrep.

By now the whole of the front of the building was flood-lit and the hostage reception were ready for custom.

'All stations, evacuate the Yankees, evacuate the Yankees.'

It looked like a human conveyor belt as we moved people out. They mustn't have time to think, they must be scared; you shout and holler to control them into the arms

of the hostage reception. Everybody was picking them up and shoving them, shouting: 'Get up, get up! Move, move, move!'

They got as hard a time as if they were confirmed terrorists, lined up face down on the floor and handcuffed.

'Stay still, no talking!'

They were covered with pistols.

The SSM came along with a torch, grasped hold of each person's head and pulled it back, shining the powerful beam into their eyes. 'Name?'

When he was satisfied that everyone was who they said they were, they were put on transport and moved away to the police cordon.

'Hello, Alpha One, this is Two. We have a possible IED [*improvised explosive device*]. We have marked it and are moving out. Over.'

They would put a small flashing yellow light on it. The same would be done for a man down; yellow light penetrates smoke better than white.

Someone else was getting direction from CRW.

'Alpha One, roger. RV with ATO, all callsigns evacuate the building, over.'

We all acknowledged, quite pleased to be evacuating. We could get back to the admin area, have a quick debrief, and then it would be wacky races back to Hereford. There was a great rule that whoever came on the helis went back on them. That was fine, apart from having to listen to Steve bang on about his latest squash game.

The exercise had gone smoothly. We'd been good, and so we should have been. We were on the ranges every day, leaping onto buildings, screaming through the CQB house, running around with the vehicles, up and down ladders, practising until we could almost do it blindfolded. The only thing that didn't improve with the training was that we lived our lives with a ring around our faces where the seal of the respirator pressed down.

The X-rays had been members of CRW apart from the

woman, who was from the Home Office. They had been working to a brief that only they knew; however, it could have changed at any time, depending on the actions of us and the other agencies involved. If they had seen anything to arouse their suspicions they would have reacted.

Part of learning to fight terrorists was knowing how to be one, and the blokes in the Regiment, and particularly CRW, were probably the most professional in the world. With our skills and knowledge we could bring down governments in months.

22

Things started to go really well with Fiona. We were sitting in the front room one day having a romantic conversation about electricity bills, and I said, 'This is quite stupid. Why don't we move in together? You virtually live in my house anyway, so why don't you come in?'

'I want to do that,' Fiona said, 'but only if you let me go halves on everything.'

'I buy the washing machine, you buy the hoover?' It sounded good to me, and being on the team at least there was the chance of some time together. We used it to the full.

The house started to take shape. It was a nice little place, in a smart part of town; we really got busy redecorating, putting new doors up, and we both chipped in to have heating installed. Gradually furniture and curtains appeared. As far as I was concerned I'd be there for ever; there was no reason to move. It really felt like home.

In June 1986 I had one of those mornings when I got into work at eight o'clock and was out again by nine-thirty. I came home; I'd been trying to fix the exhaust on the Renault 5 because the bracket kept falling off and I was damned if I was going to pay £15 to have it sorted out. I was trying to hold it on with bits of coat hanger and all sorts.

I'd spent the afternoon doing that, came in, and was sitting down having a cup of tea, watching the telly. Fiona had been down town for a doctor's appointment; she came

in, stood in the doorway, and said, 'I've got something to tell you. I wasn't too sure of your reaction, so I wanted to make sure. Andy, I'm pregnant.'

I felt as if I'd taken a straight right from Mike Tyson. I said, 'This is really good. What do you reckon?'

'I don't know. I don't know if it's good or bad. Do you think we should have the baby? I'm for it if you are.'

'Right, OK, let's do it – let's have a baby.'

Was it the right time, was it the wrong time? Who ever knows? It was scary but it was nice, a wonderful feeling of having created something worthwhile. So there I was, the expectant father.

As the pregnancy progressed Fiona started to go through a bad patch, getting very tired with anaemia. She'd get up in the mornings, walk around, then have to get her head down again. It was lucky that I was on the team, because every spare moment I had I could get back and make her cups of tea and just be there. It would have been tough for her if I'd had to go away; somebody would have had to be there to look after her.

Money was tight. I was still on trooper's pay, although I had reached the dizzy heights of lance-comical. The next step was the big one: corporal's pay was very good indeed. Hopefully I'd have sorted that out by the time the baby was born. Whatever happened, nothing could take away from me how good it felt to have a home and a child on the way.

Around Christmas time, when Fiona was about seven months pregnant, I found out that I had to go away on a team job in February. When I worked out the dates, I found that it was the day before she was due to have our baby.

'That's no problem,' she said. 'We'll look up a few old wives' tales and jump up and down in the rhubarb patch or something to bring the baby a day earlier. It might be early anyway. Let's keep our fingers crossed.'

She went for all the tests and asked, 'What are the chances of getting the baby induced a day early? My

boyfriend's got to go away, and will be away for a few months. He wants to be present at the birth.'

I was getting quite upset about it, because I really wanted to be there: this was the most exciting thing that had ever happened to me. But the team job wasn't going to be knocked back a day just because Lance-comical McNab was going to have a baby.

I started combing magazines for possible 'cures'.

'You'll have to get your finger out the day before,' I said to Fiona, handing her the latest concoction I'd read about – something like Worcester sauce and pineapple juice. 'Give this baby a good talking to. Explain the facts of life – it's got to come out early.'

Life went on. John McCarthy had been kidnapped in Beirut in April 1986. In January 1987, so was Terry Waite. It wasn't long before the press were speculating about what kind of role the Regiment might be playing in securing their release – on 28 January 1987, just a week or so after Waite's disappearance, we all got into the crew room in the morning, normal routine. It was a really miserable old day, windy and raining. Blokes had brought daysacks in as usual, with newspapers and magazines in case we got bored. We passed them around, drinking tea and chatting. The big debate was whether we should have a sports afternoon, a big tradition in the British Army.

We went down to the CQB house for a couple of hours, got back, swept the hangar out and then binned it. For once, we were all nodding in agreement: a sports afternoon, a good thing to do.

Gaz was sitting there reading the paper and he said, 'Fucking hell, look, this is news to me.'

The *Daily Express* had the headline: 'SAS scour crisis city for Waite'.

'Pity we're going on this other job,' Gaz said. 'We might have been getting a suntan soon by the looks of things.'

Nobody was really that concerned about it. If it didn't involve us immediately, we weren't particularly interested.

I said to Gaz, 'It was obvious he was going to get lifted. I don't think there's a bookie in the land would have taken a bet on him not joining McCarthy.'

'I know,' Gaz said. 'And now some lucky fucker's going to be asked to risk his life to get him out.'

Because she'd been so sick during her pregnancy, Fiona had to go into hospital for the last three or four days. I visited her as often as I could, and kept badgering the nurses into agreeing to induce.

'Don't worry,' they said, 'we'll sort it all out.'

I went into work and explained the situation to the SSM. 'What's the latest time I can get away on the Tuesday?' I asked.

The SSM went over to the clerk and said, 'Danny, what's the score on that job? What time are they leaving?'

Danny shuffled through bits of paper and said, 'If he gets his toe down, if he leaves at half past one, he'll get to Heathrow on time.'

'There you go,' said the SSM. 'Half past one.'

As I started walking out he said, 'Andy – make sure you're there. Don't fuck up.'

I went back to the hospital, saw Fiona, and said, 'Tomorrow, at one-thirty, I have to walk out of here whether we have our child or not.'

'I understand, but don't worry – we'll sort something out with the doctors.'

I was getting quite upset; I really wanted to be there when my baby was born. I kissed her goodbye and said, 'Get your finger out! Get this baby born!'

By now her parents had travelled up from Hampshire and were going to stay at the house while I was away. Her mother said, 'Don't worry – if she comes into labour now, you stay with her until one o'clock and then I'll come over.'

I drove back to work to sort myself out so everything was ready to go. I had to run around to find somebody else who was on the team job with me. Johnny Two-Combs was on

it, but I couldn't find him. I went up to the gym and there were Fat Boy and Paul Hill on the weights, taking the piss out of each other.

Paul had joined the army after a career as a croupier in clubs. He had an outrageous lifestyle and was the ultimate party animal, out every night, coming into work knackered in the morning. He and Fat Boy were in the Far East once, playing blackjack in a really downmarket casino. Paul with all his experience and expertise was counting the cards and all sorts – and losing left, right and centre. Fat Boy, so pissed he could hardly sit in his chair, walked away with a fortune.

I said, 'My kit's packed, it's in the block. When you go can you make sure it gets on the wagon?'

'No drama.'

I got back in the car, went home, and spent the night sitting by the telephone.

Nothing happened.

Next morning, the moment I got in the shower, the phone rang.

Fiona's father said, 'She's going into labour. They said there's no rush. Go down in about an hour.'

I was at the hospital ten minutes later.

The contractions started and we sat there drinking tea. She was moved to another room, they put the radio on and brought in the papers. She was scared; I was scared for her. Then she said, 'If the baby doesn't come before you have to go it's not a problem, but I'd really love you to be here.'

It was the first time ever that I'd thought: I don't want to go away. Tomorrow, maybe even in another few hours, but for this moment, I don't want to go. I so much wanted to see this thing that I had created; I had never felt so much affection and attachment as I did for this child that I hadn't even seen.

At nine o'clock a nurse came in and said there was a phone call. Fuck! Fiona and I looked at each other. We were both thinking the same, that they wanted me down there now.

I picked up the phone and it was Paul. 'There's been a change of plan,' he said.

My whole body sank.

He started laughing. 'Gotcha! Just to say, we've decided we might as well all leave together at half one.'

The labour continued. There was me drinking more tea, her getting worse with the contractions, and then at midday, all the pain started. She was swearing and hollering, even with an epidural, calling me every name under the sun. I felt useless. There was nothing I could do except hold her hand. Then she didn't want me to do that. Then she did.

It was a noisy hour. I felt guilty because she was in pain, and even guiltier that I knew I had to leave.

Ever the sensitive father-to-be, I said, 'Look, you'd really better go for it here. I'm off in half an hour.'

'I know, I know, I know.'

Her mum poked her head around the door at quarter past one.

I gave Fiona a kiss on the forehead and said, 'I've got to go.'

'I know – you bastard!'

'I'll see you.'

I got in the car and went straight down to work. Everybody was waiting by the Ministry of Defence Police lodge.

'What's happened?'

'Jack shit.'

We drove to Heathrow at Warp Speed Two, me very pissed off on the back seat and not involved in the banter.

As soon as we arrived I phoned the hospital. Nothing. I checked in and phoned again.

'Anything happened?'

'Who are you?'

'I'm the father.'

'OK, wait.'

I waited for ever. 'Nothing yet.'

I went and had another coffee. The other boys were up at the bar, having a drink.

I phoned again. Still nothing. It was time to board the aircraft. One more call. Nothing.

Just as we were lining up to hand in the boarding passes, I gave it one more try.

'It's McNab again.'

'Wait, wait. I think her mother's going to come and speak to you.'

I heard the phone go down and footsteps running along the corridor.

Her mother picked up the receiver, out of breath: 'Just happened! A couple of minutes ago!'

'All the arms, all the legs?'

'Yes.'

'What is it?'

'It's a girl. She's beautiful. I don't know the weight yet – but everything's fine.'

A girl!

I knew her name was Kate. We'd already worked out what it was going to be. It was quite a shock. It wasn't high elation. I felt numbed; I just thought, I'm a father now – and it must have been very smoky in the departures lounge that day because as I put the phone down my eyes were watering.

I joined the others on the aircraft and Paul said, 'She had it?'

'Yeah, it's a girl.'

'Congratulations, mate.' He shook my hand, all smiles. 'It feels great, doesn't it?'

Even Paul, who lived his life somersaulting from good time to good time, could remember what it felt like. He had a passion about his daughter that I'd never been able to understand; it seemed so strange, coming from him. This bloke who didn't seem to care about anything, just having fun and working and really going for it, down in his heart and at the back of his head, continuously, was his daughter. Now I understood. Now I knew exactly how he felt.

One of the benefits of going on a team job was that we

travelled Club Class, so it was straight into the little bottles of champagne as we toasted my good news. It was a long flight and the six of us got quietly pissed.

For weeks I was waiting for more news. Letters always had to go to Hereford for collation, and were then sent on to an embassy or a consulate, or the agency that we were working for in whichever country. It took a while for them to get to us, and I was gagging for a picture. At last, two letters turned up. I could feel that there were pictures inside. As I ripped open the envelopes blokes gathered around.

Two-Combs looked over my shoulder and said, 'She's beautiful, isn't she?'

'Fuck off,' I said. 'She's all greasy and covered in mucus. However, yes, she is.'

Then we all sat around cooing and admiring.

It was a really shitty job for me, tucked away on the side of a mountain for weeks on end, wishing that I was back in Hereford. But you have to make a positive out of a negative, which in this case was that at least it was another part of the world I hadn't seen.

I came back in late May 1987, having lost two stone. I was ill with dysentery, but not in such a bad way as Two-Combs, who was diagnosed as having typhoid. Two days later they decided it was a rupturing appendix.

We got back to the camp and unloaded all the kit. Fat Boy phoned his wife to come and pick him up, and said he'd drop me home.

As we drove around to the house I saw the curtain twitch, and then Fiona came out onto the path with a bundle in her arms.

I gave Fiona a kiss then took the baby, all wrapped up and asleep. I peeked inside the shawl and saw her face for the first time. I had a shock; her lip looked deformed. However, the most beautiful deformed baby in the world.

'What's wrong with her?' I said. 'Is she all right?'

'She's only sucking her lip,' Fiona laughed. 'Don't worry, she's perfect.'

Mr and Mrs Fat Boy came over, clucking like two hens. They were as smitten as I was, and that was the start of it: for the next few years they were producing children like people possessed.

It was wonderful to have some time with Kate. I spent hours watching her little hands all clenched up, and I kept thinking: I made that! I hated the time that she was asleep, and willed her to wake up; I soon learned that all they're doing at that age is sleeping and shitting, but that was beside the point.

Eno and I got an approach to take a two-year sabbatical from the Regiment and join the 'Det', an intelligence unit operating in Northern Ireland. I was on the MOE team at the time and Eno was on the sniper team.

We were having an administration morning in the crew room, dragging our kit out, scrubbing it and cleaning weapons. The clerk came over and said, 'Andy and Eno, the squadron OC wants to see you.'

'Have we fucked up anywhere?' I said.

'I don't think so.'

Eno looked as nonchalant and unconcerned as ever; he was so unflappable his heart must have only just about ticked over.

The Boss was sitting at his desk. 'Right,' he said, 'what would you say if I said to you, Do you fancy going over the water for two years with the Det?'

We both said, 'No way.'

The Det had once wanted a Regiment bloke to go and hide in Dungannon, watching people go in and out of a betting office. The OP was compromised by kids and the bloke got away, but the Det wanted him to go back the next day and do exactly the same. The ops officer of the Det was overheard saying, 'It doesn't really matter if he gets compromised because he's not one of us.' John, who was

running the troop, heard about this and went over and sorted it out in his normal persuasive manner.

Now it appeared that two blokes from each squadron were getting approached and asked if they wanted to go. Most of them were saying no; in the end the CO called in all the squadrons and said, 'The Det is something that you will do. The skills that they've got, we must have back. We're starting to lose it, yet we're the ones that developed it. One way or another, we will regain that skill. It's all part of becoming a complete soldier – we need complete soldiers.' He was quite a forceful character; you either loved him or hated him, there was no in-between.

A few days later we were called back to the OC. 'You have two options,' he said. 'You're either going over the water for two years, or you're going nowhere. You volunteered for the Regiment, you volunteered for operations. This is an operation; if you're refusing to go on operations, you're not staying in the Regiment.'

So that was us off to the Det then.

In the old days, with a division of responsibilities in Northern Ireland between MI5 and MI6, intelligence generally was piss poor. As a result, in 1972, the army established its own secret intelligence gathering unit, which was given the cover name '14th Intelligence Unit', or '14 Int' for short. Recruits were taken from regular army regiments and put through a course that lasted several weeks and covered elementary techniques of covert surveillance, communications and agent running.

Selection for 14 Int, known to us as the 'Det', emphasized the need for resourcefulness and psychological strength. There was not much call for the physical stamina needed for the Regiment. It was designed to find people – usually officers and NCOs in their mid- to late-twenties, in all three of the services – who were able to carry out long-term surveillance, sometimes only a few feet from armed terrorists.

My appreciation of what was going on at the time was

that the Det was looking for a role beyond Northern Ireland. They started saying they could do all our forward recces for us in dangerous areas around the world, but that was a load of nonsense. All their training was for Northern Ireland; they couldn't go forward and do our recces because they didn't know, for example, what our mortars or helicopters and troops would require. Little wonder they were called the 'Walts' – short for Walter Mittys.

The Regiment decided that they were going to get people to go into the Det as part of their normal regimental career. You needed an aptitude, but Eno and I didn't even want to be tested. There was a lot of anti-feeling about the Det, a feeling of 'them' and 'us'.

Four of us drove up – me, Eno, a fellow from D Squadron called Mac, and Bob P from G Squadron. None of us wanted to be there; we all felt press-ganged.

The first person I bumped into was Tiny. 'I'm on the training team,' he grinned. 'You can call me Staff.'

Eno said, 'You can shove that right up your arse – Staff.' We knew all the training teams, all the cooks, everybody who worked there. 'The next six months are going to be really intensive,' the DS said. 'There is no time off. The only time you will leave this camp is when you're working. If not, you stay in camp. There are reasons for that, and we're not going to explain them at the moment.'

The four of us looked at each other and thought, fuck this.

For the first couple of nights we were sitting there like dickheads. Finally Mac said, 'I'll get on the phone to my wife, she'll come down and pick us up.'

We put our running kit on and made it look as if we were going for a run on the training area. We jogged down the road, got in the car, and shot off to Hereford.

Another time, we organized a lift with some of the team who happened to be training in the same area as us. The getaway was planned as intricately as a proper operation;

the only problem was trying to stop people giggling as we drove out of the gate.

I got home most nights by eleven, and had to leave the next morning by six, but it was worth it. I was all bitter and twisted, and cheating the system made me feel better.

After a month of this the Det head shed got wind of it and decided we needed gripping. We were becoming quite anti and a law unto ourselves. Mac got binned from the course, which only made me even more resentful. After so long in the Regiment, living in an adult system, all of a sudden we went back ten years, and I hated it. He was chuffed to bits to be back on the squadron; the moment he got back, however, he was told he was on the next course, starting from scratch.

The rest of the people on the course were not supposed to know who we were, but this didn't work because there were people on the course who had done Selection with us and failed, as well as people from our own regiments. One evening I was sitting in the cookhouse with Eno and Bob P, slagging everybody down in Swahili. A couple of G Squadron came in, got their food, and spotted us. 'Oi, Andy, how's it going?' They came over, sat down, and we carried on chatting.

'How's it going in the Walts, then? You got your sneaky beaky kit yet?'

'Mm, yeah, it's really good.'

I made sure they knew we were press-ganged; I didn't want anybody thinking we'd volunteered for this cowboy stuff.

'Oh well, see you later,' they said. 'We're down the town now – it's Friday night. What are you doing tonight? You boys have fun polishing your pistols.'

They left and I didn't think any more about it. About a week later a couple of B Squadron blokes saw us in the gym and said, 'Remember last week, when you were talking to G Squadron boys? They got a severe fine. Somebody saw you talking together and said it's compromising!'

It only got us more sparked up and annoyed. This whole thing really was a pain in the arse.

Because the course catered for anybody from anywhere, the lessons started with things like, 'This is a bergen.' They had to do it, but we were spending this month being taught stuff that we'd been doing for years. I'd never been so bored. At last, however, the training progressed to skills that were new to me, and I started to get a bit interested. We learned different surveillance skills, counter-surveillance skills, how to give as much information as possible on the net in the least number of words. Their CQB course was pure pistol work; for us, there was no stress, no strain, it was great. We'd be on the ranges all day, come back and do surveillance skills or CTR skills at getting into factories and houses. Sometimes it was like a comedy of errors, people getting stuck halfway through windows and collapsing with laughter.

Everybody was given an alternative identity, keeping the same initials, and the same Christian name, and something similar to our real name so we didn't forget it. Working under an alias, we'd always sign our name in a way that reminded us what we were doing – perhaps it was a pen of a striking colour, or one that we kept in our right-hand breast pocket rather than the left.

We learned the skills of covert entry into a house to look for equipment. We learned how to follow a man and his family for weeks to find out what their routines were, where they went, who they did what with, trying to establish a time when we could get into the house. Does he go to a social club every Saturday night with his wife and kids? Maybe on average he gets back at about midnight, so you've got between eight and midnight to get in. But that's not good enough. If it's in July, it's not going to get dark until half ten. So you might have to wait a couple of months, or get a time when he goes away, maybe to visit his parents for the weekend.

The surveillance had to be on him all the time, to make

sure that when he did go to the club with his wife and kids, his wife didn't leave early to put the kids to bed. We had to have actions on what would happen if we got in there and somebody came home unexpectedly? It took weeks and weeks of preparation.

We had to learn how to use all sorts of cameras, including infrared equipment that would enable us to photograph serial numbers and documents – and to photograph photographs. It was a far cry from my days in the camping shops of Peckham.

I discovered it was quite an intense time, getting into somebody's house – the pressure of doing it as quickly as possible yet at the same time being methodical and not cutting any corners, because you knew that the result of carelessness could be somebody's death. By the end of the course I had learned many different methods of planning and preparation, and had acquired a whole new range of surveillance, technical attack and covert CTR skills. I realized that I was fortunate, and I looked forward to putting them all into practice over the water.

Just before it was time to leave Fiona and I had a chat.

'I've got five days off,' I said. 'Do you fancy getting married?'

'Why not?'

Indeed, why not? We were a family. By now we'd moved house again, into one of the new estates on the edge of Hereford, and everything looked perfect.

Dave, the patrol commander from Keady in my Green Jackets days, was best man. He did his duties, then spent the rest of the day trying to seduce the witness, one of Fiona's friends. Kate was the bridesmaid.

It was Kate's very first Christmas. We went to stay at a house on the south coast. Kate wasn't sleeping very well, which I thought was great. I got the pram out at midnight, wrapped her up well, and we went walking along the coastal path until six in the morning. She fell asleep after the first half an hour, and as I walked I just looked at her

beautiful little face and clucked like a hen. When we got back she woke up again so I put her in the car and we went for a drive. I kept checking over my shoulder to see that she was all right. She had fearsome big blue eyes that stared at me from inside all the wrappings of woollens and a bobble hat. It was a very special time. In the next two years I would only see her for a total of twelve weeks.

'Jarking', the planting of miniature transmitters inside weapons, more correctly known as 'technical attack', had started in the late Seventies, and offered an extra option to the security forces when they found an arms cache. The idea was that the devices would be activated when the weapon was picked up, and the terrorists' movements could then be monitored.

I'd settled into the Det and was really enjoying it. Eno and I were sent to the same Det, which was working around Derry city and surrounding county. At half past six every night we had 'prayers'. All the operators came in and we ran through administrative and operational points.

It was Easter time. We had a bar in a hut, hundreds of cans stacked up and working on a trust system. Everybody was getting a bollocking for a party that had happened the weekend before. The Det had a strong reputation for being outrageous in the bar, so much so that the windows were detachable for parties. There was a strange ritual in the bar for any new member that arrived; everybody saved up their empty cans and the Det OC would come in and say, 'Welcome to the Det. Here we have a celebratory pint of Guinness.' You had to drink it while they pelted you with empty cans. The party was one of these welcoming things for two scaleys that had turned up, but it got totally out of control. One of the blokes had a Duran Duran haircut that he was really proud of; the others held him down and started cutting it; he jumped to his feet and started punching people out. They got two planks of wood and turned it into a cross. They tied him on, hoiked it up, and left him hanging there.

In Tsodilo Hills, Botswana 1986.

Members of 6 and 7 Troop in the Okavango 1986.

Preparing for a patrol with 'the boys', Latin America, 1989. Rodriguez is second from left.

Training in typical savannah, 1989.

Members of the team posing against Huey. McNab is second from left.

'The boy': team photo.

Shantelle estate, Londonderry 1987.

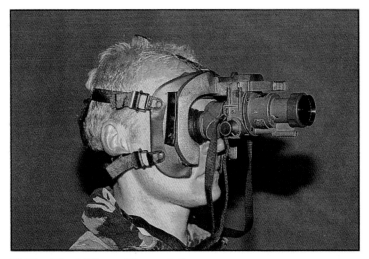

PNGs. *The Military Picture Library*

Beltkit with
tree-beater.
*The Military
Picture Library*

G3 with
collapsible stock.
Heckler & Koch

Basic beltkit.
The Military Picture Library

Flashbang.
The Military Picture Library

Beltkit and khukri.
The Military Picture Library

Red team, 1989. McNab is standing centre rear in blue T-shirt.

Sig P226 9mm.
Sig/TRH Pictures

Heckler & Koch
9mm MP5K.
*Heckler &
Koch/TRH Pictures*

Heckler & Koch 9mm MP5.
Heckler & Koch/TRH Pictures

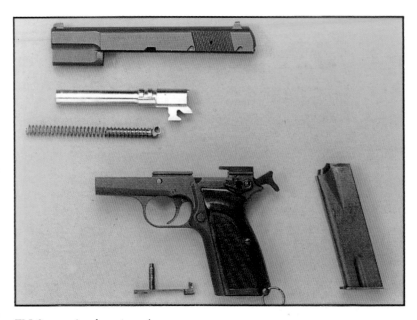

FN 9mm pistol, stripped.
FN/TRH Pictures

Heckler & Koch 9mm MP5SD.
Heckler & Koch/TRH Pictures

* * *

We put into practice all the skills that we had learned during the build-up. Covert searches of houses, office blocks, shops to gather information. It was a kick, without a doubt, going into somebody's house, finding information, and getting back out again. In the hard housing estates, places like the Bogside, Shantello, the Creggan, it was no easy operation to get into places, and it would take days, and sometimes weeks, of planning for a job that might take only thirty seconds to carry out.

At the end of the day, it was inevitable that the IRA would discover that its weapons were being jarked. These people were not idiots, they had scanning devices and all sorts. We were all playing a game; they knew that the weapons were being tampered with, they knew that their buildings were bugged. They would use countermeasures, which we would then try to counter-counter. Another possibility open to us was to replace bomb-making materials found in the hides.

A novelist wrote a book in which the coffins at an IRA funeral were bugged so that the intelligence services could hear what was being said; from the moment it was published, it became an IRA procedure that every coffin and body was scanned with location devices.

By now it was the summer of 1988 and Fiona was running around looking for a new house. Prices were going bananas, spiralling out of control. We made an absolute fortune in the space of a few months; a woman cried on the telephone because she was too late in buying the house.

'We'll now buy the biggest house we can with our money and do it up,' I said.

She found us a place while I was away, in a village about six miles from Hereford. The house was bigger, but needed some work done to it. It was really exciting. I came back on five days' leave and as soon as I got back we moved in. We got cracking. We went down to the plant hire place and

hired everything from strimmers to chainsaws for our five-day blitz. As soon as it was light we started on the outside; as soon as it was dark we started on the inside. At 4.30 a.m. one morning I painted the garage door, and at 10 p.m. was stripping wallpaper in the living room. I loved it; it was family life: I now had a three-bedroomed, detached house, a garage, a couple of trees in the garden. As a young kid I had lived in council houses or my aunty's house, and now I was looking at this wonderful place and it was mine. I had a wife, a child, a happy life in a small village, and everything was perfect. The future looked rosy. Kate was still in nappies, and just to sit there and hold her was very special. She had my eyes, and I never got tired of looking into them.

We were staking out a bomb factory in an old Victorian house that was halfway through renovation, with white-washed windows and bare floors. We knew it was a factory because Dave 1 and I had been in it the night before. We'd cleared the house, pistols in hand, in a semi-crouch. The kitchen was bare concrete. Standing in the middle of the floor was an industrial coffee grinder: there might as well have been a sign up saying 'Bomb Factory'. We knew they would be mixing bomb ingredients at some point. From now on we would have to stay 'on target', watching as people went in and out of the house. Low explosives don't last that long if not protected from the elements. Once a bomb was made, therefore, they tried to use it as quickly as possible: we had to be there to stop that.

'That's two men, green on blue jeans, brown on black jeans and bald.'

'That's them into the house. Over.'

'Alpha. Roger.'

The stake-out took for ever and we had to walk past the target to try to make out what was going on. Had they finished? Were they still at it?

'That's Delta going Foxtrot.'

Alpha replied: 'Delta's Foxtrot.' (*On foot.*)

I got out of my car. I was wearing a pair of jeans, market trainers and my blue bomber jacket. My hair looked like an eighteen-year-old football player's – long at the back, with short sides. It was greasy and I looked as if I had just got out of bed and was going to sign on. My car was old and in shit state to go with its owner.

We were in Derry, between the Bogside and Creggan estates. The names suited the area, dark grey and cold, lines of terraced houses going up the hill towards the Creggan. It was winter and I could smell peat smoke.

Alpha, who was the team leader on the ground, wanted someone to walk the alleyway that was between the back of two rows of houses. I was nearest and hadn't walked past yet.

I clicked my comms: 'Delta, check.'

'Alpha.'

As I got nearer to the alleyway I noticed two lads on the corner. They looked more or less the same as me, apart from the cigarettes in their mouths and the rolled-up newspapers in their back pockets. They were sitting on a low wall at the entry point to the alleyway. Were they dickers? I didn't know.

The weather was cold and damp. This was good; I could get my hands in my jacket pockets and get my head down, walking as if I was going somewhere.

As I turned right into the alley and looked uphill there was nothing. The alleyway was just hard mud, filled with old cans and dogshit. The two boys took no notice as I walked past. It seemed they were waiting for the bookies to open.

It was a horrible feeling going up that alleyway, knowing that these people were behind me. I walked with a purpose, not hesitating or looking behind. I kept looking at the ground, as if I was in a bit of a daze. I was a bag of shit so I walked like a bag of shit. Tucked in my jeans I had my 9mm Browning and plenty of rounds. If they said anything

to me as I went in I would have to try and avoid answering.

'Alpha, Delta, check?'

They wanted to know how I was doing.

I couldn't talk on my radio; the two boys would hear. I clicked my pressle button twice to send two quick bursts of squelch.

'Alpha, roger that.'

Everyone now knew things were OK.

The back door was closed but I could just hear the faint buzz of the coffee grinder in the back of the house: they were still making the bomb.

People were passing; I could not talk yet, but I could hear everyone else on the net.

'Alpha, November, going mobile.' Eno was off somewhere else.

'Alpha, roger that. Delta, check.'

Click. Click.

'Roger that, are you past the house yet?'

Click. Click.

'Is the grinding still going?'

Click. Click.

I went into the corner shop and got a pint of milk and the *Sporting Life*. Now I would take a walk past the front and see if I could make out anything inside.

'Alpha, Lima, I have Delta walking back to his Charlie.'

'Alpha.'

Rick had seen me and was telling everyone what was happening. He had been in the Det for years and was an excellent operator. He often had clashes with the head shed as he was a very outspoken person; however, whatever he said made sense.

'Delta's complete.' (*Back in the car.*)

'Alpha.'

I was now in my car and I drove off.

Nothing happened for about two hours. I was still part of the stake-out but not on top of the target, as I had already been exposed. This didn't mean that I'd hang slack. There

was still a job to do. Everything that passed me, I had to check it out. As well as seeing who was in the area so I could report it to others, I could also detect the mood of the place: does it look any different today? If so, why?

This was not a place that the tourist board would recommend. There was nothing passive about this work. Only a few months before, an operator was shot near where I was sitting. He'd been doing exactly the same as I was, parked up and waiting to go and do something. The players saw him, must have thought there was something wriggly, went and got their weapons and head-jobbed him.

I was parked in a line of cars outside a row of terraced Victorian houses. I had the newspaper open and was eating a sandwich. In front of me, about 100 metres away, was the road that the target was on, crossing left to right.

Alpha was talking on the net and organizing things to make sure he had a good, tight stake-out, when all of a sudden a blue flash went past me, two up (*two in the car*). I saw a face looking down the road; he was aware.

I tried to cut in on the net. 'Standby, standby. Charlie One is mobile. That's Charlie One mobile.'

I couldn't get in; Alpha was still on the net. I had no choice but to 'take' it. 'That's Delta mobile.'

I carried on talking on the net, burning up the road towards the target car. I wasn't worried about the compromise factor now. It wouldn't matter if I was leaving chaos behind me, as long as the players in front didn't notice anything. The important thing was not to lose that bomb. If we did, we were talking about a lot of dead people. Passing a junction, I looked down left but couldn't see anything. I raced downhill to the right, down towards the Bogside. As I passed two junctions I kept giving a commentary: 'Standby, standby. Charlie One's mobile. Down towards the Bogside.'

At last I got on the net. 'That's at the Bogside, still straight, still straight. He's going towards the Little Diamond [*an area of the Bogside*].'

'Lima's mobile. Lima's trying to back you.' Rick was driving fast towards me.

I found the target again just as it went into the Bogside, and closed up.

'That's possibly two up, Sierra sixty to sixty-five. He's moving!'

'Alpha.'

'November, Roger that.'

The rest of the team were now racing towards the scene. To lose contact with the bomb team could be fatal.

The passenger was turning around, looking straight at me. I tried to look casual; we had a bit of eye-to-eye contact and I looked away. I wanted the bomb to get to its destination, us to find the new hide, get the device and put a stop to their plans. To have a contact was pointless; we wouldn't know the whole picture then.

I was up at him now and he was still looking straight at me.

'That's confirmed, two up, very aware.'

We were not going to do anything yet as they might take us to another safe house. But if they were going to place the bomb, we would be there. We just had to keep with it.

By now I had the skill to give a commentary on the net, telling everyone what was going on, not moving my lips, trying not to catch the eye of the boys in the car, but at the same time stay with them.

'He's turning left. Stop, stop, stop. Delta's Foxtrot.'

He got down to the bottom past the Bogside and turned left towards the Little Diamond.

'That's now left towards the Little Diamond. He's going into the first option left.' I knew the city back to front; I'd spent so many hours learning it and walking it; I knew where all the players lived, what their kids looked like, where the kids went to school. I knew this was a dead end. 'That's a stop, stop, stop! Stop, stop, stop!'

I drove past their car and went off onto the waste area of the Rosville Flats, the area of the Bloody Sunday shootings, where there was a car park. I stopped and got out. I had to

get on the ground straightaway so that by the time he'd parked I was out and walking.

'Lima's Foxtrot.'

Rick was right behind me and stopped his car as soon as they turned into the Bogside. I saw him walking into the dead end of the estate. That took a lot of bollocks; he didn't know what he was walking into. Were they armed? Were they ready with the bomb, was it now being brought out and moved into another wagon? Was it going to be an armed bombing?

As I walked towards the open square of the estate I saw an old converted container lorry that served as a shop. Children were running around, women were hanging off the balconies. There were a few cars parked up. There was nowhere to go, but we had to make it look as if we were going somewhere. It was no good knowing just that the bomb was in the Bogside, because the estate was a warren of little alleyways. We needed to know precisely where it was, and who was handling it.

Rick walked past the shop and then saw the car. I followed to back him up in case of dickers or a trap.

He said, 'Standby, standby. Charlie One's being unloaded. That's now being unloaded.'

I said, 'Delta's backing. Delta's backing you, Lima.'

'They're loading it top left-hand side. It's getting unloaded into the top left-hand-side flat. That's confirmed. That's confirmed.'

Rick was walking through the alleyway. As he got further out he was able to talk. 'Alpha, Lima. The device was unloaded and it went into the top left-hand flat. There were about three people holding it, and there were two dickers. It looks abandoned. There's some boards up on the windows.'

'Alpha, roger that.'

By this time I could hear the other cars in the area, keeping an eye out for other players. They would be watching the entrance to the square; the players might just be putting it in there, priming it up, putting it in another wagon and

running it out. That bomb now had to be controlled all the time. It mustn't go anywhere. Not so easy in the Bogside, but we did it.

The decision was made to lift the bomb by having the police raid the square and take it. There was nothing much said in any newspaper, national or local, about the incident. It was just another 'find'. PIRA put it down to a tout, but it wasn't anything of the kind. It was the Det spending hours of intelligence gathering and surveillance. The way this was done was by people being in these hard areas and getting up against the targets. If that bomb had gone off, tens of people could have been killed.

Such incidents made me glad that I had been sent to the Det. They made me understand how professional they were and not just Walter Mittys. Having said that, I would never admit it: they were still the 'Walts'.

By now I was a corporal and things looked promising. Eno and I were team leaders in the Det and even considered coming back for a second tour. The words of the CO at the time of the great press-gang had been, 'What we want is a complete soldier, one who can operate from both sides of the coin. The only way you are going to get operational experience on the other side is by going to the Det.'

He was scoffed at then. But now, I knew he was right. The Regiment were getting the most highly trained and operationally experienced soldiers in the world, capable of manning a GPMG in a slit trench or walking around an alien environment, blending in and gaining information, and I was very proud to be part of that.

Eno, Brendan, Dave 2 and I were out on the ground one day, following two boys out of the Bogside up towards the Creggan Estate. They were moving carrying rifles and radios wrapped in black bin liners.

On the net I heard, 'Stop, stop, stop.'

The boys had stopped somewhere behind a row of buildings. Eno came on the net, 'That's them now complete.

That's now complete – one of the gardens. Wait . . . wait . . . That's now complete the row of gardens – twenty-four, twenty-five, twenty-six.'

We now knew that they were messing around in the area of those gardens and Eno could see them. As he walked past the fence that ran parallel, he looked left out of the corners of his eyes. 'They're putting it in the coalshed. They're putting it in the coalshed. Wait . . . wait . . . That's confirmed, the weapons are in the coalshed.'

Brendan, the team leader, still in his car, came back: 'Alpha, roger that.'

We'd just spent the last three hours following these people around. We'd picked them up in the Bogside, where there was a hide that we knew contained weapons. The Bogside was a maze of Sixties-style, concrete and glass flats and maisonettes linked by alleyways and dead ends. The place was in shit state. Dogs barked and skulked, kids hollered and hurtled around on pushbikes or kicked balls against the wall. Women shouted at each other over the landings. Unemployed men sat on steps, smoking and talking. It was November, and at three-thirty in the afternoon it was very cold.

We wanted to make sure where the weapons were going to. We 'took' them from the Bogside up towards the Creggan, and now they were behind these three houses.

The Creggan was on the opposite high ground, the other side of the valley, looking down on the walled city of Derry. Unlike the Bogside, it was laid out in long lines of brown brick, terraced houses – a big estate with a central grassy area and shops and a library. By the time we got up there it was just starting to get dark and I could see my breath. I was wearing an old German army parka, jeans and trainers. My hair was still long and greasy and I hadn't shaved for days; I blended in well. I felt quite happy in these areas now; we'd been on the ground for some time and were well tuned in. And at the end of the day, I had a big fat gun tucked inside my jeans.

These were hard areas and there had been a lot of contacts. I laughed to myself when I remembered the phrase 'passive surveillance'. I thought, there's fuck all passive about being in the Bogside, following two blokes with weapons, going up to the Creggan to see what they're going to do with them.

Eno came on the net, 'I'll go for the trigger.'

Alpha came back, 'Roger that. November's going for the trigger.'

We now had to control the weapons; if they were moved from that spot we had to know and be able to follow them, wherever they went. If they stayed put, the plan was to get them out of the coalshed later that night and jark them there and then on the spot. Either way, we would have control. The problem was, hanging around in the Creggan for that amount of time. Everybody on these estates was very aware, from small children to old grannies. There was always an atmosphere of high tension. Two weeks before, a soldier had got shot straight through the head, and everybody on the estate was well pleased with the effort.

Eno was at the bottom of the garden, down a little walkway that ran between some garages and the garden itself. He was tucked in to one side; if he got discovered, he'd just pretend that he was having a piss and then walk away. This was where all the CQB training and skills came in: it was deciding when the situation demanded that you pull that gun.

He whispered, 'November's got the trigger. I'm down the bottom of the path, between the garages and the gardens.'

'Alpha, roger that. November's got the trigger.'

Eno was going to stand there in the dark, about fifteen metres from the weapons. If there was no need to move until midnight, he wouldn't. Brendan was further down the road in a car, ready to back Eno if anything happened. Dave 2 and I were just swanning around, me in my eight-year-old Volkswagen GT waiting to respond.

I parked up. It was now about five-thirty in the evening and all the street lights were on. Smoke started to pour from the chimney pots and I could smell burning peat and coal. The field across the road was a jumble of wrecked cars and roaming horses. It was starting to drizzle.

I got out of the car and said, 'That's Delta going Foxtrot.'

'Alpha, roger that – Delta's going Foxtrot.'

I heard: 'That's Golf going Foxtrot.'

We were all off to the Spar shop down the road. I bought my 'blending in' items – a can of Coke and a copy of the *Sun* – and lounged against the wall. Dave 2 bought a bag of chips from the van outside and joined me for a brief chat.

I drove around the block, parked up somewhere else, and went for a walk. It was about seven o'clock when I heard Eno's voice, calm as ever: 'Standby, standby. That's two Charlies coming in.'

He gave the registration numbers and descriptions of the cars.

'That's three Bravos coming out. One with long dark hair, jean jacket and jeans; one with a blue nylon parka and black trousers, one with a green bomber jacket and blue jeans.

'It's looking all very businesslike,' he said. 'It isn't a social thing. They're very aware. Something's on.'

I sat in the car, reading the *Sun* and drinking my Coke.

Alpha acknowledged. Other callsigns went mobile, orbiting around Eno.

About twenty minutes later, I heard: 'Standby, standby. That's three Bravos Foxtrot towards the car. That's at the cars, still going straight. They're walking towards me. They're starting to put masks on. Possible contact. Possible contact. Standby.' Eno never flapped; his voice was calm and relaxed.

If they were putting the masks on and walking towards him, as far as he was concerned he'd been compromised – but maybe not yet. He hadn't seen any weapons, so it was pointless doing anything at the moment.

Very casually, he started to describe what was going on: 'They're still coming towards me.'

We were getting out of the cars; we had to start closing in, but we had to do it in such a manner that it didn't compromise what was going on. It might be a false alarm. They might just walk past, and go and do something else; then we'd follow them. As they got closer to him, Eno couldn't talk. I started to walk quite fast towards him.

Alpha got on the net: 'November, check.'

Eno gave him two clicks.

'Are they still coming towards you?'

Click, click.

'Have they still got their masks on?'

Click, click.

It went quiet for a while. I was still walking fast. As I got to the area of the cars I could see down the alleyway. I always used to carry my pistol tucked down the front of my jeans. I remembered the story Mick had told us about the boy getting pushed in the Shantello; the only thing that had saved him as he rolled was having his pistol to the front. I took my gloves off as I walked and threw them on the floor. If I had to draw my gun I'd lift my jacket with my left hand as high as it would go, with a big aggressive motion, then draw my pistol with my right. I was expecting to see these boys going down the alleyway to Eno and opening fire, but I saw jack shit.

All of a sudden Eno came on the net, 'They've gone right, they've gone down the side of the garages.'

As I looked down the line of the fence to the right of me was a line of garages. I knew they'd gone down there and were walking behind the garages. They didn't have the weapons; they were still in the coalshed. So what were they up to?

Brendan was coming from another direction, walking along the back of the garages. As soon as he heard that they'd turned right he did a quick about-turn and walked

off. He didn't want a head-to-head. However, he now had these three masked boys behind him.

He landed up walking about ten metres in front of them, down the same roadway. He could hear them getting closer and closer. He could hear them talking.

'That's it – they're right behind me. Standby for a possible contact.'

I knew Eno was off to my left-hand side somewhere. I wanted to make sure I got behind these people. Then I heard Brendan: 'I have from the front. I have from the front.'

I said, 'That's Delta backing you, Hotel.'

Dave 2 said, 'Golf's mobile.'

Wherever we went now, Dave 2 would make sure he was following us with the motor. We kept on walking. They weren't talking, and were fairly aware. The alleyway was a well-used thoroughfare that linked two sets of gardens; it wasn't suspicious for us to be there. The ground was pitted asphalt, littered with old cans. Looking to the left I saw people doing their dishes at misted-up kitchen windows.

'Golf, Delta, check.'

Click, click.

'Are you still backing?'

Click, click.

'Are they still along the back of the garages?'

Click, click.

'Are they still hooded up?'

Click, click.

The garages went on for about sixty or seventy metres. As they got to the end, they turned right. Brendan kept on going straight; I came on the net and said, 'They've gone right towards the main.' (*Main road.*)

Brendan said, 'Roger that. I'm going complete. I'm going to my car.'

I said, 'Delta has unsighted. Wait. That's unsighted, Delta checking.'

I got to the edge and turned right, just catching them out

of the right-hand side of my vision. They were opening up a garage right at the end. But they didn't have masks on. I carried on walking and said, 'That's the three Bravos, they're at the very end garage and their masks are off. I do not have.'

I had to keep going straight. This was worrying; nobody had got them now. Were they going to drive off?

Dave 2 parked up on the other side of the road and was looking down. He came on the net: 'Golf has, Golf has.'

I said, 'That's Delta going complete,' and headed for my car.

Dave was giving a commentary on what was going on: they went into the garage, put the light on, were in there for about two minutes, mucked around with a car inside, came out, and closed the door. 'That's them now walking back to the house.'

Then Eno picked them up. 'November has. They're now going complete the house [*into the house*], with no masks on.'

'Alpha, roger that.'

We didn't have a clue what was going on. This was often one of the big problems facing us: we saw things, but we didn't know what they meant because we'd only seen a proportion of the action. Why had they got masks on? Why had they taken them off? Had they just cancelled something? Had they cancelled it because they'd seen us? Or were they just doing a drill? But why practise with the masks on?

None of our questions was ever answered. The four of us had to lift off and another team come in to take over; we were overexposed in that area now and might have been compromised.

When we got back to the briefing room, the Boss said, 'We're not going to put a tech attack in. We're going to lift it tonight.'

The other team was now covering the weapons. The RUC went down and searched a lot of houses, lifted

the weapons, and that was the end of that. We never found out why the boys had their masks on.

Some of the characters got so much into the work that they didn't want to leave. Some blokes were on their third or fourth tour, completely caught up in it. There were some weird guys there as well, who couldn't cut between real life and what was going on in their work. I knew I was starting to get totally engrossed. It was exciting being in the Bogside on a Saturday night at eleven o'clock, watching known players come out of the pub, lining up and getting their food. Even if we weren't working we'd go down for some 'orientation', walking around and getting to know the places and the people. After a while, we got comfortable in these well-hard areas, and could tell instinctively when something was up.

Dave 1 was well on the road to the funny farm. The sink overflowed in his room while he was out. When he came back, the carpet was totally sogged up. Dave's remedy wasn't to take the carpet up or open the windows and let it dry out, it was to go and buy an huge bag of mustard and cress seed and sow it. Then he turned the heater up, closed the door, and proceeded to live in a room full of crops. 'Want to know how to survive, Andy?' he said to me once. 'Never eat anything larger than your own head, anything that you can't pronounce or spell, or tomatoes.'

Sometimes such bizarre things happened on operations that I'd wonder if I was in a dream. It appeared once that at some point in the next few days, at pub kicking out time, some buses were going to be hijacked from the bus station, put across the street as barricades and burnt. We put in a number of reactive OPs so that when it happened the HMSU (*RUC Headquarters Mobile Support Unit*) could steam in and do their business – and if the police couldn't get there, we'd be the last resort.

We split up into three gangs of two and were in positions from where we could trigger it. Me and Eno had MP5s and

9mm pistols. To get as close as we could, we decided to crawl into the scrubland where the concrete area of the bus depot ended, right on the edge of the compound itself. If we did get compromised we'd have it that we were on the piss, so we each took a couple of cans of Tennants lager, the ones with the picture of the woman on the back. We sat down and nursed Penelope and Samantha, keeping our eyes on the target.

Everybody started streaming out of the pubs and getting on the buses to take them out to their little enclaves around Strabane. There was a taxi rank nearby as well, and it was the typical Friday night scene. All the boys were pissed up, trying to chat up fat slags who smelled of outrageous cheap perfume and were more interested in shovelling large pizzas into their faces than in getting laid.

The next thing that caught our attention was two women, hollering and shouting with each other, laughing away and smoking. They were coming towards us, giggling about needing a piss.

We came up on the air and said, 'Standby. That's two echoes [*women*] coming towards us. Wait out.'

The next thing we knew, the pair were virtually standing over the bushes we were hiding in. Then, still cackling and shouting, they squatted and opened fire.

I was No. 1 on a job on the shore of Lough Neagh. The nearest town was Glenavy on the eastern shore.

The ops officer brought us in and gave us a briefing. 'There's the general area,' he tapped a map. 'Somewhere around the shores of the lake there, and going up in the fields in this area here, there's a fearsome hide. Apparently there's shotguns, radios, all sorts of shit – probably a complete ASU's worth of equipment. We're going to keep going in, night after night, until we find it. What I want you to do now is plan and prepare a CTR for tomorrow night.

I picked up the Hasselblad cameras and jumped into the Gazelle; minutes later we were flying over Lough Neagh,

the largest lake in the British Isles. While we did a normal flying pattern I took pictures.

We spent hours pondering over the photographs, trying to look for natural points that would be markers, or natural areas to put a hide. It could be in the corner of a field or, say, the third telegraph pole along where there was a big lump of stone. It was daunting. The area covered a square kilometre of hedgerows and shoreline. It was summertime; we weren't getting more than six hours of darkness, which meant we had to get in there, use the six hours, and get out again, not leaving any sign in the fields – all the crops were up and would easily get trodden down and leave sign. And then we'd have to go back the next night. And the next.

The ops officer was Pete. He looked like Mr Sensible Dad, happy owner of a Mini Metro and frequenter of B&Q, and wearer of Clark's shoes, Tesco trousers and V-neck jumpers – 180 degrees from my look of Mr Bag O'Shite. He said, 'You're going to be there all month by the looks of things. Just tell us what you want by four o'clock so I can start organizing it.'

I sat down and looked at all the options. Because this place was so isolated, there was no way we could get vehicles in to drop us off, for us then to patrol in. The only way we were going to get in was by Scotty beaming us – or via the loch. The only way we were going to get in from the loch was by boat, and the only people who were going to do that were the Regiment.

I said to Pete, 'You're not going to believe this. I want two boats over with some blokes.'

He went away shaking his head. Two hours later he said, 'Right, we've got a Chinook coming over with A Squadron Boat Troop. They'll be waiting for you.'

I was happy. 'I'll also need six blokes.'

'OK, there's you and Dave Two, and I'll get another four on it. I've got a Wessex coming in to pick you up and fly you down to meet up with A Squadron. The QRF you've got are two callsigns of HMSU.'

All in all, there were just over a hundred people involved, plus the expense of flying A Squadron over for the recce. Pete said, 'This is the most outrageous recce we've ever done. You'd better find it!'

When we landed in the Wessex there was a hive of activity at the SF base. The HMSU had turned up. Because of some of the experiences we'd had with the army QRF, the Regiment and Det now always used the HMSU. We had a really good relationship with them; we'd go to their houses, we knew each other, we got on really well. On jobs like this it tended to be the same faces every time.

A Squadron were on the team; they'd taken all their black kit off, got hold of the boats and got on the Chinook. They thought it was great. I found them pumping up their boats, checking the engines and putting dry bags (*diver's dry suit*) on. They didn't have a clue yet what was going on. All they'd been told was to get over here and sort themselves out.

The HMSU were unloading their bags into the accommodation. They would stay here and come screaming out in their armoured Sierra 4x4s if Dave 2 and I were in the shit. They were expecting to be there for the next two weeks and were smacking their lips at the thought of all the overtime.

I got everybody together and explained what was going to be happening. 'We're going to leave from here in the two Geminis. Once we get to the drop-off point one of the Boat Troop boys will swim and check the shoreline to make sure everything's all right for us to land.

'Once we've landed, A Squadron will stay where they are, with Rick and Eno. Dave Two and myself will then start going forward to do the CTR. The general route we're going to take is along the hedgeline here, then start working our way north.

'You can see on the map the checkpoints I've marked – when I reach them I'll radio back to the boats so you'll know where I am. If we find a hide, then depending on the

time, I'll call in Rick and Eno and they'll put in the technical attack. If not, the cut-off time stays as it is and we'll come back tomorrow night. Easy!'

It looked more like a fighting patrol than a recce patrol. We had two boats, A Squadron were in their dry bags ready for the swim; two Det blokes in each boat, both in full uniform, bergens on, carrying G3s, all cammed up and ready to go for it.

We all trundled down to the boats, only to discover that the edge of the lake further down was lined with civvies with fishing-rods. I'd wanted to start trogging down the river towards the lake so that just as it was last light we'd have travelled some of the distance. Instead, we had to sit there, waiting for the fishermen to go home.

At last light we paddled our way down river until we got on the loch, then opened up the engines. The Geminis bounced up and down in the chop, the Boat Troop wearing their PNGs (*passive night goggles*) as they navigated us to the drop-off point. It was totally dark and I felt as if we were on the sea. Finally the engines stopped and they started paddling in a bit. Two blokes, both with a weapon, jumped into the water in their dry bags and fins and disappeared.

The flash of their red torch told us that they had cleared the beach. We paddled in to the edge and the boats were tied up. We put our bergens on and set off, carrying photography kit and large radios so we could communicate with the rest of the patrol. I thought there was no way we'd find it on the first night, but at least we'd have a rough idea of the ground, and could come back time and again and dissect it.

At about twelve-thirty we were moving up a hedgeline. Ahead of us in a corner of the field we could make out the shape of what must have once been an old workshop or farm building. The ends were semicircular and built of breeze-blocks, and the roof had been corrugated iron. The metal sheeting was rusty and full of holes, and in most

places had fallen down onto old lengths of wood, broken bricks, bottles filled up with mud. Sitting to the right was a rusting, 1950s-style tractor without tyres. Debris lay all around – empty paint tins, rolls of mouldy old carpet, plastic fertilizer sacks and little piles of rubble. About fifty metres beyond was a row of four or five traditional-looking, terraced houses, probably built in the days of tenant farming. The people who lived in them now perhaps still worked the land – but obviously weren't very tidy.

As we started to walk closer, we had a good look at the layout of the buildings. Obviously they would have to be searched at some stage, but that would take a night in itself. Then I spotted something that had been obscured from our view by the dead tractor. A number of large-diameter, four-foot-long plastic drainage pipes, each with a male and female end, were stacked up against the building. There were three on the bottom of the pile and two on the top, but the strange thing about the arrangement was that the ends against the wall were draped over with newspaper. At what should have been the open ends of the pipes was a small pile of bricks; above that were pieces of corrugated iron that looked out of place, because they just didn't look ramshackle enough. I looked at the stack and thought, no, it's far too obvious – we've got that as a marker, let's carry on with the patrol and go and see what other possibles there are. Otherwise we could spend all night doing this because it would take a long time to dismantle – and if it turned out not to be a hide, we'd have lost a lot of valuable time. We kept on going and were looking at a small culvert that ran under a track. We checked a rubbish tip area, looking for large drums. It was a pain in the arse, because it had to be done slowly. We had to make sure we didn't leave sign.

Dave 2 came up and said, 'Tell you what, let's go back and have a look at that marker – you never know.'

The site was surrounded by long grass. Some of it on the right-hand side had been trodden down, but that meant

nothing. We went around the edge, crouched down, and looked. We studied it for about five or ten minutes to make sure that we could recognize exactly how it looked. I took some IR photography of it.

We then started to take off the top layer of wriggly tin. This was quite a pain in the arse: there was the risk of noise, and as we moved each sheet it scraped against the others. It was also slightly dug into the mud, so to make sure that the earth was still nicely presented, it was a lift, a push-up and a bring-out. As the wriggly tin started to come off, Dave 2 would pass it to me and I would then lay it out on the ground in order so we knew exactly what bit of which went where.

As soon as we had also got a couple of the bricks out of the way and there was just enough room to peer inside, Dave 2 got out his Maglite torch and shone the tiny beam down into the pipes. He couldn't see anything. We started pulling off more bricks, one by one. It was like a surgical operation; I was laying them in a specific order so I knew which went where and we could put them back exactly as we had found them.

Dave was taking his time, looking at every brick before he lifted it up. He took one brick off – nothing. Another – nothing. Then all of a sudden he leant back, gave me a thumbs-up, and whispered, 'Bingo!'

It was the word everybody liked to hear on the net.

'Don't know what it is,' he whispered, 'but it's definitely a hide.'

I got the radio out and communicated back to the boats. 'Hello, Lima, this is Alpha, over.' I got nothing. I tried again. The hide must be in a blindspot. I knew that without comms the blokes would be flapping because they didn't know where we were on the ground and therefore couldn't back us quickly if we had a drama. It was now about one-thirty. I sat there pissed off that we weren't getting any comms, and worked out that by the time we walked to the boats to pick the lads up and bring them back to the hide,

then jarked the weapons and replaced the hide, we'd have run out of darktime hours. That meant me and Dave 2 staying on the target and everybody else going back and then returning the following night.

We both started to put the bricks and tin back in order, Dave 2 putting his hand out for each item like a surgeon requesting instruments. It had taken us an hour to open up the hide, checking all the time for tell-tales and that the cache wasn't rigged up with a booby trap, and it now took us as long to put everything back.

'I could see some longs wrapped in black plastic bags and some more shit deeper in the hide. I couldn't make it out,' he said.

We moved back down to the boats and I explained what was going on. 'Dave Two and I'll just sleep here on the shore,' I said. 'We won't watch the hide – it's pointless, it's too exposed. But we want to make sure we can go back at last light and that gives us an extra two hours to get the tech attack in. We can get the kit out as they are moving to us.'

Next day we just sat there and laid up in the shade, watching the fishing boats and pleasure craft on the loch. One of us went on stag while the other one slept.

About two hours before last light we got back on the radio and spoke to the blokes on the boats to check that everything was OK and that they were ready to move as soon as it was dark enough.

At last light we went straight up to the hide. As we started to pull it apart, the lights of the houses were still on. It was so close I could hear a toilet being flushed.

We uncovered an Aladdin's cave of AK47s, shotguns, small hand-held radios, and ammunition wrapped up in ski masks.

Now all we had to do was wait for Rick and Eno. Time dragged on and on, and because of the blindspot we still had no comms, even when we tried moving position. It was now coming up to about one o'clock. I started to get worried. It was going to get fairly light come about four. By

374

two o'clock, still nothing had happened. We made a plan; at three o'clock, if no-one had reappeared, we'd have to block up the hide and bluff it. This was worrying. This was our second visit and this time the weapons had been unwrapped. I didn't want to rush replacing the hide if Rick and Eno didn't turn up. By about twenty past two we didn't even need night viewing aids as we watched the boys trogging up the hill.

'The fucking engine gave up halfway across!' Rick said. 'We've been paddling like lunatics for the last two hours.' Eno was by now doing his job. His annoying personal trait of being so precise and neat made him ideal for this type of work.

'We've got to rush it,' I said. 'It's going to be light soon.'

'I've got the IR photography you took last light – you might as well look at it – it's light enough.' Dave 2 and I covered them as they got on with it. It was nearly daylight when we started putting the stuff back. Cocks were crowing. By the time we finished and got back to the powerless Gemini it was breakfast time and we had to paddle in broad daylight to meet the other boat that had been sent to fetch us.

My tour with the Det finished in late 1988. When I came back, everything between Fiona and me was different. I didn't know what it was, whether it was because we'd spent so much time apart, but there was a definite air of independence between us. It wasn't a case of me coming home to Fiona and Kate, the way I was feeling it was coming home to Kate, which was the wrong way round.

Running up to Christmas, I went away on another job for a while, and it was as if I'd never been at home. I yearned for Kate, the product of the relationship, rather than the relationship itself. Fiona and I didn't exactly row about things but there were times when we sat down and had to have some really serious talks about the direction we were going. Both of us knew there were problems, but both of us

thought that we could hopefully work it out. However, my priorities were work, Kate, Fiona, and she probably sensed that.

Eno started to have a few problems with his marriage, too, and it eventually broke up. Maybe it was the same in the police force or the fire brigade, but people in the Regiment always seemed to be divorcing, remarrying, redivorcing, and always for the same reason. It took an enormous amount of effort and dedication for a bloke to have got where he was and to stay there, and almost inevitably there was a conflict.

23

Four of us were sitting in a Portakabin listening to the slime telling us what was going on. Outside the sun was shining, but it wasn't as hot as I'd expected for this part of the world. All around us on the walls were maps, magic marker boards and cork boards.

The Int boy finished off by saying, 'Well, that's it. I know you're not going to ask any questions, because it's a waste of time. I don't know the answers.'

'So basically we're going to do something but we don't know what, where, when or how. We just sit here and pick our arses, do we?'

'Yeah, that's about the size of it. Have a look at what information there is on the board, and we'll start squaring it away tomorrow. The G Squadron blokes you're taking over from are away on the ranges at the moment – they'll be back tomorrow.'

We had a quick look at the pictures of the city and personalities, but the faces were familiar enough and at this stage everybody was more interested in getting a few rays.

We walked outside onto the pan in our jeans, T-shirts and trainers. The sun was blinding. On the pan were Chinooks and Pumas and a couple of aircrew mincing around on them.

James, one of the team, said, 'Not hot enough to sunbathe in, but all right for a run.'

'Where to?' I said, looking at the barbed-wire fence that

surrounded the location. 'Talk about keeping the animals from straying.'

'A hundred and fifty two laps of that Portakabin, then,' James said. 'Come on, there's nothing else to do.'

We went back to the accommodation, another set of Portakabins. We'd dumped our kit on the beds as soon as we'd arrived an hour before, then gone straight to the briefing room. I had a nylon Parabag and bergen containing all my equipment, the most important bit of which was my Walkman, with a couple of self-compiled tapes of Madness, Sham 69, the hymn 'Jerusalem' from *Chariots of Fire* and a bit of Elgar. I pulled open my bergen and strewed everything all over the bed. Out fell my sleeping bag and running kit.

James and I ran around the perimeter fence, past Chinooks and aircrew who were busy licking ice creams.

As we turned one corner I said, 'Look at that!' Sitting on the tarmac about a hundred metres away was a bit of machinery which I knew existed but had never seen – a long, black spy plane of the USAF, all weirdly angled surfaces and very mean looking. I didn't know why, but it somehow made me feel more confident that our job would be on.

Half an hour later we were having a shower, then running around trying to find out where the aircrew had got their ice creams.

We had some scoff that night, and sorted out our kit. We'd been told to bring different types of civvie clothes with us, together with different types of body armour, overt and covert, to cater for every option. Between the four of us we had M16s, a couple of sniper rifles, MP5s, MP5Ks, MP5SDs, and a couple of Welrod silenced pistols; already on site would be different types of explosives to cover everything from blowing a wall to taking doors off. We also had all types of night-viewing aids, including passive night-viewing goggles that we might need to wear as we were moving in, and an infrared torch for our weapon, so

we could move along without being seen – we still didn't know whether we'd be wearing a pair of jeans and covert body armour and a pair of trainers, or green military kit, or going in with the full counter-terrorist black kit.

Last item in the Parabag was a daysack, stuffed with Haemaccel plasma substitute and 'giving sets'. If there were any major gunshot wounds, they'd have to be managed and stabilized until we got back.

Once the kit was checked we sat down to watch six hours of *Fawlty Towers* on video.

In the morning we read the papers, listened to the radio, watched a bit of telly. There was simply nothing else to do. In the end we dragged some of the plastic chairs outside and sat in the sun.

About mid-morning two wagons turned up and some blokes from G Squadron started piling out. They'd been down to the ranges doing some night shooting. First one out was Tony, who I knew quite well.

'Thank fuck you lot have turned up,' he said.

'I see, good job then, I take it?'

'It's a bag of shit. No-one knows what the fuck's going on. We've got two more days, I think, then you're taking over.'

'So you don't know anything?'

'Only that we're here.'

All we knew was what the Int boy had told us. John McCarthy and Terry Waite were hostages in Beirut, together with an Irishman called Brian Keenan and countless Americans, and every agency, man and dog in the western world was running around trying to find them. If any of them were found, including the Yanks, we were going to go and lift them.

We went and had a brew and I asked Tony, 'Have you been over there?'

'Yeah. Boring as fuck. There's a couple of boys over there at the moment, in the embassy or consulate or whatever. They're sorting out all the LSs [*landing sites*], and they're the

link between the embassy and us. Any information that's coming through, they're giving us a shout.'

'And have they sent anything?'

'Jack shit. We're just running around like loonies at the moment. It's the normal thing – this time next week it'll be binned, bet you anything. The only positive thing is that there's got to be something up, otherwise they wouldn't have moved us here.'

'What's it like over there?'

'Just like you've seen on the news, really. Buildings full of shrapnel, piles of rubble, loads of old Mercs. To be honest I didn't take that much interest. I'll believe it when I see it on this one. I'll spark up when they find them and want us to go and do it. All it is is another house assault. The only good thing so far is that we've got free sunglasses out of it.'

He pulled out some RayBans and put them on. 'They're all right, aren't they?'

'Freebies? How come?'

'We were practising this assault on the ranges, coming in on a Chinook. The idea was we'd come in near the building, and as the heli landed the tailgate would come down and we'd just pile out and do it – running or in the light strike vehicles. It's all dark inside the Chinook of course. There's twelve of us sitting there with beltkit and body armour on, everybody's carrying MP5s and G3s and all sorts – we were ready to start World War Three.

'The tailgate comes down, we run out straight into the sun and – fuck! We're blinded! We couldn't see jack shit. It was a live attack, and all we heard was "Stop! Stop!" Sean was going apeshit. "Stop! Unload!" We unloaded and he said, "What the fuck's going on? Fucking hell, call yourselves Special Air Service soldiers?" "But we can't see fuck all!" We'd missed all the targets. So the pilot saunters up and says, "Well, you've just come out of a dark aircraft, haven't you, you dickheads?" We ended up being given aviator glasses. Mind you, we had a honk.'

'Why's that?'

'RayBans. We wanted Oakley Blades.'

What Tony was saying reflected the attitude on a lot of jobs, which was very downbeat. We were going to do a house assault in Beirut and bring home the bacon. So what? It was pointless getting excited or concerned until we found out what was going on and where they were – if they were still alive. Nobody had even confirmed that much. So no-one was hyper, running around and screaming: 'We've got to do this, we've got to save the hostages.' When the job happened, the job happened.

All the principles were exactly the same as for any other house assault. Only the area was different, and it was in a hostile environment. Again, so what? We'd got guns, we'd got the aptitude and the attitude, we had body armour and we had aircraft – what more could we ask for?

G Squadron disappeared for the rest of the day. Sean got the four of us together and said, 'We're going to have this trickle system going through. You four from B Squadron will take over, and in two days' time we'll send back four from G Squadron and just have a gentle tick-over so we've got continuity on the ground. The score's the same as normal. You're in isolation, and you stay here. Mail can come in and out every day, you've got phone calls, and there'll be a run to the market every morning for soap and shit.'

'What about the aircrew – where are they?'

'The aircrew are staying down town in a hotel.'

'Ah, lovely,' we honked. It was always the same; we'd be in isolation, but the aircrew, who knew as much as us, were put up in hotels or messes.

I turned to James and said, 'Please do not feed the animals.'

That was it for the day. There was a little multi-gym to fuck about with, but we soon got bored with that. I sat on my bed listening to the Walkman and reading the paper, then I wrote a letter home to Fiona. 'Hopefully that insurance claim will come through,' I said. 'Just go ahead

and get what colour you like.' We'd tipped some paint on the kitchen carpet and I'd only got around to doing the claim form the day before I left. 'PS: I promise I'll fix that leak in the roof.' Every time I got organized to do the repair, I'd been called away. It had become a standing joke.

Next morning everybody was got together in the briefing room. Tony was given the good news that he wasn't going back, his four were staying and another four of G Squadron were sent home. It was funny, it always seemed that we took over something that G Squadron had initiated. Still, it was a good chance to take the piss out of them for being so incompetent that they had to be replaced.

A television set and video machine had been set up on a table in one corner. The slime stood up and said, 'This is a video run of possible areas in Beirut where these people might be held. Nothing's confirmed, but these are the general areas so you can orientate yourselves a bit.'

He started to run the videotape, which had come from the guys on the ground in Beirut. They'd been looking at the areas, driving them and walking them. They were taking photographs and doing video runs with covert cameras, looking at landing sites in and around possible targets, and security – both building-wise and physically, with guards. They even studied the state of the traffic out-side. Was it busy, was it quiet, were there little sidestreets? Was there a good escape route in and out? They'd rigged up a camera in a van and driven around the areas. The place was in shit state. The video was bouncing up and down, occasionally showing a glimpse of a dirty wind-screen. It looked like something out of a *World in Action* report.

There's quite a skill to operating undercover in an urban environment. It's a matter of trying to do normal things, while working to a different agenda; how you do this will vary according to the climate, prosperity and traditions of the country you are operating in. A large city like Cairo or Bangkok is an anonymous place with a large population

of floaters or drifters and plenty of public transport and public facilities. People keep themselves to themselves, and as long as the way you look and behave doesn't attract attention you can move around freely. A place like Beirut, however, with strong family networks, local loyalties or a repressive political regime, will be much harder to move about in – and movement is important: it's easier not to be asked questions if you're not standing still.

Simon, the Int Corps fellow, spoke fluent Arabic and had spent most of his working life in the Middle East, including a long tour with the Sultan of Oman's forces as an Int collater, and a spell in Beirut itself when the Brits supplied people to the UN forces. Now a warrant officer, he had been with the Regiment for many years.

He said, 'I'll warn you of something now. It's such a fucking maze and there's so many different factions running around, that if you're in the shit – if the operation goes wrong and you're not killed and survive – I can promise you you'll land up best mates with Terry Waite. The sooner you're in, and the sooner you're out, the better.'

I wondered, what would happen if I did become a hostage? I knew that I'd have a hard time initially, getting filled in, but after that I'd land up sharing a piss-pot with old Tel. At that stage I didn't really worry about it; the moment I knew the exact location we were going to hit, I would make it my business to learn by heart the locations of all the embassies and consulates, and the location of the American University of Beirut and the main areas where all the reporters lived. But, I told myself, and it was a big but, there was no way I was going to get captured. I had a big gun, loads of rounds, and it would all be over and done with in a quarter of an hour. No fucker was going to stop me getting back on the heli.

James sparked up and said, 'When do we get over to Beirut then and have a look?'

'That's being organized now with the embassies. The boys over there at the moment will rig it all up and

orientate you quickly. The helicopter's going to be doing some more practice runs in the next couple of days. As soon as that happens we'll get you on board and off you go.

'The people in the embassies are trying to organize some tennis courts as an LS. A friendly power wants to pull its embassy staff out of the area as a cost-saving measure, but politically they can't be seen to withdraw. By letting us use their embassy gardens and tennis courts as a helicopter landing site we're getting two birds killed with one stone. We secure a method of infil and exfil, and as part of the bargain we'll pick all their people up and bring them back with us. They could then say that they'd had to withdraw because they'd helped the Brits.

'We can get some helis in there easily and quickly, which will obviously make it easier to get into the centre of the city. Or we might have to go in covertly, we don't really know yet.'

Sean stood up and said, 'If you G Squadron lads want to bin it then, see you!'

He then started to give the rest of us a brief. 'What we're looking at just now are three main options. Once intelligence comes in and it's confirmed where they are – assuming that they are alive – we'll then get the OK to go. Depending on where it is and the numbers required, we might have to call in the standby squadron. However, that's where you come into it: you're here and you've got the continuity, so you'll be able to take them in.

'At the moment we're looking at going straight in and doing a big crash and bang. Pumas or Chinooks, depending on where the target is and where we can get the aircraft in – then straight in and take it out, grab the hostages, into the aircraft and back over. The most important part of that for you is not so much getting in and getting them, because I know you can square that away – it's if they're in shit state or if they're wounded, and need to be sorted out on the aircraft. We've got some major trauma care gear to go on the aircraft. You'll be taking the medic packs on target as well

because we don't have a clue what state they'll be in. You might have to bung them on a stretcher.

'There's a problem with refuelling. We're just trying to work it out – hopefully we can get in with the Chinook, because they've got internal fuel tanks on board. If it's Pumas, we might have to refuel in Beirut – but again, that's being organized at the moment. Another possibility is that the Americans will refuel us at sea.

'So that's the first, and most ideal, option – a straight-forward, hard-hitting, quick attack: get in there, get them, and get out. But until we know where they are, it's one for the back burner.

'The next option is again to go in by heli – there's normal helicopter traffic going in and out, so no problem there – landing, and moving covertly in vehicles.

'The way we're looking at it at the moment is that the boys already there will get us on target; we don't even have to know where we're going. It would be a green option [*in normal army uniform*] – the vans stop at the target, we go straight in and do it. Then back in the vans and go for it back to the nearest safety area and organize the helis to get us out. At the moment that's not our problem, that doesn't interest us. All we want to know is where the target is so we can hit it and get these people out.

'The last option is a covert entry and covert exfil. How we'd do that I don't know – whether we go over by boat and get picked up by the boys from the embassy, I just don't know.'

James said, 'There's nothing I like more than taking over a well-organized job. Good one, G Squadron!'

'Well, that's all we know,' Sean said. 'The one and only thing we do know for sure is that we've been sent here. There might or might not be a job on in Beirut, but if there is, it's to rescue the hostages. You four,' he said, pointing to us, 'get your weapons, go down the range, and re-zero and check them out. I then want you to see Tony, he'll show you the four G Squadron blokes who are leaving,

and they'll start handing over the medical kit and HE.'

Still in jeans and trainers, we drove down to the range. We zeroed G3s, 203s, MP5s and tested all the magazines. Everybody was fairly nonchalant and bored. We knew our weapons were zeroed, but we had to check them.

We cleaned the weapons and went over to G Squadron for the equipment handover. We checked all the Haemaccel, all the giving sets, the fold-up nylon stretchers, first field dressings, oxygen sets. We also had little miner's lights to wear around our heads for working on somebody at night, and inflatable, anti-shock trousers, an excellent bit of American kit, which are wrapped around the lower body and then pumped up to restrict the flow of blood and keep fluids in the top half of the body; the basic aim of trauma management is to stop the loss of blood and replace fluids, and that'll keep them alive. If we can keep them screaming, they're breathing.

The blokes from G Squadron were well pleased to be off. Later in the day, as they boarded the aircraft, they thought they'd got away with not giving their RayBans over. But Sean appeared from nowhere and said, 'And don't forget the glasses – they're squadron property.'

For the next couple of days we were hanging around again. If we weren't eating we were going for a run around the compound, and if we weren't doing that we were training. We had to practise all the different options because we still didn't know how we were going to get in – and at that stage we didn't even know exactly where the hostages were being held or the layout of the buildings.

Everything was getting in motion. All we had to do was jump in the aircraft and go in and do the option that had been decided on. The objective never changed; that had to be to drag them out of there as quickly as we could, and get away. We had no idea of the condition they were going to be in; they might need stabilizing, they might be in shit state, they might be drugged, they might be totally exhausted and incapable of moving. So we'd have to take

the lot – even down to bolt-cutters so we could cut them away from whatever they were chained to.

We had computer-enhanced pictures of what they might look like now – with beards, without beards, having lost weight, lost some hair, some with greying hair, some with scarred faces or wearing glasses.

We would be going into a hostile environment quickly, so it very much had to be a matter of speed, aggression and surprise. By the time they were starting to react, we'd be gone. For ten minutes of work, it might take ten weeks of preparation to get it right. We were practising, practising, practising, but as soon as we got the OK, we would be ready to go.

We practised going in by helicopter, then moving into vehicles and dropping off at different points around the location, and all walking in at the same time. We'd done it plenty of times over the water; everybody just casually walks in and *bang*! It then goes overt as soon as everybody's in the area. You're banging and crashing, you're getting through to the target, and there's either vehicles or a helicopter coming in to get you out.

We also practised going in by boat. We'd meet somebody at the beachhead, who would then put us in vehicles and drive us off to the target. At the same time, a helicopter would be holding off; as soon as we went bang, crash, the helis would come in; they would either lift us direct or get into the embassy and wait for us to arrive by vehicle.

Another version we tried was for the heli to go straight in. People already on the ground would have marked the area. We'd fast-rope down, take the building out, and whilst that was happening the heli's either still airborne, waiting, or it goes and sets down. The people on the ground covered the helicopter, and that became part of the exfiltration.

Eventually it looked as though it was going to be a heli-copter going into the embassy; from there we would sort ourselves and go in on target by vehicle. We'd get in there,

get McCarthy, Waite and anybody else who wanted a free ticket out of town, and come back in vehicles to the embassy. As soon as the first heli lifted off, there would be another one holding up to come in. The priority would be to get the hostages out on the first heli, with any other civilian personnel that were there. The assaulters would get on the last helicopter.

It looked as if we were going to go in on a green option with body armour, and then over that we'd have coats for the covert infil (*infiltration*). We were going to drive up to the building and do an explosive entry. We'd need information on the doors – we didn't know what was on the other side. We didn't want to start killing the people we were supposed to be saving. The charges for that were all made up. We were going to drive along three different routes, and everybody would have personal comms, on one frequency.

Then it was a question – as so often – of hurry up and wait, and check-and-test, check-and-test – and yet another six hours of Basil, Sybil and Manuel.

Finally we were told by Sean, 'OK, they're going in tomorrow night – the pilot's going to practise going in on NVGs. So if you want to go along for the ride, away you go. You've got to go in uniform, no weapons. Carry an ID card with you, and ID tags.'

All four of us met the aircrew near the Puma.

'How's it going?' I said.

'Boring as usual,' was the reply. 'These luxury hotels all look the same to me.'

'Fuck you.'

'Right, we'll go in about three quarters of an hour. Basically, all we're trying to do is practise going in on NVGs, and do some time checks. We'll land on a new LS.'

They were in flying suits and life jackets, pens and bits of paper dangling off all over them. We put on life jackets and sat in the back.

The flight was uneventful. There was nothing to see as we flew over the Mediterranean. Then, as we approached Beirut, I craned my neck to look out of the window. Disappointingly, it looked like any other Middle East city. There were lights in houses, car headlights carving their way through dark areas. What we couldn't see with the naked eye was the infrared flash of the 'Firefly' equipment that was guiding the pilot into the middle of the city.

I heard the rotors slowing down and we lost height. Minutes later we were on the ground; the rotors kept turning as the loadie opened the door and two blokes from G Squadron came running towards us. Being the liaison, their job would be to mark the LS for us and bring the aircraft in. The loadie waved for two other boys to come forward. They, too, were G Squadron, and what they were after was the mailbag we were carrying. They grabbed it and ran hunched double into the darkness. I saw a vehicle's headlights go on, and watched it drive off. At almost the same time, the heli lifted; we did a big circuit and flew on to our refuel point.

I turned to James and said, 'Er, so that was us in Beirut then?'

'Never mind,' he said, 'at least we know the flying times.'

Everybody slagged us off the next morning about our big sortie.

'How was Terry then? Any messages for the archbishop?'

There was a cross-section of people who were feeling sorry for the hostages, and those who simply didn't care. 'What the fuck was Waite doing there anyway? He didn't have to be a brain surgeon to know that he was going to get caught.'

Then, at about four o'clock one morning, one of the scaleys on stag on the radio net came screaming in. He threw all the lights on and shouted, 'We've got a standby! It's on! They want you in the briefing room now!'

Good news!

We pulled some kit on and ran down to the briefing

room. Simon was there to greet us with the words, 'It's on: we're going in at oh eight hundred.'

He was standing there in running shorts, flip-flops and a big baggy T-shirt, and his glasses were on wonky from all the rushing around. 'They've got the location. We're just waiting for it to be confirmed. It's coming to us now.'

Sean stood up and said, 'Everybody, listen in. What we're going to do is a smash and grab. The aircrew are coming in now – as soon as we know the location we'll have a look at it. No time to fuck around. If we can get on target in the helis, we're just going to go straight in.

'I want to go through the rules of engagement before we start. Do not shoot at anybody unless he's firing at you or putting someone else's life in danger. I repeat, do not shoot unless there's somebody putting your life or someone else's life in danger. We don't want the fucking OK Corral down there, all right? Just get in there, get it done, and get on the aircraft. The mission is to get the hostages. As soon as we know the location, we're going to run through a quick set of orders. We've been told it must be done today. OK, sort yourselves out. It'll be a green option.'

There wasn't an air of excitement or tension. After so many weeks of practice we just wanted to get it done. I put on my green DPM and smock, and the lightweight boots I used on the team. We wouldn't be tabbing great distances; we were only going to be on the ground for maybe half an hour. Over my smock I put my chest harness with ten magazines of 7.62. I took the G3 with a folding stock because it had more firepower than anything else. In a bag, I took an MP5. If things changed while we were in the air, I had to make sure I'd catered for it.

On my back I had a small daysack containing two litres of Haemaccel plasma replacement and four giving sets. The rest was packed out with field dressings and a nylon fold-up stretcher.

Around my neck I had my dog tags and my ID card, through which I had burned a small hole and put some

string, and two syrettes of morphine. The drugs were unlikely to be used: it's not good to use morphine for gunshot wounds to the chest, stomach or head. In any event, we should be back drinking tea and ordering our duty frees before it was needed.

We came back over to the briefing room.

'Still waiting,' Sean said.

By now all the aircrews had arrived and I could hear rotors turning. The aircrews came in, flying suits, pistols tucked in their harness, maps and chinographs and bits of paper and radios all over them.

We sat there. After ten minutes somebody said, 'Let's get a cup of tea.'

Sean said, 'Yep, fuck off. But the only places I want you to be are in the cookhouse, the living accommodation, or here.'

The scaleys said, 'Let's sort out these radios while we're waiting for the brief.'

We checked that our radios between us and the helicopter were working. The helicopter would be relaying everything. On the ground, we'd only need comms between us personally, working one-to-one with an earpiece.

We sat there and waited, cups of tea in hand. It was now six o'clock. The start time was eight o'clock. Sean let us go to the cookhouse. A couple of people wandered back to the living accommodation, had a wash, brushed their teeth.

Then what we got from Sean was: 'Bin it. It's cancelled.'

Oh for fuck's sake. So near and yet so far.

We kept all the kit in the ops room, went for a run, watched more TV, read the newspapers. Later that afternoon we went for another briefing. We were told, 'It's finished. It's binned. We don't know why, so don't ask.'

We packed all our own kit and handed the other stuff in to the stores. We had two days off, so the most important thing, now that the weather was hotter, was getting the wagons and having a couple of days on the beach.

At the end of the day we weren't that particularly fussed about it. It was just another job that we'd got pretty bored practising for.

Soon afterwards, an article appeared in *The Times*, accusing the government of 'squandering chances' to rescue the hostages. A Foreign Office spokesman was quoted as saying, 'We have vigorously followed up the many approaches which have been made to us. All of these have, sadly, run into sand for a variety of reasons.'

Oh well, we never found out what the sand was, but at least we'd tried – and got a nice tan.

24

The lecture room in Hereford was full as Bert from Int Corps gave B Squadron the background.

'As you are aware, the Regiment has been involved in many anti-narcotic measures. We have worked with a number of American drug agencies, such as the DEA, whose personnel have visited Hereford on a number of occasions. Members of the Regiment have also assisted the US Coastguard with anti-drug patrols. On the domestic front, the Regiment has been involved in drug-busting operations in London, mainly to stop PIRA's fund-raising drug operations.

'The main market for narcotics is still the United States, but Europe is catching up fast – the inner cities have become major distribution points, and it's feared there could be a major epidemic. Now it has been decided at the highest levels that several UK agencies will join in the fight, and you are one of them.

'So, gentlemen' – Bert pulled down a roller map of Central and Southern America and jabbed at a specific region – 'I give you a theatre of operations that is so secret that anyone heard discussing it – even in camp – will be RTU'd on the spot.' Then, allowing himself a brief, tongue-in-cheek grin, he said, 'So to get you into the habit straightaway, even I am only going to refer to this place as: "a certain Latin American country".'

His face serious once more, he went on, 'This is not going

to be easy. Our "certain Latin American country" is one of the most violent in the world, apart from those physically at war. There were more than twenty thousand murders last year – at least three thousand drug-related killings in one town alone. In fact these days, a local male between the ages of eighteen and sixty is more likely to be murdered than to die of any other cause.

'The Latin American drugs trade has developed from a small cottage industry in the early Seventies into a multi-billion-dollar enterprise, with its own distribution network and armies of "narco-guerrillas" to make sure it stays that way. The chief villains of the piece are the cartels, associations of drug producers and smugglers, who have combined to divvy up the market and intimidate the authorities. Their vast profits have brought them power; they've killed politicians, judges and senior army officers – and got away with it. Measures have been taken, but it's like pushing water uphill.

'All efforts must be made to fight the drug trade in its own backyard. If we can hit them at source and slow down the growth and production we will then see the effect back in the UK.'

Bert distributed photocopies of an intelligence report that showed that, according to the US State Department, three Latin American countries between them produced enough coca leaves in 1988 to yield 360 tons of pure cocaine. At $14,000 for a kilo at one-third purity, the suppliers' income would be $15 billion from cocaine alone – and that took no account of the massive quantities of marijuana grown and processed. However, since the cartels also controlled distribution and retail sales, their profits were, in fact, much higher – an estimated margin of 12,000 per cent from production cost to street value.

'Looking just at cocaine for a moment,' Bert said, 'it takes two hundred kilos of leaves to produce one kilo of paste. The leaves have to be converted into coca paste in their

country of origin because the sheer volume and weight of leaves make it impossible to move them very far.'

The plantations were scattered in the valleys, with thousands of collection points at which the leaves were rendered down. The coca paste was then taken to one of thousands of small dirt airstrips hidden in the jungle, and from there to drug manufacturing plants to be converted first into cocaine base (it took 2.5 kilos of paste to produce 1 kilo of base) and then into cocaine hydrochloride – pure cocaine.

To run the drug production-line the cartels had imported skilled technicians, many of whom were Europeans, as well as specialized equipment and supplies. They also handled the smuggling operation and had even set up their own distribution networks in America and Europe.

Bert said, 'In the last two years, the number of addicts in New York has trebled from one hundred and eighty-two thousand to six hundred thousand – and that's without the up-and-coming generation of heroin users. Just looking at one of the problems that we've got – cocaine – the size of the job can be measured by a recent seizure: in September, police in Los Angeles impounded the largest single consignment ever discovered, over twenty tons. Its value was about two billion dollars wholesale, yet the seizure had no effect on price. In other words supply still exceeded demand.

'Our "certain Latin American country" is itself not a fantastic producer. However, rather than try to convince other governments to defoliate millions of acres of marijuana and coca, it makes sense to attack further down the chain, at the drug manufacturing plants.

'We don't want that sort of problem to happen in the UK. We need to hit the problem at source. It is a proactive strike, a first strike: if we are successful in our task, we will cut down the stream of drugs into the UK.'

G Squadron had been the first to deploy. I didn't mind going in after them a few months later; in many ways it was

better to take over from somebody else – they'd have had all the cock-ups and found out all the little bits and pieces that we needed to know, and squared them all away.

B Squadron started to plan and prepare for the takeover. The first priority was to learn the language to a passable standard, as it would obviously make our job easier if we could communicate directly with people rather than have to go through a third party: what is said can be wrongly understood by the interpreter, and his translation can't be confirmed.

I seemed to live in the language lab. All around me blokes in headphones were shouting, 'Fuck it!' in frustration, and either storming off for a brew or binning it for the day. Personally, I used to go for a run when the grammar got too much for me. I wasn't that fussed about getting it exactly right, I just wanted to get to grips with the verbs. When I'd learned Swahili I'd found that if I got hold of those, I could work around everything else. Spanish is in fact not that hard to learn; within a few weeks I could hold my own in any conversation about the price of tomatoes or the time of the next train.

Some of the blokes picked it up really well, and one of them in particular even appeared to have the accent down to a T. I thought, great, if ever we get time off I'll stay near him. I changed my mind when I heard him trying to chat up a Spanish au pair in the town one day. 'Hello, love,' he said. 'At what time this evening do you terminate?'

We were also doing all the normal planning and preparing that we'd do for any operation, as well as making sure the weapons were OK and the equipment was sorted out. Bert gave us detailed in-country briefs, teaching us more about the main players.

The Int people dragged in all the local newspapers and weekly news magazines. A couple of the blokes had Spanish wives and they came in and chatted to us. It was all part of the process of getting tuned in to the country, which we took seriously – so much so there was a strong

rumour going around at one stage that the boys in B Squadron were taking lambada lessons at Bartestree Village Hall. It all went back to the way people looked at the squadrons, and B Squadron was definitely seen as the yee-hah party squadron.

Some of G Squadron were going to come back with us to ensure continuity in the task. They started briefing us, confirming what we had been taught but also giving their version of what had gone on and suggestions as to how we could make things better next time around.

Our job was going to be in two phases. First, we were going to grab hold of the paramilitary police and assess their standard of training. Then we would start training them from that baseline, taking them through all the basic skills that were going to be required, such as aggressive patrolling, OPs and close target recces. The object was to show them how to find the DMP (*drug manufacturing plant*), then stay in close proximity and send back the information. It wouldn't be an easy task.

'A lot of DMPs are deep hides in the jungle,' said Tony from G Squadron. 'Fantastic set-ups, well guarded and well alarmed. They have a system of tunnels and escape routes for leaving the plant in the event of an attack. By the time they hear the aircraft bringing in a heli-borne assault, they'll be away – down the tunnels, into other hides, or along the escape routes.'

We were going to enter Bert's 'certain Latin American country' covertly; not exactly sneaking in like spies, but the Regiment's experience was that if a trip was unannounced there was less to go wrong.

The first leg was by C130 to St John's, Newfoundland, for an overnight stop. The interior of a Hercules is spartan, not much more than rows of nylon seats and luggage racks, and this one was also bulked out with equipment. I tied my hammock to the aircraft frame and climbed in with my Walkman and a book. By the time we all had our hammocks

up the interior of the aircraft looked like a nest of hanging grubs waiting to grow into something nice. Slaphead nabbed the prime spot near the tailgate, where there was plenty of room for a hammock and all your gear; the only problem was the proximity of the toilet, a curtained-off oildrum full of chemicals. The stench was grim.

We stepped off the aircraft in summer clothes to find that it was winter in St John's. We made our way to the hotel in temperatures of minus twenty.

'We've got to go out on the town,' said Slaphead, 'get a few bevvies down us.'

During the mad dash from the hotel into the town Slaphead's dome froze over and I grew ice on my moustache. By the time we reached the drinking district everybody was purple.

Slaphead strode up to the bar, ran his eye along the optics of sour mash whisky, and said, 'Hot chocolate, please.'

The following morning we took off again, finally reaching the military airfield in darkness. We flew in with the aircraft unlit and the crew on PNG. As we landed and were taxiing along the runway, I saw the silhouettes of twenty or thirty aircraft parked up on the grass – small jets, twin-engined, an old Junkers 88, a couple of Dakotas.

'Some of the aircraft that've been confiscated from the drugs boys,' said Tony. 'Now they're just sitting there, rotting.'

Despite Bert's briefing sessions, we'd all had visions of being in a nice warm place – balmy South American climate and all that. In fact it lay high up on the plain and was anything but tropical. As we stepped from the aircraft into a freezing cold night, B Squadron's OC and the SM, who had gone out the week before with the light HQ group, were there shivering inside their Gucci leather coats.

Vehicles were there to collect half the squadron and our equipment and take us to the camp. 'It's about twenty minutes from here,' said the sergeant major. 'If there's no traffic.'

'And if there is traffic?' asked Slaphead.

'Three hours.'

There was traffic. Even so, we were the lucky ones. The other half of B Squadron were going elsewhere, and that was four hours away – 'when there is no traffic'.

We arrived at first light at the police camp where we'd be staying. As we came up the drive it looked quite a pleasant site. The paramilitaries' camp looked well-maintained and very clean, with large, long buildings that were old but in good repair. Then we turned left and landed up in a minging old hut the size of an average sitting room. There were bunkbeds and a table, and shower room off to one side. There was no storage space. It felt like we were living in a submarine.

'We've had to use the shower as a store room,' I honked to Gaz.

'Just as well,' he said. 'There's no water anyway.'

We soon found out that the toilets didn't work either, so they also became a cache for bergens and other kit. I put my sleeping bag on the nearest bed and that was it: home.

In the morning we had a walk around the camp with Tony, who had been on my second Selection but failed. He had come back straightaway and passed the second time.

The police were very much the paramilitary force I was expecting to see. Their equipment was mainly supplied by the Americans but I also spotted a lot of European kit. Their weapons were also a mixture of US M16s and Israeli Galils, and quite a few Russian AKs. However, the patrols that we were to be training just had the Galil – basically AK47 parts with a different barrel and furniture.

'An excellent weapon,' said Tony as he stopped to shake hands with people that he knew. 'Unfortunately they don't know how to use them yet.'

The boys were dressed smartly, and all looked very organized. He introduced me to them, and they struck me as very open and sociable people.

'The camp's looking good on the outside,' Tony said, 'but

in fact it's a heap of shit once you scratch the surface. Their living conditions are not very good at all – better than ours, but still not good. The food is absolutely heaving, even by their standards.'

I wasn't sure whether to believe him, until we went past the cookhouse and two boys who had just eaten breakfast came out and puked it all up again on the ground. The building reeked like a shithouse in an abattoir.

'These people are the *crème de la crème* but they aren't particularly well treated,' he went on. 'However, if you're a peasant farmer with jack shit, six kids and a donkey, why not become part of the system – at least you're getting paid and in theory the family are getting looked after.'

Having seen the people outside the cookhouse, I decided to stick to what we'd all brought with us. As usual, we had arrived laden down with tins of tuna, bags of pasta and bottles of curry sauce.

Billy from G Squadron, the world's smallest and most aggressive curly blond-haired Jock, was sleeping on the bottom bunk. As soon as he woke up in the morning he unzipped his sleeping bag and got his little petrol cooker going on the floor. The water went on for his brew, then he mixed his porridge up.

I peered over the edge of the bunk. 'Oh good, what's for breakfast?' I asked pleasantly.

'I'm surprised you're hungry, you bastard,' he said. 'We've spent all frigging night chewing on your farts.'

'Sorry,' I said. 'Jet lag.' I got up, sat next to him, and then kept looking at him and smiling until he gave me a mug of hot chocolate and some porridge. Over the next few days he got more and more annoyed that I wasn't making my share of the breakfast – which was exactly my intention. Finally, honking at me for being a lazy bastard, he picked the cooker up to throw it at me and forgot that he'd just used it. There was a sizzling sound, the smell of burned flesh, and the shape of the cooker top burned into his hand. It made quite a nice pattern, I thought.

Since the shower room was now the store room, we had to go and wash at outdoor taps around the corner. The water was freezing.

The weather was a bit nippy in the morning but then wonderful when the sun rose in the sky. We were high up in the hills, and were warned that we'd be getting out of breath for the first couple of days until we acclimatized. Of course no-one took any notice and all went up the hills for a run. Billy was loving it as we were all in shit state. Everything was a competition to him and he enjoyed stopping and shouting, 'B Squadron, a bag of shite.'

I watched the arrival of the people we were going to train. There were about forty or fifty of them all told, and they swaggered malevolently about the place like a convention of nightclub bouncers. The mentality of the Latin American male was very macho; we were somehow going to have to harness the machismo and try and turn it into something of substance.

We were sitting against our hut wall watching them assemble. Billy started to laugh and said, 'If they stick their chests out any more they're going to explode. I love this part – watch this!'

He then got up and walked into the middle of them and started shouting out commands to get them organized. After all this macho stuff they were getting ordered about by a 2-foot midget barking at their kneecaps.

Whenever I met troops that I was going to be staying with, their body language was nearly always: 'We don't need you, we're hard as fuck.' Above them, the prime personalities in the organization also resented us to an extent because we were undermining their authority. We'd have to be really tactful in the way that we treated them; no lording it over them and playing the Great I Am, because that wouldn't get the results. We'd have to show respect to their leaders at even the lowest level so they didn't turn against us – but at the same time, we had the problem that familiarity breeds contempt. By and large, however, we'd

just make sure we were friendly and approachable; everything was a learning opportunity, and we hoped to learn as much from them as they from us.

The paramilitaries were an incredible sight. They were wearing the world's supply of beltkit and webbing, with knives hanging off them everywhere and six-shooters in holsters around their hips.

Gaz and I swapped glances. We couldn't just say, 'This is a heap of shit – get rid of this, get rid of that,' because it wouldn't work. They'd go against us and we wouldn't get what we wanted. So to start with we didn't say anything.

Each one of us was given ten blokes, and it would be our responsibility to take them from the basics and build them up. The very first thing to do was sort them out with some equipment. We gave each of them a bergen, a sleeping bag, a sleeping bag liner, a waterproof outer, and a compass. You'd have thought we were giving them the crown jewels. A compass to them was gold dust. Even at officer level, none of them could read a map or use a compass, so these blokes had credibility straightaway with all their contemporaries: they were the team with compasses. Nobody knew what to do with them yet, but that was beside the point.

Before we could start teaching them any sort of tactics we had to get to grips with their shooting. Their idea of firing a weapon was to loose off countless rounds on full automatic and make lots of noise. It was totally ineffective. The weapons started to go high and they mostly missed the targets.

'Very good,' I beamed. 'Now can I show you a few little tricks somebody taught me recently?'

The camp we were in was built on the top of a hill of sandy soil, the sides of which made excellent ranges.

The first lesson was to teach them to conserve ammunition. 'It's a good idea to make every round count,' I said. 'If you're getting through a magazine every five seconds your ammunition won't last long. If you

want to look after your ass, look after your ammunition.'

We took them back to first principles, starting with how to lie down with a weapon and fire at a target, nice and controlled. Once we'd got to that stage we taught them in the kneeling and standing positions. We taught them on the ranges, not under pressure, but in a friendly atmosphere – no shouting, no hollering, just attempting to get good results.

These boys were soon starting to perform well on the ranges and the other police who were not part of our group were jealous, especially those of higher rank. None of them knew how to use their weapons properly; I saw some Galils and M16s that were still smeared with the grease they had been packed in when they arrived.

I was on the ranges one day with the boys. We'd got to the stage where they were moving from the lying position into the kneeling position, and then into standing, doing timed shots at about a hundred metres. The equivalent of a sergeant major from another group came storming over and said, 'My weapon does not work. Every time I fire it, it aims off. I need you to correct it.'

It was nothing to do with us but I got the zeroing tool out and did a couple of twists to the foresight and rear sight. I looked through and said, 'Yep, that's much better. You have a look, see what you reckon.'

He got the weapon into the shoulder, looked through it, and was as happy as a sandboy. As far as he was concerned he was ready for Bisley.

Just as with young recruits at Winchester, there was no such thing as a bad soldier, only a bad instructor – once you had the right material. We got them to the stage where they could fire their weapons and frequently hit what they were aiming at. Whether they could do that under pressure was another matter – and our lives could depend on it at a later date.

We started incorporating live firing exercises. The average contact in the jungle was going to be at a range of

about five metres; they'd have to recognize a target and shoot quickly and accurately. We'd go out into the hills and rig up a scenario: they'd walk down it first as individuals, recognize a target, snapshoot and kill it, then move back. Then we'd do it in pairs, firing and manoeuvring, moving down the range. It reminded me of Selection.

When we sat with them at lunchtime we'd be chatting away, trying to find out how they lived. It was easy to see what the food was like. The storeroom their ration packs came from was obviously infested with rats, because everything that wasn't canned was chewed to bits. They threw it away and opened the cans.

We were away from the camp training one day. The air was crisp, the sky more blue than I thought possible. Everybody was boiling water on hexy burners, us for our pasta, them for their coffee.

'What about all this fantastic coffee I've heard so much about in television commercials?' I said.

I knew there were some coffees that you couldn't take out of the country, the penalty being something like a six-year prison sentence. They were throwing out tons and tons of drugs all over the world, but if you took coffee beans home you landed up in prison.

'Yeah, what's the best coffee to take home from all the different blends and roasts and so on?' Slaphead asked.

'You don't want any of that shit,' one of them said. 'Our favourite is Nescafé instant.'

And as we found out, they were right. Some of the coffee was dire.

The first morning I took the group, I'd asked their names. 'I am one of three Josés,' this boy had said; in my confusion at using Spanish for real for the first time, I took it to be one of those long compound Spanish names and replied, 'Pleased to meet you, One-of-three-Josés.' The name stuck.

We talked about the situation here with the cartels running everything and the fact that all the farmers were working for them.

'If you're a farmer,' he now said, 'and the government come along and they give you two dollars an acre to grow corn – and that's it, no health system, just a little bit of schooling, and you're living in a tin hut in the middle of the jungle – and then along come a cartel and they say, "You grow for us, we'll give you seven dollars an acre; we'll also build a football pitch, we'll give you medical care, and we'll also educate your kids," what do you do? Of course you grow coca leaf – you don't care about what happens to the gringos. The farmer just thinks, where's it going? It's going to America. I hate the Americans, so I'm getting my own back – fuck them, it's their problem, the monkey on their back.'

The police knew they were losing the battle, but most of them were there for exactly the same reason – job security. They had families to feed and they didn't particularly give a tuppenny damn if the Americans had the cocaine or not. All they knew was that they were making money out of fighting it and securing food for their families.

They'd got the nation behind them, and quite rightly so – if I'd been a farmer, I'd have been growing for them. Their whole culture revolved around the drug trade. Marijuana and coca plants were a part of everyday life, so plentiful they even grew at the roadside. In fact the police themselves used to wrap coca leaf around sugar lumps and suck away: they believed it would make them macho and virile. As far as they were concerned it kept them strong and alert to go and fight the cartels, and nobody seemed to spot the irony.

'The whole culture is based on violence,' they said. 'In the towns the secret police will drag young street urchins out of the sewers where they live and kill them.' At night, apparently, the ordinary sounds of the cities were punctuated by gunfire.

'A bus crashed over a hillside in the jungle about a month before you arrived. When the rescue services arrived on the scene they found all the local villagers scavenging through

the wreckage. Many passengers had survived, but were injured. The villagers ignored them in the rush to rip the watches and the rings and wallets off the corpses.'

'It's true – the police had to cock their weapons and start shooting the villagers to get them away,' said One-of-three-Josés. 'And as soon as they left, some of the police started doing exactly the same.'

'There is a disregard for life,' another fellow said. 'Life here revolves around death.'

We had two interpreters with us to get all the technical details over. Bruce was from D Squadron, and had only one arm – the other one had been blown off. The Regiment always kept its cripples. We had blokes with one arm, one eye, one leg; two blokes in B Squadron only had about six fingers between them. There was a wonderful picture in the interest room of them on a mountain-climbing course, trying to tie knots with only a couple of fingers each. Some blokes had lost legs, or suffered disabling gunshot wounds. One bloke who turned up for every Selection to run around the hills and man checkpoints had only one arm and one eye.

It was just part and parcel of life; if they're living quite a harsh existence and spending time on operations, people will get injured or shot, or collect diseases that impair them at a later date. They were kept in the Regiment for two reasons. First, if we were ever in the shit, we'd know at the back of our mind that even if we were hurt we'd have a future. Second, why pension off somebody who has experience and knowledge that could be used in training?

We started looking at the tactics we would need to carry out the task of attacking a DMP. At this stage we didn't know exactly what we were going to be attacking, so there was a bit of guesswork involved. We took it from the real basics, looking at the sort of equipment they had – which was essentially a bit of beltkit, a weapon, and their uniform and that was it. Then we looked at how they were going to move with it, and how they were going to live in the field.

They had a problem with hard routine. They liked to have the big fires going at night to keep themselves warm and boost their morale, and couldn't immediately see the tactical benefits of shivering in a sleeping bag and eating cold food. This was where the bonding and the friendship came in. We did hard routine ourselves, and they copied us.

We got out in the field for days on end and practised moving tactically around the jungle and the savannah. They learned to hole up before last light, get into a little LUP and stand to; at first light, they stood to again, ready to move off. After a while they actually enjoyed it; it was something different, it looked macho, and everybody else wanted a piece of the action.

We spent weeks teaching them OPs and how to hide up and watch locations. They'd be holed up for a couple of days and have to report what they saw, and they got very good at it.

We also taught them how to do close target recces on locations – to go in, try to get as much information as possible on the target without being seen, then watch it and when the time was right, to hit it. They could destroy all the ether, chemicals and processing equipment, but what they really wanted were the skilled people who did the processing; once they were out of the picture, the cartels would have to replace them, and we presumed the supply wasn't infinite.

Map-reading lessons were hilarious. There's a big myth that the natives of a country will know their way instinctively around the jungle. The fact is, nine times out of ten, they're as stuffed as everybody else is without a map, and they just stick to high ground, tracks and rivers. In my experience of people in the Middle East, the Far East, Asia and Africa, the locals always knew the easiest route – and they found it by following the animals, which always take the easy option. Take the boys off that route and they're scratching their heads. When they travel across savannah for hundreds of miles they're not navigating,

they're following animal herds. If the animals got lost, so would they.

We got all forty or fifty of them together in the cookhouse after breakfast because it was the biggest sheltered place where we could get the maps spread out on tables and get them around. I hated the sessions, because the place was minging.

Gaz taught the map-reading. 'This is the compass,' he'd say. 'We take a bearing like this.'

The rest of us would be moving up and down the tables, checking and helping where we could. It was a total gang fuck. We had to interpret to the soldiers what was going on, they then had to come back with any questions, which had to be answered. It just went on and on. In the end we'd just start laughing, and they'd join in. Gaz would go mad and shout: 'Stop! Come back in half an hour.' He would then compose himself, after giving us a bollocking for not taking it seriously.

We had to teach them how to look at the ground and interpret the map – to be able to say, 'OK, we found a DMP, now we've got to tell people where it is.' It's hard enough in the British Army to teach soldiers how to map read; it's not a science, it's an art, and the only way a recruit can get a feel for it is by getting on the ground and practising the skills.

Once they'd got the basics of using the compass, that was it – as far as they were concerned, it was the best lesson of their lives. Officers started calling by, saying, 'Any chance of one of these compasses?' Not to use, mind – they just wanted it dangling on their uniform to make them look good.

These guys were going to be fighting in a 'real time' war and they needed a taste of realism. More important, though, we were practising in the areas where they would be operating anyway, so if the shit hit the fan during train-ing we had live ammunition on hand. They weren't too impressed to start with, most of them looking very worried

about the possibility of shooting themselves. After a while, however, they got into it, and then started to come over all macho, swaggering all over the camp.

'They think they're going to go off and kill every fucker,' I said.

Gaz said, 'We'll soon put paid to that.'

He got some PE and we rigged it up around the training area. We had all the boys lying down ready to go forward, as if they were on a start line. One or two of them were lying there giggling and chanting, 'Rambo! Rambo!'

As they started to move forward we initiated the explosives. There was shit flying everywhere; they could feel the pressure of the explosives, and then dirt and bits of wood showered down on them. They hit the ground, then looked around sheepishly, suitably cut down to size. Some of them looked as if they were going to cry. They quit the Sly Stallone routine after that.

We had to knock all that shit out of them because as soon as the first one of them got killed, and there probably would be quite a few killed, they would be in for a very nasty shock.

We were getting invitations back to their houses when they had their two days off every couple of weeks. We had to try to dodge and weave as diplomatically as we could, because we didn't really want to get too familiar. We wanted the bonding relationship, but we wanted it in slow phases – otherwise it would affect the training. Apart from that, we wanted to get down town, have a shopping frenzy, and generally get around and see the place and have some fun.

By now we'd gradually weaned them off the great big daggers and six-shooters that had been hanging off their kit. We'd convinced them that the thing about kit dangling all over the place is that it gets entwined in the under-growth and leaves sign. We'd actually got them looking fairly professional.

We'd got them tactically OK and they were doing live

attacks on different targets, training for every eventuality. What we now started looking for was certain aptitudes required by a recce-cum-OP-cum-attack force. Their job would be to find the locations, look on the map, find out where they were, and get as much information on the place as possible. They would then go forward with an attack force to take the place out, or put in an OP and gather more information.

OP work calls for people who are naturally quiet, not active or hyper sorts. They have to spend a long time in a cramped position, just observing – two, three, maybe four of them in a location, gathering as much information as possible and sending it back over the radio so that the FOB (*forward operations base*) can plan and prepare. The ideal is to attack when the processing personnel are there and all the equipment is in place. Then you can get the personalities as well as the kit, and close the place down.

The people in the OP might be there for two or three weeks, living on hard routine, shitting in plastic bags, pissing in water canisters, not moving around, and under severe pressure because they were right on top of the target: because they were operating in the jungle, they were going to be much closer to the target than if they were out on the savannah.

We were also trying to pick out the natural leaders. There were designated leaders with ranks, but that didn't mean to say they were the right ones; people got ranked for certain things, not necessarily their command of man management or leadership.

It was a pain in the arse trying to bring on the natural leaders, because the system was so regimented. Everything had to be done diplomatically, and by giving the prospective leaders responsibilities rather than stripes. By picking the most capable blokes, we had more chance of getting the result that we wanted – the successful completion of a task. And because it was highly likely we would be there with them, we'd also stand more chance of

getting out alive. The best man in my group was One-of-three-Josés.

Every chance we had we'd get down town. I found it quite a modern, cosmopolitan city, with mega-office blocks, big shopping centres and good class hotels. But as in many other places, it was very evident that the locals either had enormous amounts of money or absolutely none. Ultra-modern skyscrapers stood next to derelict shanties; Mercedes limos drove over holes in the ground where the sewage system had collapsed and kids had taken shelter.

The city was also one of the dirtiest and noisiest places I'd ever seen. People seemed to throw away their rubbish wherever they were standing, and music blasted out in the streets, restaurants, and long-distance buses – it seemed to be an integral part of daily life, culminating at night in discotheques, tabernas and private parties. The blare of TV was just as bad. It appeared that sets in Latin America had two unique features: it seemed impossible to switch them off until late at night, and the volume control only had two settings – very loud and deafening.

The traffic noise was something else. I'd heard anti-quated APCs that were quieter than some of the deathtraps running around. Traffic jams seemed frequent, and the etiquette if you were stuck in one seemed to be to lean on your horn until you moved. When vehicles were not stuck in a traffic jam it seemed important to the locals that they be driven at well above maximum recommended revs. I'd already seen buses flying at breakneck speed down twisting mountain roads; in the city, they speeded up. There was an amazing variety of taxis, ranging from old American Fords, made during the time of JFK, to brand new Mazdas. There were traffic lights everywhere. You could cross the road on either green or red, and have an equal chance of being hit. I found it paid to look both ways several times before sprinting across, even if it was a one-way street.

Living and working in Dodge City, we all needed to wear

concealed weapons. I was sitting in the breakfast bar of the hotel one morning when a couple of white eyes turned up. Normally I'd have just given them the once-over, but this time it was a double take. By the way they wore their shirts I guessed they were carrying weapons. Then it dawned on me that I knew their faces: they were two ex-members of G Squadron. Sometimes, on different jobs around the world, we'd be working and see somebody we knew. Nothing would be said, everybody would ignore one another: they didn't know what we were doing or who we were supposed to be, and vice versa. Until one approached the other, there'd always be a silly little stand-off.

Eventually the ritual finished and it was OK. They came over and sat down.

'How's it going?'

'Not too bad.'

Another part of this ritual was not really getting straight down to what you wanted to talk about. Most people were cagey when it came to discussing their activities.

We chatted away about normal things, as you do when you bump into ex-members of the Regiment on the other side of the world. We slagged everybody down that we knew, and discussed what was going on in down town Hereford.

After a while I asked the question, expecting a 'Fuck off, big nose' in response: 'So, what are you doing then?'

'We have a close protection job here for a while, up north. Are you still in or are you working?'

Straightaway I realized that they were having the same doubts about me. I decided to play them along for a while.

'Yeah, I've been here for a few weeks now on a training job. The money is good but the people can be a pain in the arse.'

'What's the money like? Maybe we could get a job with you?'

'Same as if you were a corporal in the Regiment.'

Their job, it turned out, involved protecting people against the cartels.

I wondered if ex-members of the Regiment really were working for the cartels, earning fantastic amounts of money, adopting the same attitude as everyone sitting around us in this hotel: if these people want to use drugs, more fool them. Allegedly, lots of Americans and Canadians were working for the drug barons; the Yanks were advising, teaching and sorting out the business end. The cartels had fantastic wealth; working for them would probably be a cosy number. But lucrative as it might have been, I didn't think it was for me.

A meeting was fixed for the following week but by then other events had overtaken us.

25

Things had not been going well. We'd been in-theatre for a while now and every time we'd gone in against a DMP we found we'd captured the *Marie Celeste*. Security had been fearsomely lax. Corruption appeared to be a part of life; it wasn't unknown for helicopters, on the way to pick up troops for an attack, to fly over some of the processing factories as an early warning. I felt we were fighting a losing battle.

However, Gaz got us in the hut one day and said, 'Right, there's a change in the system. We're going to go and look for a plant over in the west. We'll get you in there covertly – you go and find the place, take it on, and then and only then will we bring the helicopters in. What's more, you'll report directly to us on the net back in HQ.'

We looked at a map that was spread out on his table. 'We know there's a plant in here somewhere,' he said, indicating an area of about sixteen square kilometres. 'We'll take four patrols in to go and look for it – that's four Ks each. The patrols are Tony's, Andy's, Rod's and Terry's. If we find it, we'll take it, because this is getting to be a pain in the arse.

'Once any of you find the target I want you to put a CTR in. I want photography, I want video, and I want as much information as possible sent over the net to me. I'll then organize the helis. We'll keep it strictly between us – the boys are not to know until we actually go on the op. Once we're on the ground we'll give them orders. Helis will be

on standby, but they won't know where or when they're going. The only people who'll know what's going on are us, and the head shed at HQ.'

None of us had any questions, and everybody probably felt the same as I did – absolutely delighted that we were breaking out of the vicious circle and that everything suddenly looked so positive. 'All we have to do now is find it,' said Rod.

I sat on the steps of the hut and ate some food as I watched Wayne, who had chatted one of the policemen into letting him ride his horse, come screaming past on an animal that was well and truly on Zanussi. Wayne was tall, dark, good looking, funny and intelligent – all the things you hate in a person. He had been brought up with horses, which was probably why he hated everything about them apart from riding. They disappeared from sight behind some buildings, and the next time I saw him, about an hour later, Wayne was covered in cuts, bruises and abrasions.

'Fucking thing,' he said. 'How come of all the bloody nags in this country I get the one that's just snorted a nose-bag of white powder?'

Each recce patrol, consisting of four policemen and one of us, would search an area of four grid squares – four square kilometres. Time out on the ground would be anything up to ten days and the object, as always, was not to kill the people in the manufacturing plant but to arrest them – especially the European chemists – and then to destroy the equipment.

At the muster parade the next morning Gaz announced to our trainees, 'We're going to go out and do some training. We're going to be away for about two weeks. Pack your kit and be ready at lunchtime to move off.'

We drove to an area about an hour away that we had been using for training. Gaz told the boys to relax and get a brew on, then said, 'We're not going training. We're going out on another operation. The lack of success that we've

415

been having is because of leaks by informers in the system. We're going to take you out of here now, and you're going to go and look for a DMP that is to the west.

'It's up to you to make sure that you put in all your best efforts. You've done all this training, and you're getting really well paid. We're expecting you to perform – we know you can do the job, we know you're good, and we're going to be with you all the way. Hopefully we're going to find the target – imagine the prestige when you succeed. All you have to do is exactly what we tell you, and everything will be fine. Now let's get out there: the quicker we do it, the quicker we can all get home.'

We got into our own little groups around the wagons and started to do our orders. I could hear the others talking to their groups around the area of the wagons. Wayne and Gaz were sorting out rations for the patrols.

To my four boys I said, 'Once we've succeeded, you will have all the credibility that you want and deserve. If we fail, maybe they will disband the paramilitaries.'

I saw four worried faces, perhaps picturing themselves back on traffic duty.

I said, hopefully in my best Spanish, 'So, we're going to go and locate a drug manufacturing plant. We've been told that it's roughly in an area sixteen Ks square somewhere in the west. We don't know where it is or how big it is. We don't know if people are still there. If we find it, we're going to put a CTR on it, bring all the other patrols in, and then we'll get a plan together to go and attack it. There'll be lots of helicopter support coming in, and plenty of other troops. If another patrol finds it, we'll go to meet them, join forces, and attack it.'

The boys were still looking worried. This operation was going to be totally alien from what they were used to. Usually it was the helicopter screaming in on top of the location, and everything all over and done within a couple of hours. What we were looking at now was a prolonged operation, a very different kettle of fish.

'Another change is that this time we're not going to helicopter in, we're going to drive in the vehicles down to the area, and gradually patrol in. We don't want anybody to see us or to know that we're there. This time, we might find something. Do you say yes to that?'

Four nervous smiles and a chorus of 'Yes!'

'It might take a couple of days to get into the area,' I went on, 'but it will be worth it. We'll be taking our time, we've got plenty of food, we know what we're doing. There'll be no problems.'

I laid out as much information in front of them as possible – a small-scale map, some drawings, the area in general, and then a large-scale map for the detailed briefs. I had to keep reminding myself that I wasn't dealing with professional soldiers. I had to sit them down and say, 'Before we start, does anybody want to go to the toilet? Anybody need to do anything before I start?'

After every phase of the orders I made a point of pausing and asking, 'Are there any questions?' They had to feel comfortable about asking, no matter how stupid the question. It was important not to take the piss out of them when they did come out with something really bone, and not to allow others to, either.

I first gave them all the political and military factors and made sure they realized how important it was that they pushed themselves forward to stop the trafficking. I then talked about the ground, starting with the area in general – all known enemy locations, all old processsing sites, and all our own locations.

We didn't have a target as yet, but I talked about the terrain, the weather conditions, what we expected the going to be like, what the locals were like, the names of any towns and villages, the direction of the main rivers. If the shit hit the fan and they were on their own, they would know that if they followed a certain river downstream they were going to hit a town. As I spoke, they checked everything on their maps.

I then went into the Situation. I told them everything they needed to know about the enemy in order to carry out the task – including the fact that the local barons were feeling pretty confident at the moment and would fight if we came up against them. I described what weapons they had, and what they dressed like.

'Now – friendly forces,' I said. 'There will be another three patrols that are going to be patrolling in other grid squares.' On the detailed map I showed them the rough area where the other patrols would be operating.

Next came the Mission. 'Mission – to locate and CTR the DMP in these grid squares here.' I repeated it, then went into the Execution, which I had broken down into phases.

'Phase one, the infiltration. We're going in by vehicle. As you know, once the stuff is ready, it has to be moved out by aircraft or vehicle. There is usually a road within ten to twenty kilometres of one of these plants. With trucks, we'll keep control of security. It might take us two or three days to patrol into the area, but that's what we get paid for.'

We'd be on hard routine. 'I'll have a scout out at the front, and I'll be doing the map-reading myself, with the local patrol commander checking. There will also be pacers and check pacers. If it's dense canopy we'll probably patrol in daylight and bin it at night-time. If the terrain allows us to patrol at night-time, all well and good, we'll do that as well. But in that sort of terrain I don't anticipate any movement by night.'

We understood the boys well by now, and they understood us. We had mutual respect that bordered on friendship; when we said we wanted something done, we expected them to comply – and they did. They no longer questioned our orders because they trusted us.

The slings had disappeared long ago from the 7.62 Galils, following our example. The swing swivels had also been taken off or taped down: they were designed to move, and therefore they made noise. Every man had about four to five metres of paracord, so if we had to do any river crossings

they could tie their weapon securely. As a navigation aid, I had taped a Silva compass onto the stock of my weapon, with the big arrow covered up to avoid having a fearsome luminous object moving through the jungle. If I was moving forward as a lead scout, I knew the rough bearing that I wanted to go on and the compass supplied an instant reference. As the patrol commander, with the scout out in front of me, I could also give an immediate indication of direction if required.

When the patrols were first issued with magazines for their weapons, they started taping them together because they'd seen a few Oliver Stone movies and they thought it looked rather macho. We discouraged them as much as we could: 7.62 are heavy rounds, and a 20-round magazine is a hefty object: when they were down on the ground, some of the lads could only just about lift the rifle up, let alone deal with the weight of a double magazine.

The Regiment blokes all took 9mm Brownings. The pistols the rest of their patrol took were weird and wonderful. Some had cowboy six-shooters, some had Colt .45s. What they expected to do with them probably even they didn't know.

We carried plenty of plastic explosive for destroying the DMP and also we had the means to burn down any fields that we came across – PE4 mostly and American C4, and all the odds and bods that went with it such as detonating cord, detonators, and claymores for our own defence.

Once we'd found the target, we'd put in a CTR. A picture speaks a thousand words when it comes to reconnaissance, especially if the troops you're briefing don't speak your mother tongue. We therefore also carried cameras and video recorders, and portable darkroom equipment to produce negatives. I favoured a Nikon with a zoom lens, plus a 28mm lens for IR photography, and a Canon point-and-shoot, also fitted with an IR filter for night photography. A video camera was excellent for CTRs, and we also had with us a little Sony play-back machine; with it, we could brief

the patrols with visual reference, so they'd know what they were looking for when they got onto the ground. The video had a manual-focus lens; an auto-focus lens latches onto the nearest object in the centre of the field of vision, which in jungle is almost always a leaf.

We also took night-viewing aids, either pocket scopes or weapon-mounteds, and all the kit had to be waterproofed.

Almost more important than the kit we took was what we didn't take: everybody had to go out sterile, apart from any obvious documentation. The boys carried their police warrant cards, but no home addresses or pictures of the wife and kids. They all knew the statistics; they'd all had family, friends or colleagues gunned down in the street.

We set off that afternoon in a convoy of four cattle trucks and travelled through the night. Everybody was subdued; nobody was talking much. The occasional fag flared in the darkness. It reminded me of Selection and the long drives to the Elan Valley and I tried to get as much rest as I could; I knew I'd be running around like a lunatic for the next couple of weeks.

For most of the next day we travelled through towns and villages, the roads getting more and more outrageous. A couple of hours before last light we stopped and had a brew. Gaz came over and said, 'We're going to split off about three Ks up the road. I'm going to take two groups, Wayne's going to map-read your lot. If there's any dramas, get on the net, because we've got the helicopters standing by. Don't fuck about, just get on the net and get the people out. See you soon.'

We got back on the wagons. I was in Wayne's vehicle, which was leading. The road was metalled but badly pot-holed. The suspension was shaking itself to pieces and we were getting shunted about in the back; soon everybody was standing up to save themselves from a battering.

It was coming to last light. The vehicle stopped, the engine was turned off. It went very quiet and the noises of

the savannah took over. Wayne got out and said: 'This is your drop-off point.'

I got the blokes off the wagon. They looked as if they didn't want to get off, but at the same time knew the job had to be done. Shades again of Selection.

'We aren't going to do anything tonight,' I said. 'All we have to do is tab into our area.'

It was all in slow time. We got our bergens on, sorted ourselves out, and started to walk off towards the cover about half a kilometre away. Once we'd gone a couple of hundred metres we heard the engines start up then drive away. After a minute or two there was total silence. I watched the headlights threading their way along the road and disappear into the distance.

I could hear my breath. I'd had twenty-four hours of total inactivity, and now I was starting to get my second wind.

The weather was very warm and moist. The night was full of jungly sounds, though we were still in savannah. I could hear crickets. There was a very light breeze. It was moderately cloudy but I could see stars.

I was feeling fairly comfortable. We had plenty of food and water, and were going to get our heads down for the night. I was actually looking forward to a few hours in my hammock.

In the morning, because we weren't in any immediate danger, I let the guys start with a brew and hot scoff.

One of the blokes in the patrol was called Rodriguez. He was about twenty-two, tall, black, and rather effeminate. He had unnaturally long eyelashes and very fine, defined features, a pianist's hands and immaculate nails. He spoke with a soft tone, and seemed to apologize for everything he did. He was, however, very good at his job and I wanted him to be the scout.

I said, 'I want you to set off on this bearing, Rodriguez. We're going to go forward, and after about an hour we're going to stop and have a brew. Keep your eyes open and

keep on the bearing – we don't want to start getting lost. Do you understand? We are depending on you!'

'Si,' he smiled. 'Si, sorry, no problem.'

The scout kept far enough ahead to give advance warning of a problem, but close enough for me to see him and signal occasional directions. He really dictated the movement of the patrol as he moved along – if he wanted us to stop, he'd tell us to. If he stopped dead, I'd also stop dead, and everybody else would do the same. He was the first set of eyes.

After an hour Rodriguez stopped in a dip in the ground under a large tree. We hunkered down and got a brew on. Birds twittered in the branches overhead; some form of wildlife rustled in the undergrowth. We talked in quiet whispers.

'This will be the last brew,' I said. 'Make sure you don't tell anyone I let you have it!'

They were pleased to think it was our little secret.

I looked at them and said, 'Let's crack on and do it – nobody let me down. Any problems with that?'

'No, no problems.'

Rodriguez wanted to be the scout again, so I let him. Normally I'd have changed the scout every couple of hours because it was a strenuous job. Chopping his way through would have made noise and leave sign; the scout had to move the vegetation out of the way as he patrolled through. He was on the lookout for movement, or any sign of there having been movement. It could be ground sign, such as mud prints, or it could be top sign, such as leaves overturned. A large rubber leaf or fern, for example, doesn't naturally turn up onto its underside and after a short while it would turn its way back to the sun – so something must have turned it, and that meant that somebody had been there quite recently.

The scout was looking, too, for any signs of animal traps. Indigenous people leave signs that these things are around, and we didn't want to land up in a net dangling from a tree.

He was also looking for any signs of the DMP: this could be a lot of footprints going in one direction, it could be a noise, it could be a smell. If he spotted people we wouldn't take them on; the object was to avoid them, to see where they went, and to follow them.

It took us nearly half a day to start getting into the rough area of our four grid squares. By now we were all wet with sweat. It hadn't rained; I was just hoping that if it did it was before last light so we didn't have to sort ourselves out that night in a downpour. Then we started our search pattern, which varied with the terrain. Sometimes we might be paralleling along grid squares, at others we'd fan out from prominent objects. About once every hour we'd stop for five minutes. That gave us time to tuck our shirts in, pull our trousers up, have a drink, refill the water bottles. Every time we came to a source of water we'd fill up; if the bottles were already full, then we'd drink as much as we could. Some of the blokes put lemon powder in one of their water bottles and had the other as plain water. I preferred both to be plain.

For the first afternoon all the blokes were keen, but then fatigue started to take its toll – the mental fatigue of continually looking for sign, and the physical fatigue of carrying a bergen in the heat. It was showing on these people quite a lot.

About an hour before last light it was time to look for a place to LUP, but first we'd need to break track to make sure no-one was following us. Gonzalo – 'Gonz' – was the scout. I gave him the signal to stop and went forward.

'We're going to look for an LUP,' I said into his ear.

A big smile came up on his face. He had massive tombstone teeth with black marks between from chewing tobacco.

I said, 'Follow me,' and he tagged on behind.

Gonz was about twenty-three or twenty-four. He had a really youthful look on his face as if he still had puppy fat, and was always smiling. At times I didn't know if he was

stupid or just happy. It was a mischievous sort of smile; I never really knew what was going on in his mind, but I hoped there was a lot more tucked away than there appeared to be.

We looped the track and put in an instant ambush on our own trail, because no matter how carefully we went through the jungle, we were always going to leave sign. Then, when we were happy, three blokes stayed with the bergens, while Gonzalo and I went to look for an LUP. The ideal site was not necessarily somewhere that could be defended; the main consideration was concealment. Everybody knew what was going on now and was happy at the prospect of getting their head down.

At the site, we took our bergens off again and got into all-round defence, standing-to until last light. First, however, came a good dousing of mozzie rep. All around my head I heard the steady buzz of insects. Standing-to in the jungle, you always see and hear a lot more than you realized was around you. You think you're moving covertly, but the wildlife has you sussed, and by the time you get there they're well and truly gone. Now, just sitting there, doing nothing, I could hear everything around me. Apart from the mosquitoes it was lovely, being sort of embraced by the jungle.

As soon as it was last light we put up our hammocks and ponchos. There was no need to talk; everybody knew what to do, taking it in turns. While two of us got ourselves organized, the other three looked and listened.

I put my dry kit on and got into my hammock, and fell asleep listening to the hums and rustles and the rain that came about midnight.

About an hour before first light we packed our equipment up. Again, there was no reason to talk; we just did everything slowly and carefully to avoid making a noise. We left as soon as it was light enough to move.

We patrolled for about two hours, then stopped to make

our sitrep to the FOB, giving our location, any enemy location or activity that we'd seen, and our own activity and future intentions, which in this case was: 'Carry on patrolling.' Back at the HQ the blokes would then plot us on the map; if the shit hit the fan later in the day, at least they'd know where we'd been at 0800.

The boys sat there eating sugar and corned beef.

For the next few days that was the routine – moving off, changing over scouts, changing over check pacers.

Once or twice we got lost. We stopped, moved off track, sat in all-round defence, and got the map out.

'Where were we last time we definitely knew where we were?' I said to Gonz.

We methodically worked it out from there – it was no good running around like lunatics, chasing shadows. I sent two boys out on a short recce to confirm that the next feature was 500 metres further along. Hopefully they'd come back and report, 'Yes, there is a river and it flows from left to right.'

On the third occasion I sent out Gonz and One-of-three-Josés on a recce patrol. 'Go down there no more than four hundred metres. As you start moving down towards the low ground we should be on the highest point. Look around and there should be no higher ground around you. If not, we have *una problema*. And there should be a river about three hundred metres further down, running left to right.'

Off they went, Gonz with a big black toothy smile on his face. They came back much sooner than I had expected, and Gonz's smile had vanished.

Putting his mouth to my ear, Gonz said, 'We got down there. We were on the highest ground, but there's movement ahead. We heard a sound of metal and some shouting.'

I got everybody together and said, 'There's something down there. We don't know what it is. What we're going to do is move forward as best we can. Gonz is going to take us down there to the area where he heard it, and we'll stop

and take it from there. Is everybody ready? Just take your time, there's no need to flap.'

Everybody started to switch on. We moved down the hill very, very slowly. Gonz was ahead of me, the others behind. I couldn't hear anything.

Gonz stopped and pointed forward.

I motioned for him to come with me, and the other three to stay with the bergens. 'If there's any problems you're soon going to hear. If we're not back by last light, wait until midday tomorrow and then skirt around the noise, hit the river, and turn right until you hit the road. We'll sort ourselves out. Leave our bergens where they are.'

We crept forward through the vegetation, with nothing but rifles and beltkit. We were going to go just far enough to confirm; it would be no good jumping up and down thinking that we'd found it, after only a cursory look.

I inched through the jungle, following Gonzalo. My eyes were darting around all over the place. He was looking ahead, concentrating on trying to remember where he had heard the noise. Every now and again he looked back for a bit of reassurance, and there was no smile.

At a point about 200 metres from where we'd left the bergens, he stopped and held up his hand. I stopped. As a technical advisor, I should now have been helping him to go and do the CTR, but I had to make sure the job was done and we all got out safely. Motioning for him to stay where he was and give me cover, I signalled that I was going to go and have a look.

I got down onto my belly and crawled forward very slowly. I took three or four little crawls, stopped, listened, looked around, and crawled again. After about twenty minutes I couldn't believe what I saw.

I was looking through about two metres of brush, and then the area opened up into almost a small industrial complex. I saw three or four buildings. One was a long, low one, which I knew was the trademark of a DMP. Inside, the coca paste would be laid out on long tables. Two other

single-storey buildings were higher. They had corrugated iron roofs, with attempts to camouflage them with leaves and branches.

I heard a South American voice shout a question. The answer, in Spanish, was slightly drowned by the sound of a generator, but it had a strong, almost Afrikaans twang to it.

I saw an old boy walking between two of the buildings. He wasn't armed.

I stayed there for about half an hour, watching and listening for more activity, not believing our good luck. It was the first manufacturing plant I had seen in operation; I didn't want to fuck up. I couldn't see much from my perspective, but heard another couple of people and the occasional banging of a door. The mosquitoes loved what was happening. They could land on my face and it would take me long, slow seconds to bring my hand up to wipe them away. I didn't want to move to another position or kneel up to get a better view. I didn't need to do that at this stage; all I needed to do was make myself happy that it was indeed a DMP.

I crawled my way back to Gonz. I put my mouth to his ear and gave him a thumbs up. 'Bingo!'

He gave me a flash of blackened tombstones, but I knew he was thinking, 'Oh fuck, we've found one . . .'

We moved back to the rest of the patrol. I got everybody around and said, 'We've found it – it's down there.'

I told them exactly what I'd seen and heard. There was an air of disbelief, together with a mixture of happiness and apprehension. Now something had to be done about it.

We moved right out of the area to avoid any chance of a compromise. I told them, 'I'm going to go in tomorrow at first light with One-of-three-Josés. The other three are going to guard the equipment at the final RV, which is where we stopped with the bergens earlier on. This might take a couple of days. You're to stay there for two days if we don't come back. On the morning of the third day, if we're not

there, you're to head down to the river, turn right, and hit the road. If you hear any firing, you're to come down and help us. Got that?'

The fourth member of the patrol, nicknamed El Nino, was about nineteen. He was about 5'7" and had a skinny, bony body. He found it very difficult to look at anyone when he talked, looking above or to the side of their face; maybe he was self-conscious of the jungle of zits that covered his own. He didn't have a clue what was going on. He was always left to do as little as possible. He was all right, just inexperienced and worried. He would rather be at home with his mum than doing this shit. However, he always tried to act the macho bit in front of the others, who took the piss out of him non-stop. He was looking severely worried, but happy that he was in the final RV group.

'Don't put your ponchos up in the final RV,' I said. 'All I want you to do is stay with those bergens. It's going to be a long day – might be two days. Make sure you look after the kit and you'll be looking after us.'

I got the radio out and sent a sitrep back to the troop HQ. It was in a rush because I wanted to bang it out before last light. I told them what we'd found, what I'd seen. 'Unless I'm told otherwise,' I said, 'we will CTR it tomorrow.'

I knew that back at the squadron HQ they would be making the decision as to whether to tell the other patrols on their next sitrep, or wait until it was confirmed that it was the target. If they told the other patrols to stop and wait out, they'd be losing time. Not our problem; we started planning and preparing for the CTR.

I'd go in myself with One-of-three-Josés; the other three would guard the equipment at the final RV. A set of orders would have to be produced, covering all eventualities – how we were going to get there, what we were going to do when we got there, what we were going to do if the enemy opened up on us. What would we do if the final RV group had a contact? How long would the RV be open for before we changed to another RV? What would

428

we do if there was a contact and somebody got caught?

We would plan and prepare in the area where we were now, and then move forward to the final RV, which would be the jumping-off point of the two-man CTR team. The CTR might take one or two days, depending on what we could see and where. We'd just have to make sure that if we were out during daylight hours, we came back an hour before last light; then we could move off and LUP somewhere else. The ponchos wouldn't be put up at the final RV; the boys would just place out a couple of claymores, sit with their backs to the bergens, their beltkit on, and then between themselves alternately stag it and get their heads down, which wouldn't be good news.

The teaching went to bollocks now. In theory it should have been the patrol doing the CTR and conducting any attack, but we'd only get one chance and it had to be done properly.

We were about 500 metres from the DMP and were going to stay there for the night. We got our ponchos and hammocks out and settled down. One-of-three-Josés wasn't getting his head down, that was for sure. He was tossing and turning all night, obviously flapping about what was going to happen the next day. The others were apprehensive; they looked almost lost and lonely, as if they wanted everybody else there as reinforcements.

I was apprehensive myself. I didn't know what to expect; all I knew was that if they got hold of us we'd be in the shit. I lay there covered in cam cream and mozzie rep and thought about Kate. I tried to work out the time difference and wondered what she would be doing. I worked it out that she'd probably just finished her breakfast and was getting ready for playschool. I just wanted to get this over and done with as quickly as possible, so we could get back down town and have a good time on the beach with the ex-G Squadron boys. I knew it wouldn't be long until I was back in the jungle again.

* * *

'We'll take the minimum amount of equipment with us,' I said to One-of-three-Josés at first light. 'Basically just beltkit, plus the cameras, and a pistol and rifle each.'

We had already spent lots of time making sure that our equipment didn't shine, by blackening it with spray paint.

Now we cammed ourselves up, too. Skin is a reflective surface, no matter if you're black, Asian, or white. When the sun shines, your skin shines. At the beginning of a jungle patrol, cam cream is difficult to keep on because of the sweat. After a few days, however, when the face started to get a bit of growth, the stuff congealed into the beard and got engrained in the creases in the forehead.

It wasn't a matter of just a few dabs on the face like Indian warpaint. We daubed it on all over the face, the ears, behind the ears, all around the neck and the back of the neck, below the line of the collar, down the V of our chests, on our hands and up our wrists. I had my shirt sleeves down to protect me from all the jungly nasties as I was crawling about, but I still took it up past the wrists because my hands would be moving and therefore the material would be moving.

The way the cam cream goes on is always a sign of a good professional soldier. There was no need for all the magic colours – dark green, brown, and light green – all in weird and wonderful patterns and shapes. It wasn't there as camouflage, it was there to mask the shine and break up the lines of our face.

We now checked each other's cam cream in the buddy-buddy system. I checked One-of-three-Josés, and he did me.

'Everything OK?' I asked him.

'Is OK.' He smiled nervously.

We all moved down towards the final RV at about 0700. Rodriguez was the scout, and this time he was really taking his time. He was stopping every five minutes, looking and listening. In my mind I was thinking about many things: about the CTR; about One-of-three-Josés – I knew he was

going to hold back and I'd have to do everything – and about what would happen if he or I got caught. I decided that I would not get caught and that was that.

A very cautious two hours later we reached the final RV, took our bergens off, sat down on them and waited five minutes for everybody to settle down and stop panting. I took the camera equipment out of my bergen, already stowed in a little daysack. I checked all our equipment again to make sure that everything was tied down and secure, that we didn't have any rattles. I also made sure One-of-three-Josés knew where all my first-aid kit was. I ran a discreet eye over his uniform and kit to make sure all his buttons were done up, and that he wasn't taking anything with him that was unnecessary.

'We are at the final RV,' I said. I confirmed our patrol and emergency RVs and all our directions – the direction we were going out on, the direction we'd be coming in from – and the time we'd got to be in by. Then it was time to go.

I looked at One-of-three-Josés. I knew that if I was captured they'd take their frustrations out on me; there was a good chance of being held hostage for a ransom. But for him the downside was much nastier and he was sweating buckets. The police were getting knocked out left, right and centre: even before they finished training many tens of them had been assassinated. The cartels spared no effort or expense when it came to reprisals. If a member of the police was caught he knew he was guaranteed a slow and painful death. Many of them had been found dead at the roadside, having had not a good day out on the receiving end of a chainsaw and hammer.

Rodriguez insisted on going through all the details again. 'We're there for two days? On the third day we go to the river? Is that right? Sorry for asking.'

I had built up the task at the original briefing to make them feel that they were special. I went over to One-of-three-Josés and said into his ear, 'You are Number One, the best.' I hoped that would stop him from hyperventilating.

He tried to grin, but it came out looking more like a grimace.

We moved very slowly; there was no rush. It was hot and damp; mozzie rep was running into my eyes. My feet and boots were soaking wet.

CTRs in the jungle are very scary things. We would be getting right onto the target; if we couldn't see what we needed to see from the perimeter, we'd have to go forward and then even more forward until we did. It would be no good getting just half of the information; that could mean having to go back in.

When I thought of CTRs, I always imagined one of those toys that motor forward on little electric wheels until they hit something. They turn around, come back, and then they bounce off into it again. The two of us would be going in, coming out, going back in at a different angle, bouncing off, going around. We'd go around the entire camp initially, looking for routes in and out and any signs of security. If we saw people on guard, we'd note what weapons they were carrying and what they were dressed like. Did they look switched on, or were they casual and nonchalant? Were they young, were they old?

Were the tracks in and out well worn? Were there fresh marks on them? Could we tell by the sign how many people had been going through?

What sort of noises can we hear as we're going around? Whereabouts can we infiltrate into the camp? Has it got barbed wire up, or rattan, or is there nothing?

Is it in a small valley and camouflaged? How many people are in the camp? Are there any communications? Are there any antennas? Are there any vehicles, are there any aircraft?

What vantage points are there? Are there places where we could locate fire support groups? Are there places where we could put an OP in – the decision might be not to attack it now, but just to OP it and watch it for weeks. Where would be a good start line for an attack? Where

could we bring people in? What are the main processing areas? Where is the living accommodation? All these questions would have to be answered from where I was lying on my belly and looking up, from maybe a dozen or so metres away.

We got to about fifteen metres from the edge of the camp and stopped. Very slowly, I got down and took my beltkit off. I handed it and my rifle to One-of-three-Josés, then pointed to him and pointed to the ground, motioning for him to stay put. I did a little walking sign with my fingers to show him that I was going to go forward and have a look. I pushed the camera around to rest on my back, got onto my stomach and started edging myself forwards.

Somewhere a generator was chugging. There were snatches of conversation and the sound of a radio, playing pan pipe music. As doors were opened and closed the music got louder, then died a little.

My breath came in pants; the crawling was hard work. All I had to protect myself with was my pistol as I kitten-crawled towards the perimeter. I put my hands out, put pressure on my elbows and pushed myself forward with the tips of my toes. Six inches at a time, I moved through the undergrowth. I stopped, lifted my head from the dirt of the jungle floor, looked and listened. I heard my own breath and it sounded a hundred times louder than anything around me. The leaves crackled more than they normally would; everything was magnified ten times in my mind. I inched forward again. It took nearly an hour to cover the distance. I was right on top of the DMP now and movement was the thing that was going to give me away. If one of the guards saw movement even just on the periphery of his vision, he would be instantly drawn towards it. I stopped, looked, moved forward, constantly looking for alarm trips – whether they were wires, pressure pads, infrared beams or maybe even a more sophisticated method based on empty tin cans. I was right up on top of it now. If there was an opportunity, this was the time to start

taking pictures of any personalities in the camp – especially Europeans or gringos. If it all went to ratshit, at least we'd have some sort of evidence of foreign involvement that the police could use.

The sun was very bright, making it easier for me to see the target and harder for them to see me in the gloom of the forest. I could see some buildings, each about thirty feet by twenty. They were built of vertical wooden planks with corrugated iron roofs and leaves and rattan as a crude form of camouflage over the top. The iron sheeting had lost its shine and was rusting, indicating that the camp had possibly been there for quite a while. Some of the slats had gaps between them, some were close-joined. All the buildings had windows, covered with mosquito netting. There were two doors, a wooden inner and a mesh outer, an anti-mosquito measure which seemed strange given the gaps in the wood.

There was intermittent noise – music, a bang of metal, a bit of shouting – indicating that there weren't that many people there. Very slowly, I eased the camera bag from my back. If we were going to hit this place, people had to have a firm idea of their targets and what the camp looked like. Hopefully this would be the first of many pictures as I moved around the camp.

I got the camera off my head. The biggest danger would be the lens reflecting the sun, so the whole camera was wrapped in a face net. It wasn't a problem; the photographs would still come out. Really slowly I put the camera on the ground, aimed and gently squeezed the shutter release. Nothing happened. With my thumb I tried to move the film winder along but it was stuck. There was no time to muck about with it; I put it down by my side and kept on looking. This was going to be a pain in the arse. I cursed myself for not bringing the video camera; I'd wanted to save the batteries for any OPs that we might have to put on.

I stayed where I was, watching and listening. I could see four main buildings. To my left was the long low building,

of which I could see about a third. I was assuming that it was the DMP. To the right of that were two other buildings; one was definitely the kitchen and administration area. The door opened and out came an old boy of about fifty or sixty wearing a football T-shirt, a pair of shorts, plimsolls and a fag in his mouth. He was carrying a pile of pots and pans, which he just threw onto the ground. There were small piles of kitchen rubbish strewn around within easy reach of the door.

There was also a generator running, the noise seeming to come from the other side of the cookhouse. I could still hear odd bursts of shouting, but had only seen the old boy. I wanted to know what the protection looked like, how many of them there were, and what weapons they had.

After about an hour I backtracked out. Whether it was too early in the morning or there simply wasn't a lot going on, I didn't know. I backed out until I reached One-of-three-Josés. He was sitting there grinning away. I took the camera off and gave it the cut-throat sign. I put my beltkit on, pointed to him and showed him the way we were going to go, which was anti-clockwise.

It took us about twenty minutes to travel 30 metres to be near the edge of the camp again. We stopped, I signalled to One-of-three-Josés to stay where he was, and I inched forward. This time I was facing the living accommodation, and almost immediately I saw a white face. He was small, about 5'5", in his forties, and in the process of throwing away a bowl of water. He was wearing only a pair of shorts, boots, and dark glasses. His hair was wet and pushed back; I guessed he'd just had a wash. His arms were darkly tanned up to the T-shirt line and he had a big white ring around his neck. He hadn't shaved for about a week and looked in shit state. He put a fag in his mouth and lit up, and then walked back into the hut. I was pleased: at least one European. I just wished the camera was working and knew I'd get a bollocking from Gaz.

I had been waiting there for another forty-five minutes

when two players appeared. One had a long, a G3 automatic rifle, the really old type with the longer muzzle and solid stock. The other one wasn't armed. They moved from the living accommodation over in the direction of the processing hut, which I couldn't see. They were very casual, smoking, talking and laughing, obviously very confident about where they were.

That was three characters, not counting the old cookhouse boy. I stayed. I didn't move to swat the mosquitoes that were landing on me; I just kept my head low, looking up and listening, trying to take in every detail. My head was starting to fill up with lumps but I'd given up by then. I was lying there with my hands in front of me, resting my chin on my hands.

To help me listen, I opened my jaw a little to close off any swallowing sounds.

I was trying to get a mental picture of exactly what this place looked like. I only had about 20 per cent of the information at the moment, and I had to get as much as I could.

I could see where the generator was now. It was between the two buildings. I could also see antennas on the roofs. There was a satellite dish, which could have been for television or comms. There was also a normal whip antenna.

I could hear music playing, and everyday routine noises. Plates clattered, men laughed. I heard two men talking in their own language, which was possibly Dutch or Flemish – I was no expert. I didn't particularly care; all I knew was that there were Europeans in the camp.

I was starting to get really tuned in now. I could picture this side of the camp, where the doors were, how they opened up. It was fairly good construction and had been there a long time. The areas where they walked were well trodden down.

It started to look as if something was happening. From the direction of the processing hut I heard another

generator sparking up. I decided to give it half an hour. The European came out, now wearing a grubby-looking T-shirt, and sauntered over towards the processing hut. Then another two came out. They weren't talking, but they were white. One was rubbing his hair as he walked, obviously having just got up. He, too, was in his forties, but much taller than the others. He wore American combat trousers and a dirty Smiley face T-shirt. His hair was long and dark blond, and either wet or greasy. The other was about two paces in front of him and enjoying a cigarette. He was in his late twenties or early thirties and looked much smarter, and was carrying a leather bag. Something was about to start.

I now knew there were definitely at least six people in the camp, but there were still people in the accommodation and I needed to know how many. All I'd seen so far was one G3; I also needed to know how many weapons there were.

I waited for another half an hour but nothing happened. I could still hear music and the sounds of the cook throwing around his bits and pieces, but it seemed that everything was happening around the other side. I crawled back out. One-of-three-Josés was really happy to see me this time; he'd been sitting there for what must have seemed like hours, and in his head he didn't know what was happening. I motioned for him to stay still and then set off.

I mooched down a few more metres, following the rough line of the camp perimeter. I moved on my hands and knees, trying to find another point to move in. I couldn't see the camp, but could hear it. I was now getting down near the river, which was the original feature that the blokes on the recce patrol had gone to find. I moved between the water and the camp and came across a well-worn track with tyre marks. Have they got a vehicle? I decided to go down to the river and follow the track. On the opposite side of the track were two rubber Geminis with outboards. They were beached on the bank, and

concealed in undergrowth. I still couldn't see where the vehicle tracks came from. It must have been something that was carried on the boats, and then used as transport.

I now wanted to get onto the other side of the DMP to see what was going on and how many people were involved. There obviously weren't going to be that many, because there wasn't enough accommodation. I went back, spoke right into One-of-three-Josés's ear and said, 'We're going to go back around the other side.' He nodded, turned, and off we went in really slow time.

Every time there was a noise we stopped and listened. Once it subsided, we carried on, keeping far enough from the camp not to be seen, but close enough so we could hear what was going on.

When we were right on the opposite side I stopped, took my beltkit off, and kitten-crawled in. There was a definite amount of activity. I wasn't bothering to look up at the moment; all I was doing was getting as near as I could. As soon as I could hear clearly what was going on, I stopped and listened.

It looked as if things were about to spark up in what I presumed to be the actual manufacturing area. As I got closer and closer, I could see that the manufacturing building, about two thirds of the height of the other buildings, was in fact an open hut with the roof supported by posts and walls that only went a third of the way. In the shadows, I could see people moving around. There wasn't a massive hive of activity but there were certainly other generators running. I could see the heat now coming off the ground in the exposed camp.

To the left of the processing hut was another building. I guessed that it was a storeroom of some kind. Also on that side, I saw a three-wheeled trike with a trolley.

I waited another ten minutes, took a deep breath, and started moving again. By now it was starting to get pretty hot. The sun was up and I was on the edge of the cleared canopy. I could feel the heat on the back of my neck and on

my shirt. I was a bit worried at one stage because I thought that if my stuff started to dry out, they might see the steam.

I was stinking. The bottom half of my body was soaking wet and I was covered in mud and bits of twig and brush. I kept wanting to scratch it, and rub at the mozzie bites that felt as if they covered every exposed inch of flesh. But the only thing I wanted moving were my eyes.

I was breathing really heavily. I didn't want to go further forward, but I knew I had to. We needed information, otherwise we'd just have to go back the next day.

The next thing I saw was a weapon. It was an old-type M16 with a triangular stock, left-leaning against the trike. It meant these people were fairly non-fussed; they were obviously feeling comfortable with their situation.

I still couldn't see how many people there were. Probably some of them were still in the huts. All I could see from this perspective was the processing hut; I couldn't see the living accommodation. I'd fucked up; I should have stayed on the other side for longer so I could see people coming and going.

I was annoyed with myself. I didn't want to stay there any longer than I had to, and I didn't want to come back another day. I imagined what the people at the final RV were thinking. They'd be sitting there doing absolutely nothing, frustrated as hell. I knew; I'd done it myself often enough. I hoped they felt confident enough to sit and wait.

At last there was movement. A boy came out to the trike and sat on it. He lit up a cigarette and leaned back on the seat, soaking up a bit of sun. He had sunglasses on and a pair of jeans that were rolled up to halfway up his calf muscles, and trainers but no socks. He had a light-coloured denim shirt hanging out of his jeans. That was one more narco.

He shouted at somebody, went around the back, and disappeared. He then came back into view and started to walk towards me. He didn't pick his weapon up but I was flapping. One thing I didn't want was eye-to-eye contact; I

439

kept looking at his feet. I had my chin on my hands; I kept still, taking really slow, deep breaths. I thought: if he walks much closer he's going to see me. What then? Am I going to drop him and run? Or am I going to draw the pistol and shoot him and run? Or do I just take him, get him down, tie him up, and keep him quiet? I wasn't too sure. I decided to play it by ear; it certainly wasn't a good day out at all.

I was sure he hadn't seen me, or he would have picked his gun up. He didn't look inquisitive, he was just walking. But the closer somebody gets to you, the more chance there is of being seen. He got so close I was bracing myself for a shout. Suddenly he veered to the left-hand side of me. Fuck, I thought – if he's going to start mooching in the jungle he'll find One-of-three-Josés. Was he going for a shit? They must have some facility, probably for shitting into the river. What the hell was he doing?

He walked past, no more than two metres away from my face. At that stage I put my head down, closed my eyes, and kept as still as possible.

I heard his trainers kicking the ground, then he shouted back at somebody. I was looking on the jungle floor, trying to keep my breath as slow and controlled as possible. I wanted to start going slowly for my pistol. But it was in a shoulder holster, and to get it I'd have had to cross my hand over my chest and go down for the pistol grip, which was going to create movement and noise. If he came over, I'd just have to spin over and draw it. Mentally I was running through it – the safety catch was on, the hammer was back. All I had to do was drive it out, flick that safety catch off and I could shoot him. I'd turn over and push my foot up, because if he started lunging at me I could keep my foot up and keep him off my body, and then drop him. And then I'd just run for it – and hopefully not get shot by One-of-three-Josés.

He carried on moving to the left. About two minutes later he came back, carrying a small cardboard box. There must be another part of the camp that I hadn't seen, another

storeroom or something. So could there be more people up there? Could it just be a storeroom? Why would they have a storeroom that far away?

He went back to the trike and dropped the box onto the floor. It split open and cans fell out. He picked one of them up, stabbed it, and lifted it to his mouth. Yet it wasn't a drinks can, it was small and flat, more like a can of tuna. Then it dawned on me – it was milk. It was condensed milk.

After about another hour I decided to move. I wasn't seeing that much and it was starting to get really hot. People weren't moving around. I didn't know how much activity it took to manufacture drugs. All I knew was that I'd seen people doing things in the processing hut.

I had a good idea of the layout of the camp, but not what lay to the left-hand side.

My heart was pounding severely. I was pleased that we'd found a plant, and revved up because now we had to do something about it.

I eased myself back and got back to One-of-three-Josés. We had eye-to-eye and I gave him a thumbs up before quietly putting my kit on. I pointed up to the area where the character had been walking, and further to the left of the target. He didn't seem too pleased, as he'd obviously assumed that the recce was over; time was pressing and if we didn't get back soon it meant a night in the FRV. We mooched on very slowly. We started going up a gentle rise, and then we hit a track. The trees and vegetation were very sparse now, and we had beams of sunlight coming down on us. It was boiling. It was obvious to me at once that this must be the track the character had gone to. Up to the left was flat ground; we doubled back on ourselves and went up onto the high ground. We stopped, I took my kit off and went forward on my hands and knees, pistol in my hand.

It was a clear, flat area with a wooden platform – a helipad. There were odds and bods scattered around, including cardboard boxes. Some food must have come in by

helicopter and been left there. A helipad was excellent news; it meant we could get helicopters in right on target.

By now I was sweating good style in the heat. Crickets were chirping away; the noise was different outside of the canopy compared with the inside. I could feel the wind, and the light was hazy, shimmering. It made me want to go and stretch out in the sun before I went back into the other world of doom and gloom.

I got back to One-of-three-Josés and sat there for a while. Back in the relative safety of the undergrowth, I allowed myself a few deep breaths. José was grinning again, and this time it was pure relief. He knew that we must have finished. In my mind I ran through whether we knew everything we needed to know. I came to the conclusion that it was pointless coming back in the next day; I knew as much as I was going to know, unless I sat there all day again and tried to count people. It wasn't a mass of activity, which made it difficult to count. I knew there were at least two weapons, and I could only guess that the guards would use them to defend the plant. There was a lot of money at stake. Some of these people would stay and defend the plants at any price; they knew there couldn't be an unlimited supply of men coming in and attacking the place – so it might be worth their while just taking us on.

I was satisfied that we had all the first-phase information that we needed. I tapped One-of-three-Josés on the boot and nodded towards the FRV. He was happy now as we made our way carefully back to the others.

We met the bergen cache from exactly the same direction we had left. I passed on all the information so that everybody would know exactly the same as we did. If One-of-three-Josés and I suddenly dropped dead, at least the information would have been pooled.

'We're going to stay here for the night,' I said. 'I want to go forward again tomorrow morning.'

Their faces fell and it suddenly dawned on me that I'd

forgotten who these guys were and had been treating them as members of the Regiment.

I changed my mind. 'We're going to leave from here in a minute and go back to the LUP.'

The relief was evident; as far as they were concerned they were being cut from the danger area. Rodriguez flashed me a brilliant smile.

We got back to the LUP. I was going to send a sitrep out that night but it was getting too dark. I decided to prepare it and encrypt it, and bang it out first thing in the morning. I'd tell them what I'd seen of the camp, the numbers, the grid of where we were going to sponsor the troop RV, which was where we were. Once the four recce patrols were assembled, we would become a fighting patrol. I'd also say that I was going to send an OP out the same day to go and get more information. I decided not to use the video the next day as I didn't want to put them under pressure to use it and then fuck up.

It felt good to know that the other patrols would be on their way, and all we had to do now was gather as much information as possible. It was going to be difficult to decide who was going to go down on the OP the next day; it couldn't be me because the priority was to stay put and sponsor the troop RV and prepare for the attack.

I decided one of them had to be One-of-three-Josés, because he'd been down there anyway and knew the area; the other would be Rodriguez. I didn't want to send El Nino, purely because the strain would have been too much. I didn't particularly want to send anyone down there, but we needed more information – the other patrols would expect it. In any event, these guys would have to do it themselves sooner or later, so they might as well crack on and do it now.

I got everybody together just before last light and said, 'Well done, everybody – excellent. Tomorrow we're going to send this information. Everybody's going to come to us, we're going to show them where it is, and we're going to

443

hit it. It's been a really good day – well done! Tomorrow, we need people to go down there. I want responsible people, and it was really difficult to decide who, but I want you, One-of-three-Josés, and you, Rodriguez, to get down there and get as much information as possible. It's your job, it's your responsibility. Think of how good it will be to get down there and do it.'

Their faces were a picture.

'I want to know how many people there are, and what weapons,' I said to them. 'I want to know if any boats come in, if they use the trike, if a helicopter comes, what time everybody goes to dinner – I want to know everything you can see. But most of all, how many narco-guerrillas and how many weapons. If you think you can't do it, don't push yourselves. Try to listen to what they're saying, but only do enough to get the information – is that all right? Everybody is depending on you two to get that information.'

We had rain in the early evening and everyone lay there absorbed in his own thoughts. In the morning, Rodriguez and One-of-three-Josés set off towards the camp. I stayed behind to sit on the radio because I was waiting for a reply about what was going on. Two hours later, Gaz came back on the net and said, 'Let's go for it. I'm going to tell the other patrols to start moving in towards you, and you sponsor the RV.'

On Day One, he said, which was the following day, the first patrol would be coming in between ten o'clock and midday, on a bearing of due south. If they didn't make that, the next window would be the next day, at the same time. He then gave timings for the other two patrols to arrive in the afternoon. If they missed their windows, they too would wait until the next day at the same times.

With Gonz and the Nino I began preparing for the other patrols to arrive. We dug up an area the size of a dining-room table to make a sand-box model. I made model buildings in the soil, together with a river and helipad.

When that was done we sat around drinking water and eating biscuits.

I spoke with El Nino. He was very quiet and insecure. He wasn't happy about what was going on. He didn't want to be there; it had probably all sounded good fun in the beginning, but now the realities of it were living in the field, wet and stinking, and going in against a violent enemy. The only thing he was pleased about was being part of the final RV.

'Where do you come from?' I asked.

As we chatted on, he started to come out with some fascinating stuff about malaria. 'The strain is very weak in Latin America, compared with South-East Asia, so it's easier for scientists to work on. That's what I really want to be. I want to go to university and study medicine. But I can't afford to – so here I am.'

I put my bergen next to a tree and sat against it. It was wonderful to relax and listen to the birds in the canopy. The only drawback was that I could smell myself, and I stank like an old mether.

About two hours before last light Rodriguez and One-of-three-Josés came back. I was on stag, still sitting against the tree but watching the area of the plant.

'What did you see?' I asked.

They spoke quickly, saying a lot that I didn't understand. I went back to basics. 'Narco-guerrilla?'

'Ocho.'

'Fusilos?'

'Ocho.'

I asked what the narco-guerrillas had been doing. Rodriguez grinned, tilted his hand and said, 'Cerveza.'

So there were eight men with weapons and three white-eyes. On the model, they showed me that the people were just wandering around doing nothing in particular. Maybe they were waiting for a delivery or a pick-up, but there didn't seem to be much going on. It would be quite worrying if they were waiting for a pick-up – did

that mean that boatloads of people would be turning up?

My concerns were suddenly put in the shade. The sound of gunshots echoed through the canopy, coming from the area of the camp. Birds screamed and lifted from the trees; the whole forest was alive. Single shots followed, then a quick burst, and another burst. Then silence, and another couple of single shots.

The boys looked at each other in alarm, then to me for reassurance. We all had our beltkit on and weapons; we got down by our bergens and stood-to, trying to listen.

I couldn't work out what it was all about. There were no other patrols in the area; they weren't arriving until the next day, so they wouldn't have stumbled on it. So what the hell were they firing at?

Five minutes later there were another two single shots, followed by another two. This went on for about twenty minutes. I thought, do we go down there tomorrow and find out? Were they arguing amongst themselves? Was it another gang coming in to steal their supplies? It was quite worrying.

The only thing I could put it down to was that they were pissed and doing target practice, or firing into the river. Whatever, it confirmed that the weapons worked, which was a bit of a shame.

That night, we got the ponchos and hammocks up. I didn't get much sleep. I was running through in my mind exactly what I had seen, and hoping that the model was right. Everybody was hopefully going to start coming in tomorrow. The first patrol, Terry's, wasn't that far away. I knew he'd be cracking on, no longer concerned about being tactical, just making distance. They'd be holding up for the night, then motoring on again at first light. I felt sorry for his patrol; I knew what it was like. I imagined the big sweaty messes sorting themselves out after a hard tab through the jungle.

We were up at first light. I spent some time at the model, trying to come up with some sort of plan so I could start

talking as soon as the other patrols arrived. At half past nine we covered all the arcs and waited for Terry's patrol. They arrived just over an hour later. Looking down at the slightly lower ground, I could see Terry looking up with a big bone grin on his dark, sweaty face. It was obvious they'd been screaming along.

Terry was twenty-nine, tall, blond, had sticky out ears, and was madly in love with his wife and two kids. He had the sort of West Country accent that only bad actors put on. He'd come from the RAF Regiment, having decided that he either wanted to be in the Regiment or become an accountant. Many a time he was told that he might have been better off as an accountant.

'How's it going, mate?' I said.

'Fucking good one.'

'You're looking a bit fatigued. A long distance for those old legs, was it?'

'Fucking distance – tell me about it,' he said, bent double, leaning on his weapon.

The rest of the patrol tabbed in, breathing heavily, their faces and hair soaking wet. As soon as they stopped I saw steam rising from their heads.

I turned to Terry. 'What I want you to do, mate, is get the patrol down where you see that big crooked tree. There's no big rush, so get some scoff and we'll get together later on.'

'I'll get the boys sorted out then I'll come up and see you.'

His patrol were grinning at my lads and giving them the thumbs up. My group looked happy to have support, the other patrol were happy to have finished the tab.

I started preparing the sitrep I was going to send out that night – hopefully it would say that everybody was in. If not, we still had the window open the next day. It was important to stagger the arrivals, to prevent a blue-on-blue.

The next two patrols arrived on time, between twelve-thirty and two-thirty and three and five; they

all looked knackered after the fast hike without stops.

I said, 'I'm going to send the sitrep off now, then I'll show you what we've got and see what you reckon.'

An hour or so later we sat on our bergens around the sand model and did an appreciation. I explained the layout of the camp and said, 'It's obvious that the majority of the stuff comes up and down by river. They've got the two Geminis down at the bottom there, and there's the helipad. We're looking at eight narcos with 5.56 and 7.62. There's three Europeans – German or Dutch, who knows. Do you reckon we've got enough people here? There's twenty of us, against eight. They're extremely casual; they're walking around leaving their weapons all over the place, and it looks like they've even been on the piss.'

Terry muttered, 'Lucky fuckers.' He went on, 'I reckon twenty is enough, no problems.'

Rod had mixed us up some cold Camp coffee. As the mug was handed round he said, 'Let's bin it now. We'll stand-to, then crack on with it in the morning. Anyone want a sip?'

Rod was the cleanest, tidiest and most organized man I'd ever met, with the possible exception of Eno. He was thirty-six going on sixteen and seemed to care about nothing. His hair was always very short and fashionable, and he was forever moaning about his chapped lips, carrying a jar of Vaseline with him everywhere. To Rod, the operation seemed secondary to making sure his lips were OK and that there would be some time off to buy some new fashion clothes.

As I lay in my hammock I mulled everything over again in my mind. It seemed really straightforward and I wasn't particularly worried about it. We had four Regiment blokes and sixteen well-trained policemen, and we had the element of surprise. I was looking forward to getting it all over and done with and having a few days off before we came back to find some more.

My thoughts drifted to Kate and domestic things. Our

house still had bits and pieces to be done to it. The garage roof was starting to leak, and we'd been talking about painting the hallway when I got back. I thought about wintertime in Britain. I loved walking through the town at the dead of night, when all the shop lights were on and it was drizzling. I thought about taking Kate down to the shops. We used to go to a penny sweet place and pick and mix all her favourites, which seemed to be everything in the shop.

At first light we packed up and sent a sitrep to Gaz, telling him all the patrols were in. By now my patrol were used to this place; it seemed we had been there for weeks, not just days. It was the same feeling as going into a strange house, which becomes more and more familiar as the evening wears on.

It was quite a boring time for most people, but they didn't mind as it was better than tabbing like a man possessed to get to an RV. They had been given a warning order about an impending attack and were now sorting their kit out and cleaning their weapons. Strictly speaking, they should have been field-stripping the weapon, taking the working parts out and cleaning them. But as long as a weapon was well maintained there was no need to do that. All that was needed was a quick squirt with something like WD4O around the working parts so they knew the thing was going to go backwards and forwards. The blokes were checking their magazines, making sure they weren't damaged, since most stoppages came from the magazine. Apart from that everybody was just generally resting, waiting for any tasks before the orders, such as patrols being sent back to confirm information.

The police carried pounds and pounds of sugar with them and seemed to eat it with everything. The one good thing they carried in their rations was a small can of condensed milk. Years before, we used to have condensed milk in a tube in our rations, but that was taken out – which

was a shame, because it was lovely. We mixed up the milk with Camp coffee and lots of sugar and settled down around the model to get to grips with what we were going to do.

Rod finished putting Vaseline on his lips and said, 'We know what the mission is – to arrest the occupants of the DMP and destroy their equipment. We know we've got three Europeans, who are unarmed. Shame we haven't got any negatives of them. Chances are they're just there to work on the processing. They won't resist an attack.'

'What comms have they got?' Tony asked as he passed the mug around and opened a packet of boiled sweets.

I said, 'We saw some antennas and a satellite dish. We don't know if it's TV or comms. Chances are it's a TV dish – however, that can't be confirmed. But if we're going to bang them at first light, they're not going to have time to get on the net. Even if they do, nothing's going to happen – Gaz'll get the reaction force in very quickly.'

I looked at Terry and had to smile. He'd been rubbing his chin and had come across a zit. Now he was squeezing it and inspecting the yield.

I carried on: 'There's one building down the bottom that looks like the cook and bottle-washer's area. There's been someone seen going in and out. He hasn't been armed – just an old boy in his sixties. About five metres to the south of that is another building that looks like the administration block. It has its own generator. The one above it is certainly the living accommodation.'

'What makes you think that?' Terry asked, wiping pus on his shirt sleeve.

'That's where they all were coming out of, and I saw the boy coming out after his wash. The other hut is definitely where they do the business. It's low and long, it's only partially walled. There was a lot of movement in and out during the time we were watching. There's one other store-room, but I couldn't make out what was in it.'

I took a swig of Camp coffee and pointed at the model.

'As far as I could see the perimeter isn't protected, but I didn't see jack shit. The area was cut out of the forest, and that's it.'

'Whereabouts did you hit the perimeter, mate?' Rod was looking at the model and making more coffee.

'Here was definitely OK.' I sat, pointing. 'And here's definitely OK. We then moved around left and went up near the helipad, and that was fine.'

'What's the going like in the camp – is it well trodden or do we have to start scrambling over shit?' Tony said. 'I'm fucked after tabbing here yesterday.'

'Well trodden. It's been used for ages. There are no duck-boards, but it's old baked mud because it's exposed to the sunlight. It looked like it was cleared and burnt, like the farmers do. There's some stumps around from when it was cleared, but apart from that, it's OK.'

'What are the buildings made of?'

'They're solid wood, with atap and palm-leaf coverage, over corrugated iron. They're obviously trying to cam it up.'

'What's the walls like and the doors?'

I explained about the inner and outer doors.

'We need to make sure we can get into these fuckers,' Rod said. 'We'll go for an explosive entry anyway.'

'Yeah, why not?' Terry took a mouthful of cold coffee and passed the mug around. 'That'll fuck 'em up.'

Having looked at the camp, we looked at the enemy. 'What do you reckon their intentions are?' Terry said; he couldn't resist it – he had to keep playing with his zit, hoping for more to come out. The thing was bleeding.

'I don't know,' I said. 'Basically, there's nowhere for them to go. I think they'll take us on. They'll protect it. There's a lot of money involved, so they'll look after the produce. That's why they've got so many people armed. What do you reckon?'

Rod jumped in. 'I agree. All they're going to do is blat off loads of rounds and try to leg it, but they'll retaliate,

451

without a doubt. We might get one or two runners. I think we need to get right on top of these fuckers.

'We know they've got 5.56, and there's a G3 running around, so we know we've got that coming down on us. We don't want to take them on, because we don't want to start taking casualties. We want to hit them as early as possible, bang them while they're sleeping. Then let's get the fuck out of here for a few days because I think I have a zit coming up and we can't have that now.' As ever, he looked completely relaxed and there wasn't a hair out of place.

Now we looked at their relative strengths and capabilities, which were basically that they just killed every fucker. Their tactics, if they were members or ex-members of any narco-guerrilla organization, would be very John Wayne: just loads of rounds going down everywhere.

Then we looked at the ground – the terrain and vegetation – then 'vital ground': if we got a certain bit of ground, would that dominate the whole area? 'I had a look around,' I said. 'There's no vital ground. The helipad might have been OK because it was higher than the camp and in theory overlooked it, but in fact I couldn't see jack shit.'

'So there's nowhere we can put a decent cover group in high ground. The only way it could happen is by it coming into the camp.'

'Andy, tell us how we can get in.'

'When I went down there,' I pointed, 'there weren't any obstacles. It was quite easy to get to. There's just one small river to the east of it, but that's knee high and slow flowing, not a tactical problem. I've got an area for the FRV; I've also got an area for the start line. I reckon that the cover group needs to go in with you to be right on target – I don't think I can go anywhere to get the high ground.'

' Tony said, 'OK, no drama. So do you reckon we need more people in, or what?'

Rod cut in, 'I don't think we need it at all. If we hit these fuckers at first light and go for it, we'll get them while they're still in their little old beds.'

Terry nodded. 'If we get that explosive entry on, we can sort it out there and then, in two or three minutes,' he said.

'Sounds good to me,' I said. We could get it done, get the reinforcements in, then we could withdraw and get back for tea and cakes.

We then had to look at time and space: what was the earliest time we could get the attack in?

'I don't particularly want to rush this.' Rod had made up his mind what he wanted to happen. 'I don't want to go in tomorrow morning; I want to spend the day planning – we've got to get our guys sorted out. If we go straight in at first light, it means we've got to move before last light tonight. Let's go in the day after tomorrow.'

Everybody was in agreement.

'If we move from here to the FRV tomorrow, spend the night at the FRV, and then go and do the attack at first light, then we've cracked it. So we've got tonight and tomorrow to sort our shit out.'

More nods. 'I'll send the sitrep in a minute. If they want us to move earlier, they'll tell us. But by the time we get an answer, we won't be able to move for first light tomorrow morning.'

'We've got enough PE and all the kit we need,' Rod said. 'We don't need anything bringing in apart from Gaz and his gang.'

'Easy one,' Tony said. 'Just get them straight in on the helipad. We'll get that cleared as soon as we take the camp.'

The last item on the checklist was the assessment of tasks. 'We've got the two huts people are staying in,' I said. 'And we've got the river and those boats. I don't know what was down there with the boats, I couldn't see far enough. I don't know if people were staying there, or what. But the only escape route I can see is from the camp down to the river.'

'I think we do need a cut-off group,' Rod said. 'If there's any fuckers coming down that river and we're mincing

around, we've got no early warning and nothing to stop them. We could be in the shit.'

'I agree,' said Tony.

'So one patrol will become a cut-off group down the bottom there,' Rod pointed. 'Their job is stop any runners, take control of that northern end of the camp, and give us early warning along the river.'

We'd made a guess about how the enemy were going to react to an attack. They'd got the weapons, and it wouldn't be the first time they'd used them. The effect of that would be that we might have our own casualties, so we'd got to cater accordingly. We had the patrol medic packs, which for this sort of task mainly contained trauma management packs. We'd got a helipad, so all we had to do was make sure that squadron HQ had a heli stood by to casevac – where it was going, and why it was going there, the pilot wouldn't know yet. All he would know was that his aircraft was stood by.

The next stage was to summarize all the deductions that we'd come to, and to look at the different options open to us; it was a matter of weighing up the advantages and disadvantages and selecting the best course. That then became the plan, and from that plan Rod would make orders.

There were going to be four groups: a cut-off group by the river, two assault groups that were going to take the houses, and a cover group that was going to cover the advance up to the two buildings and dominate the area in case there were runners. On top of that, Gaz was organizing everything back at the FOB. He had helis stood by to bring in a force to burn down the camp, and the publicity machine to film it.

It was now past midday on Day Five since finding the camp. Rod had to put it in some form of orders that the patrols could understand. This was quite difficult, because our Spanish was only good enough to get by. We needed to involve them as much as we could, because in the near future they would be doing this themselves.

Everybody assembled around the sand model with their weapons and beltkit. Some of the boys were interested in it; others looked tired and indifferent. Terry spoke the best Spanish, so he did the talking.

'We have found the camp,' he said, 'and this is what it looks like. Tomorrow morning, we're all going to leave here, and go to the final RV. From there, my group will move to the other side of the camp and become the cut-off for the attack. Everyone else will stay at the final RV. The following morning, the three groups will move to the camp. Andy's group will be the cover group; Rod's group will attack this building, and Tony's group will attack this one. Each patrol commander will show you what he wants you to do. In the camp, there are about eight armed men. We will go in there early in the morning, when they are asleep. There will be no problems. All you have to do is listen to what your patrol commander is telling you.

'In a minute, when we've finished, the patrols will get together in their areas and the patrol commander will tell you what he wants done. Are there any questions?'

They all shook their heads and split into their groups. The four of us got back together to confirm what would be going on.

Terry's cut-off team would move to the north of the camp. They would be in position as a cut-off if anyone legged it from the camp to the boats, their only known escape route. It would be no good them going to the helipad; there was nothing there, and it was surrounded by jungle. 'I won't bother trying to rig the boats,' Terry said, 'because of the compromise factor during daylight hours.' If anybody found the boats had been tampered with, they'd be suspicious and on the alert. The cut-off team's other job was to give an early warning of anything coming down the river. We could be sitting there in the daytime in our FRV, ready to do a first-light attack, and six boatloads of narco-guerrillas could slip quietly into the camp for a big piss-up. There'd be twenty of us screaming in there big time,

suddenly confronted by a defending force of eighty. Not to be recommended.

It was now starting to rain and it was a funny sight watching all the normal activity going on with water dripping off people's noses.

The cut-off team would take their bergens and beltkit with them, because they would be working independently. They would split off from us as soon as possible once we'd reached the FRV, because they needed as much daylight as possible to get there, sort their shit out, and do their recce so they'd know what they had to do and where they had to do it. As they moved into position, the rest of us would be in the FRV, acting as the immediate action: if they were compromised, we'd soon know because we'd hear the shooting and commotion. We'd then just have to go for it, straight into the camp and do it there and then.

'As soon as you're in position give us a shout on the Motorola channel six,' I said. 'If we don't hear anything we'll just carry on as planned, because we might not get the comms.'

All the patrol commanders had Motorola comms that we had brought with us from the UK. They gave us about a kilometre and a half in good open countryside; sometimes we'd get comms in the jungle with them, sometimes we wouldn't. If we didn't get a report from Terry, and hadn't heard any gunfire, we would have to assume that he was OK anyway and carry on.

One-of-three-Josés would take Tony and Rod down to the camp and show them the start line and the two buildings. Once they came back, we'd wait until first light the next day, when we'd start moving off. 'Once the camp attack goes in,' Rod carried on to say, with the rain still falling and being ignored by everyone, 'the cut-off will stay put until it gets the all clear from me. If I can't raise you on the comms, I'll send a runner down. Make sure your patrol knows! Once the buildings are secure, I want Andy's team to clear the work hut and then go up to the helipad. If you

move in once it's secure, we'll centralize all the boys, get them down, and I'll call Gaz in with the aircraft, so I want you, Andy, to take the comms with you. Once Gaz comes in we'll get back to the bergens and sort ourselves out.'

'That's that, then,' said Tony. 'We'd better get the sitrep off to Gaz and make sure he knows when we're going in. Then sort the boys out and get our heads down.'

The sitrep stated what we were going to do, what time the camp attack was going in, the way we were going to do it, and how we wanted the helicopters brought in – which was on orange smoke. We said that we'd open up the net the following morning to get a confirmation that everything was OK before we went in. We wouldn't move until 0900 hours to the final RV, and from there we'd go ahead with our plan.

We went to our own individual patrols and started explaining what we wanted them to do. 'When we get to the FRV tomorrow morning,' I said, pointing to One-of-three-Josés, 'you will take Tony and Rod to the camp and show them the edge and where the two buildings are. It's a very important job. If they want to see anything else, show them where it is, then come back to us. Is that all right?'

He grinned and nodded, proud to shoulder the responsibility.

'When he comes back,' I said, 'we're going to wait there all night, back to back, and wait for first light. We'll then move forward – it's our job to make sure everybody else is protected while they're going into the position. What I want you to do is follow me; I'll put you in the position and show you where the rest are coming in, and where to be looking. If you see anything, I don't want you to shoot, I just want you to tell me, and I'll decide if you shoot or not. If you hear me shooting, you shoot. Is that OK?'

They nodded; they were happy with that because there wasn't much to think about. I really wanted to labour this point, because I didn't want them flapping and landing up shooting one of our blokes as they were coming in. 'When

we get into position, you will see our people coming from your right-hand side, going towards those buildings. Anything else could be the enemy. But I don't want you to shoot unless I shoot or tell you to.

'Once the attack has happened, we'll then have to do two other things. We'll have to move to the long building here, check the storeroom, and go to the helipad. But I'll tell you where to go and when. Keep nice and calm, and if you see something, shout: "Get down! Get down!" If they shoot at you, you shoot back. You must be very careful. You'll hear lots of explosions and maybe other gunfire. Don't worry about that. You just keep looking at your job.'

I looked at each of them in turn. 'Rodriguez, any problems?'

'No.'

'Nino?'

'No.'

'Gonz?'

'No.'

'One-of-three-Josés?'

'No.'

'Good. Tomorrow, Gaz comes in with helicopters and more men. We put our bergens on and fly out. Then – party time!'

Rodriguez whispered, 'Yee-hah!' and everybody gave a low laugh.

I liked these guys. I enjoyed talking to them; they had a really good sense of humour. We were very much on the same wavelength; all they wanted to do was get the job done and then get back and have some fun. They were very much into dancing and whisky; me, I couldn't dance but I did like Famous Grouse.

The blokes in charge of the assault groups had a harder job getting across what they wanted their boys to do. Looking over from our position, I saw Rod's group standing in a line, as if there was a door; he had them walking in and practising their moves, all in slow time and very quiet.

It was still raining and their drenched uniforms were clinging to them. Some had packed their issue sombreros with them and now I saw why; they were perfect for keeping the rain off their faces.

It was getting to last light. We stood to and then put the hammocks up. I lay in my hammock, eating cold bangers and beans. For pudding, I'd swapped some of my food for a can of condensed milk, which I poured over some hard tack biscuits. It made me think of *Tiswas*, where Lenny Henry played a reggae bloke called Winston; he used to eat condensed milk sandwiches. I thought about other kids' shows, and then I thought about Kate, and how much having a child had changed my life. In my early days I'd have been relishing the task and looking forward to a lifetime in the Regiment – I used to take the piss out of people on jobs who talked about their kids or said, 'My boy's got his piano exam tomorrow – I hope he's OK.' Now I could see their point. Such apparently trivial things were in fact very important. Kate was walking, talking and being stupid, and I was missing quite a bit of it. I decided that when I got back the three of us would go off on a holiday. And this time I meant it.

It had stopped raining by first light. I told my group to make sure their weapons were oiled up and had a round in the chamber. I checked for rattles amidst lots of thumbs up and winking.

The Regiment blokes met up and we got the radio out. As soon as Gaz had confirmed, we could go in.

It came up: 'Yes, go ahead. The helicopter reaction time will be about one hour. It will come in on your orange smoke. If there's no sitrep sent by ten hundred hours on the morning of the attack, we will come in anyway to take it.'

We were going to move off half an hour later for the final RV. The order of march was my patrol, then the cut-off group, and finally the two assault groups. There was an air

of excitement and acceptance that finally the show was on the road.

I told Rodriguez that he was going to be lead scout for the whole troop, and that sparked him up into being very official and important.

Everybody was leaning on his weapon, bergen on, ready to go. Rodriguez was at the front, checking his compass. He already knew the way, but it looked good.

We set off and Rodriguez became the world's best scout. We were stopping every 15 metres for him to check for movement or sound.

When we got to the area of the FRV we stopped and everybody knelt down. When Terry came up I pointed, 'It's in that direction; that'll take you round the right-hand side.'

We checked the maps and he said, 'I'll get down to the line of the river and go left, and see where I can get in. Once I see the Geminis I'll sort myself out from there.'

'Right,' Rod cut in. I could see the shine on his lips; it was a wonder they didn't stick together with all that grease on. 'We'll open up our Motorolas at five o'clock tonight. We'll keep it open until last light. If we haven't heard anything from you, we'll just take it that you're there and we're not getting the comms. If there's been a change of plan, to-morrow morning when the attack goes in just sit tight and there'll be a runner down to get you. The helis will be in at ten o'clock anyway if we fuck up. If I don't see you then – *mañana*, we'll see you at some other time. I take it you'll chuck a right and go down to the road.'

My lot and the two assault groups sat in a large circle, resting against our bergens in the FRV.

Tony turned to me and said, 'I suppose we'll be off now – we'd better go and have a look at this place, hadn't we?'

I went over to One-of-three-Josés and said with a thumbs up, 'You ready?'

'I'm ready.'

I had a quick check of his kit and that his safety catch was on, and he mooched into the canopy with Tony and Rod. I

could see him stopping every six paces, probably to show off to his mates that he was big time now, he was leading a recce patrol. Tony went up to him and pointed in the direction of the camp with a motion of 'let's get on with it', and they disappeared from sight.

The aim was to confirm what had been seen. If there was any change, we'd have to reassess and hopefully tell the cut-off that night. If not, too bad, the attack would still go in.

Tony and Rod needed to be on this recce because they needed to know where exactly the two buildings were located. They'd seen models of them, they had an idea of where they were; however, it was a lot easier to see them on the ground, for somebody to point them out and say, 'That's your one, and that's yours.'

The rest of us just sat there for the next five hours, eating biscuits, drinking water, swatting flies and rubbing on mozzie rep. There was no talking, no smoking, no brewing up. The odd one or two were nodding off. It was a really boring time, as it so often was. My mind drifted to Hereford; for the first time ever in my life I felt pangs of homesickness. I missed family life; I missed our times together. There were a couple of trees that needed to be chopped down because the roots were going to affect the foundations of our house at some stage, so I was going to have a look at that. I thought about the holiday; then I had a chuckle to myself, thinking about Rod and Tony on their stomachs, puffing and panting, kitten-crawling through the mud and gunge.

It looked as if we were in for a downpour, which wasn't the most exciting prospect, seeing as how it was the equivalent of a night out on beltkit. I told the boys to get their ponchos out, really nice and slowly, and prepare for the rain. It came, not too hard, but insistent.

The recce patrol came back in at about four-thirty, looking like drowned rats.

'What do you reckon then?' I said.

Rod was drinking some water from a bottle, then pouring it over his head to sweep his hair back. He said, 'There's no problems with that. We'll just bung an explosive entry on there. But you will get in position first, because we go over that open ground – if we're seen, we're in the shit.'

'We saw the cook and bottle-washer running around in that first hut,' Tony said. 'Then we saw a boy coming out with a Car 15 [*a small version of the M16*]. And that's all we saw. The generators were going, and there was activity, but not much. Good here, ain't it?'

Rod grinned with a face full of mud and said, 'We should be down there on the piss with those boys, not sitting here waiting to jump on them. We're on the wrong bloody side here – look at the state of my kit.'

We had a little giggle at the thought of Terry; his boys wouldn't even have their ponchos out, they'd be sitting on their bergens, ready to go, probably shivering their cocks off.

We got our Motorolas out and put our earpieces in. At five o'clock we switched on to see if Terry was going to come on the net. We got jack shit.

There were no big problems with that. Maybe it was the distance or the weather – or maybe they were all hanging upside down from a tree having their bollocks tickled. There was nothing we could do about it now. If he was there in the morning he was there. Nevertheless, we kept the net open.

Just before last light, Tony tried again. 'Terry, Tony, check?'

Nothing. Everybody hunched up in their ponchos as the rain fell harder.

Back at the squadron HQ there would have been maximum activity going on. Gaz would have been getting everybody geared up, and everybody would now be stood to. Gaz had said it would take them about sixty minutes' flying time to get to us. He wouldn't have enjoyed having to involve other agencies but there was no option; we

needed the aircraft – especially if the shit hit the fan and we needed some casevac aircraft in.

We settled in for the night. We had our beltkit on, we had our weapons, and everybody was just resting against their bergens, getting their heads down as best they could, waiting. First light would be as soon as we could see well enough to walk without knocking into each other or the vegetation.

I listened to the buzzing of insects and swatted the occasional thing that crawled on my skin. Nobody was really asleep; I could sense their anticipation about the next day. There was the occasional light snore until a pal gave a quick little shake or pinch of the nose – being careful that they didn't wake up with a startled cry.

The temperature dropped a bit and it was pretty wet and uncomfortable. I looked at my watch; it was one o'clock. Half an hour, I looked again and it was ten past. I nodded off, woke up, nodded off.

About an hour before first light I nudged Rodriguez and motioned for him to pass it on. He leaned across to the next and gave him a little shake, and so on round.

I hated peeling off my poncho and getting that first whiff of the coldness but at least it had stopped raining. We started sorting ourselves out in our area, plastering the cam cream on top of our own dirt and grime. After so many days in the jungle, we were in shit state. I couldn't see the DPM on my trousers because they were caked up with mud. My hair was greasy and flat on my head; I had days of growth on my face and it was thick with cam cream. No doubt I'd be de-zitting with Tony in a few days' time.

As soon as we could see 3 metres in front of us we began to move out. The order of march was first the lead scout, One-of-three-Josés; I followed, and behind me were Rodriguez, El Nino and Gonz. Behind them came Rod and Tony's assault groups.

There was no need to communicate with the cut-off group. If there had been a drama during the night we

would have known about it. And regardless of them, this was going to go ahead.

We all knew what to do; there was no need to talk, and there was no banter – it was pretty serious stuff now. One-of-three-Josés led us to the start line. There, Rod and Tony would get hold of their assault groups and move them forward to the edge of the forest. They wouldn't move towards the huts until my cover group were in position.

I looked at them, pointed, and they nodded. They knew where they were, they knew what they were doing. Then I led my group away.

From now on I was in front because I knew where I wanted to go. I was covert in my movements, but at the same time forceful. I wasn't too worried about disturbing the brush; the attack was going to happen now come what may. The priority was to get to the cover position. My weapon was in my right hand, I was moving the vegetation with my left, looking around all the time. I wasn't even checking that the others were behind me.

I knew that all the commanders had their Motorolas on, waiting for me to get in position. I knew that as soon as I was sorted out I would push four clicks on my radio. Rod, Assault Group 1, would come back with one click. Tony, Assault Group 2, would come back with two.

Then I would know everybody was ready, and would give another four clicks in two sets of two.

Click, click – click, click: 'Standby! Standby!'

The groups would then start to move forward from the rolling start line; ideally they would be covert right up to the doors. However, if they were compromised on the way, it would just be shit or bust and they'd have to go for it, and it would be time for the cover group to earn their wages.

In my mind's eye I pictured Rod and Tony, each with his patrol behind. They weren't wearing beltkit; all they had was their rifle, pistol and ammunition. On their rifles some had mounted a Maglite torch with masking tape around

the stock and, between the Maglite and the stock, a little wedge of wood to keep it at the right angle. The Maglite would provide a crude form of zeroing as they went through the door. It was first light; it was going to be dark inside the buildings. And with the explosive charge going off there would be clouds of dust and debris; the Maglites might be needed to penetrate them.

The second man in each group would be carrying an explosive charge. I imagined the commander pointing where he wanted the charges to be put. Everybody else would be covering the windows and the general area, pressed right up flat against the door itself. All it would take was a small dab of PE with det cord running through it onto a clacker – the same as used on the claymore. At the end of the wire of the clacker there was a detonator, which was clipped onto the det cord. Once the explosive was in position, the figures would move back a couple of feet and turn their backs. The commander held the clacker. Whoever was doing the firing would have to hold the wire, keep the connector into the clacker, and squeeze it – or put the wire in and give it a good dose of masking tape. Whatever, but they had to make sure they got that good connection, because it had to go first time.

I imagined the two loud thuds, doors caving in and the boys disappearing inside.

We got to our area, on the side nearest the processing hut. As I looked forward I could see no change, except that the ground was wet with a thin film of mud. The trike was missing, but the cardboard box that had contained the tins of condensed milk was still there. The cans had gone.

It was more or less full light now. Within the hole in the canopy I could see it was a beautifully clear day, a deep blue sky without a cloud. It was going to be really hot. Soon the mud would start steaming.

It was quiet; none of the generators were running. As I panned from right to left I could see the cook's hut, and beyond it the roof of the other one. I knew the assault

groups would be lining up on the edge of the canopy, ready to come forward to place the charges. I knew everything was all right; I knew we could cover.

I said quietly, 'Here we are going to cover. El Nino, keep your eyes on that building going left towards that track. Understand?'

Everybody nodded. El Nino knelt down, his weapon in the aim.

To the others I said, 'I want you, Rodriguez, to watch from that building to there. If there's shooting, shoot back. One-of-three-Josés and Gonz, I want you to look for anybody running up towards the heli—'

BANG!

What the fuck was that? When you hear a gunshot totally out of the blue the whole body jerks. As I turned around I saw Nino looking like a puppy that knows it shouldn't have pissed on the kitchen floor. He started gobbing off: 'It fired! It fired!' As he took the safety catch off he must have had his finger on the trigger and had an ND (*negligent discharge*).

My mind screamed: 'Fuck!' as I went straight on the net and shouted: 'Go! Go! Go! Go! Go!'

To El Nino, I motioned with my thumb to put his safety catch on.

It had been initiated now. It was pointless staying there. I waved them on and we moved towards our target. 'Go! Go! Come on!' I knew we were heading for a total and utter gang fuck.

It wasn't slippery underfoot but I found it difficult to get my footing in the slime. I was expecting to hear the explosions or gunfire. Just as we approached the hut there was some automatic fire and single shots coming from the area of the huts. I wasn't bothered, I kept going forward. My eyes were focused on the building and who might be coming out of it.

I got there first, followed by Rodriguez. 'In, in, in!' I said. He hesitated, not understanding what I wanted.

466

I pointed at him, then at me, and I went in.

There were long tables with trays stretching to the far end. Butts in the shoulders, we moved down either side.

I was shouting at Rodriguez. He was shouting in Spanish: 'Stand still! Police! Police!'

To the far right I heard Rod shout: 'Move up! Move up!'

The firing had stopped now; there was just yelling and shouting, and the sound of metal falling and furniture being overturned.

There was something coming on the radio but I couldn't understand what it was.

In the semi-light inside I saw large, oil-drum-type barrels, empty packets of cigarettes, beer cans lying on their side.

I was hoping the other three were outside and covering our arses. All I wanted to do was get to the other end of the hut and get out.

I heard more shouting, then gunfire. Fuck! As I looked around in a semi-stoop, I saw a figure running down the path towards the Geminis. Then there was more gunfire. I knew it was Nino, Gonz and One-of-three-Josés firing but the boy kept running. I knew the cut-offs would take him down.

I shouted at Gonz and the others to go to the storeroom. They ran up to it, but there was no way they were going straight in. They shouted and kicked against the wood. They worked their way to the door, gingerly opened it and took a tentative peep.

'Get in there!' I shouted. 'In, in, in!'

They crept inside and reappeared two seconds later. It was full of barrels; there were no people.

To the right there was shouting but I ignored it. 'Helipad! Helipad!' I shouted, chest heaving as I tried to catch my breath. I had a pain in my throat from all the shouting and running around. I told Nino and Gonz to stay where they were; Rodriguez and One-of-three-Josés were to come with me.

We ran across and started going up the track. There wasn't time to get them to cover each other; we just ran as fast as we could towards the helipad.

I was flapping and breathing hard, my face drenched with sweat. This time I was checking behind me as I ran, to make sure the other two were with me. As we hit the rise, we could see the opening of the helipad itself. I could now feel the heat on my back.

I was going to run around the edge of it to make sure everything was clear. There was no time to tell them; I just hoped that they would be there.

We started to move around the line of the pad, just waiting for someone to run or fire – I couldn't care less either way, I just wanted to get this over with and recover something from the shambles. The area was clear.

The sun was burning the mud; the floor was covered with mist, like ankle-deep theatrical smoke on a stage. Standing on the edge of the helipad, I heard screaming from somewhere down near the living accommodation. I got on the net and said, 'Rod, check? Rod, check?'

Nothing. Then, 'Send! Send!'

'We're up on the helipad – that's clear. I'm now coming down.'

'Roger that. We've got a man down. Get down here, we need help. Out.'

That explained the screaming. Having a man down made me seethe even more about Nino having an ND. He'd fucked everything up; blokes were getting hit, and the chances were people were getting away.

We got down to find total chaos. Rod was controlling and looking after the casualty. The boy was on his back, screaming his head off. A 7.62 round had hit him in the wrist and travelled up his forearm, exiting just below the elbow. He'd lost all the muscle mass on the lower arm. He was screaming like a pig. He was going to live, but he must have been in agony. All the other boys were clustered around, looking very sick.

It was a matter of controlling the people who were in the huts, and also controlling our own people who looked as if they wanted to bolt back into the jungle and run and run.

'Get back!' I shouted. 'Cover that hut!' My ranting and pointing meant more to them than what I was saying.

Rod had the medic pack with him. He looked up at me and said, 'It's just a matter of plugging up the holes to stop the blood. If he stopped screaming he'd see he's OK.' Then he looked at the boy on the ground and screamed: 'Shut up!'

He unwrapped more field dressings and pressed them hard onto the wound. He grabbed a pack of Haemaccel and tried to get an IV line into him. The boy had lost a lot of blood and needed more fluids fast. He was going into shock. Still some people just stood around; perhaps they were in shock, too.

Tony was in the huts, controlling the people inside with lots of shouting and kicking. I heard a shout of, 'Shut the fuck up now!' His group had plasticuffed them, picked them up, grabbed them by the hair or their clothes and got them on the ground, hollering and shouting to keep them scared and under control. Now they were man-handling them out of the door and making them lie down on their stomachs in the mud. While some of the police covered the prisoners with their weapons, others searched them. Some of the boys started to kick and rifle-butt them. There was no time to stop it – and why should we? We were not interested in names, who they were, what they were – that was someone else's job. All we wanted to do was control them and make sure they hadn't got any concealed weapons or run.

'We are now going to search you,' one of the police said, slapping the back of a narco's head. 'If you resist, you will be shot. Do you understand?'

I called over to Tony, 'I'll just get the people out of the other hut.'

As I went in, I saw wooden beds with tables, a couple of

old chests-of-drawers, ashtrays full up, cans of beer. The room stank of sweat and farts. A group of people lay on their beds, faces down, hands on the back of their heads. There must have been two weapons pointing at every prisoner.

I went back outside, got hold of Nino and said, 'Help me put the antennas out for the radio.'

I started to get the sitrep ready. Originally it was going to be a proper sitrep, saying: Done, we need the helis in now, how many people we'd caught, how many casualties. But instead I just banged it out: 'We've got a man down. I want the aircraft in on the orange smoke.'

Rod was still with the casualty. He called out, 'Everything all right? We got the aircraft coming in?'

'Yep, just waiting for the auto-acknowledgement.'

I got it. The helis were on their way in. I left the radio where it was; we might be needing it in a minute.

On the Motorola, I heard Tony talking to Terry: 'Terry, check?'

'Yep.'

'Come on in now, mate. Move down the path.'

'Roger that. We've got a dead runner. Do you want him brought in?'

'Yeah, bring him in.'

Tony was shouting to make sure everybody knew the patrol was going to be coming up the path. Everybody was so hyper at the moment, chances were they'd just turn around and shoot them.

A couple of minutes later I heard them shouting that they were coming in; then I saw them. Two of the policemen were dragging the dead man; Terry had his weapon, a G3.

Terry's patrol were really happy with themselves. They had the air of hunters home with the kill. They left the body to one side, giving him a quick macho kick and a prod. Then they found out that somebody on their side had been dropped and their expressions changed to one of concern.

By now he'd been stabilized. He'd gone into shock but Rod had got some Haemaccel into him. He wasn't going to lose any more blood, but he was down – he was severely down.

By now everybody had been sorted out, trussed up with plasticuffs between the two buildings. I went over and had a look. There were three narcos, the bottle-washer, and one white-eye.

'Fucking hell,' I said to Tony. 'We saw eight. We've got some runners here.'

Tony kicked one of the narcos and shouted: 'Gringos? Where are the gringos?'

He shouted to the European, holding his head up by the hair: 'Where are they? Where are they?'

The white-eye said nothing.

'Look, if they're running, they're going to get shot. Tell us where they are. We might be able to save them.'

Nothing. It was the boy I'd seen on my first CTR, still in the shitty T-shirt. He was severely scared.

Tony started on the old man: 'Where's the gringos?'

He started gobbing off, indicating with his head that they'd gone towards the river.

'Fuck!' I said. I couldn't believe they'd got past the cut-off group. Straightaway I blamed it on Nino. The stupid wanker.

The wounded boy had been sorted out and another couple of lads were looking after him now. Rod came over, looked at me hard and said, 'What the fuck happened?' with a look that blamed me.

'That cunt had an ND.'

Nino sat on the steps of the hut, severely pissed off.

'Get him out of the way,' Rod said. 'Tell him to sit by the radio.'

He stormed off and checked the casualty.

Terry came over. 'Right. I'll get my lads down to the river and tell them to keep their eyes open. They will knife up the boats, so if we have got runners they aren't going to

take them. We're not going to get jack shit out of this lot. The white-eye's a pain in the arse. He knows the score – he knows he's going to get away with it. This is fucking annoying.'

Rod agreed. 'Yeah, do that and we will get a brew on.'

I went over and cut the plasticuffs off the cook. He went up on his knees doing all the signs of the cross and putting his hands up to heaven. I didn't know if he thought he was going to get shot, or what. I picked him up and dragged him into the kitchen. '*Café*,' I said. '*Café con leche*.' He looked at me in total surprise.

Rodriguez stood over him while he sparked up the generator and got the brews on.

Tony was running around placing people in case we had any fire coming back at us. 'You go there, look that way! You stay here, look this way!'

We passed the brews around. The sun was beating down and it was boiling hot. Everybody was trying to get into the shade. My eyes were stinging; my mouth tasted foul, my teeth had sheepskin coats. My shoulders, arms and legs were drying off but the crotch area and bits under the webbing stayed wet. It was starting to itch where the wetness had dried.

I was feeling a bit pissed off with myself, purely because it was a member of my patrol that had had the ND. It wasn't anything to do with me but I felt responsible all the same.

The other patrols didn't know yet what had caused the problem, but I kept Nino away from the others for his own safety.

Tony and I stood near the casualty, who by now was pumped up on morphine.

'He's looking better,' I said.

'Won't be wanking for a few days though,' Tony said and I had to turn away so the boy didn't see me laugh.

Rod was trying to get information from the white-eye but

he said nothing. They searched him but he had nothing on him; he was sterile.

We went back into the hut and had a look around. Porn mags lay on the floor by the sides of some beds; old copies of *USA Today* and *Herald Tribune* were piled up on a chest-of-drawers; one or two short wave radios were on tables or by beds. We still couldn't work out what the satellite dish was for, because there wasn't a TV set or any sort of satellite comms, just a short wave set. We weren't worried about finding out what radio frequencies they were on or whatever – that would all be discovered later on.

Some of the police had helped themselves to cans of food from the cookhouse and were passing them around. They were munching and smoking themselves stupid with the packs of 200 Marlboro they found in the huts. Now and again there was a volley of excited, relieved laughing.

If any of the narcos had been wounded, we would have treated them. It would have been pointless letting the characters die: quite apart from humanitarian considerations, the police were scared enough as it was about reprisals. Police students were being killed by the cartels as soon as they started their training. Four out of a group of thirty had been shot with their families in the time we'd been there. It was good for the police that the narcos were seen to be getting medical treatment; it meant that the police were looking after their prisoners humanely, and obviously this would be reported.

We started to hear the helis coming in. I ran up to the helipad and threw out an orange identification smoke; besides giving them a precise location, it told them the wind direction.

We had line of sight so I got on my Motorola to talk them in for the final approach, in case they hadn't seen the smoke. 'Gaz, Andy, check? Gaz, Andy, check?'

There was no reply. I tried twice more, but by then the helis had seen us because they started to turn towards the smoke.

Rod and a couple of his patrol were lifting the casualty and walking towards the helipad. The first Huey landed and Gaz jumped off with the first replacement patrol, his clothes smelling all rather nicely of washing powder.

Gaz came up to me, really serious. Behind him were the two colonels in charge of the unit. 'What have you got?' he said. Then he spotted the casualty: 'OK, let's get him in the aircraft and gone.'

Tony told Terry to take the new patrol down to the cut-off position near the river to give us early warning, and bring back the two lads who had stayed there on stag.

The two officers went over to the narcos. Pointing at the European, one of them turned to Gaz and said, 'He'll be out very soon. He won't go to jail. There's so much corruption, he will be out. The important thing is that we've stopped all this.' He walked off and started to look around.

The officer was quite tall, about 6', and in his early thirties. He wore glasses with square, gold-wire rims. He had an American twang to his accent and had probably been educated in the States. All the times I'd seen him, he'd sounded very conscientious and straight-to-the-point, as if he really did want to stop the drugs trade. The other one was in his late forties, early fifties, and was more of a realist. He knew what was going on, and he knew the business was never going to be stopped. He got his cigarettes out, lit one up, and walked around talking to the boys.

Five heli-loads came in, about forty blokes in total. The aircraft took off again and headed for the nearest refuelling point.

The younger of the two officers was sorting them all out. They had their own command structure. I watched the changeover; I didn't understand exactly what was being said by the boys who'd done the attack, but by their body language I could see it was very much along the lines of how fucking good they were.

The new boys went over to look at the body, and some of them gave it a little poke.

I went over to Nino and the radio. He was still pissed off. I gave him the daysack and told him to pack the radio up and put it on his back, because we'd be going in a minute. He looked as if I'd just told him he'd won the state lottery; he had a second chance now, an opportunity to show me that he could do something right – even if it was just to put a radio in a daysack.

'On me,' Gaz called to all the patrol commanders. 'Right, this is what's happening. It's being handed over now to the police. I want you to get hold of the patrols, bring them all in together, make sure that you've got everybody, and go back to your FRV. Pick up the kit, and wait over in the corner there.' He pointed at the edge of the compound. 'Get under the canopy, get some scoff on, and once the helicopters are refuelled they'll come back and pick you up.'

Terry sparked up, 'Well, chuffed to fuck – we've already got our kit so we'll go over there and wait.'

We went back to the FRV and then we trogged back and joined him. They were brewing up, everybody very jovial and having a laugh.

Gaz was still outside doing his liaison with the two police officers. After a while he came over and sat down with us, helping himself to some of my brew.

'What happened then?' he asked. I told him about El Nino and the ND.

Rod jumped in and said, 'As soon as we get back we need to fuck him off. Once everybody knows, especially since this boy's been shot, he's in severe shit.'

'I'll sort that out now,' Gaz said, going over to talk to the older of the two officers.

I spun the shit with One-of-three-Josés and the others, and told them they mustn't say anything to anybody about what happened. I said it would get everybody into trouble. They thought it was great; they had a secret now.

I could hear the helis returning. Gaz came back. 'The first heli is going to lift the prisoners off,' he said. 'The next ones are for you.'

We walked up to the helipad and watched the narcos getting loaded on, everybody wanting to hit them on the way. All the boys then had to unload their weapons and put all their live ammunition in the top flap of their bergens. The last thing we wanted now was another ND.

Aboard the helicopters, all the euphoria had died down by now. We were all realizing how tired we were, and probably thinking about what we were going to do when we got home. I dozed off, waking with a jerk each time my head fell forward.

The first thing we had to do when we got back was sort out our weapons and equipment, and ourselves. That only took a few hours, and then the boys got stuck into a barbecue of fresh and a massive piss-up on beer and whisky.

Everybody was best mates. 'Come to my village, it is really beautiful,' said One-of-three-Josés.

'Not as beautiful as the women from mine,' laughed Rodriguez.

Everybody got completely pissed and had a good old night. Nino, however, wasn't there. He had been told he was out on his arse; by the time we were on our third can of beer he was probably already back on traffic duty.

At midday the next day the Regiment blokes started our debrief. We went through it all again – what we did right, what we did wrong, how we could improve.

'The only improvement I can suggest is to get our finger out and learn better Spanish,' Terry said.

'And to make sure the safety catches on the Galils are harder to get off,' I said.

Gaz told us that under interrogation the narcos had revealed that after a big farewell piss-up the day before the attack, some of their number had left the camp to escort the other two Europeans down river. The European

we had captured had already been released on bail.

The next day our patrols were all off home as war heroes, and we screamed down town for three days of eating ourselves half to death trying to put back on the weight that we'd lost in the jungle, buying cheap emeralds and leather jackets, and going down to the embassy area where all the nice bars were and saying hello to ex-members of G Squadron. And at last Rod was happy because he'd got out of the jungle without a zit and now his hair wasn't flat and greasy.

Within hours of Iraqi troops and armour rolling across the border with Kuwait at 0200 local time on 2 August 1990 the Regiment was preparing itself for desert operations.

I was still 3 i/c of the team, and my gang were unfortunately not involved. I watched jealously as G Squadron drew their desert kit and departed 'on exercise'. Our nine-month tour was coming to an end and we were looking forward to a handover, but as the weeks went by rumours began to circulate of either a postponement or cancellation altogether. We got all the bullshit: 'If it starts, there's still the anti-terrorist threat in the UK. You'll still be needed here.' I just kept my fingers crossed that the squadron changeover would happen as planned and G Squadron would be the pissed-off ones for a change.

My marriage to Fiona had broken down and I'd made the decision that it was better to go while Katie was young rather than have her grow up in an atmosphere of rowing and honking. Although her mother and father would have split up, at least she wouldn't be experiencing bad feeling in the house, and maybe going through the trauma of us parting when she was eight or nine.

There was no way I wanted to go back to living in the block. One of the scaleys was getting out to be a mature student, but couldn't afford to keep up his mortgage on his student allowance; I said I'd rent the house off him, and if eventually he did want to sell it, to give me first refusal. So

there I was, back in a two-up, two-down on a Westbury estate near the camp.

I threw myself into my job on the team. Everybody was mightily pissed off that we were probably going to miss out on the Gulf. We were sitting drinking tea in the hangar one morning, honking severely about what was going on.

Harry said, 'I remember talking to A Squadron after the Falklands. They were severely pissed off because they were on the team at the time. And now it's going to happen to us.'

At that moment Gaz walked in with two strangers. 'These blokes have just come from Selection,' he said. 'This is Bob, and this is Stan. Bob's going to go to the sniper team, and Stan, I want you to latch on to Andy. He'll show you the ropes – get all the kit; I bet you don't even know how to put it on, do you?'

This fellow turned round and said, in a thick Kiwi accent, 'No, I don't actually.'

Bob Consiglio and Stan were to have a good effect on us all. Straight out of Selection, they were raring to go; they loved being on the team and their enthusiasm was infectious.

It was round about this time that I spotted a gorgeous girl at the local gym. We were both sweating buckets, attending a new session which was particularly difficult. She was working out in front of me and I couldn't help appreciating the styling of her leotard.

After I'd seen her five or six times at the gym, I came across her one Saturday evening in a wine bar down town. She was with a girlfriend, and they were being chatted up by a bloke in D Squadron. It was the first time I had seen her fully dressed, and again, she looked great.

A tinker came in selling roses. I bought one, and asked her to take it over to the girl in the corner.

She came over afterwards, gave me a radiant smile, and said, 'Thank you.'

'It's nothing,' I said. 'I only did it to annoy the bloke you're talking to.'

'So charming,' she said. 'Your name must be James Bond?'

'No – Andy, actually. Look, your friend is getting on really well with that bloke. Seems a shame for you to go back and break it up. Can I get you a drink, Miss Moneypenny?'

'Jilly, actually – and yes, a bottle of Pils.'

That was how it started. We talked to each other now at the fitness centre, we saw each other in the town a couple more times, no dates or anything or phone calls. But about three or four weeks after that things just snowballed and towards the end of October I asked her to move in.

On Remembrance Sunday the Regiment gym becomes a church. Every member of Stirling Lines – Regiment and attached personnel, serving and retired – who can be there, is there. So, too, are their wives, girlfriends and families, and the families of people who have died. Serving members of the Regiment wear full dress uniform, the only time it is worn. This year I was in civvies as I was part of the protection outside the camp during the service.

After the service, everyone moved outside to the Clock Tower. Wreaths were laid by all the different squadrons, and all the different departments and organizations that were in and around supporting the Regiment. There was a two-minute silence and then it was into the club for drinks and food. Many saw it as a chance to talk to retired members – the old and bold – because a lot of them only appeared for this one occasion a year. The party would go on for the rest of the day and well into the evening.

Instead of doing all that, I went with Jilly down to the graveyard.

The regimental cemetery isn't in the Lines, it's in the local church; the Regiment has its own plot, and it was almost full.

'They'll either have to buy a bigger plot or stop all the wars,' I said.

Jilly gave a smile that was more of a wince.

One or two other people were there to pay their respects to old friends. One of them was an ex-B Squadron warrant officer who'd got out a couple of years before. It was the first time that I'd seen him in a suit. He had nothing with him – no flowers or anything like that. He wasn't going to any grave in particular; he was just walking up and down, alone with his thoughts. His shoes and the bottoms of his trousers were wet from the grass and his suit collar was turned up against the cold.

Jilly and I fell in step beside him.

'You going up the camp?' I said.

'Fuck that. There's too many people up there as it is, desperate to be part of the show. This is where people should be.'

He was right. The Remembrance Day service was packed with camp followers and hangers-on who seemed far less interested in what was being commemorated than in being able to say afterwards that they'd been there.

Blokes who really are in the Regiment either feel sorry for, or loathe, those who've had some sort of contact and make themselves out to be more than they are or were. They must have very low self-esteem if they feel the need to bluff, but what they perhaps don't realize is that they are normally found out. It is a very small world and everyone knows each other or can connect. Such characters would not be worthy of licking the mud off the boots of the people in the 'plot'.

I thought about the blokes I worked with. They were as much of a cross-section personality-wise as would be found in any organization. They ranged from the slightly intro-verted who kept themselves to themselves – to the point of training in the gym at 1 a.m. – right the way up to the total and utter extroverts who moon-danced all over the place. There's a hill outside Hereford called the Callow; as you hit

the brow of it at night, you see below you the lights of the town. On their way back from a trip, a lot of the singley party animals call it Hard-on Hill: they've been away for six months, and all they want to do is get into camp, have a shower, and scream down town. At the other extreme was a single bloke I was flying back with from a trip who turned to me and said, in his thick Birmingham accent, 'I can't wait to get back to clean my windows.'

Then there were all the people in between. Everybody from a Hell's Angel to an exotic butterfly collector, and men of all colours and creeds – Australians, Kiwis, Fijians, Indians from the Seychelles. Blokes were doing Open University degree courses; one wanted to become a physics teacher when he left. People who'd really got into the medical side had gone on to become doctors. There were other blokes who really got into a country where they'd been operating – in particular, the Arab countries. A lot of them became very proficient in the language and got interested in the culture, the people and the country itself, and ended up going and living there.

In B Squadron there was a former taxidermist who was also an ex-convict and boxer. He had a deep freezer in one of the spare rooms in the block where he lived. Inside, instead of frozen pies and fish fingers, there were dead foxes, owls and salmon, and cartons of chemicals. Some blokes would bring him back dead animals from trips; others would use his services to get their pet dog stuffed.

A lot of people got into anything to do with the air – once they joined a freefall troop, they got this fixation with anything to do with flying and freefall. Nosh had bought himself an old Cessna in the States and flown it over to the UK – an outrageous journey on a single engine. The fuel bladder in the back was leaking, it looked like the thing was going to fall apart, so he put his parachute rig on, took out all but two screws in the door, and flew high enough so if the bladder went he could just jump out. The radios were not the sort for transatlantic flights, so he put out the

antenna, which was a wire tied to a brick, and then measured it out to get the frequencies to hit the stations.

There were people who were severely into the old jap-slapping; they got to international level sometimes. Others got into weird, obscure sports, especially the Mountain Troop blokes. They nearly always got into sheer face climbing, and developed an obsession with climbing Everest.

There was also Mr Normal, Mr Family Man with the house and 2.4 kids; he'd get back from a job, do all the debriefing, and then it was a total cut: he went home, mowed the grass, found the lost cat and replaced the tile on the roof.

A major part of what made the Regiment more professional than the normal military unit was that it was staffed by people who could tell the difference between work time and play time. When you're working, you're working, when you're not, then it's time to be the idiot – you can do whatever you want, you can go and get drunk out of your head or you can go home and mow the grass, it really doesn't matter. But everybody has to be able to cut between when they're working and when they're not.

There was one particular crowd that came from all squadrons, called the Grouse-beaters – all the Highland jocks who used to get together and go down town and drink. At New Year, the Grouse-beaters would hit the town with their skirts and fluffy shirts. Such occasions apart, the ordinary man in the street would find it very difficult to pick out Regiment blokes. Anybody seeing a squadron away would probably think it was a school outing.

With such a cross-section, there were bound to be personality clashes now and again; it's just a normal human reaction, and it clears the air. Fortunately, the Selection process cancels a lot of that out, because they're looking for blokes that can mingle with each other in closed environments, but it's bound to happen. We'd just come back from over the water one Christmas and were in one of the bars down town. Eno the midget was drunk; he was

getting behind Regiment blokes that he knew, jumping up and slapping their heads, then disappearing giggling into the corner. It pissed off one of the blokes so much that he turned around and dropped him. In the morning Eno phoned me up and said, 'I don't know who it was, but I was obviously out of order.' A couple of days later he found out it was one of his really good mates out of the same troop that had decked him. 'Ah well,' he said, 'that's all right, as long as I know.'

The culture is downbeat. Élitism is counterproductive, it alienates you from other people, and we depend on a working relationship with many other groups like Special Branch or the security services: after all, the Regiment is there as strategic troops, to do tasks that enhance other groups' capabilities. It was always hard, however, to break down the barriers. I remembered going on courses, or being seconded to other units: I'd be sitting there on my own for a couple of days before anybody would talk to me. Everybody would stand off because of the mystique that was created in the army about the Regiment. We had to make an effort to go and talk to people, to show them that we were normal, approachable and just like everybody else – we had grass that was overgrowing, we had a cat that was missing.

That wasn't to say that we didn't know we were very professional and very confident in what we were doing, but that had nothing to do with élitism. Blokes just looked at it as a job, as a profession. Soldiering was something that they found they had the aptitude for, and they wanted to take the profession to another level.

It was sadly ironic that because they were so good at what they did, they were more likely to be at the sharp end; because they were so good, they were more likely to end up getting killed. What it all boiled down to was that if we were there shooting at somebody, chances were that he'd be shooting back at us – which meant that we were in the shit, and we could die.

A lot of the time, to be shooting at somebody means that the task is being compromised; the Regiment is not a big, aggressive, overt force looking for trouble, it's about small numbers of strategic troops, a covert force that spends as much time intelligence gathering as anything else.

The Regiment's roots were in the Second World War and the Malaya conflict, both of which involved a lot of information gathering and quick strikes. It wasn't about inflicting massive casualties, it was about destroying equipment and communications, and lowering morale. As a small force during the Second World War, killing forty Germans meant little in the scale of things. Destroying forty aircraft, however, was a different matter: it embuggered the enemy, and it saved Allied lives.

My own ideas about killing had changed a lot since I was young. I killed my first man when I was nineteen. There was a big celebration, purely because I'd done what I'd joined the army to do. But now, I got a kick from stopping death, not causing it.

It certainly didn't worry me when enemy were killed in contacts. I didn't celebrate the fact, but there again I didn't lose any sleep about it. I understood that they had sons and daughters, mothers and fathers, but they were big boys like all of us and they knew what was going on. They knew that they stood a chance of being killed, the same as we did.

I'd never met anybody who kept a running total or said, 'Yeah, good stuff, I've killed so-and-so.' If it had to be done, I didn't know anybody who wouldn't try to make it as quick as possible – not so much to make it a nice clean way of dying for them, but to make it safer for himself. The quicker they were dead, the less of a threat they were; it's no picnic getting shot. In the films, it's all rather nice – the guy takes a round in the shoulder and is still running around shouting good one-liners. Load of shit: you get hit by a 7.62 round and it's going to take half your shoulder off.

During the Second World War, David Stirling, the founder of the Regiment, threw a grenade into a room and

killed several Germans. He didn't need to do it to achieve his aim, and he bitterly regretted it. He said it was a waste of life and it pissed him off.

We walked home through the park, taking the cold November wind full in the face. Leaves swirled in small typhoons and it started to pour with rain.

'I love this weather,' I said. 'Best part is knowing I'll be home in a minute with a brew in my hand.'

Jilly turned to look at me. She looked strained.

'It's going to be a bit hotter where you're going, isn't it?'

'You what?'

'Kuwait. You can't kid me you won't be going if it blows into a war.'

In the short time that I'd known her, she was always all right if she wasn't aware of the dramas. She knew very little of what I did, and had never asked questions – because, she told me, she didn't want the answers. 'Oh, you're off, when are you coming back?' was the most she would ever ask. But this time it was different. For once, she knew where I might be going.

I didn't want to mess things up between us. I wanted this to be it. My marriages had failed mainly due to my commitment to the army. Now I realized I could have both – a career and a strong, lasting relationship. Our future was together.

'Don't worry, mate,' I said. 'There's more chance of Maggie getting kicked out of Downing Street than there is of me being sent down town for a new pair of dessies and some factor twenty.'

As I put my arm around her, I only hoped she didn't notice that my fingers were firmly crossed.

Glossary

203	*M16 rifle with 40mm grenade launcher attached*
2 i/c	*second-in-command*
66	*lightweight, throwaway anti-tank rocket*
109 or Agusta 109	*type of helicopter*
ARF	*Airborne Reaction Force*
APC	*armoured personnel carrier*
Atap	*foliage covered*
ATO	*ammunition technical officer*
Basha	*shelter*
Beasting	*army slang for a beating or very hard run with kit*
Bergen	*pack carried by British forces on active service*
BG	*bodyguard*
Bivvi bag	*GoreTex sleeping-bag cover*
Blue-on-blue	*friendly fire*
Bone	*naff*
Brick	*four-man infantry patrol in Northern Ireland*
C130	*Hercules transport aircraft*
C4	*US plastic explosive*
Can	*Saracen APC*
Chinstrap, be on your	*really knackered, as in 'I can't go on, I'm on my chinstrap here.'*
COBR	*Cabinet Office Briefing Room*

CQB	*close quarter battle*
CRW	*counter-revolutionary warfare*
CTR	*close target recce*
CT team	*counter-terrorist team*
Cuds	*countryside*
Delta Force	*US equivalent of 22 SAS Regt*
Dicker	*IRA observer*
DMP	*drug manufacturing plant*
DPM	*disrupted pattern material (camouflage)*
DS	*directing staff (instructor)*
DZ	*drop zone*
Dry bag	*diver's dry suit*
E&E	*escape and evasion*
Eppie Scoppie	*tantrum*
ERV	*emergency rendezvous*
Exfil	*exfiltration*
FOB	*forward operations base*
Foxtrot	*on foot*
Fresh	*fresh food*
FRV	*final rendezvous*
Fuddle or kefuddle	*getting together and having a brew*
Gemini	*inflatable assault boat*
GPMG	*general purpose machine-gun*
Green slime (or slime)	*member of Intelligence Corps*
HE	*high explosive*
Head Shed	*nickname for anyone in authority. From Malaya days, this is what any form of leadership in the regiment has been called, after the term for the start of the river course*
Hexamine (hexy)	*small block of solid fuel*
HMSU	*Headquarters Mobile Support Unit*
IA	*immediate action*
ID	*identify/identity*
IED	*improvised (or identified) explosive device*

IJLB	*Infantry Junior Leaders Battalion*
Infil	*infiltration*
Int	*intelligence*
IV	*intravenous drip*
Jark	*technical attack on weapons or IEDs*
Leak	*sweat*
LMG	*light machine gun*
LOE	*limit of exploitation*
Long	*rifle*
LS	*landing site*
LUP	*lying-up point*
MM	*Military Medal*
MOE	*method of entry*
Mozzie rep	*mosquito repellant*
ND	*negligent discharge of weapon*
Net	*communications network*
NVA	*night viewing aid*
NVG	*night viewing goggles*
OC	*officer commanding*
OP	*observation post*
OPSEC	*operational security*
PE	*plastic explosive*
Pinkie	*110, a long-wheel-base Land Rover*
PIRA	*Provisional IRA*
PNG	*passive night goggles*
QRF	*quick reaction force*
RTU	*return to unit*
Rupert	*nickname for officer – not always derogatory*
RV	*rendezvous point*
Sat nav	*satellite navigation*
Scaley	*signaller*
Scaley kit	*signals equipment*
SF	*security forces*
Short	*pistol*
Sitrep	*situation report*
SLR	*self-loading rifle*

SM	*sergeant major*
SOP	*standard operating procedure*
SSM	*squadron sergeant-major*
Stag	*sentry or sentry duty*
Stand to	*prepare to defend against attack*
Tab	*hard long-distance march with kit*
TACBE	*tactical beacon radio*
TCG	*Tasking and Co-ordination Group*
VC	*voluntary contribution to squadron funds*
VCP	*vehicle checkpoint*

Andy McNab's mind-blowing non-fiction bestseller

BRAVO TWO ZERO

In January 1991, eight members of the SAS regiment embarked upon a top secret mission that was to infiltrate them deep behind enemy lines. Under the command of Sergeant Andy McNab, they were to sever the underground communication link between Baghdad and north-west Iraq, and to seek and destroy mobile Scud launchers. Their call sign: BRAVO TWO ZERO.

Each man laden with 15 stone of equipment, they patrolled 20km across flat desert to reach their objective. Within days, their location was compromised. After a fierce firefight, they were forced to escape and evade on foot to the Syrian border. In the desperate days that followed, though stricken by hypothermia and other injuries, the patrol 'went ballistic'. Four men were captured. Three died. Only one escaped. For the survivors, however, the worst ordeals were to come. Delivered to Baghdad, they were tortured with a savagery for which not even their intensive SAS training had prepared them.

Bravo Two Zero is a breathtaking account of Special Forces soldiering: a chronicle of superhuman courage, endurance and dark humour in the face of overwhelming odds. Believed to be the most highly decorated patrol since the Boer War, BRAVO TWO ZERO is already part of SAS legend.

'The best account yet of the SAS in action'
James Adams, *Sunday Times*

'Superhuman endurance, horrendous torture, desperate odds –
unparalleled revelations'
Daily Mail

'A gripping account of special forces at work . . . a tremendous
adventure story'
Duff Hart-Davis, *Daily Telegraph*

'One of the most extraordinary examples of human courage and
survival in modern warfare'
The Times

0 552 14127 5

CORGI BOOKS

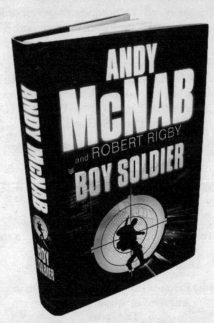

**Andy McNab's
new Nick Stone novel**

AGGRESSOR

Ex-deniable operator Nick Stone seems to be living his
dream, not a care in the world as he steers his camper van
round the surfing and parachuting centres of Australia. But
when he witnesses on TV the massacre of children in a
terrorist siege on the other side of the world, long-suppressed
memories are triggered. Once more Nick is catapulted into
working for the American secret services – only this time, of
his own free will.

As events unfold on the bleak, medieval villages of
Azerbajhan and teeming streets of modern Istanbul, it isn't
long before Nick discovers the true objective of his mission.
His talents are being misused by those who stalk the
corridors of power . . . and this time he is determined to make
a stand.

0 593 05031 2

COMING IN NOVEMBER FROM BANTAM PRESS

BANTAM PRESS

Andy McNab's Nick Stone novels

FIREWALL

Helsinki, December 1999. Nick Stone, ex-SAS, is now a 'K' working for British Intelligence on deniable operations. Offered the lucrative freelance job of kidnapping a mafia warlord and delivering him to St Petersburg, it seems to Stone that his problems are over. In fact, they are only just beginning. Stone enters the bleak underworld of the former Soviet republic of Estonia, where unknown aggressors stalk the Arctic landscape. Russia has embarked upon a concerted cyber-espionage offensive, hacking into some of the West's most sensitive military secrets. American and British intelligence agencies are determined to thwart them. And the mafia are waiting in the wings with their own chillingly brutal solution . . .

0 552 14797 4

'Gripping stuff . . . Nick Stone makes Action Man look like a couch potato'
Daily Express

LAST LIGHT

Aborting an officially-sanctioned assassination attempt at the Houses of Parliament when he realises who the target is, Nick Stone is given a chilling ultimatum: fly to Panama and finish the job, or Kelly, the 11-year-old orphan in his charge, will be killed. Stone is on the edge, struggling to pick up the pieces of his shattered life. By the time he arrives in Panama, he is close to breaking point. And in the sweltering Central American jungle, Stone finds himself at the centre of a lethal conspiracy involving Colombian guerrillas, the US government and Chinese big business. At stake are hundreds of innocent lives.

0 552 14798 2

'McNab's great asset is that the heart of his fiction is non-fiction: other thriller writers do their research, but he has actually been there'
Sunday Times

CORGI BOOKS

Andy McNab's Nick Stone novels

LIBERATION DAY

A Zodiac inflatable slips away from a submarine off the North African coast. If he hadn't needed American citizenship so badly, Nick Stone wouldn't have agreed to do this one last job, but the CIA's offer of a new life in the United States, and the chance to share it with Carrie, the woman he's fallen in love with, is one he cannot refuse. The job seems simple enough for a man of his particular skills: infiltrate the hostile and violent republic of Algeria, kill a money-laundering local businessman, and bring back his severed head to the West. Stone isn't told why the man has to die like this, and there are some questions you just don't ask. But with events unfolding dangerously fast, Stone realizes that he has by no means been told the full story.

0 552 14799 0

'McNab is a terrific novelist. When it comes to thrills,
he's Forsyth class'
Mail on Sunday

DARK WINTER

When maverick agent Nick Stone is despatched to Malaysia by the CIA to assassinate a shadowy biochemist, he expects his mission to be a straightforward part of the fight against Osama Bin Laden's network of terror. Target neutralised, Stone returns to the USA and a maelstrom of personal problems. Kelly, the fourteen year-old orphan to whom he is a joint guardian, cannot escape the ghosts of her traumatic past. He takes her to recuperate in England, but the terrible consequences of what happened in Penang are never far behind. Before very long, the conspiracy he has uncovered unravels to reveal a doomsday threat against the populations of New York, London and Berlin.

0 552 15018 5

'Andy McNab knows where his strengths lie, and it's not just in his biceps . . . Only people who have not read this book could suggest that he is not a fine writer. It is a heart-thumping read'
Daily Express

CORGI BOOKS

A LIST OF OTHER ANDY McNAB TITLES
AVAILABLE FROM TRANSWORLD AND
RANDOM HOUSE CHILDREN'S BOOKS

15357 5	BRAVO TWO ZERO	£6.99
15018 5	DARK WINTER	£6.99
15235 8	REMOTE CONTROL	£6.99
15236 6	CRISIS FOUR	£6.99
15237 4	FIREWALL	£6.99
15238 2	LAST LIGHT	£6.99
15239 0	LIBERATION DAY	£6.99
15019 3	DEEP BLACK	£6.99
05031 2	AGGRESSOR (Hardback)	£17.99
60803 9	BOY SOLDIER (Hardback)	£10.99
60804 7	PAYBACK: BOY SOLDIER (Hardback)	£10.99